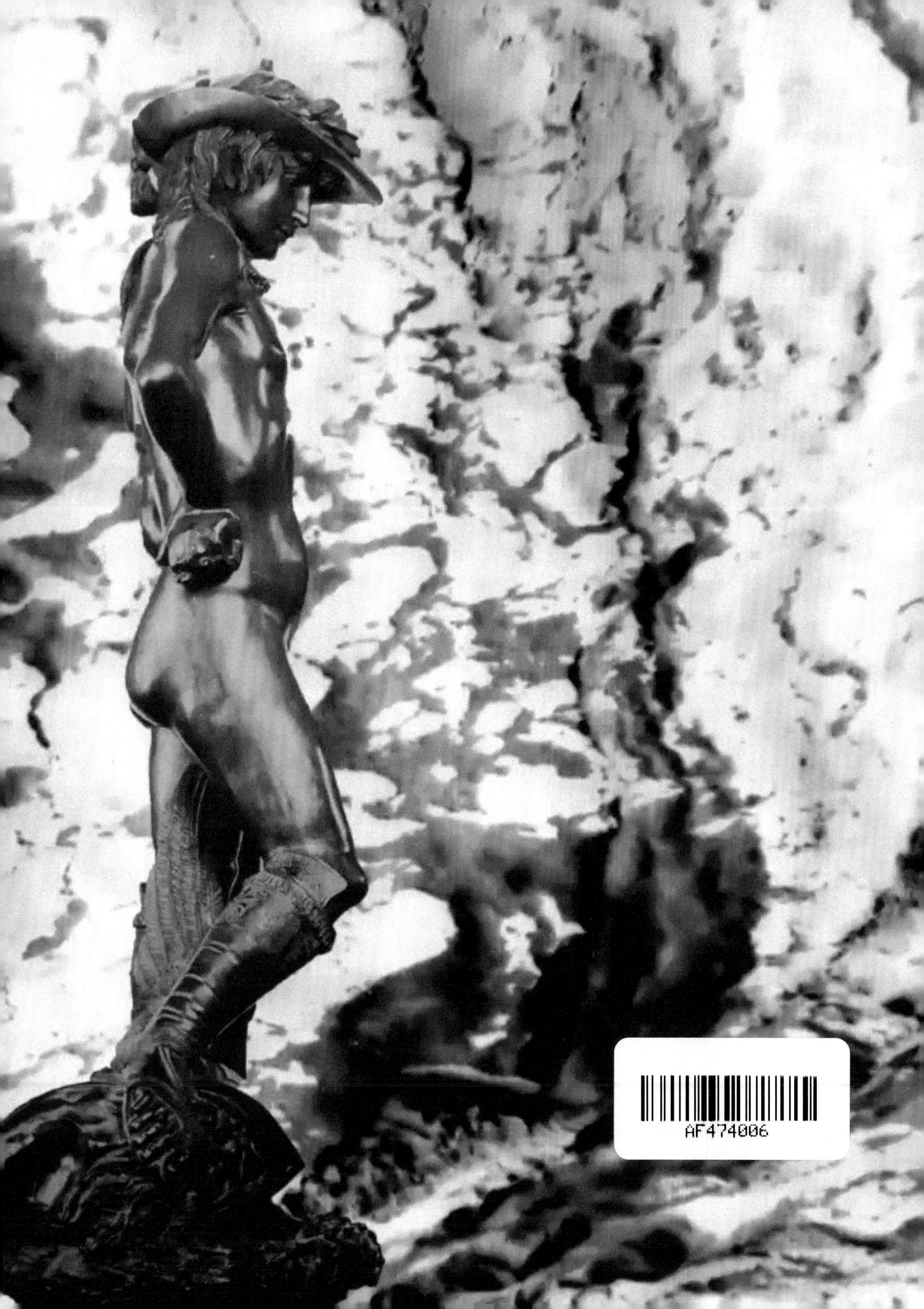

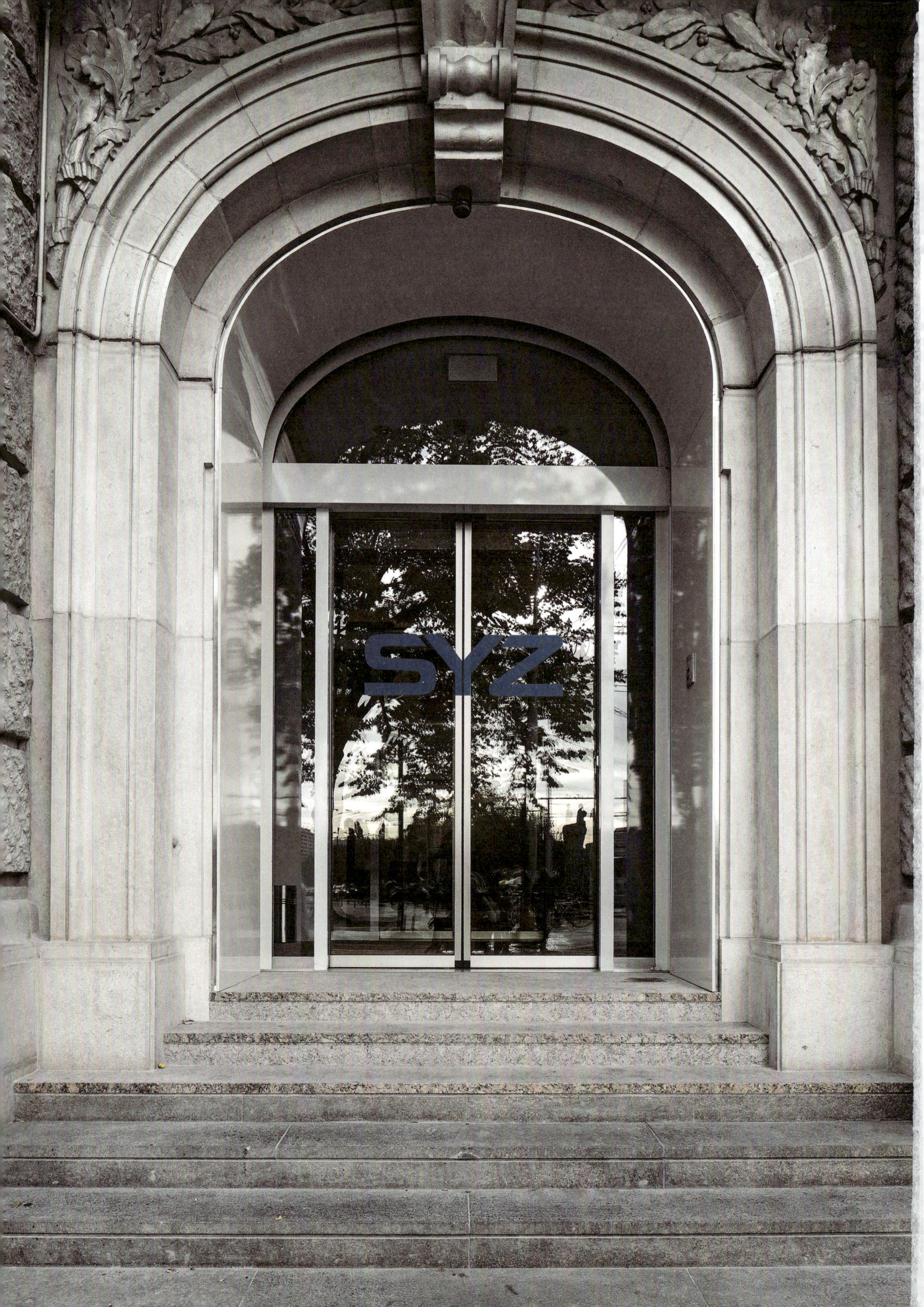
SYZ

the syz collectio

Edited by Nicolas Trembley

on

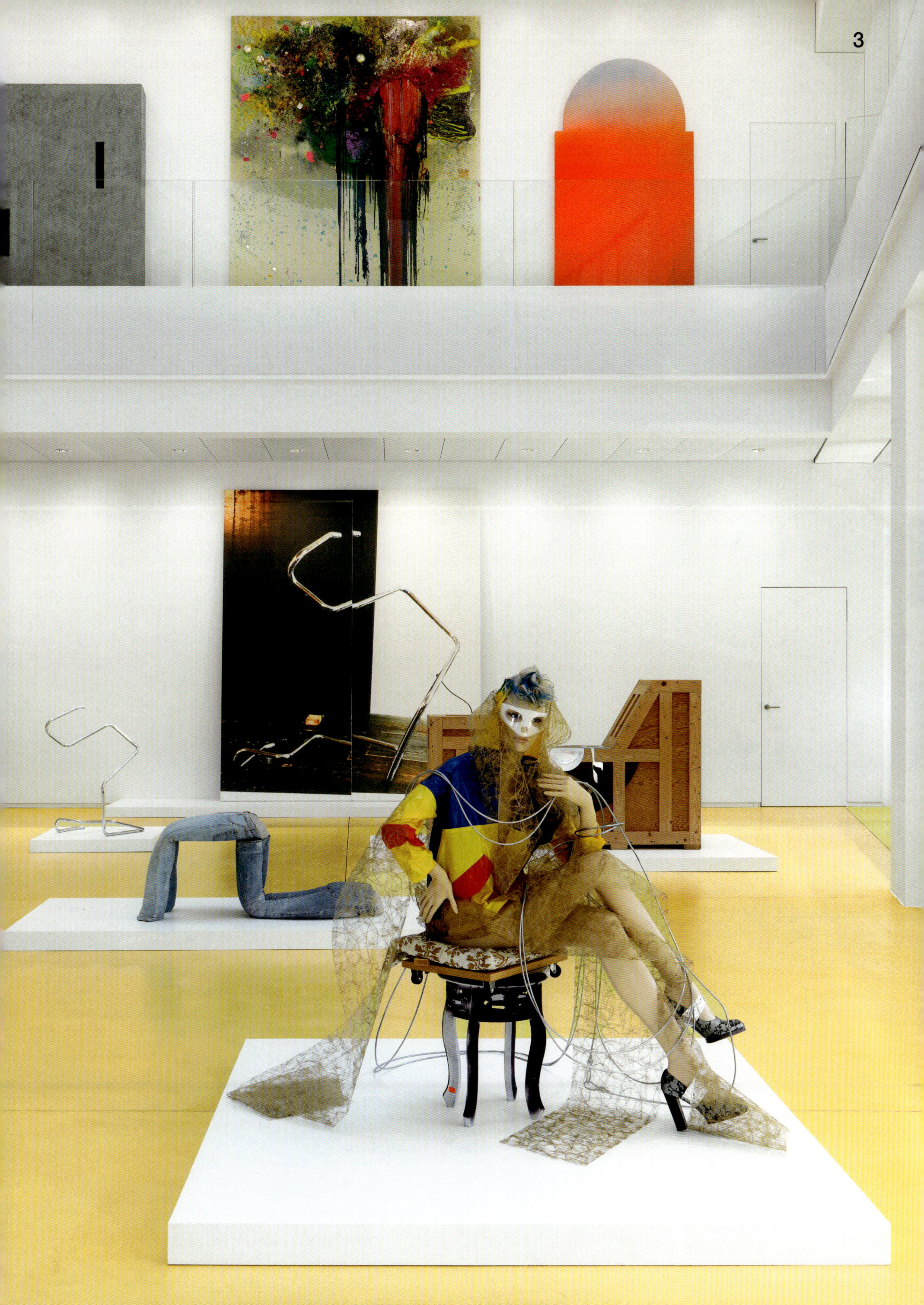

3

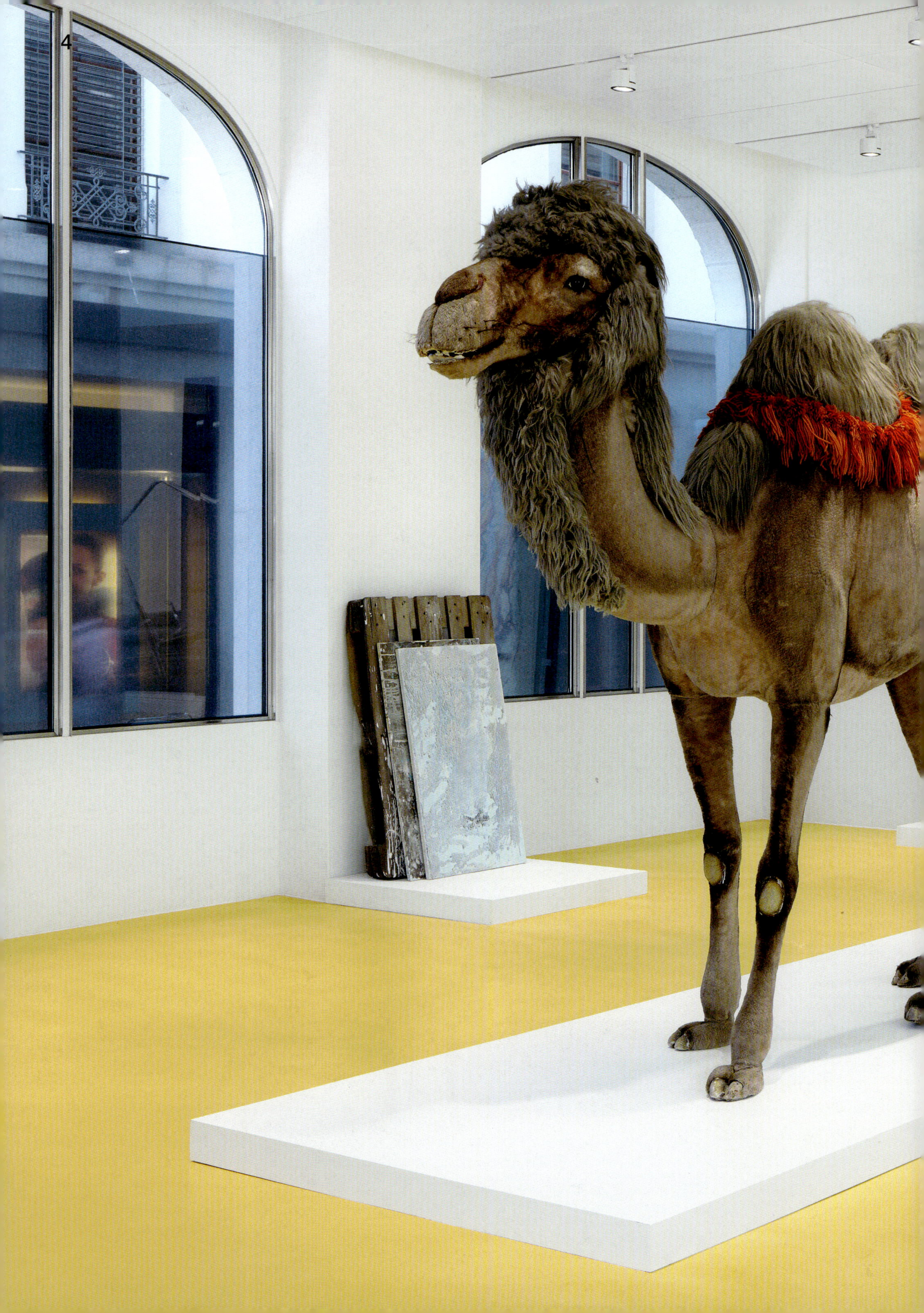

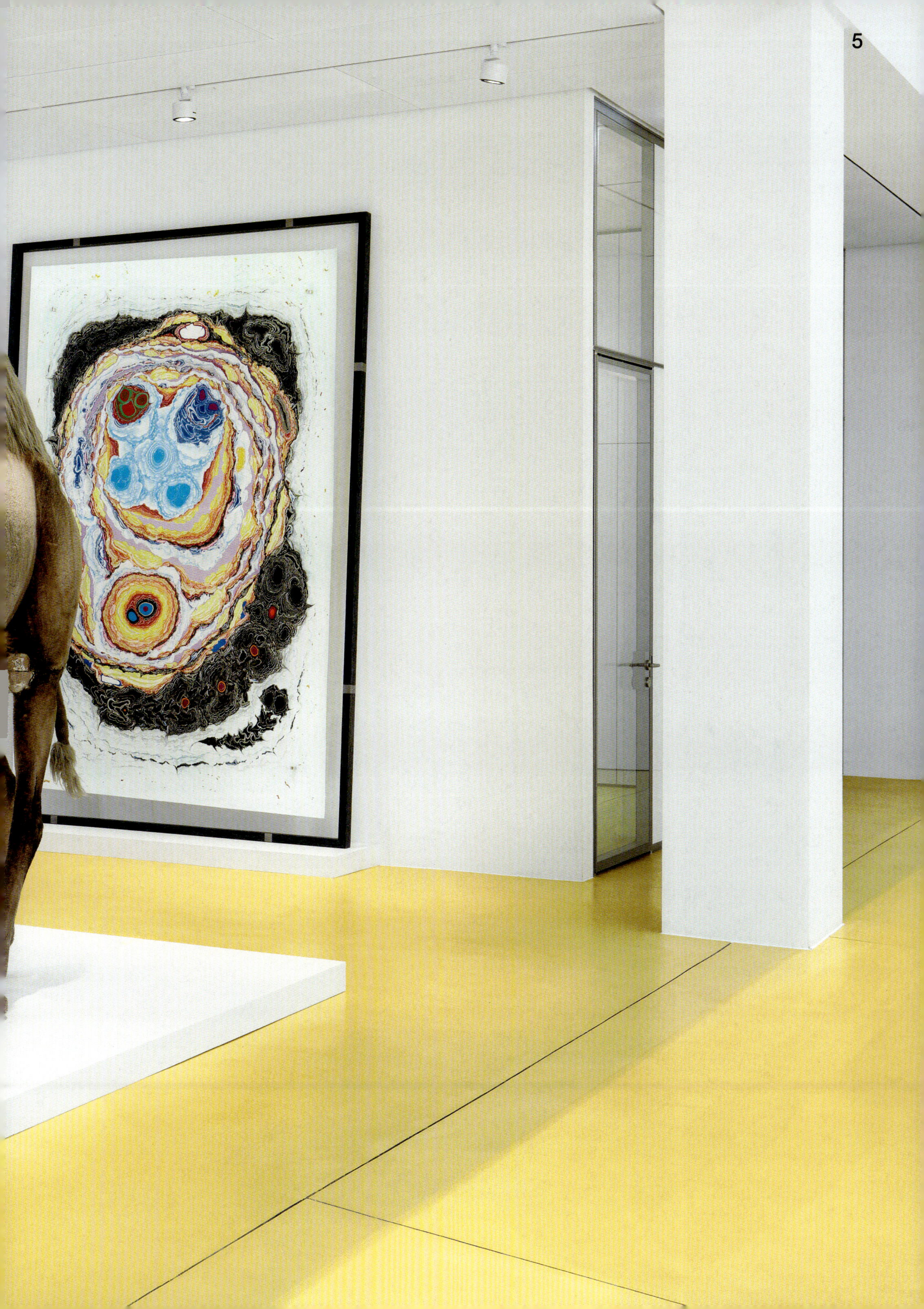

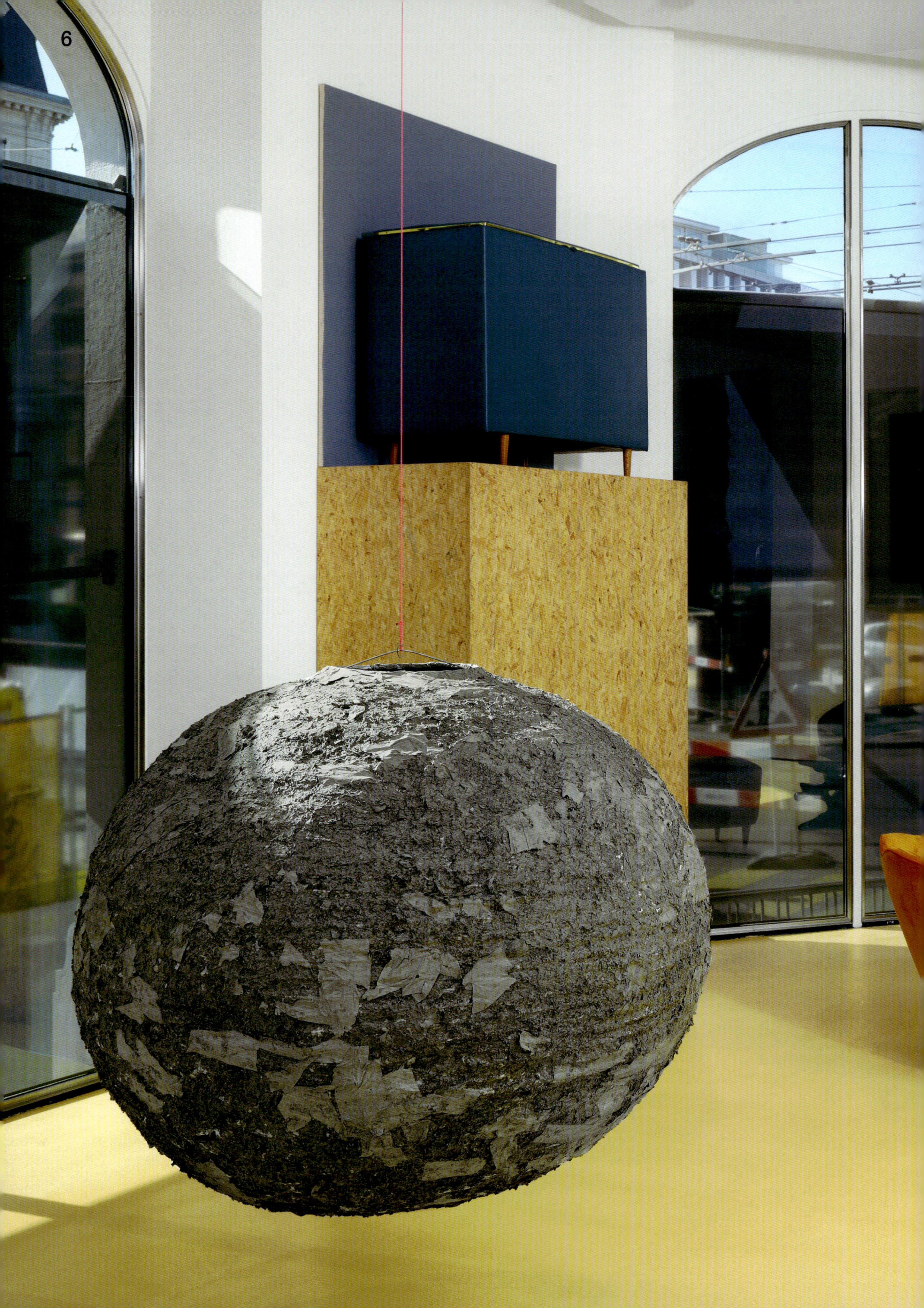
6

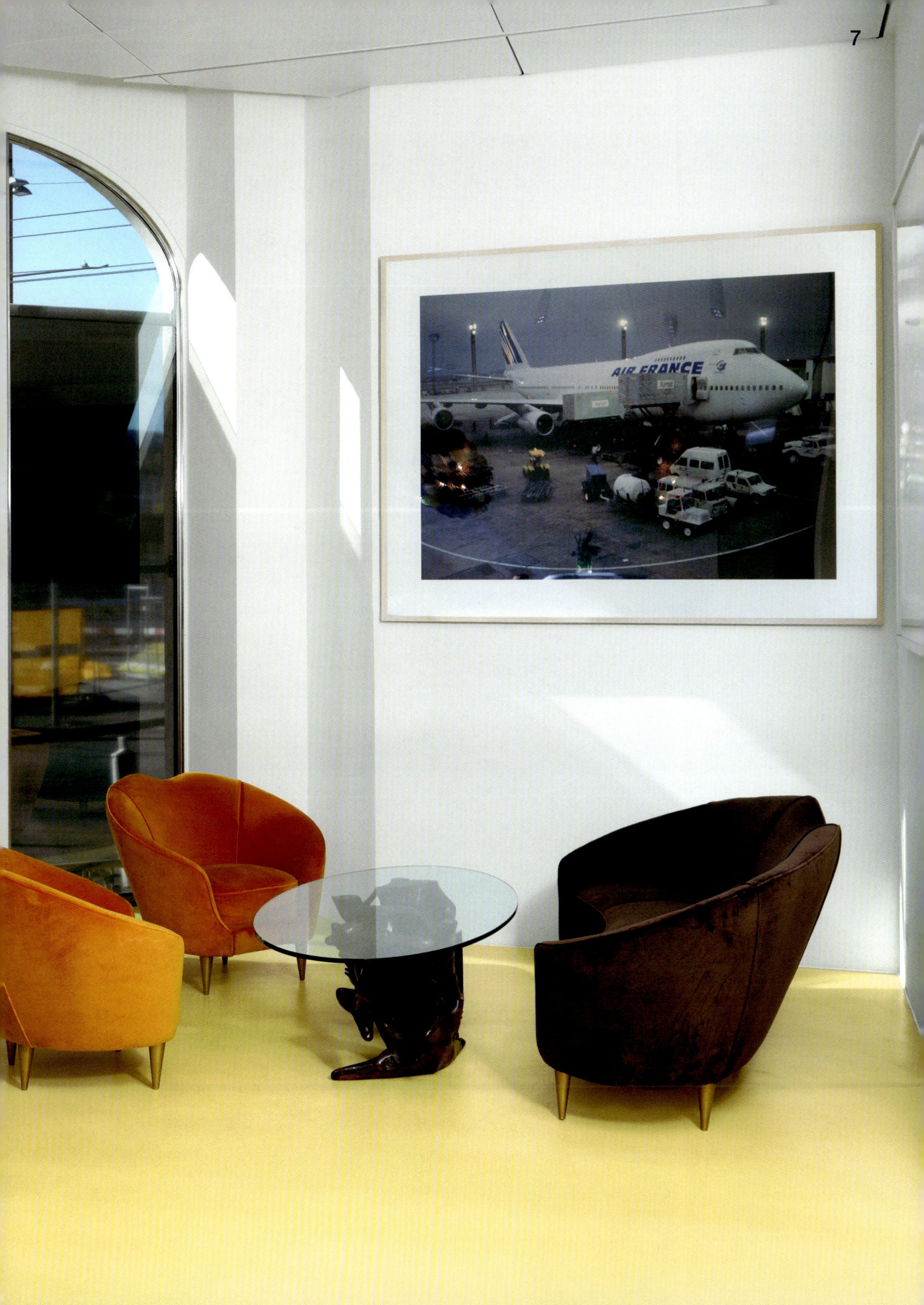
AIR FRANCE

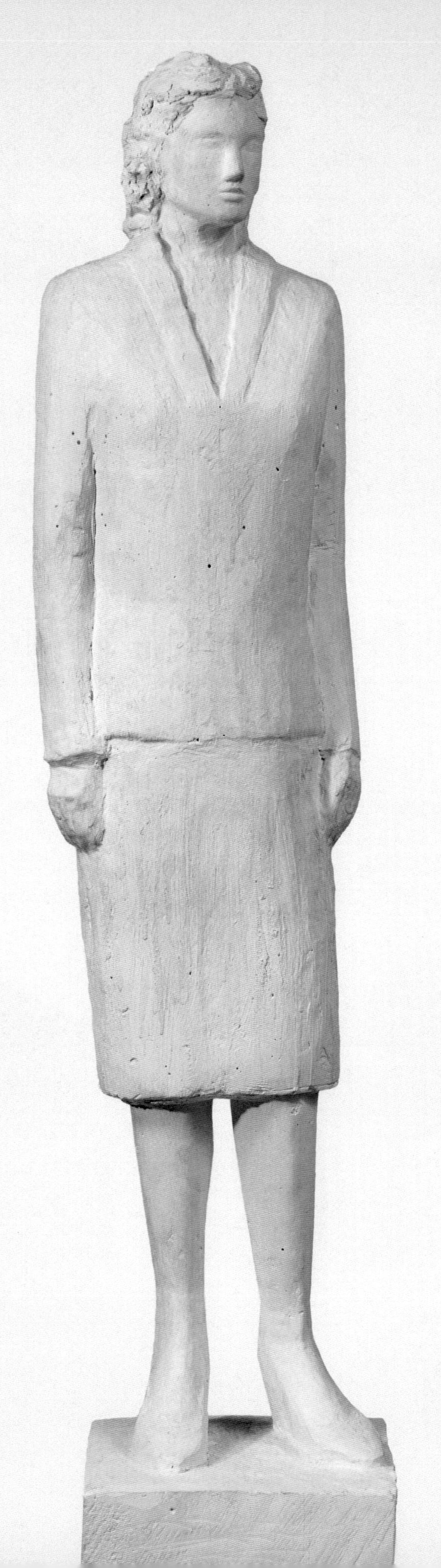

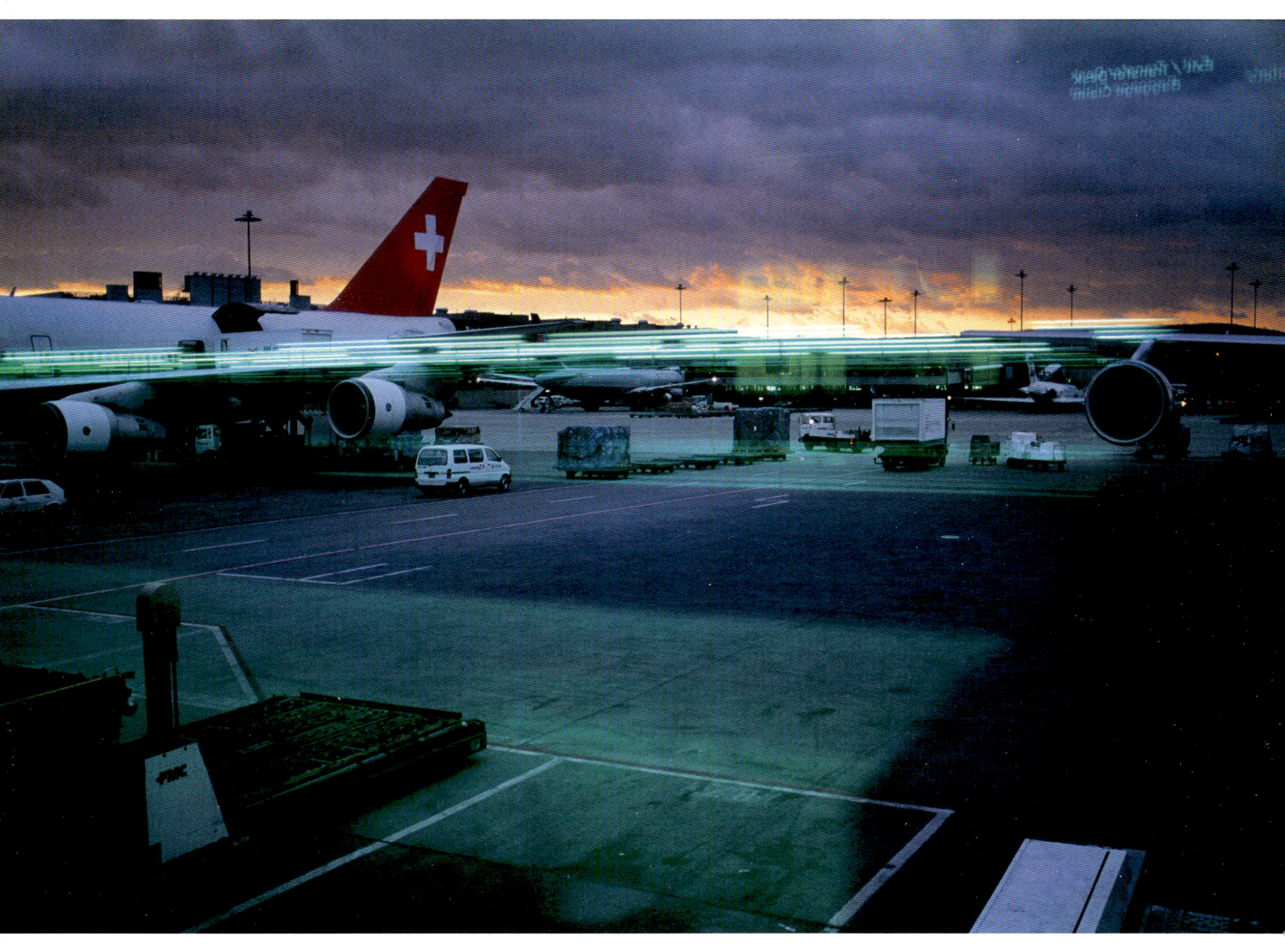

Stewardess I, 1989
Plaster
111.8 × 24.1 × 24.1 cm

Zürich (grüne Linien), 2000
C-print
124 × 190 cm

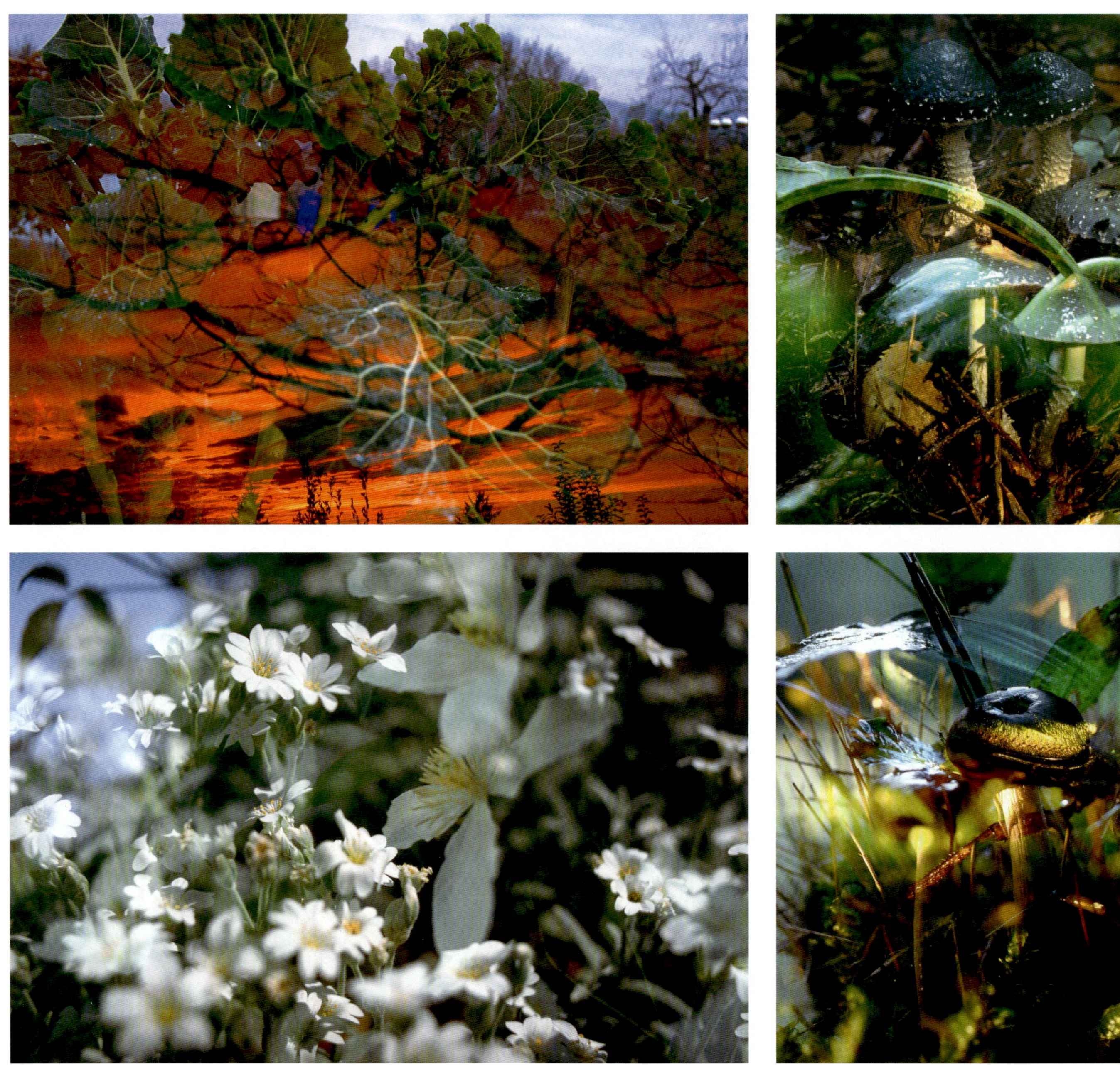

From top to bottom, left to right
Ohne Titel (Blumen); Ohne Titel (Pilze); Ohne Titel (Pilze);
Ohne Titel (Blumen); Ohne Titel (Pilze); Ohne Titel (Blumen)
All: 1998
Inkjet color print
74 × 107 cm

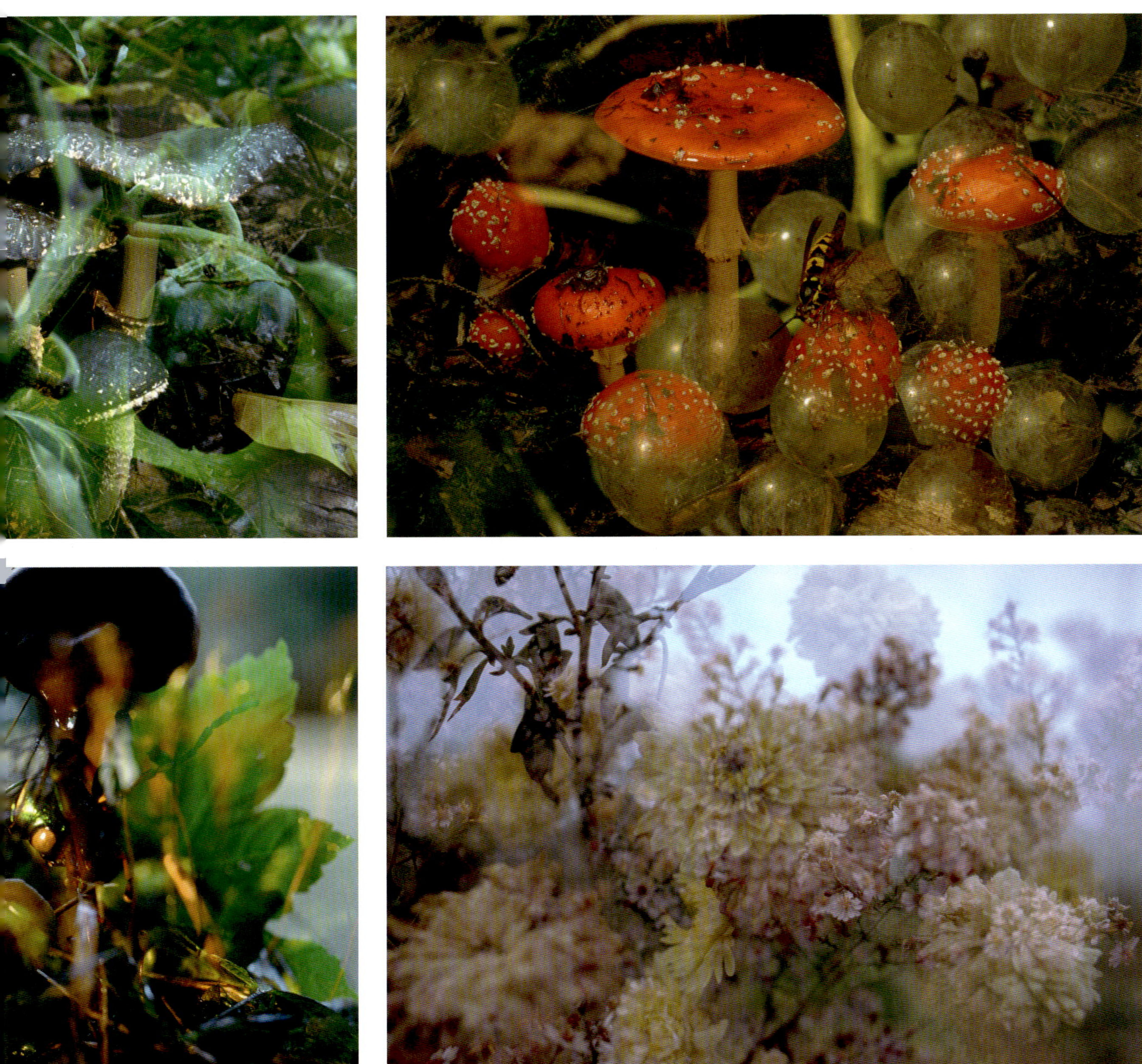

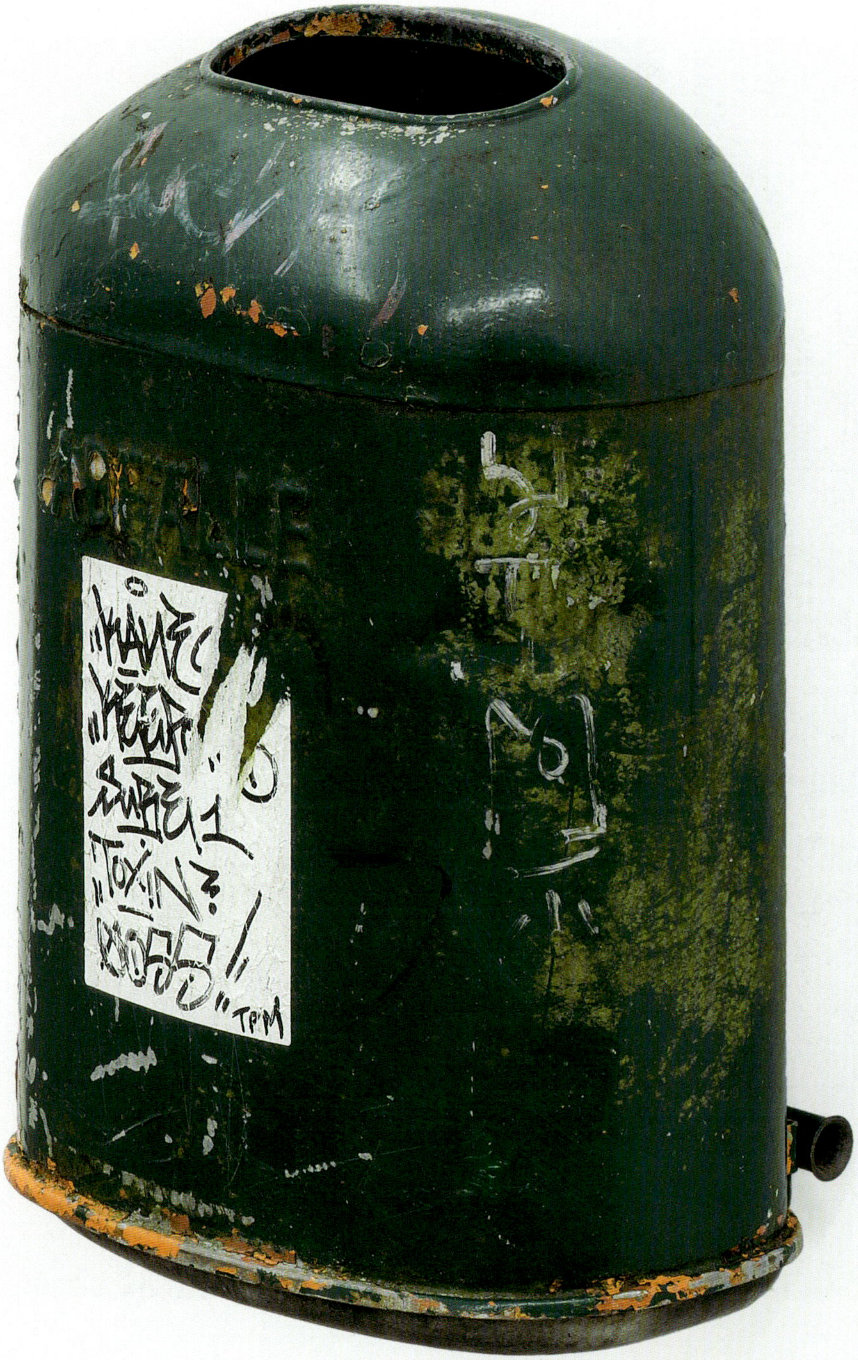

Untitled (Trashcan), 2015
Mixed media
71 × 45 × 36 cm

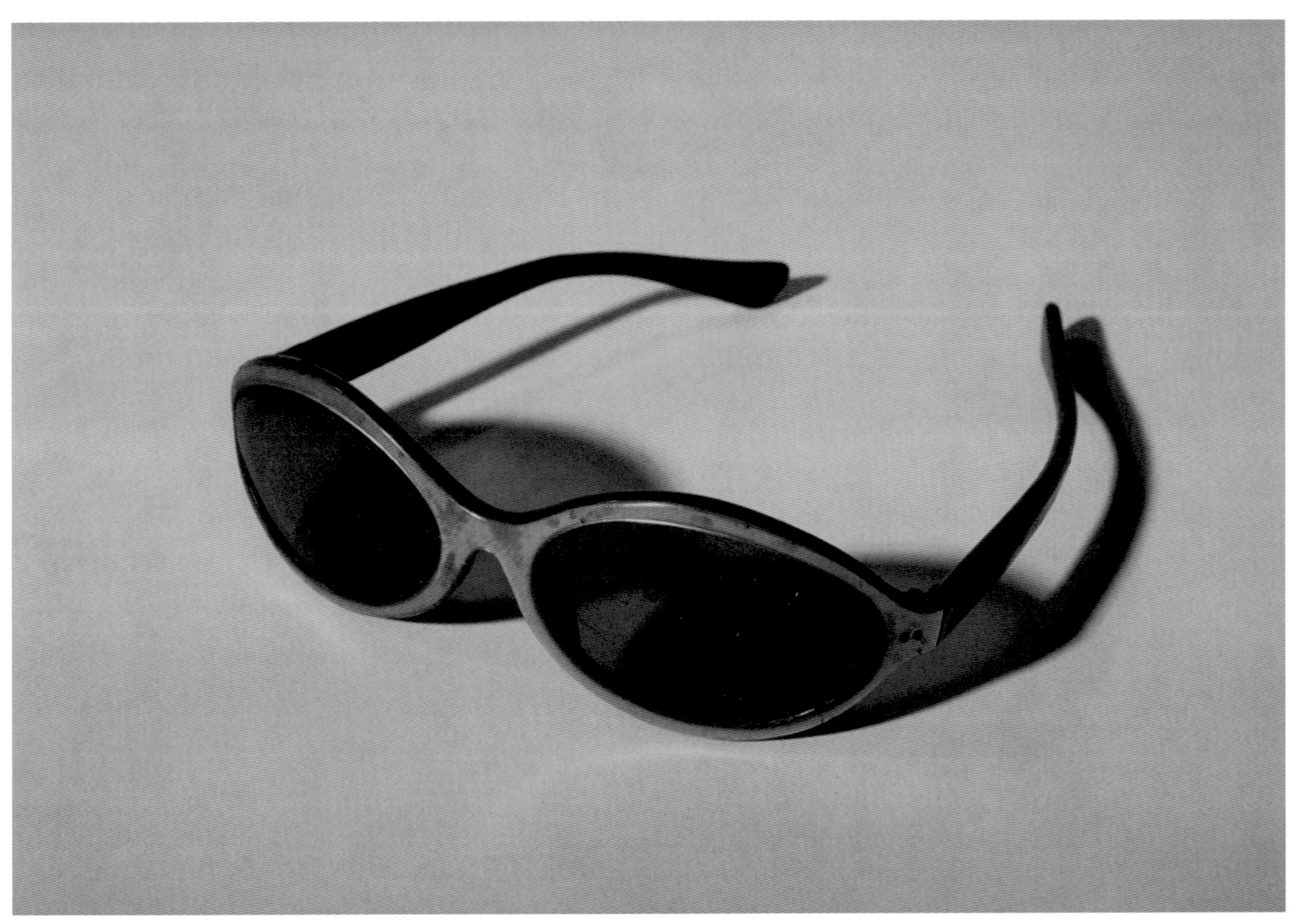

Untitled (from Propo Series) (Sunglasses), 1972–1994 (2007)
Cibachrome print on aluminum
122 × 183 cm

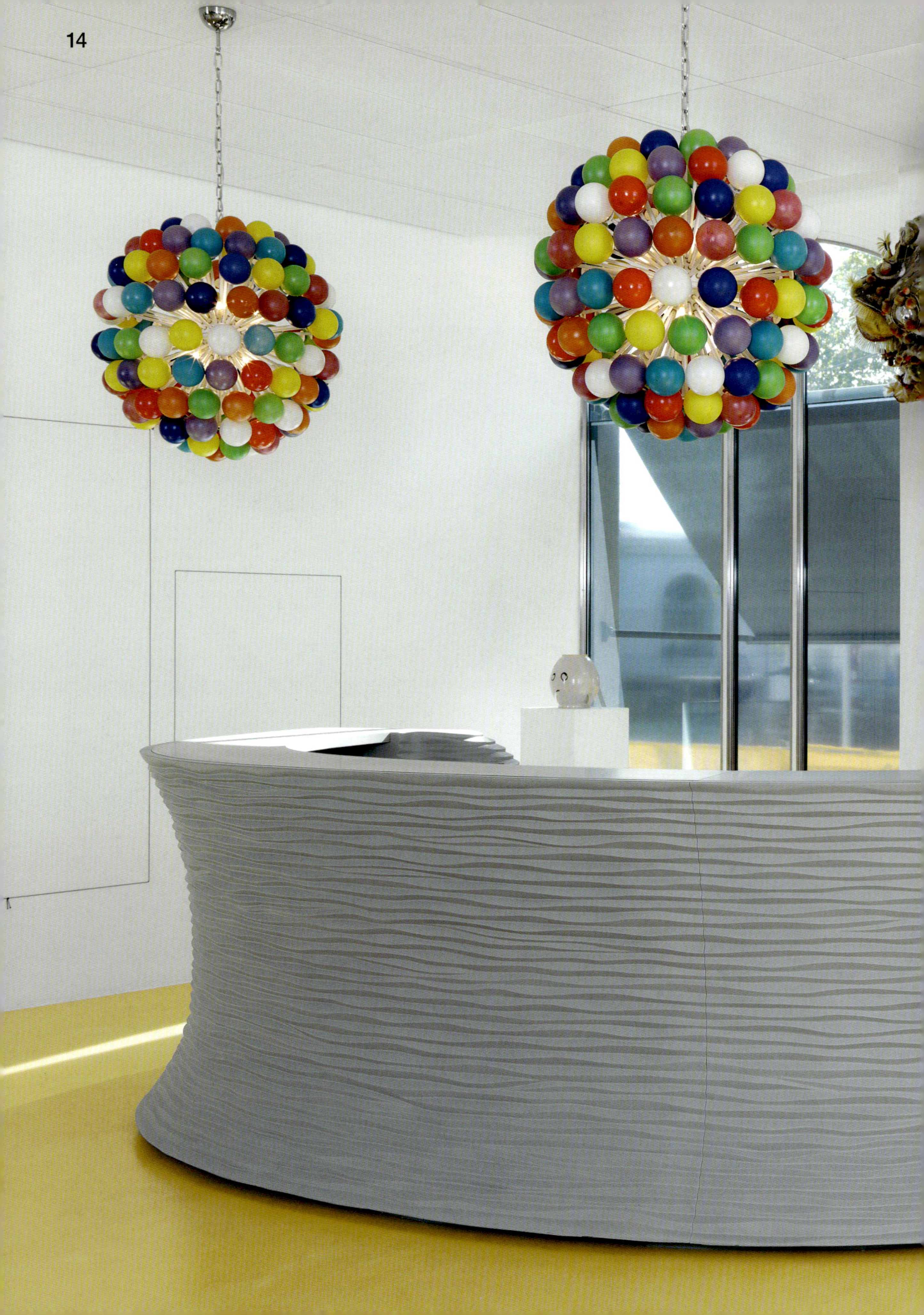

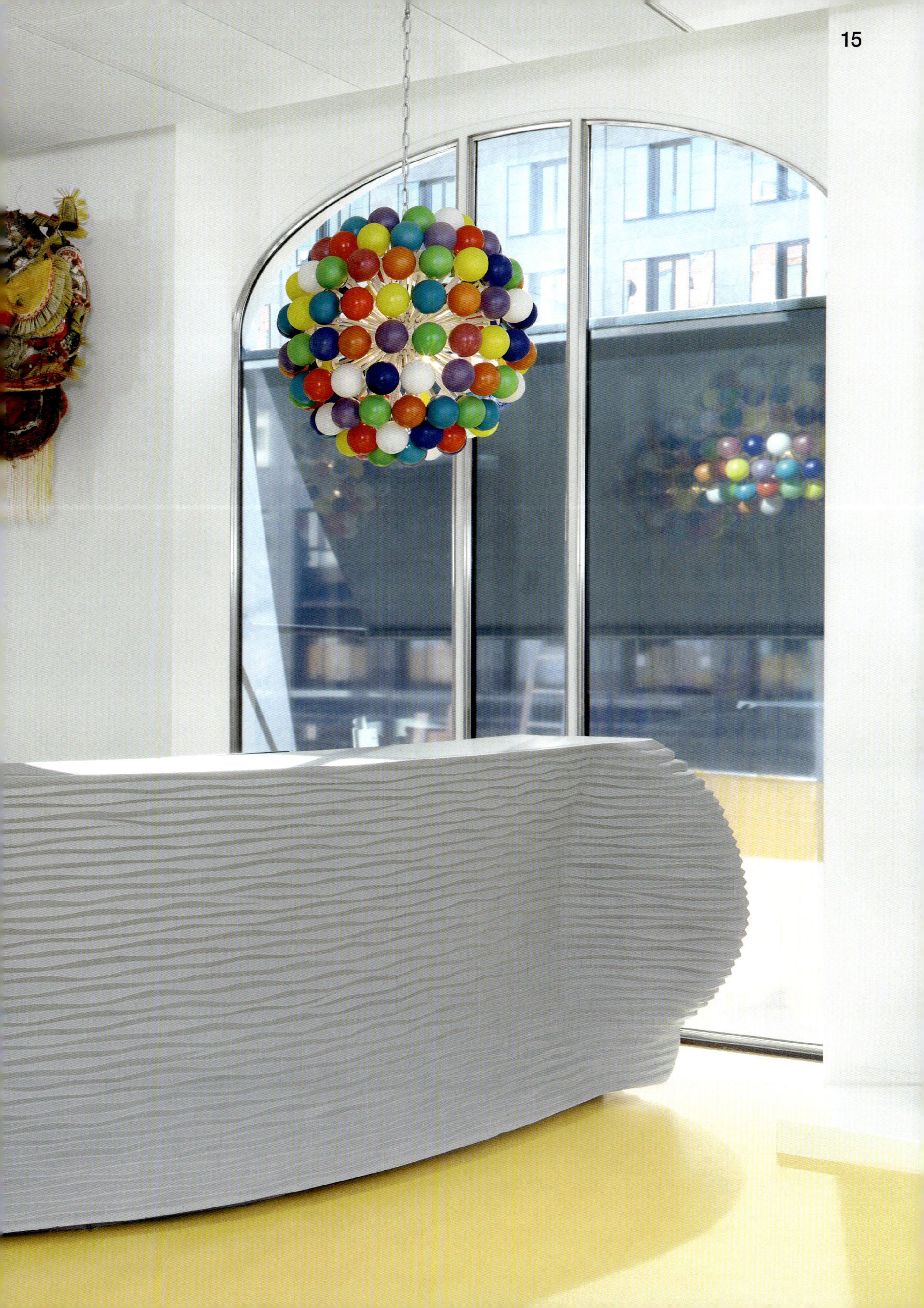

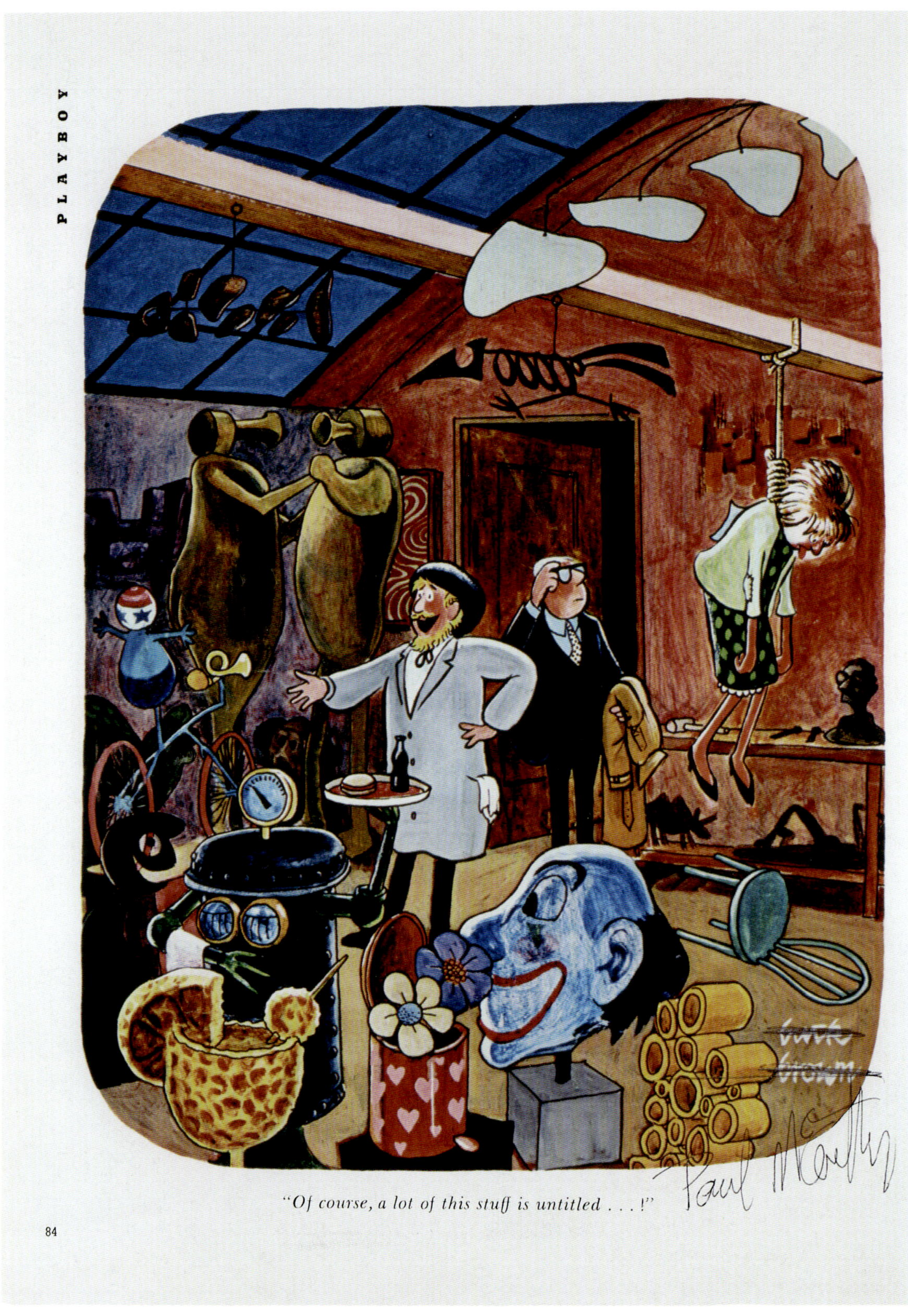

Artist's Studio (from Playboy Comics), 1976–1980/2004
Cibachrome on aluminum
204 × 151 cm

Initiated in New York by Eric and Suzanne Syz in the early 1980s, the collection was first composed of works created by the artists they met there. With the complicity of Bruno Bischofberger, whom the young couple frequented, they became interested in the major artistic trends of the time, from Neo-Expressionist painting to the legacy of Pop art. It was with paintings by Jean-Michel Basquiat, Julian Schnabel, Francesco Clemente, George Condo, and Andy Warhol that the core of what would become the Syz Collection was formed.

In the mid-1990s, on their return to their native Switzerland, Eric Syz founded the Geneva-based financial group that bears his name. Suzanne Syz meanwhile created her jewelry brand, Syz Art Jewels, in the early 2000s.

The presence of art in the premises of the SYZ Group has always been a priority: a way of being permanently connected with contemporary creation since, for the Syz couple, there is no evolution without creativity.

In Fall 2017, the SYZ Group inaugurated its international headquarters located on the Quai des Bergues in Geneva in a historic building that has undergone spectacular interior renovations.

This particular setting was designed to showcase part of the Syz Collection. Since the 1990s, the collection has been gradually enriched without ever favoring any particular medium or artistic trend. Composed of installations, sculptures, and paintings, as well as photographs and works on paper, its ambition is to bring together key works that mark the history of contemporary art, and document some of its essential artists.

With rare exceptions, Eric and Suzanne Syz always favor works that are contemporary with their acquisition; this is the founding principle of their collecting activity. In the 1980s, they bought works from that decade. In 2018, they are perpetuating this principle. It is thus a question of reflecting the narrative of the fractures and artistic evolutions of these last decades thanks to the proximities and discontinuities that emerge between different generations of artists. Their collection shows the taste of an era, their own taste, as well as their constant desire to support emerging figures.

The first publication dedicated to the Syz Collection, this book is mainly devoted to its presentation in the new SYZ Group building. However, some works not on display there are also reproduced because of their significance.

The installation of over three hundred works, as well as numerous design pieces chosen or created by Suzanne Syz, was a real challenge. The building may look like a museum from certain angles, but this is obviously a corporate environment, a place where more than two hundred employees live and work daily. Organized around a central atrium, the building comprises seven floors of varying heights. On either side of the large central wall designed to hang the works, there are open spaces, as well as private offices and reception rooms.

One of the challenges of this presentation was to conceive it as a true exhibition, to give it an artistic consistency, in order to overcome the practical spatial constraints.

It seemed necessary that the multiple groupings constituting this particular history could be understood as a whole, one that can arouse the interest of art professionals as well as the curiosity of collaborators less accustomed to contemporary artistic language. The dense hanging thus offers several levels of reading intended for different audiences, while privileging an undeniable visual pleasure.

In developing this site-specific presentation of the collection, Eric and Suzanne Syz never imposed or refused anything in principle in preliminary conversations, and no work has ever been acquired because of its relation to the financial context of the group. The Syz Collection is thus an open collection, which makes it possible to reproduce, in an obviously subjective way, the vitality of the last 40 years of contemporary creation.

To elucidate this journey, we asked Emmanuel Grandjean, Editor-in-Chief of Culture at *Le Temps*, to lead a discussion with Eric and Suzanne Syz and myself, curator of the collection, on its genesis and development. Together with Matthieu Neyroud, who assisted me throughout the project, we describe the main axes of presentation of the works within the building. Finally, the visual strength of the building and its unique way of presenting artworks inspired Clément Dirié to write an essay on the hanging of artworks in the corporate world.

I am extremely grateful to Eric and Suzanne Syz for their trust, and to their children, Marc and Nicolas, who have just joined the SYZ Group and who will inherit this collection and develop it in the future.

I would also like to thank all the artists and people involved in this adventure and this publication, without whom this project would not have been possible.

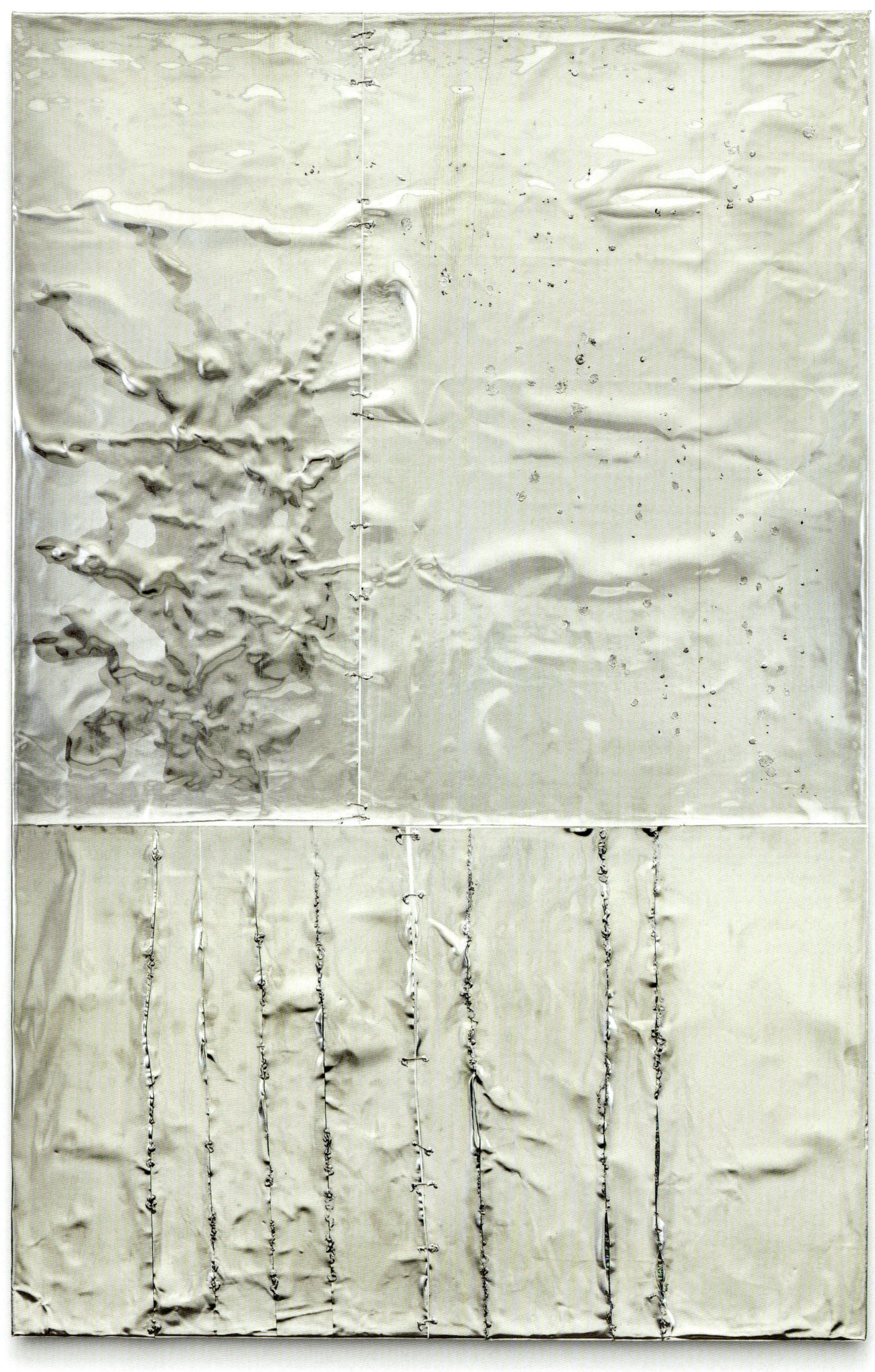

Samurai Among the Reeds, 2015
Tin, mother of pearl plates, and solder on canvas
120.5 × 80 × 3.5 cm

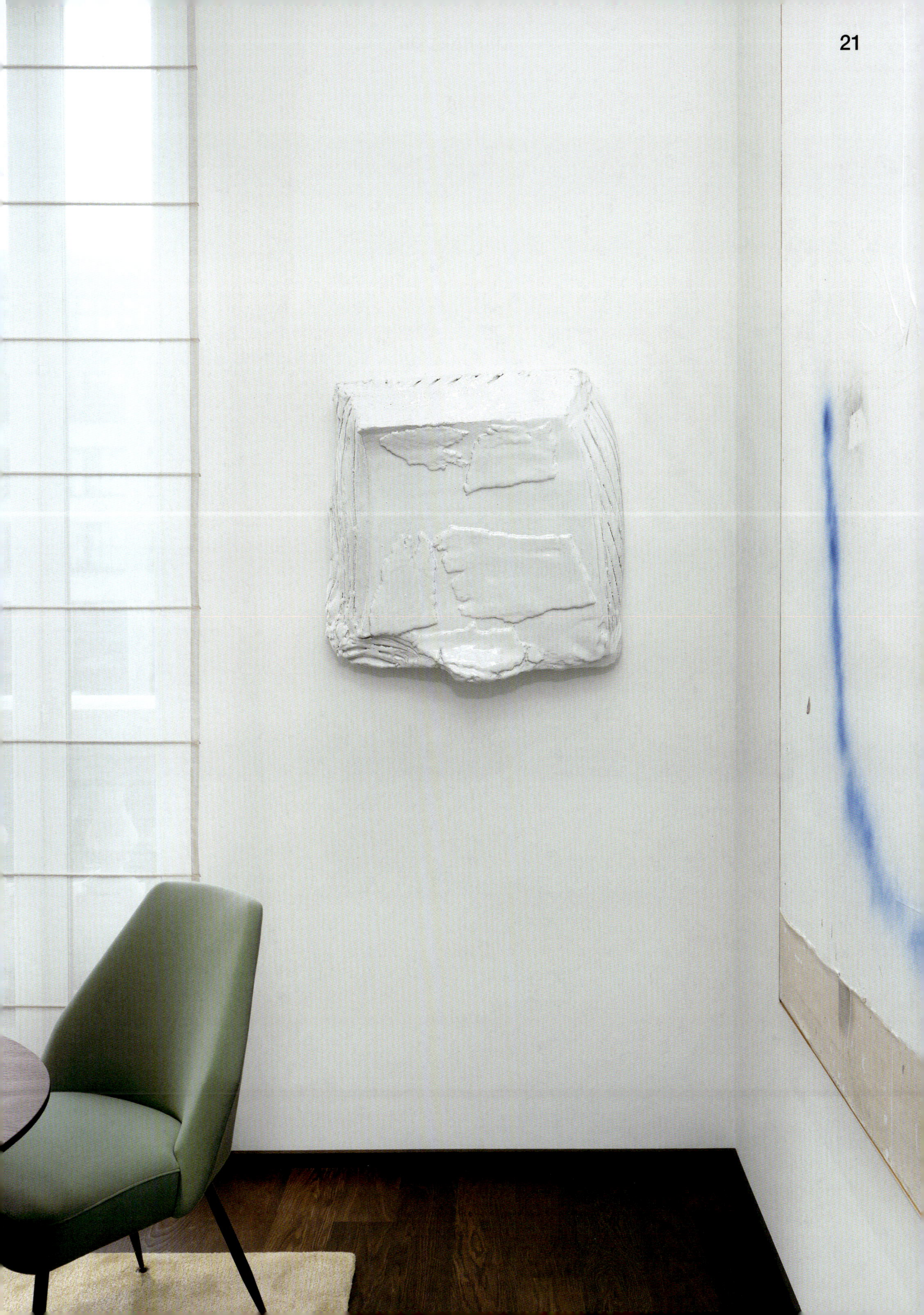

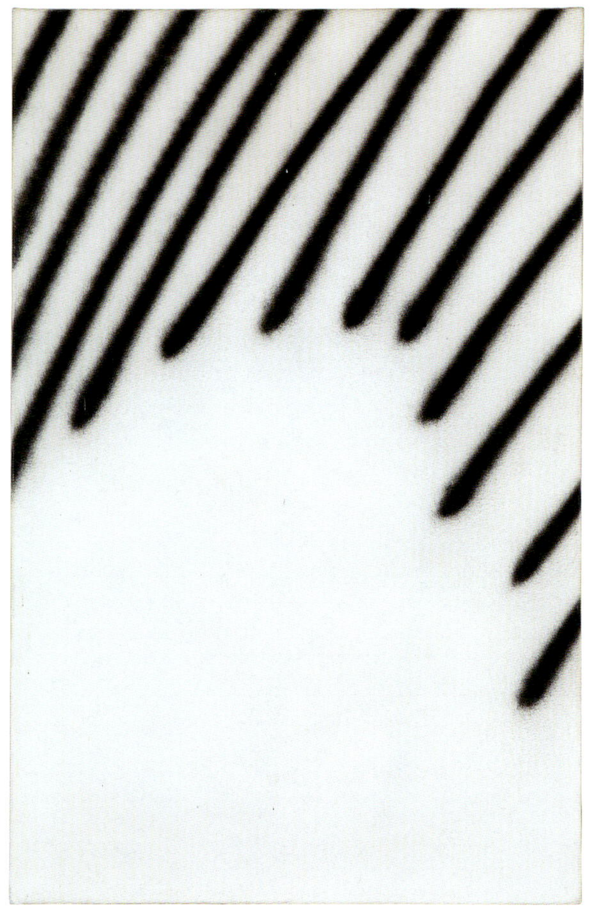

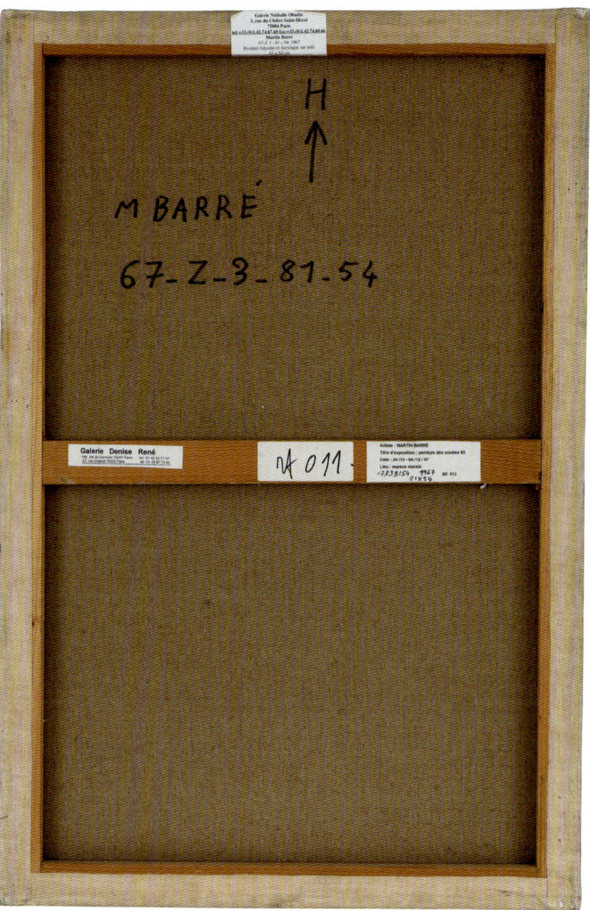

67-Z-3-81×54, 1967
Spray paint on canvas
81 × 54 cm

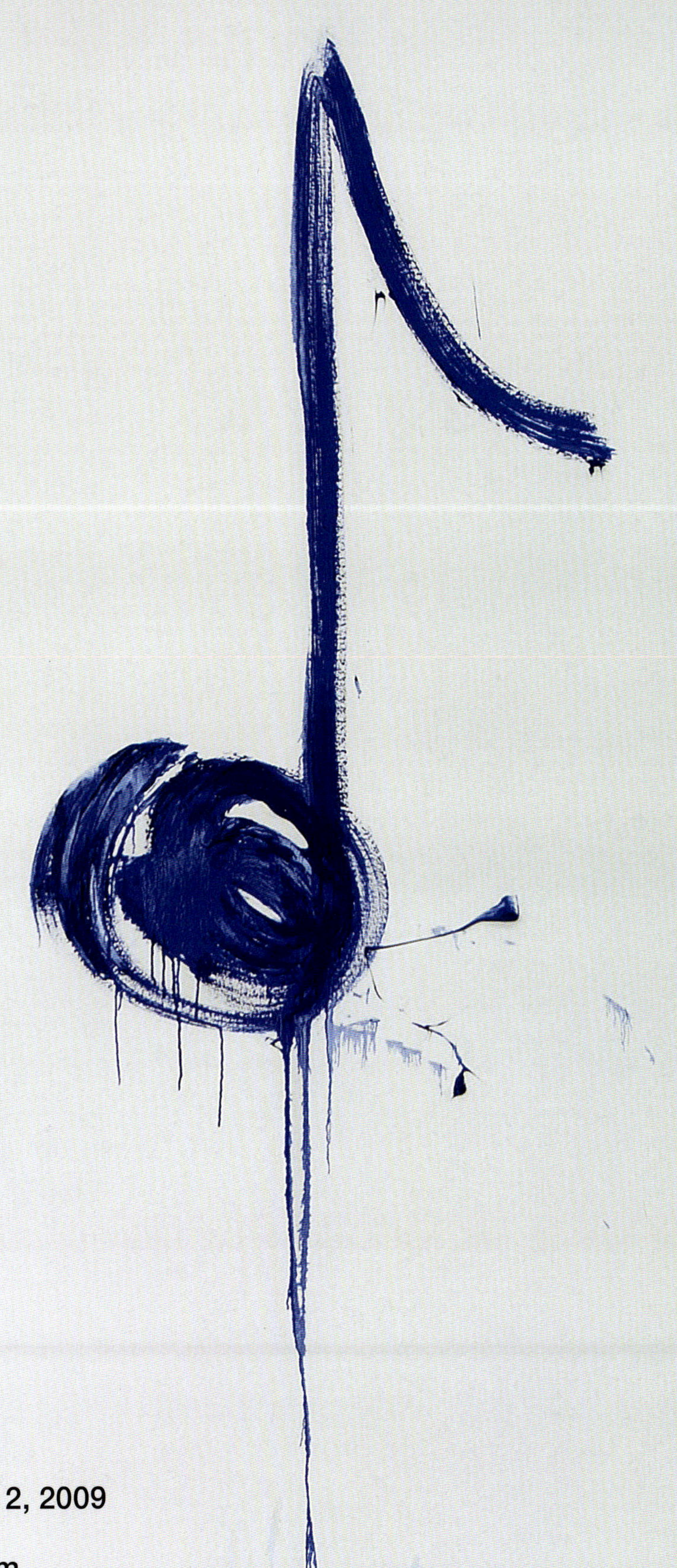

The Opening:
New Museum: 2, 2009
Oil on linen
213.5 × 152.5 cm

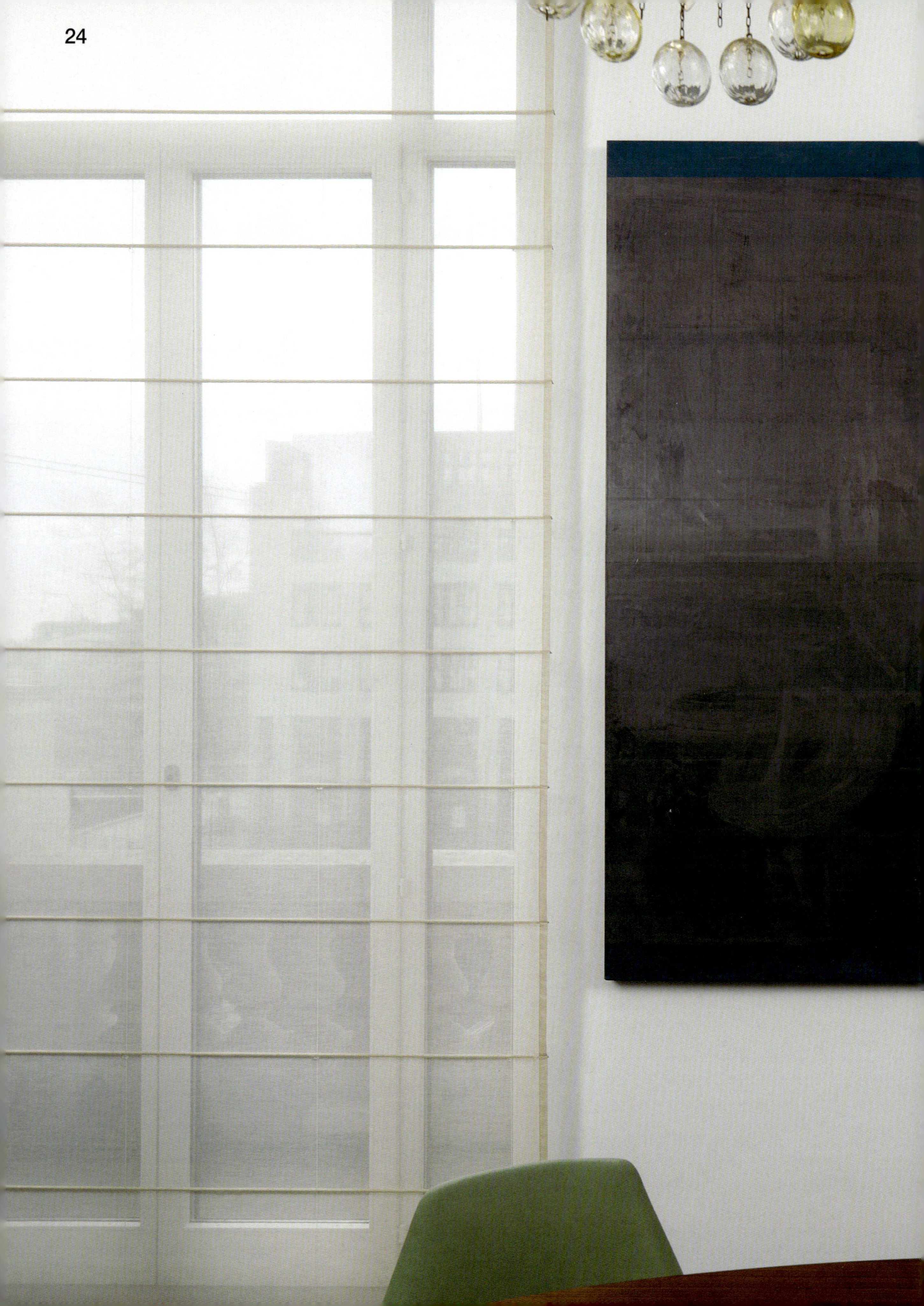

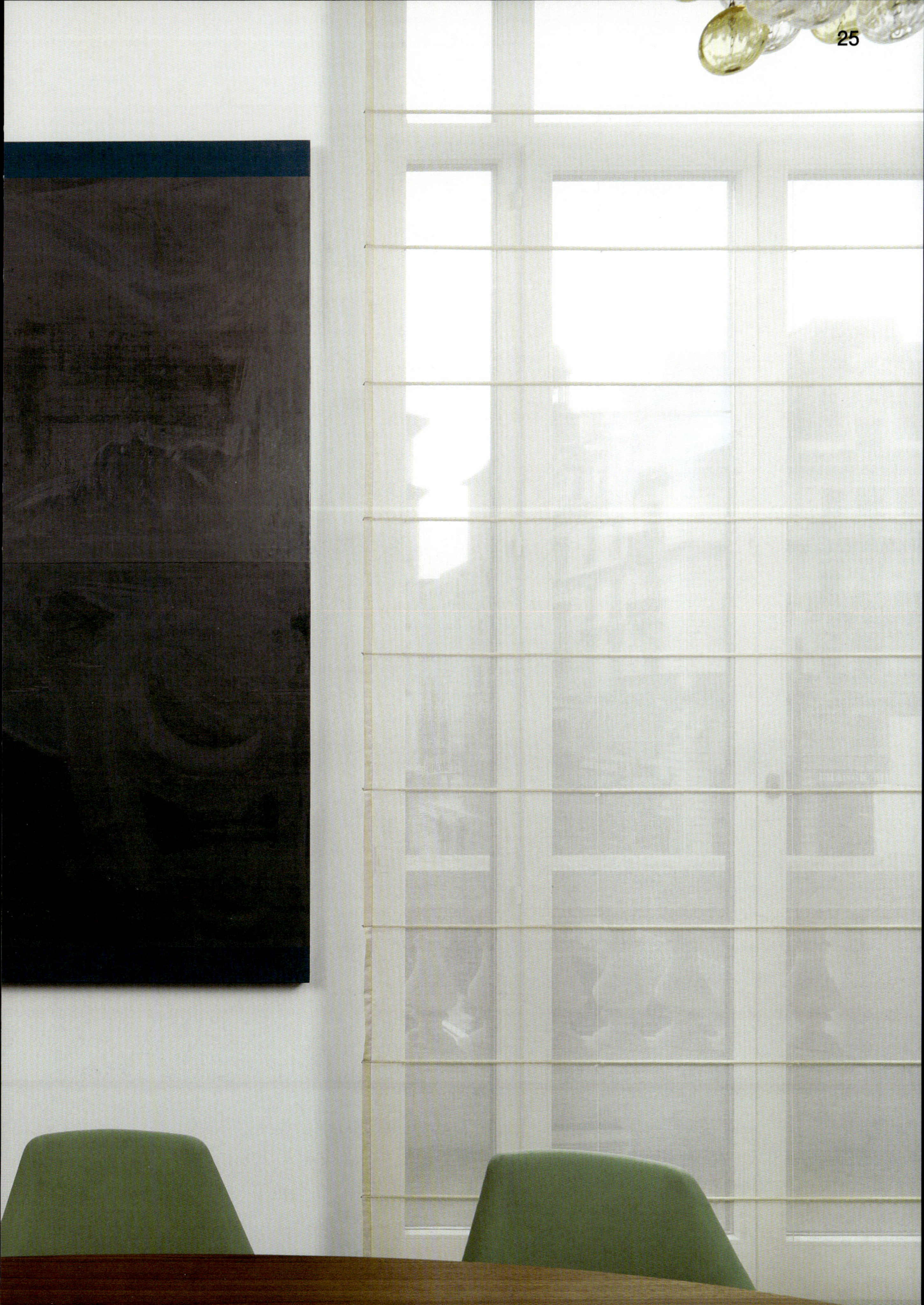

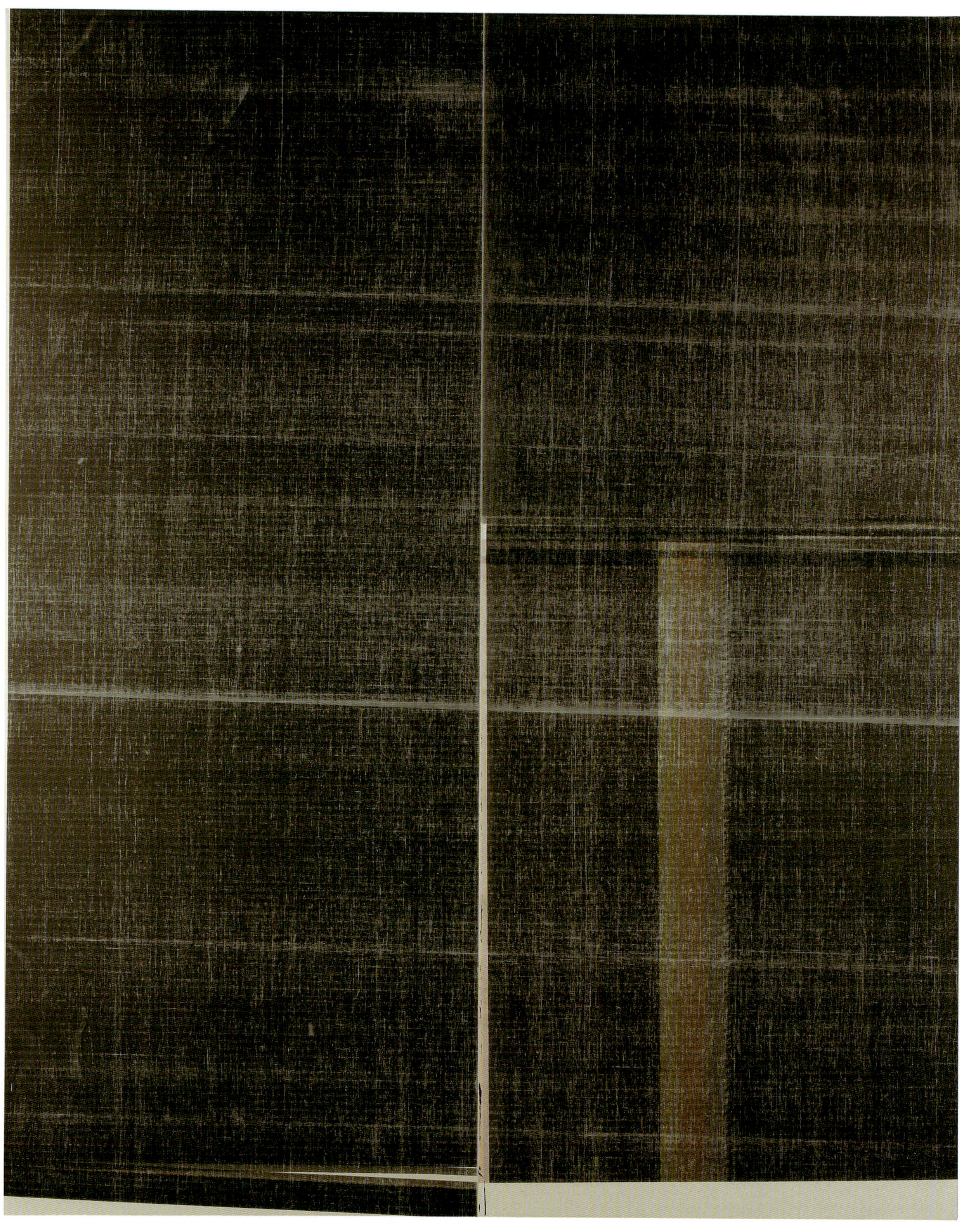

Untitled, 2011
Epson UltraChrome inkjet on linen
213.4 × 175.3 cm

Dark Threat 2, 2010
Wool on canvas
200 × 200 × 3.5 cm

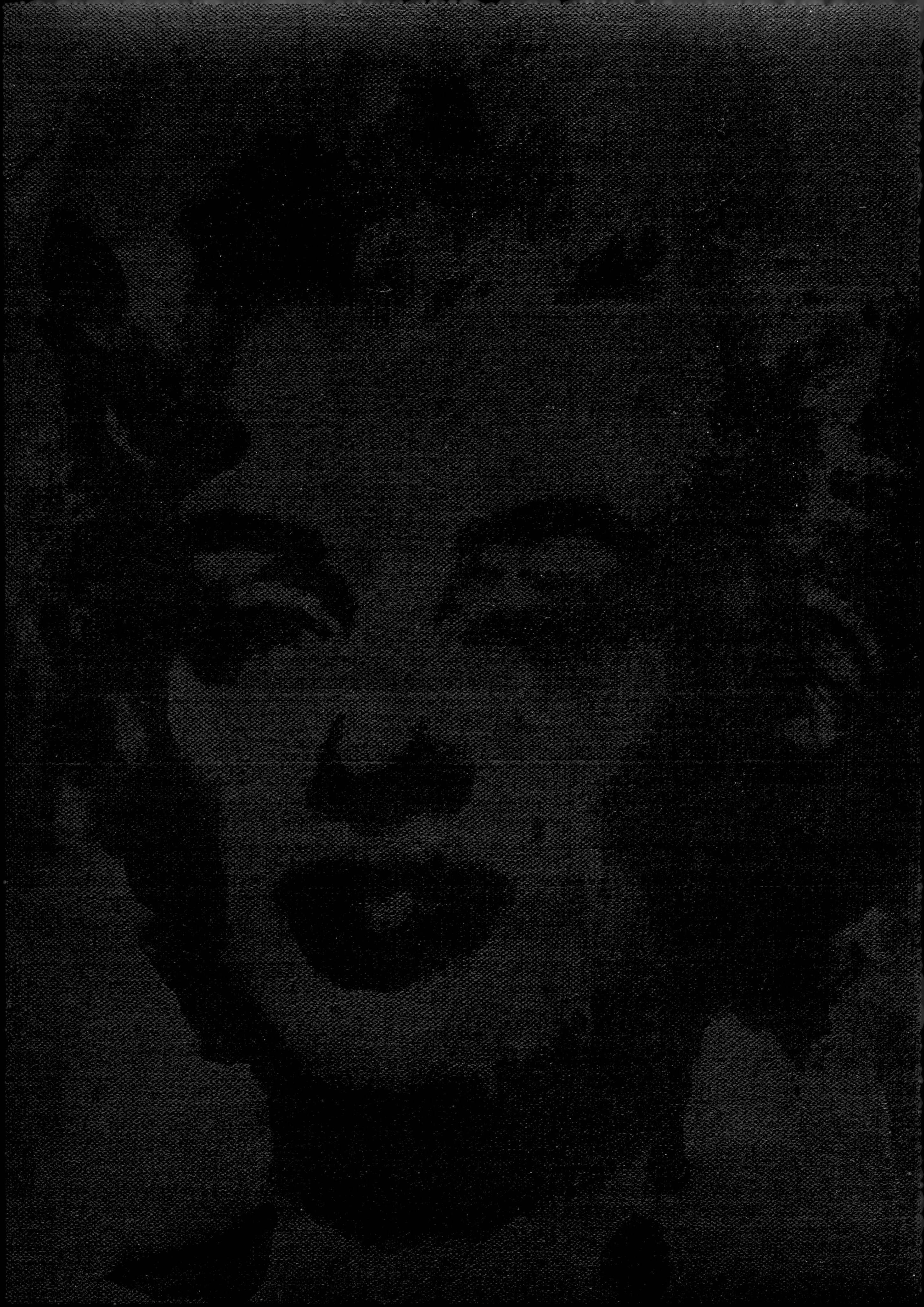

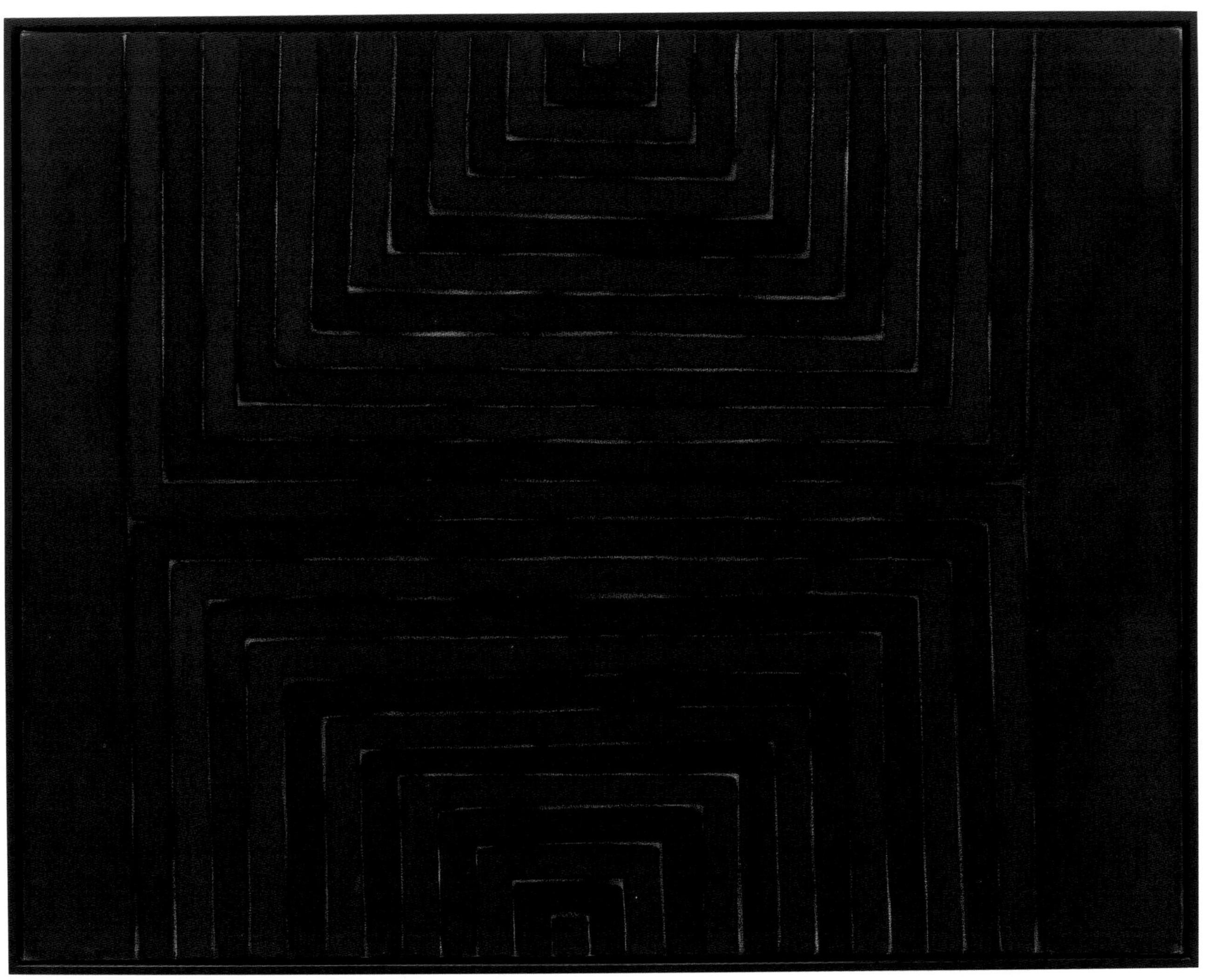

Warhol Black Marilyn, 2004
Synthetic polymer silkscreen
and acrylic on canvas
41 × 33 cm

Stella Morro Castle
(First Study), 1990
Black enamel on canvas
105 × 138 cm

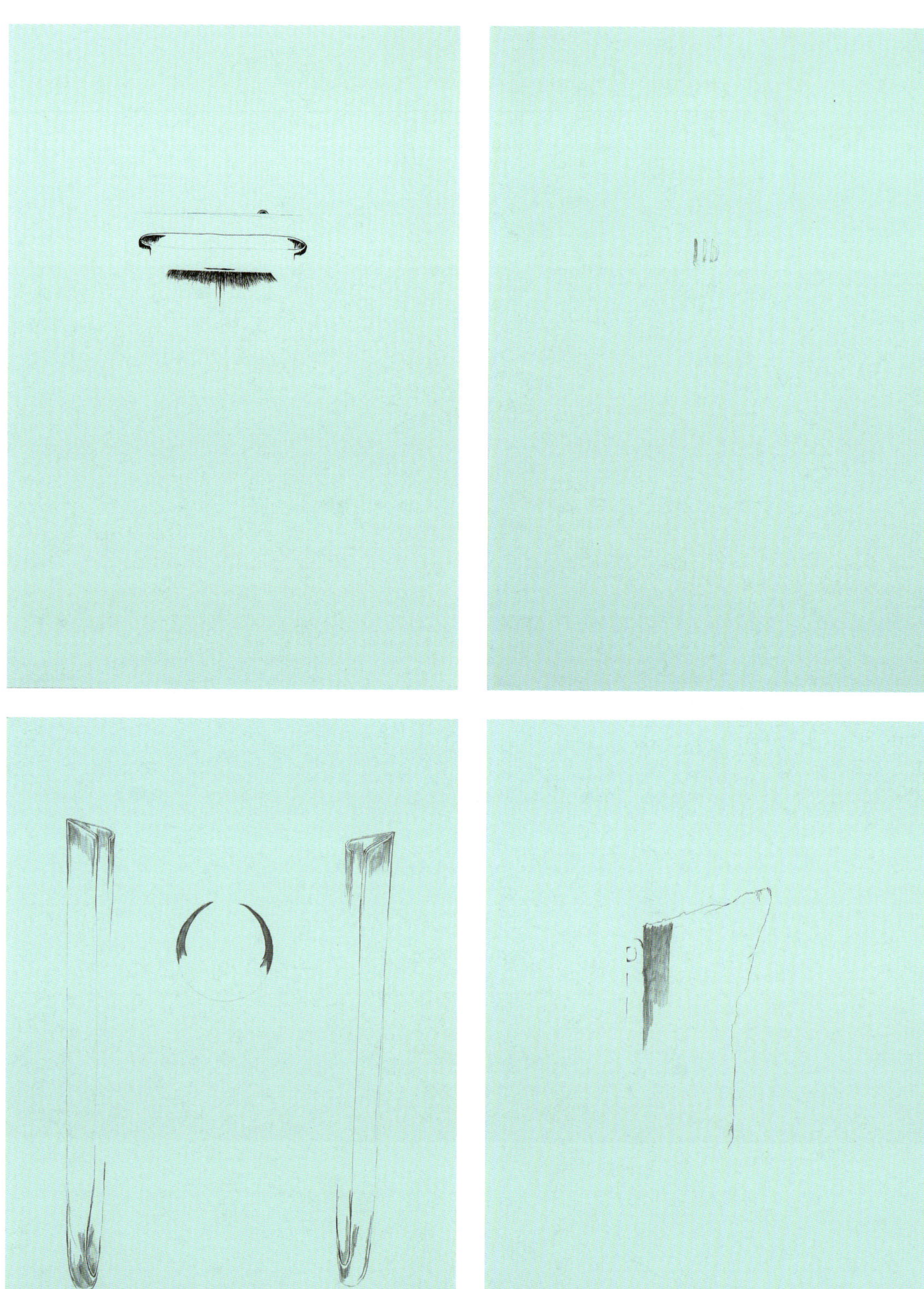

Untitled, 2007
Ink and pencil on paper
84 × 59.3 cm each

Untitled II (Peralta), 2007
C-print
158.8 × 111.8 cm

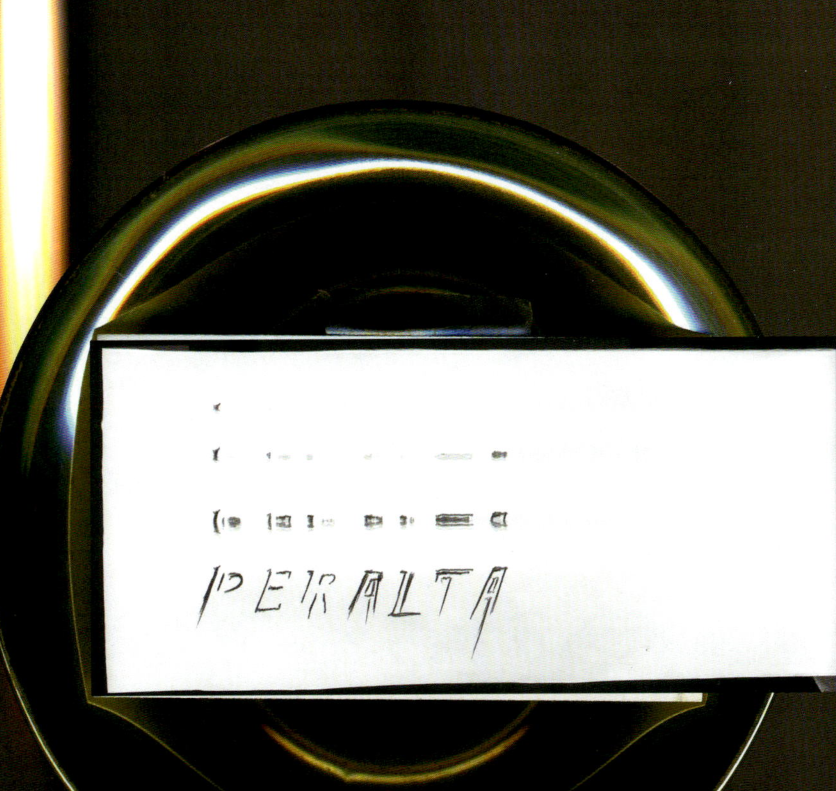
PERALTA

johns target with four faces, 1987–1990

Encaustic and collage on canvas with objects
95 × 56 cm

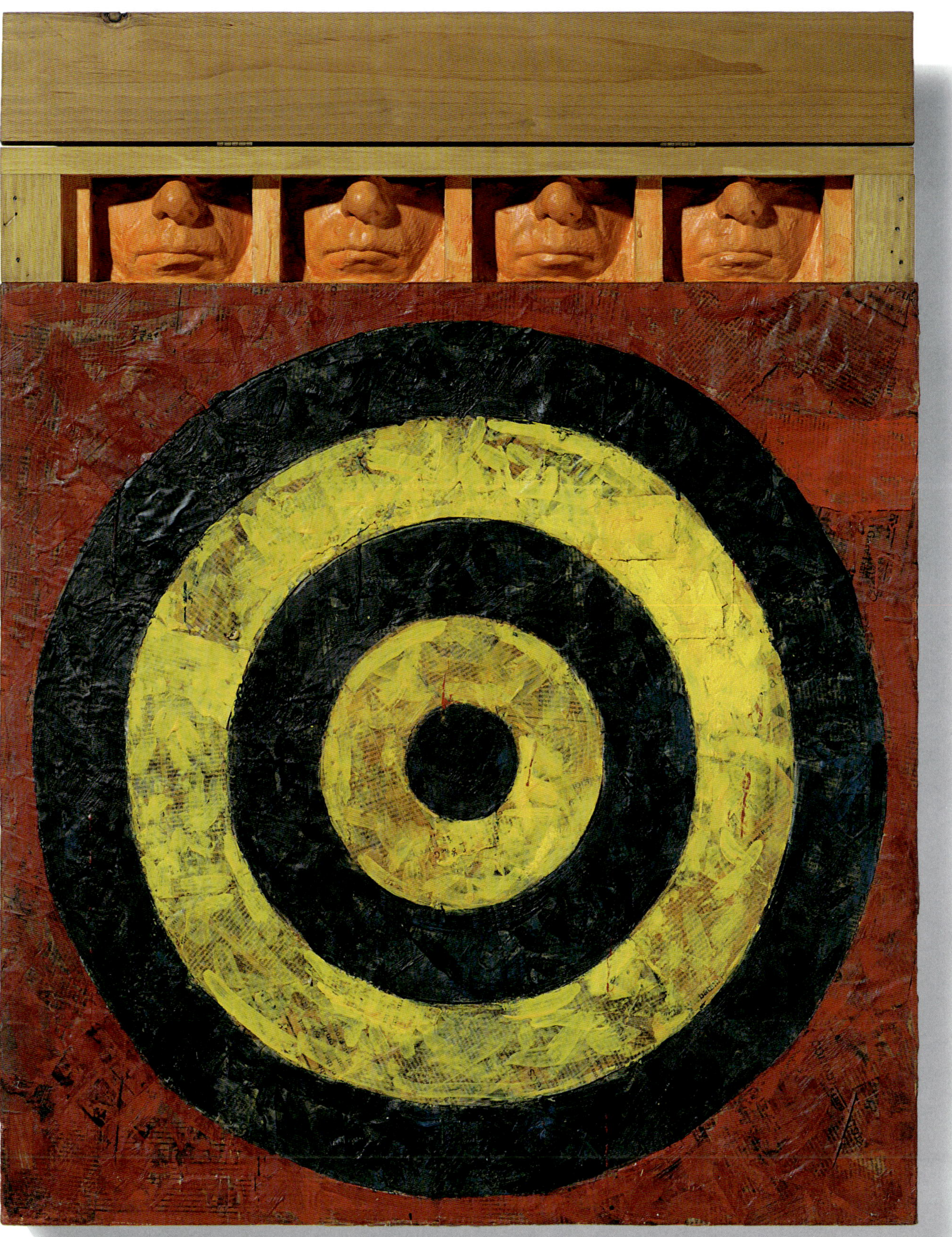

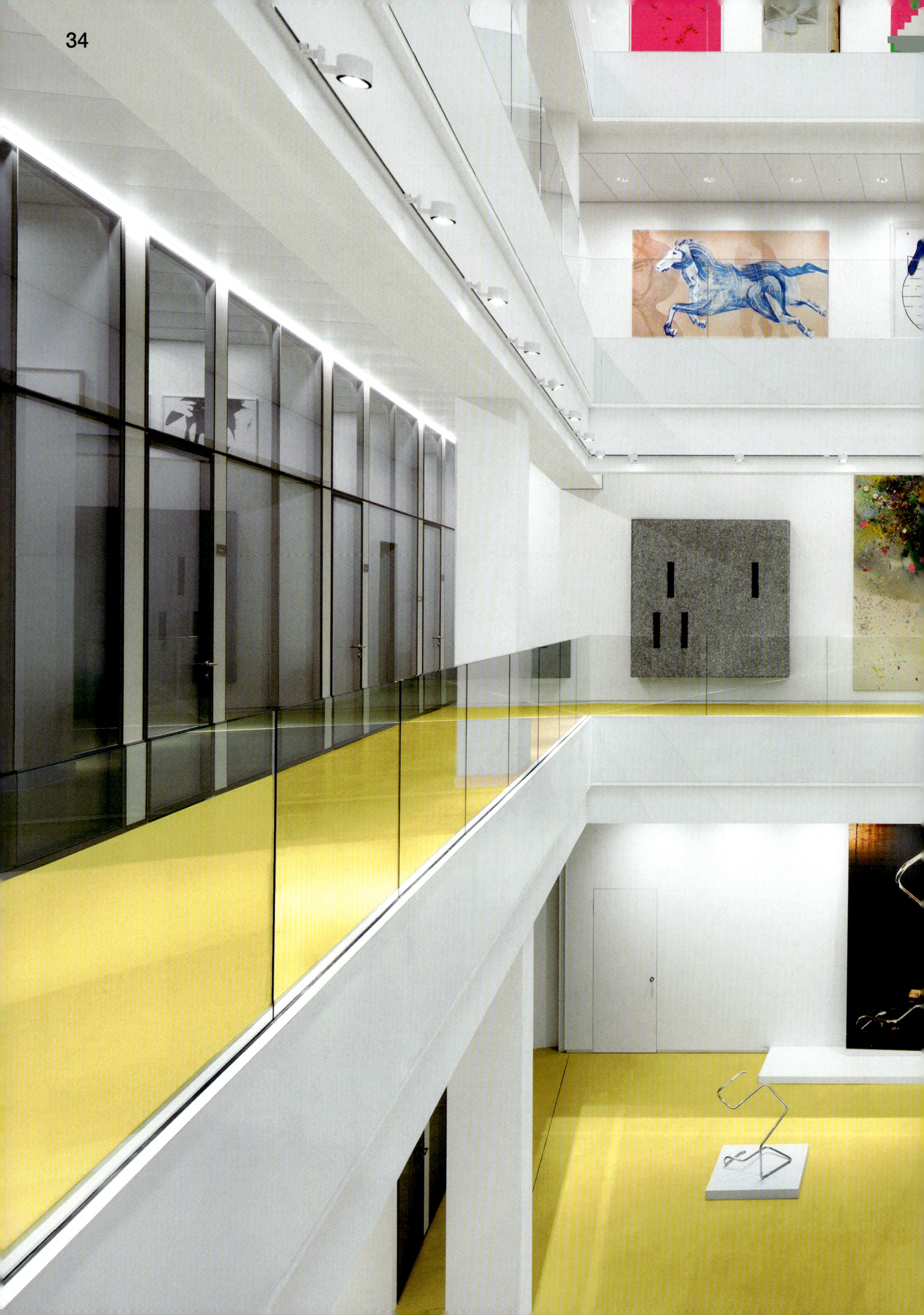

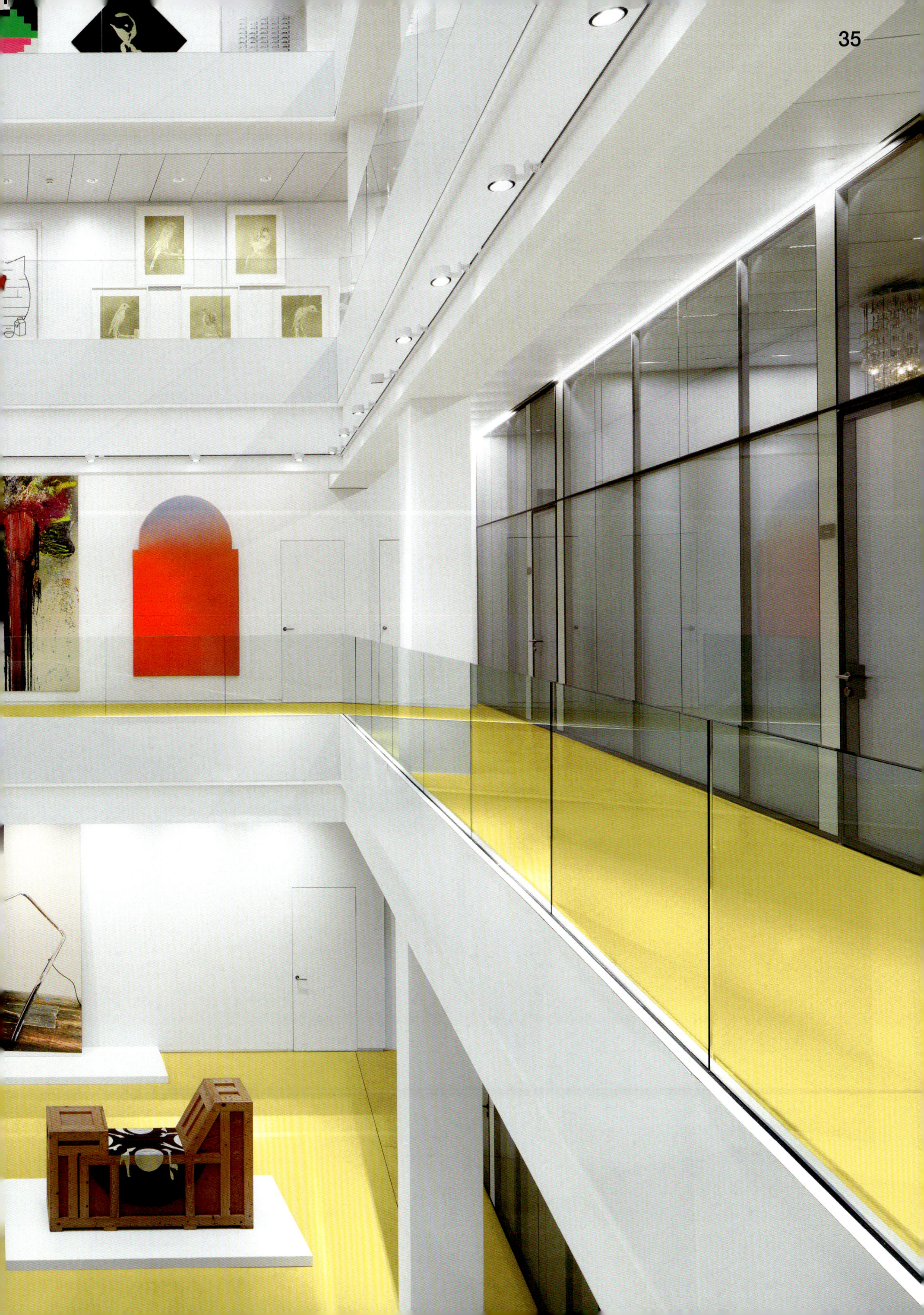

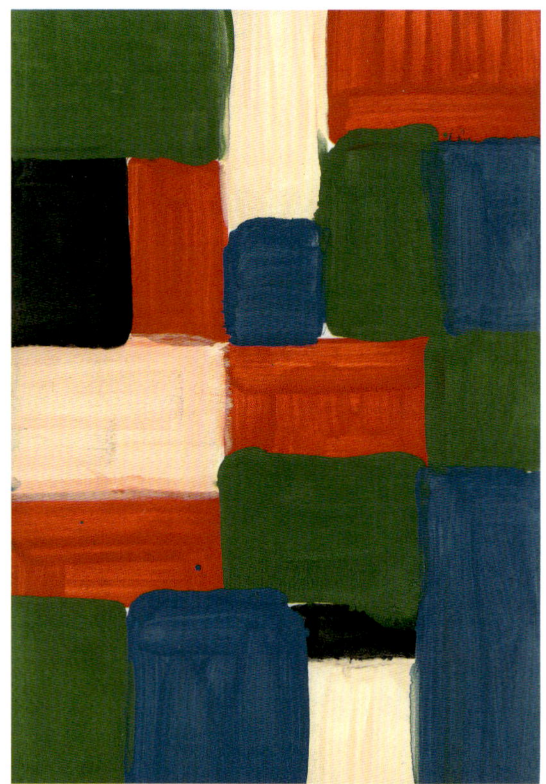

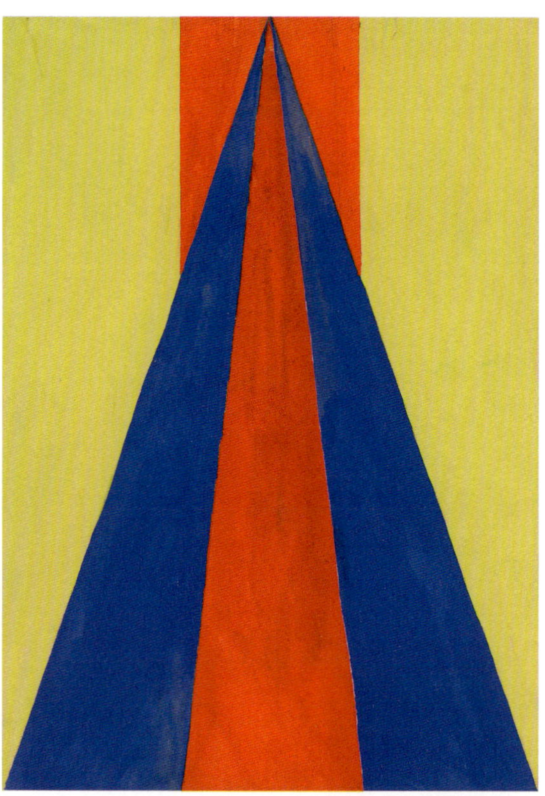

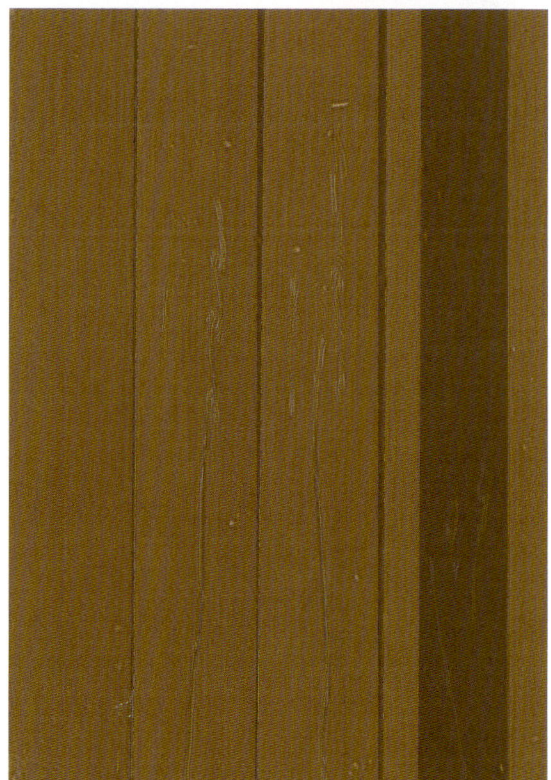

Untitled, 1986
Gouache on paper
30.6 × 21.4 cm

Untitled, 1985
Gouache on paper
29.7 × 21 cm

Untitled, 1986
Adhesive tape on paper
29.7 × 21 cm

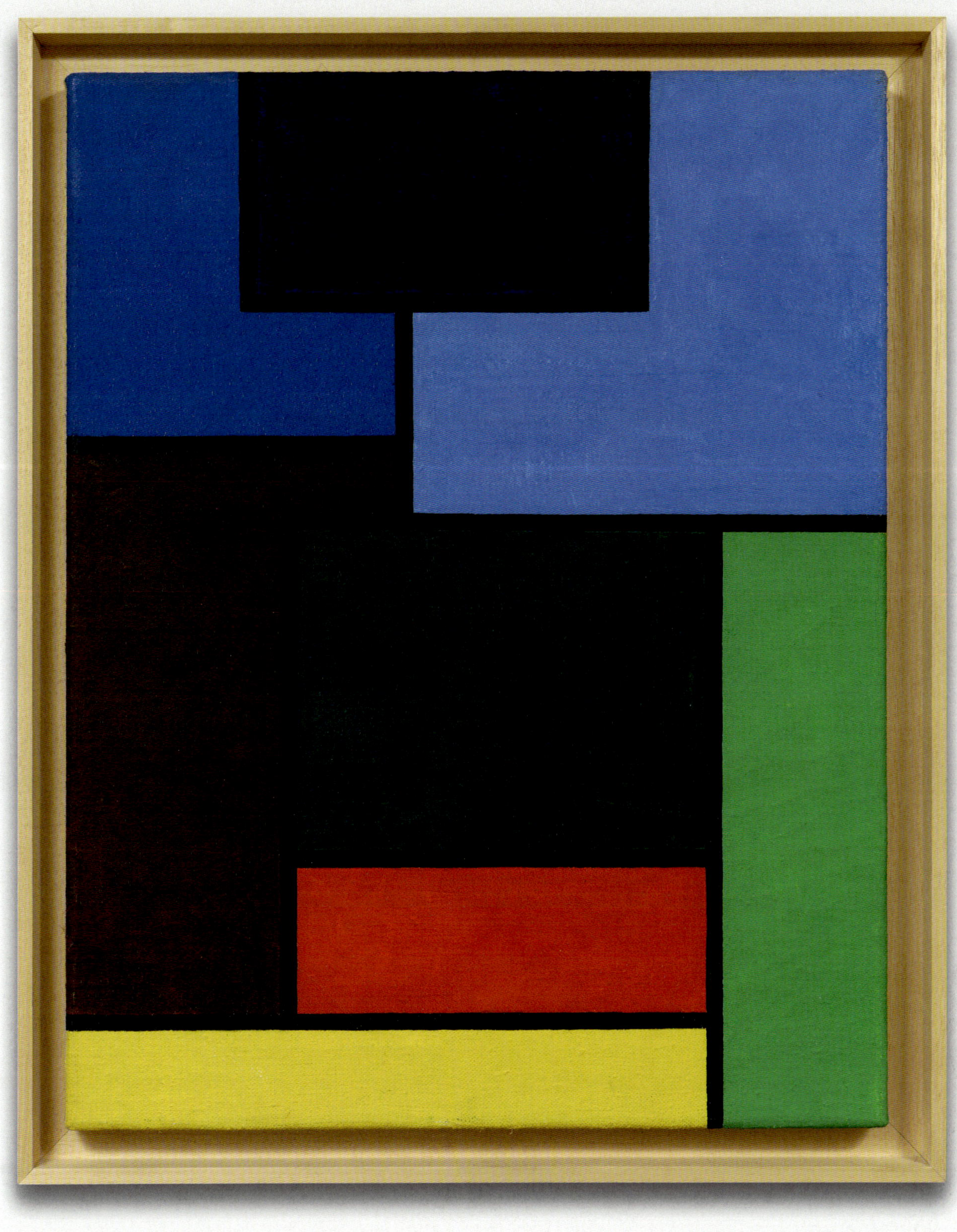

Untitled, 1985
Oil on canvas
50 × 40 cm

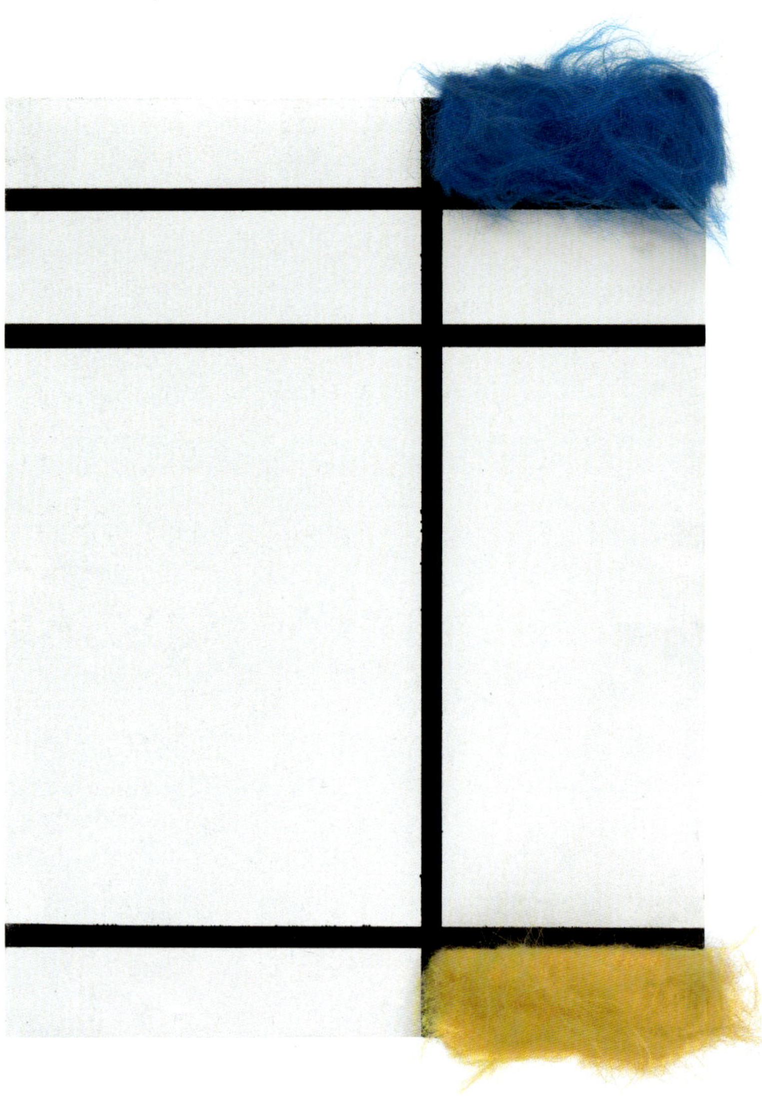

Composition avec bleu, jaune et blanc, 1992
Acrylic and synthetic fur on wood
43 × 33 cm

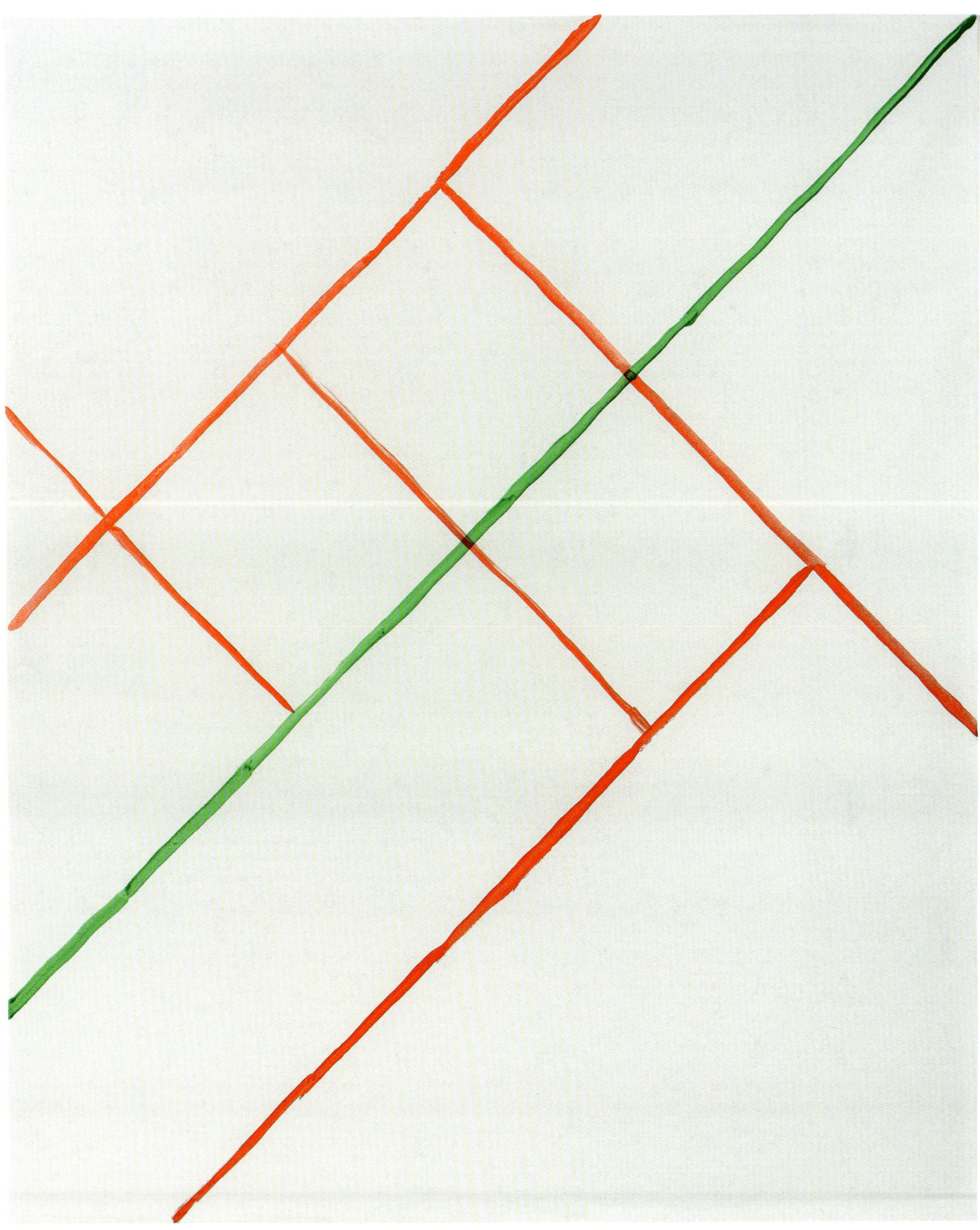

Cartouche Painting N° 8, 2017
Acrylic on canvas
120 × 100 cm

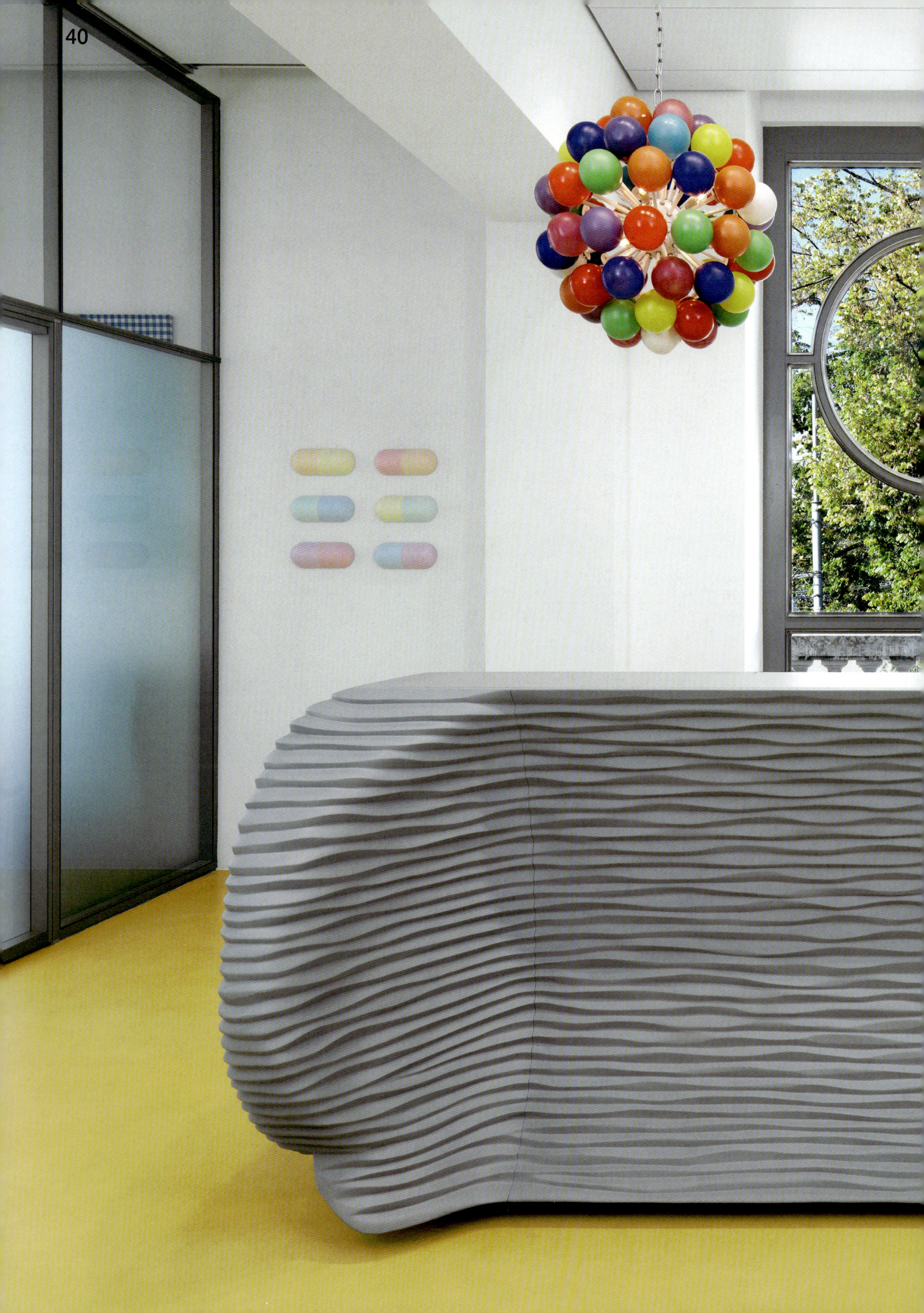

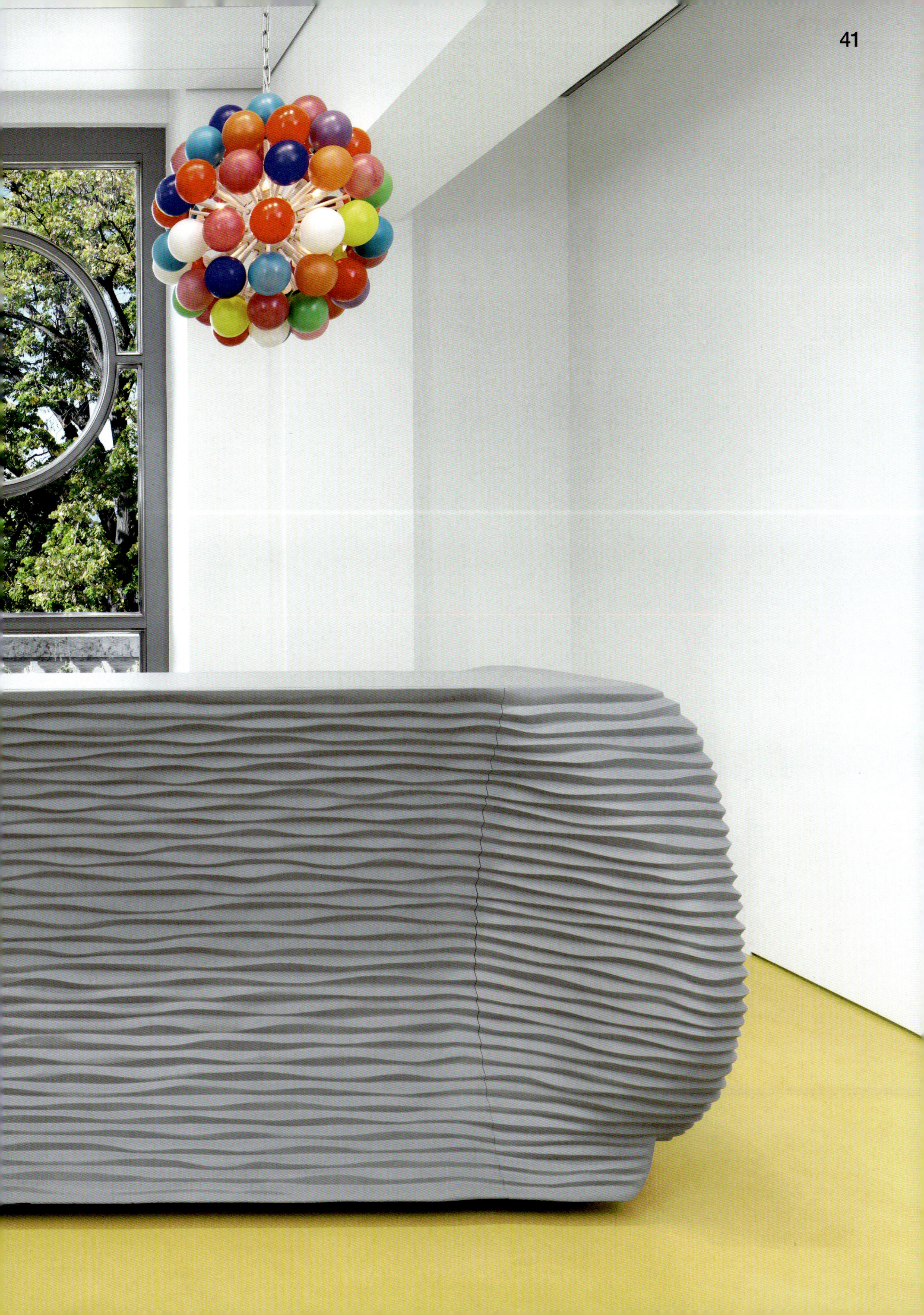

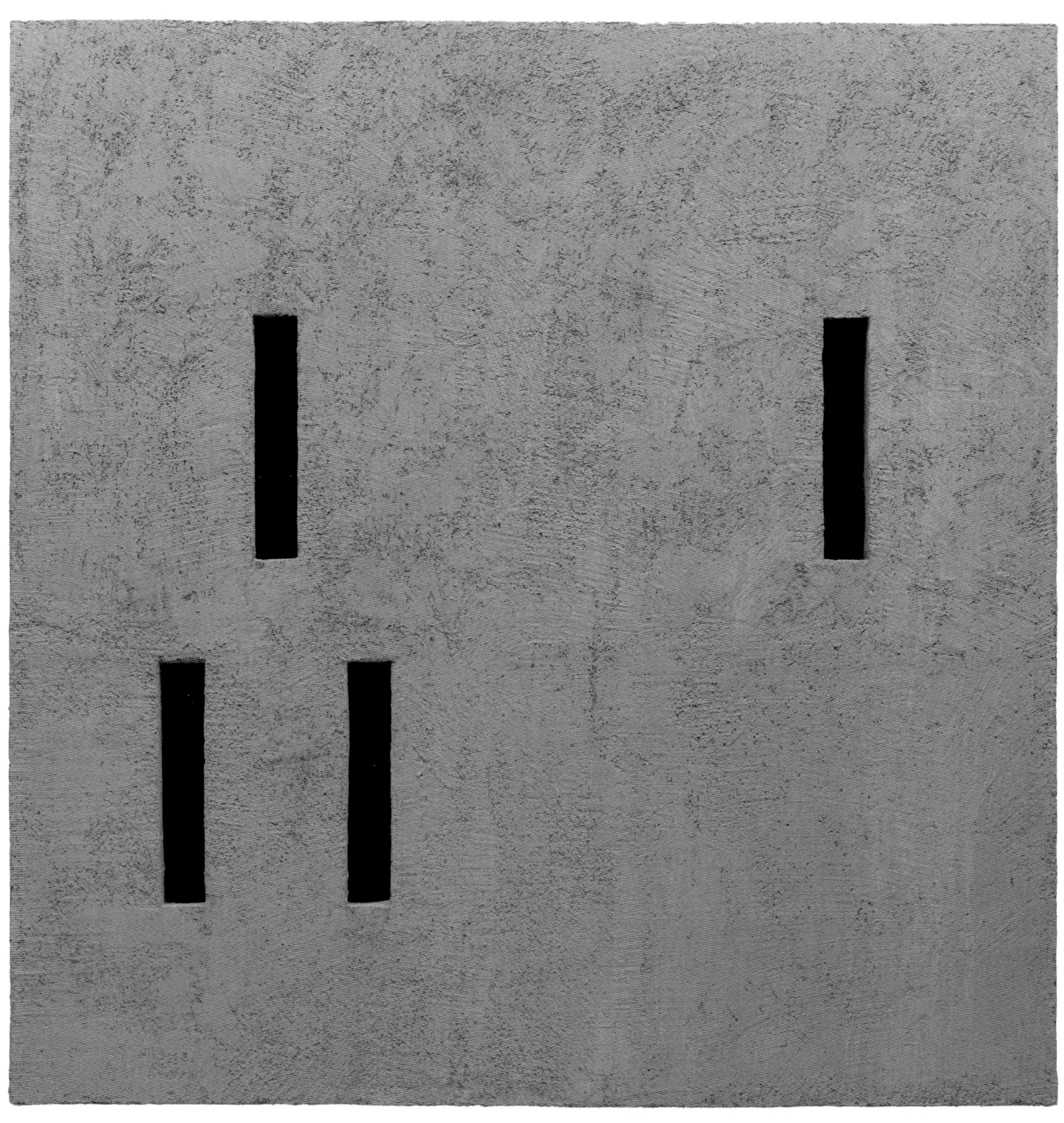

Bleue bleue brune infâme, infâme, 2009
Styrofoam, fiberglass, wood, resin, metal, acrylic paint
220 × 220 × 30 cm

Untitled, 1967
Acrylic on canvas
200 × 200 cm

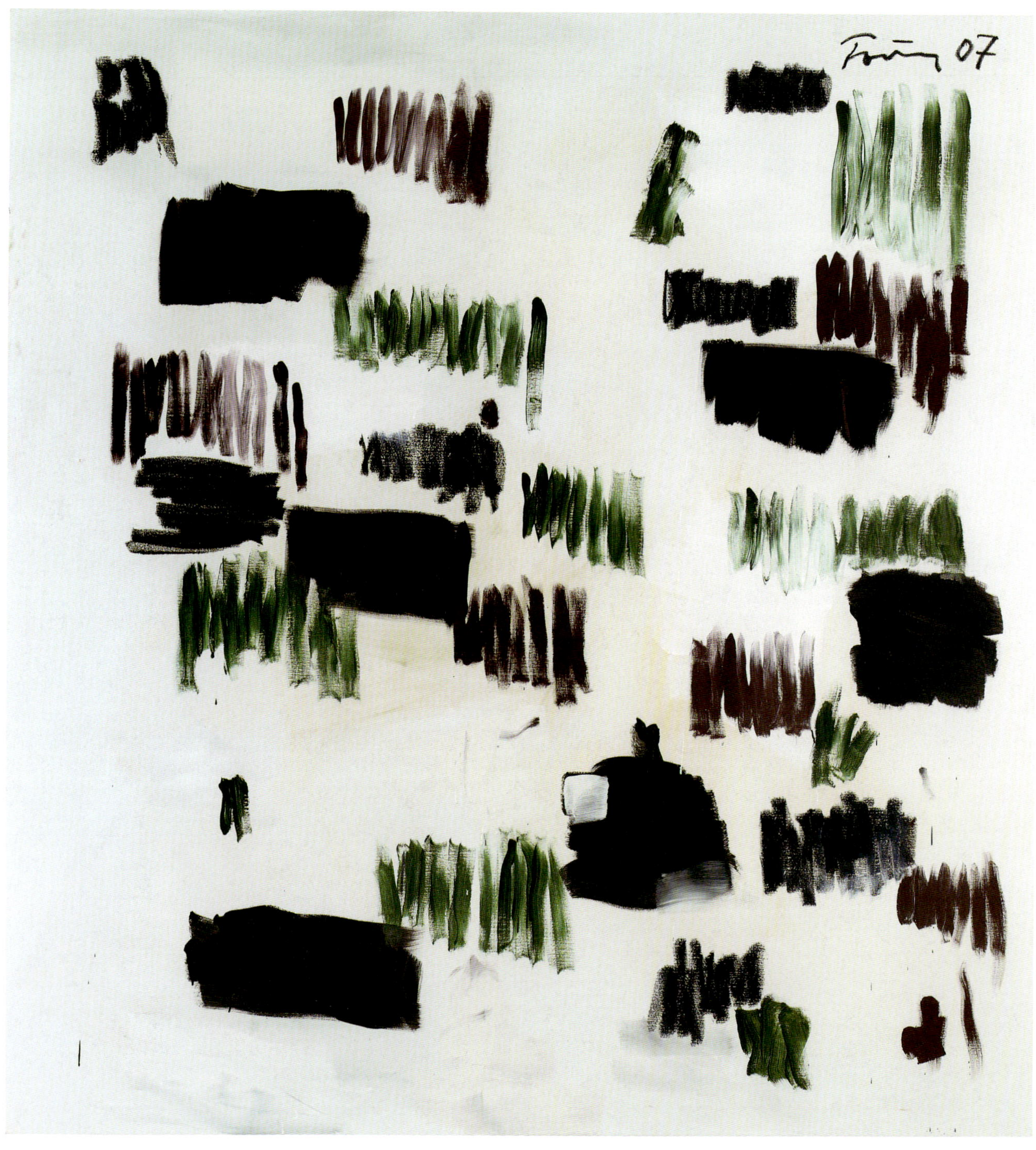

Untitled, 2007
Acrylic and oil on canvas
200 × 190 cm

grosse röhre aus gummi, liegend. 2012

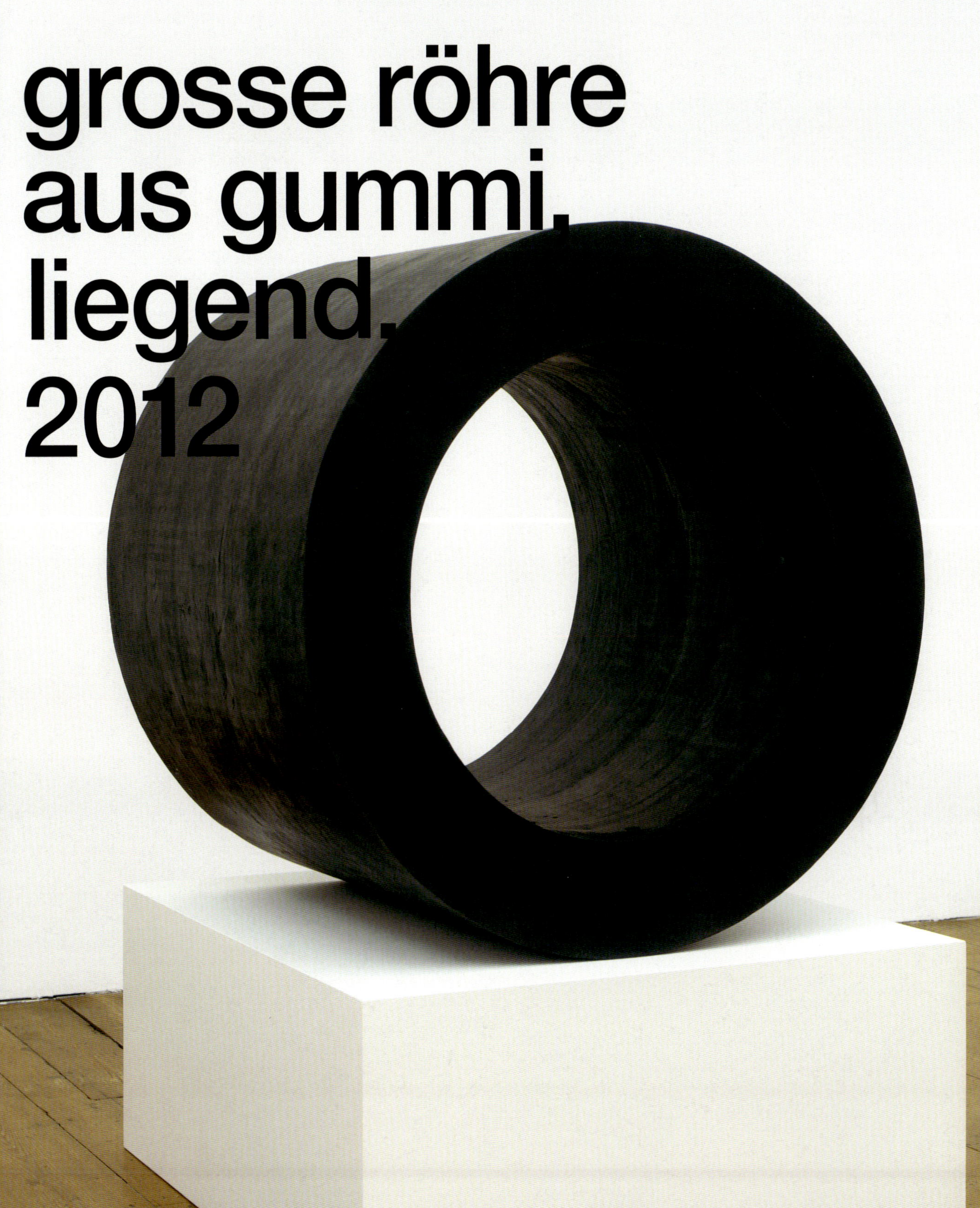

Rubber
71 × 71 × 60 cm

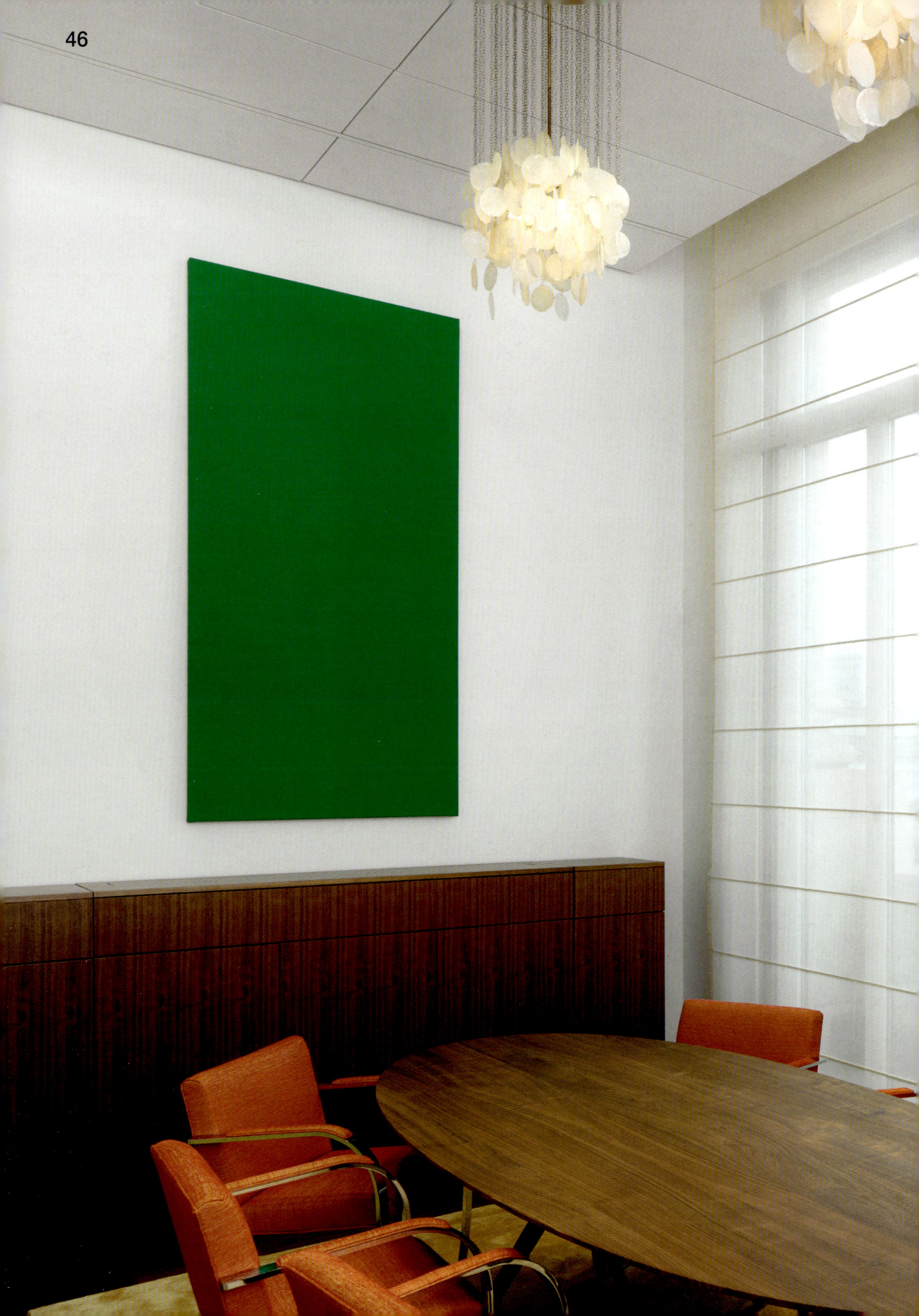

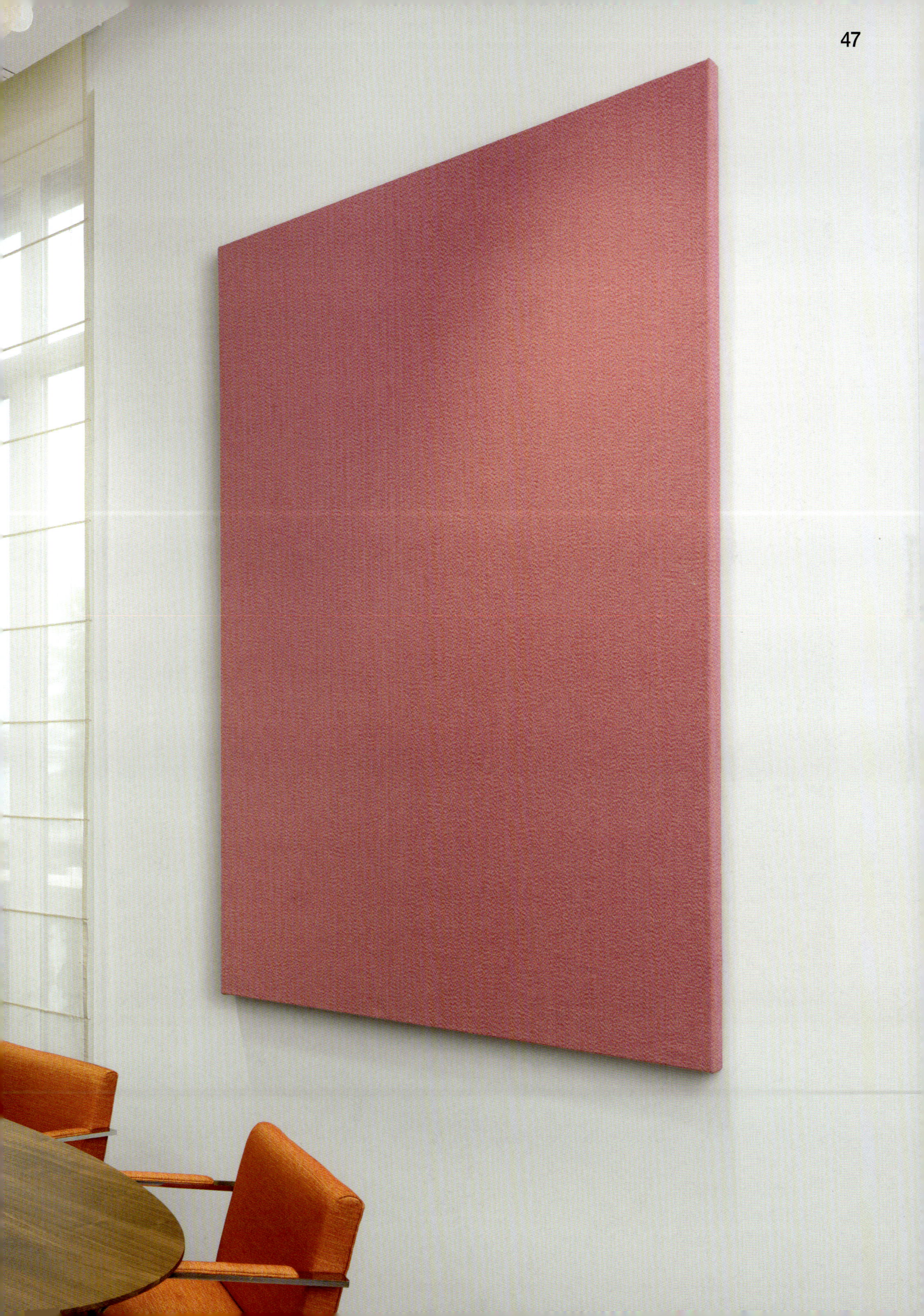

Untitled, 1988
Oil on canvas
100 × 100 cm

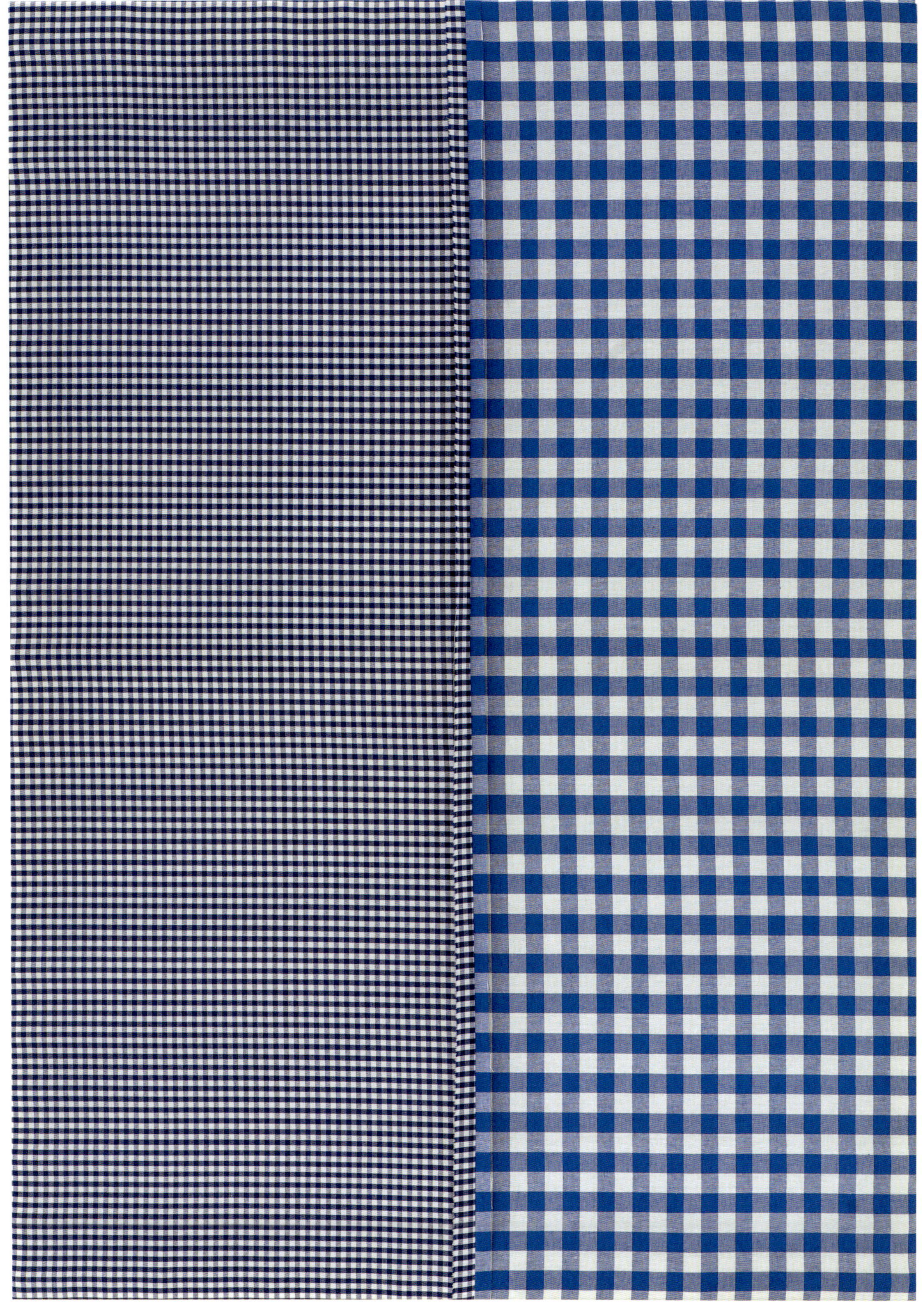

Untitled, 2006
Fabric
120 × 90 cm

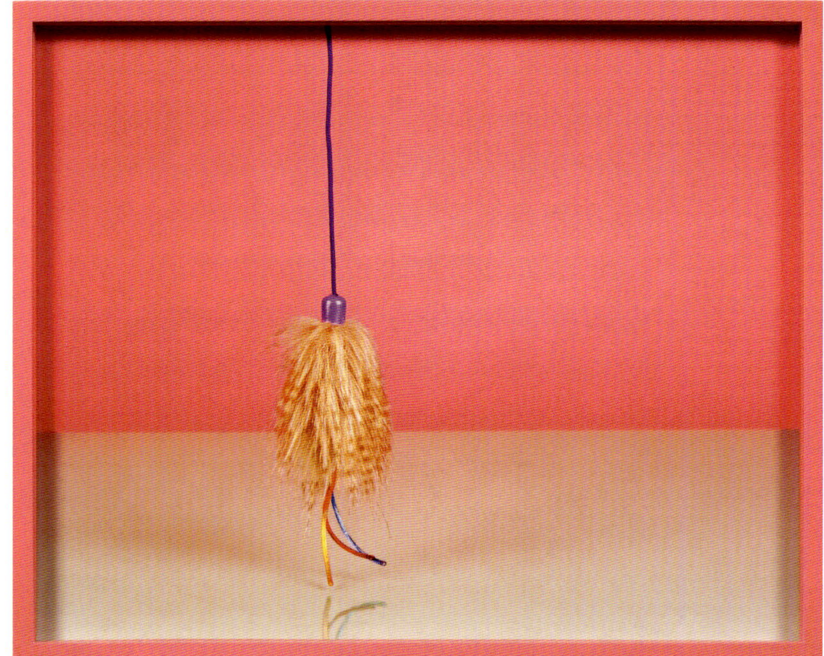

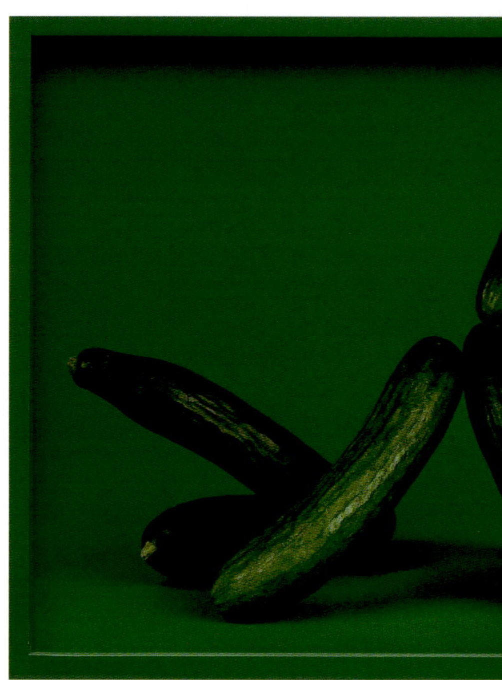

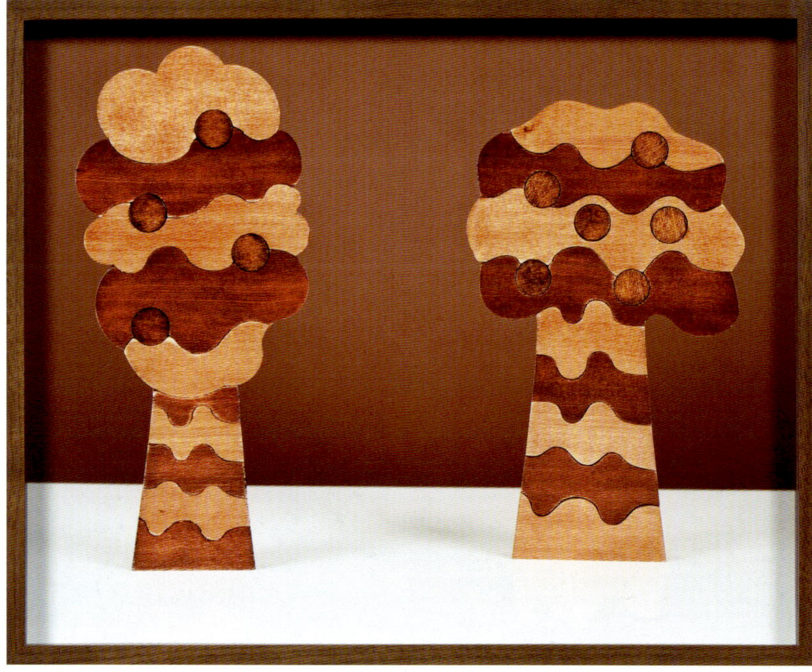

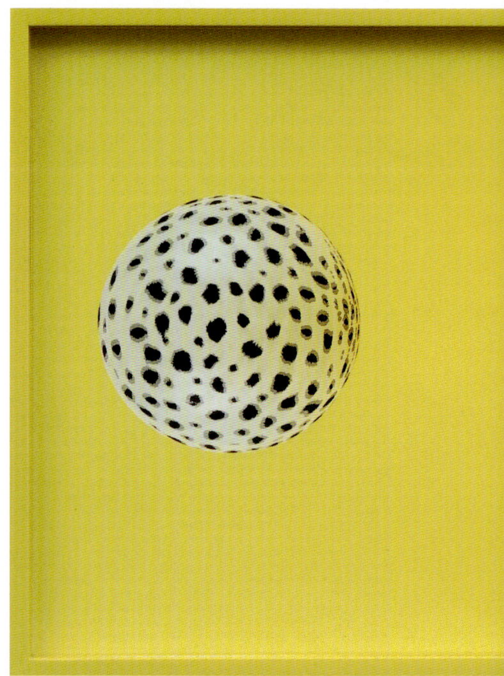

Cat Toy A, 2010
C-print
29.2 × 36.8 cm

Two Trees, 2010
C-print
29.2 × 36.8 cm

Persian Cucumbers, Shuk Hakarmel, 2008
C-print
24.1 × 27.9 cm

Untitled (Cheetah), 2008
C-print
29.2 × 36.8 cm

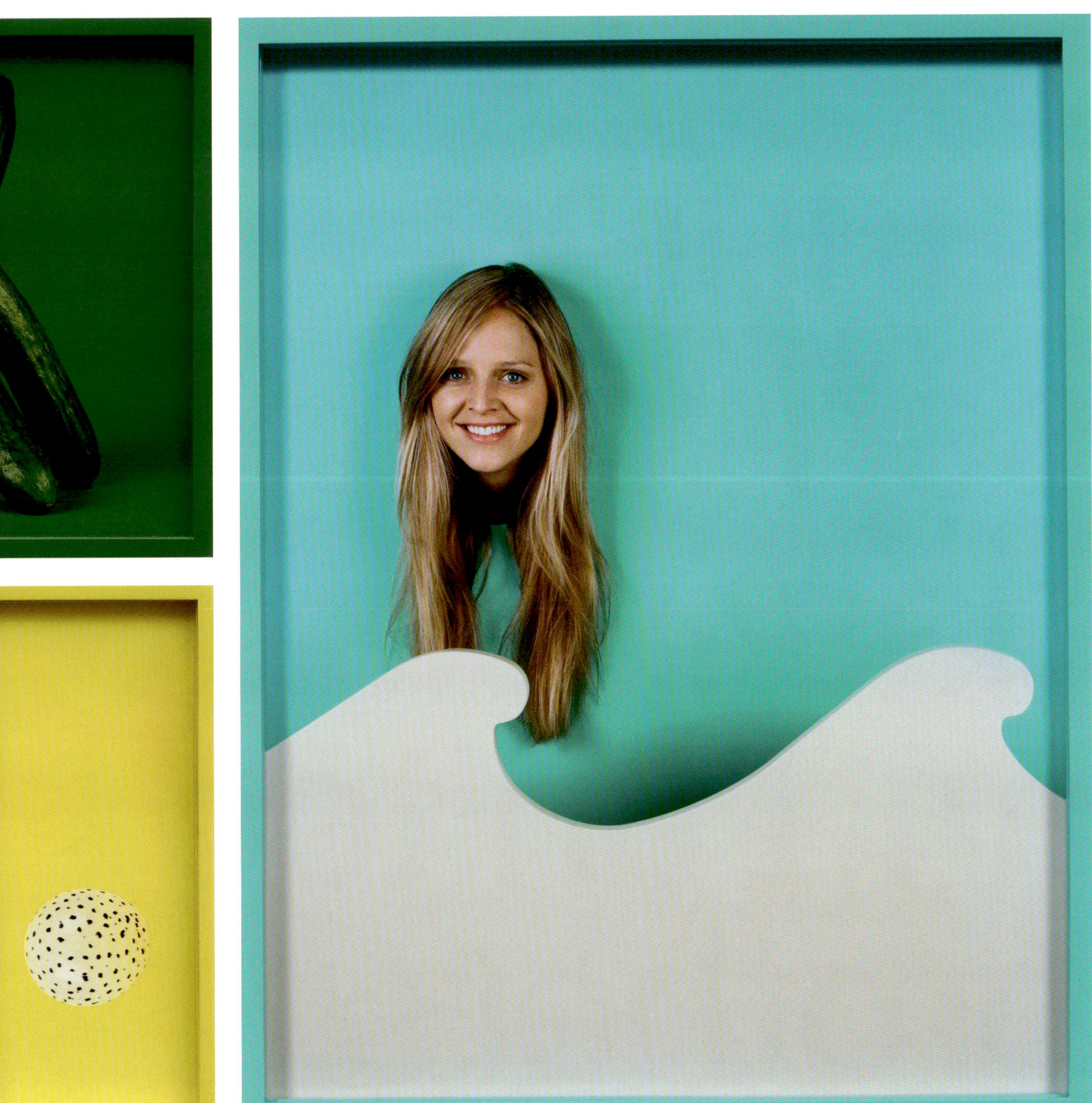

Angela, Waves, 2010
C-print
36.8 × 29.2 cm

glow rod tanning series for das institut and united brothers, 2011

Oil on Mylar
160 × 135 cm

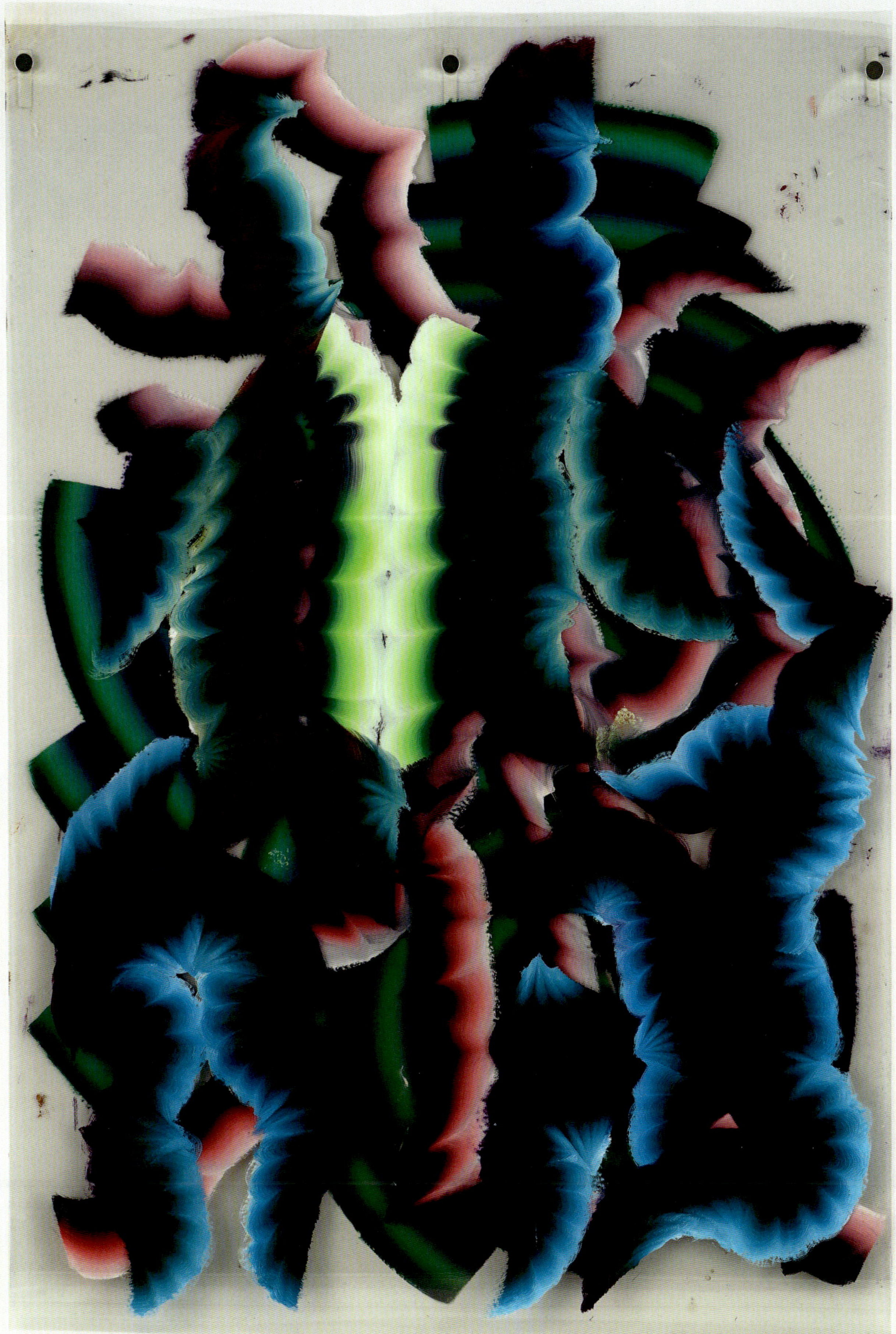

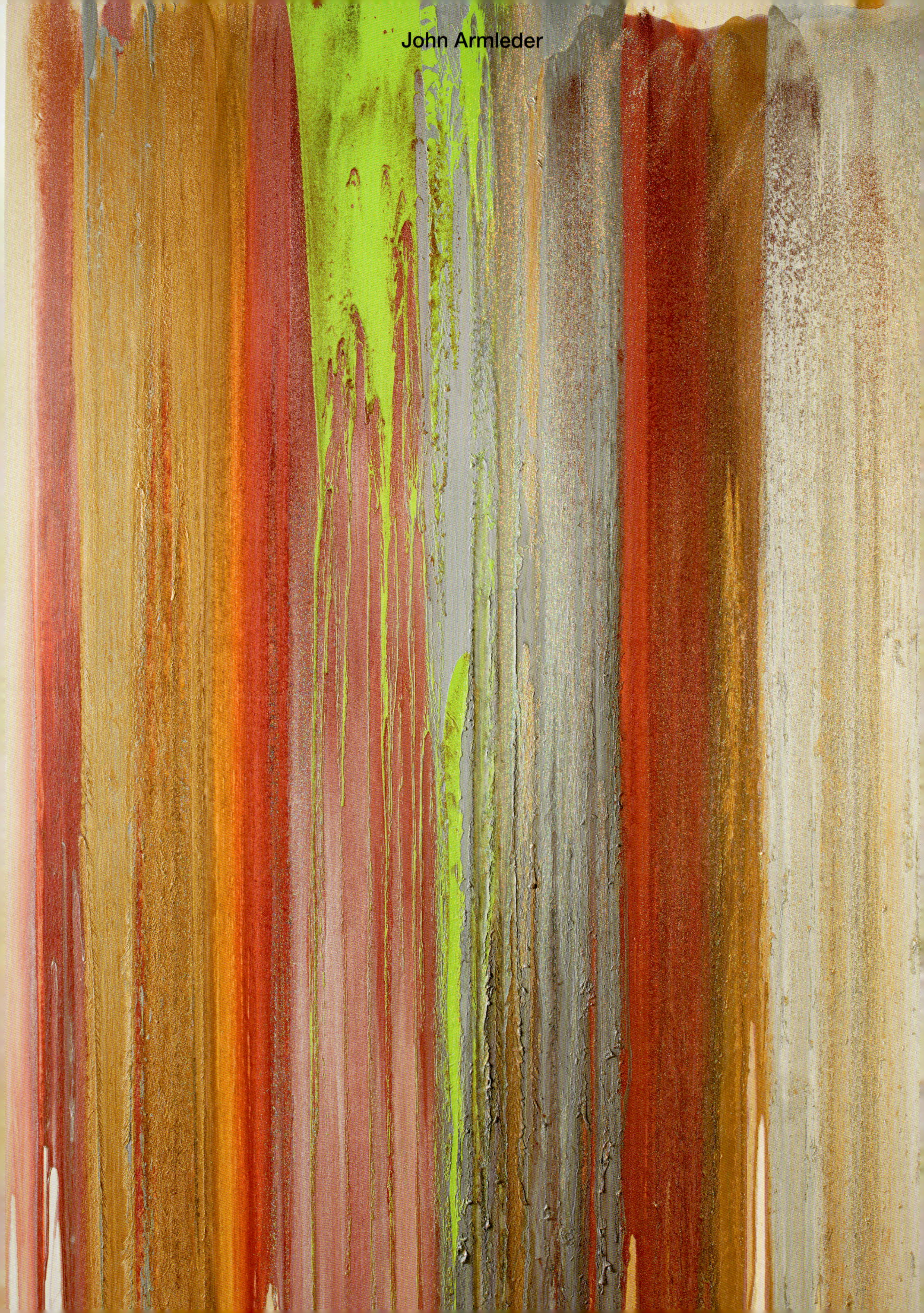
John Armleder

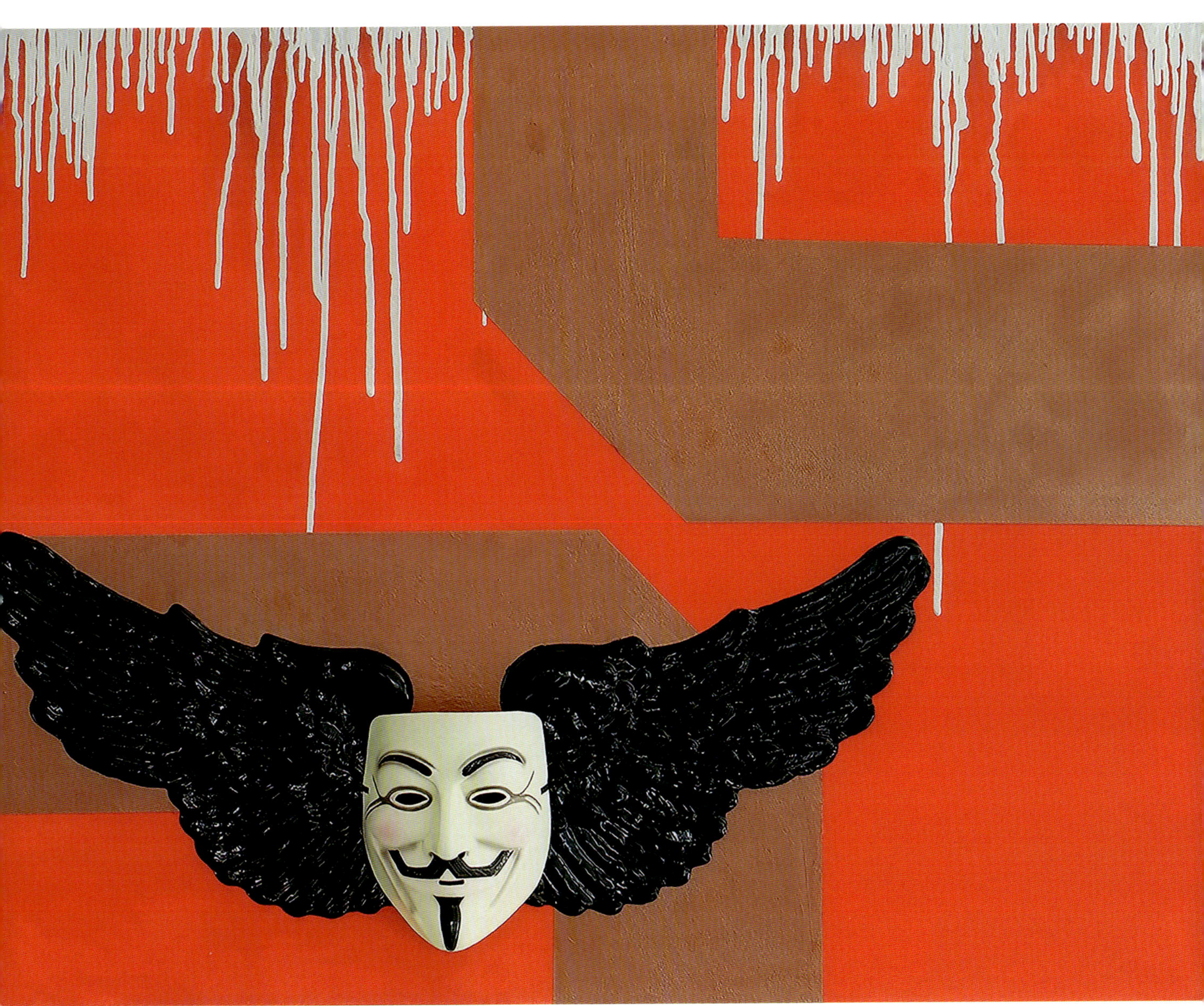

Sent With Thanks, 2015
Mixed media
89 × 116 × 16 cm

Left: Antennaria dioica, 2008
Mixed media on canvas
300 × 200 cm

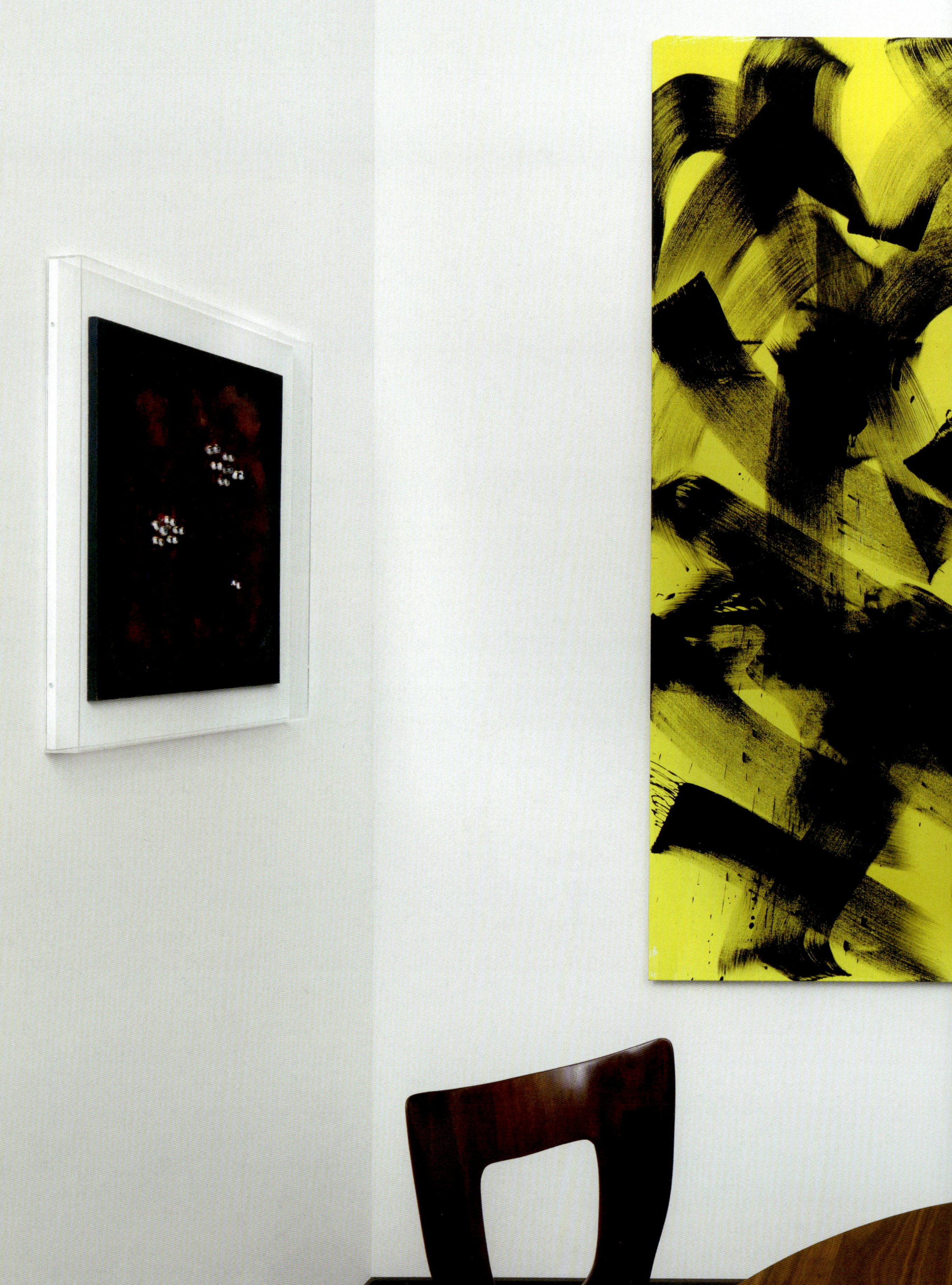

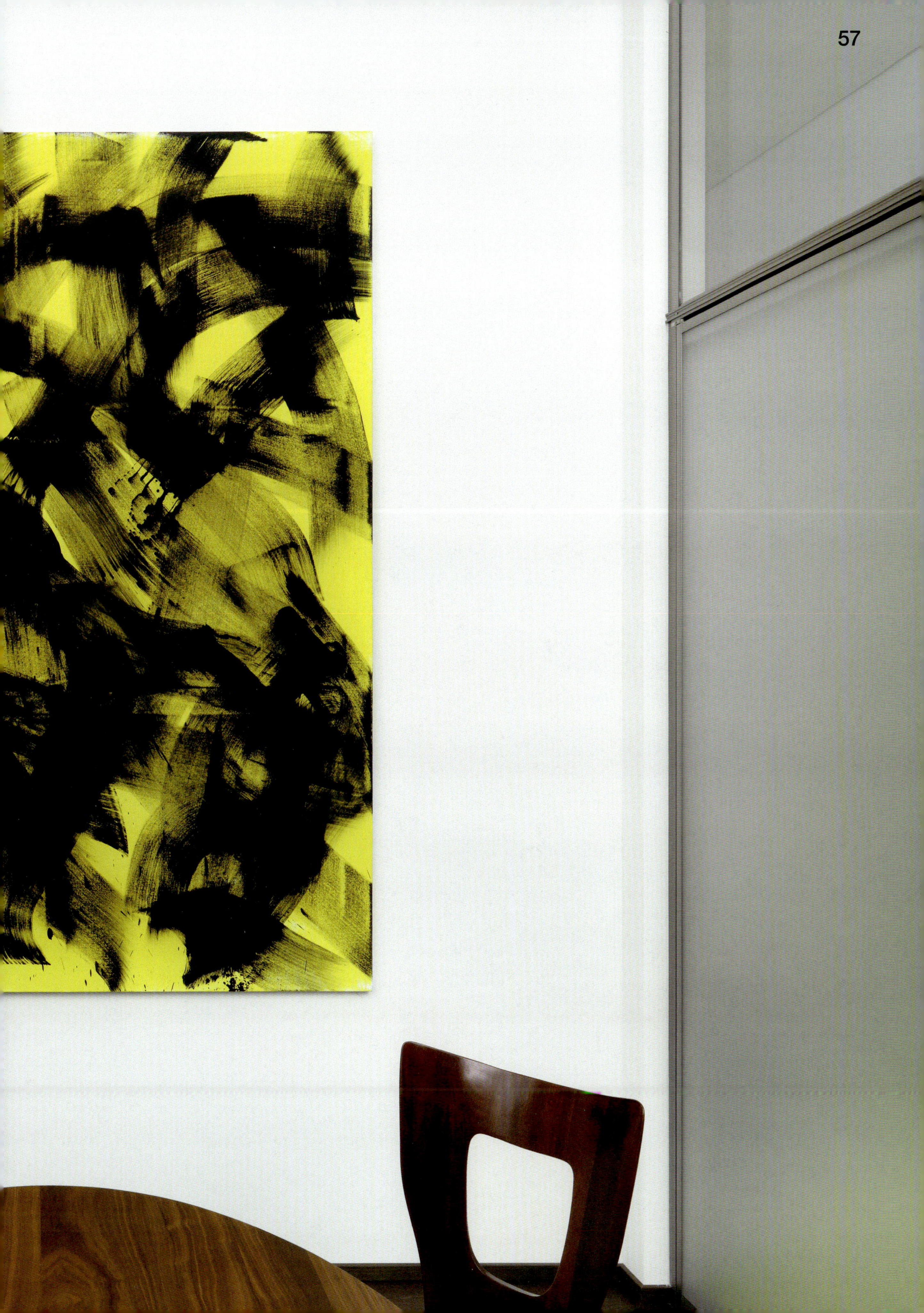

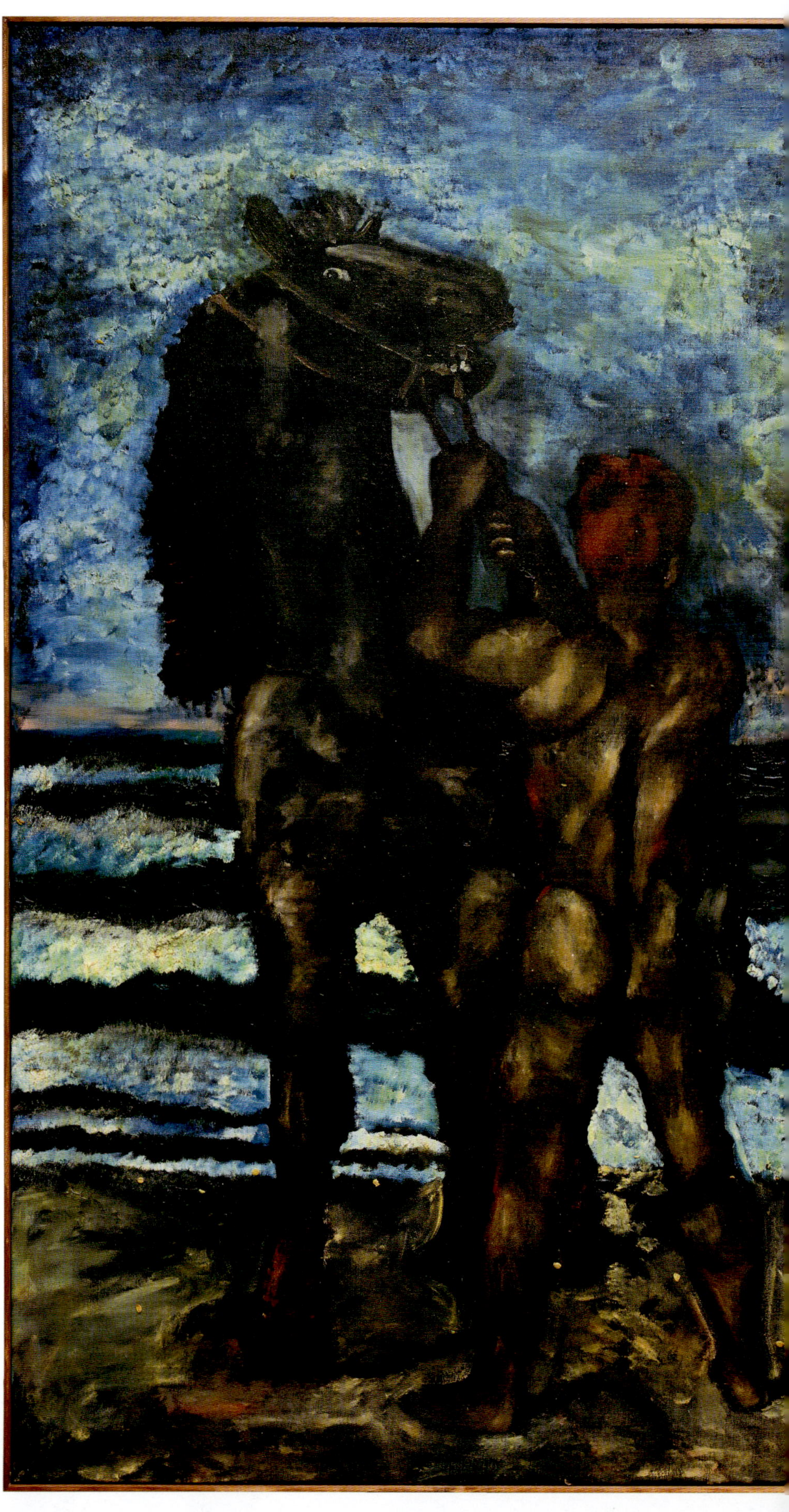

Fire Island, 2017
Oil, varnish,
rye flakes, and
wood on canvas
150 × 200 cm

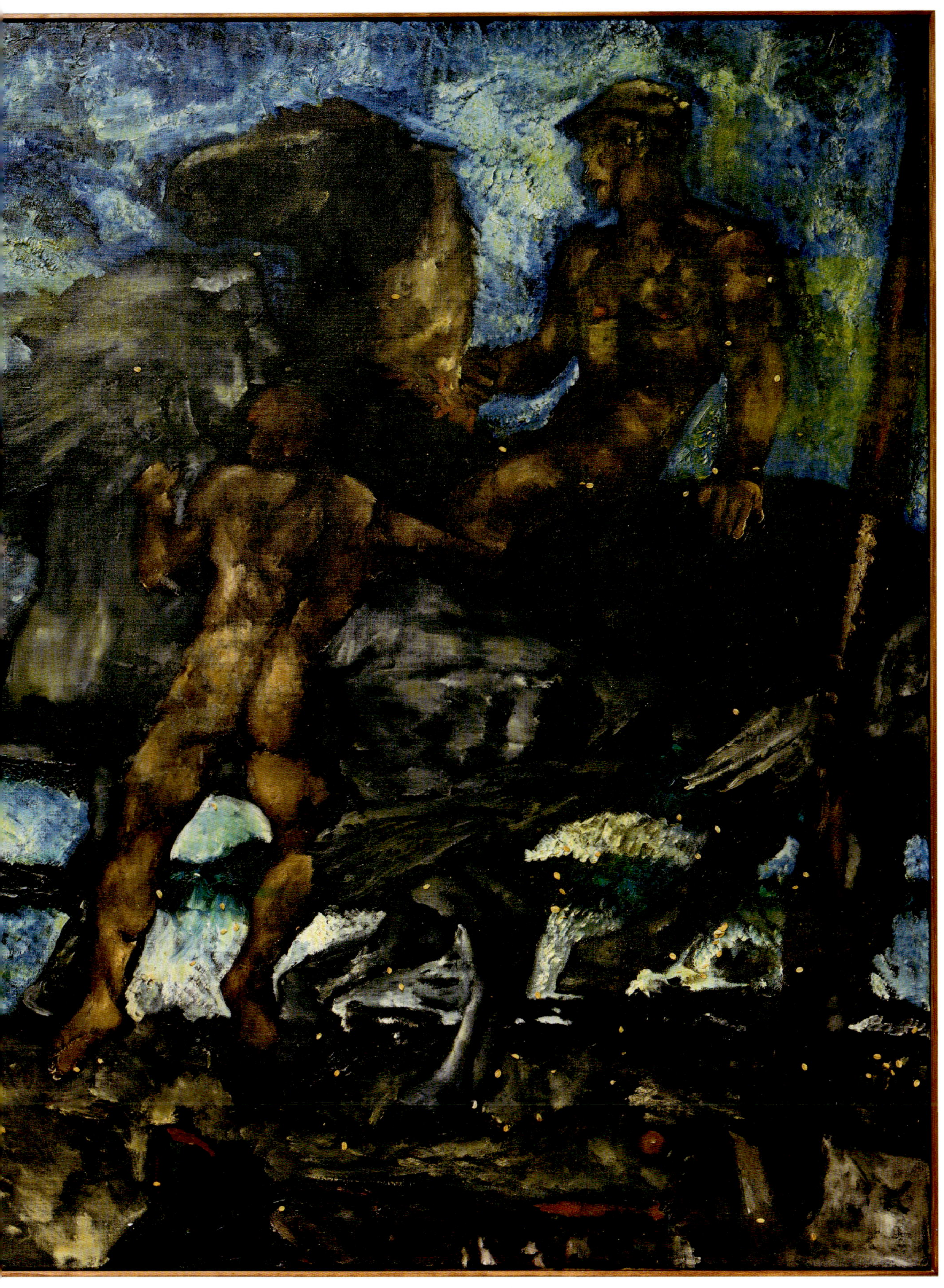

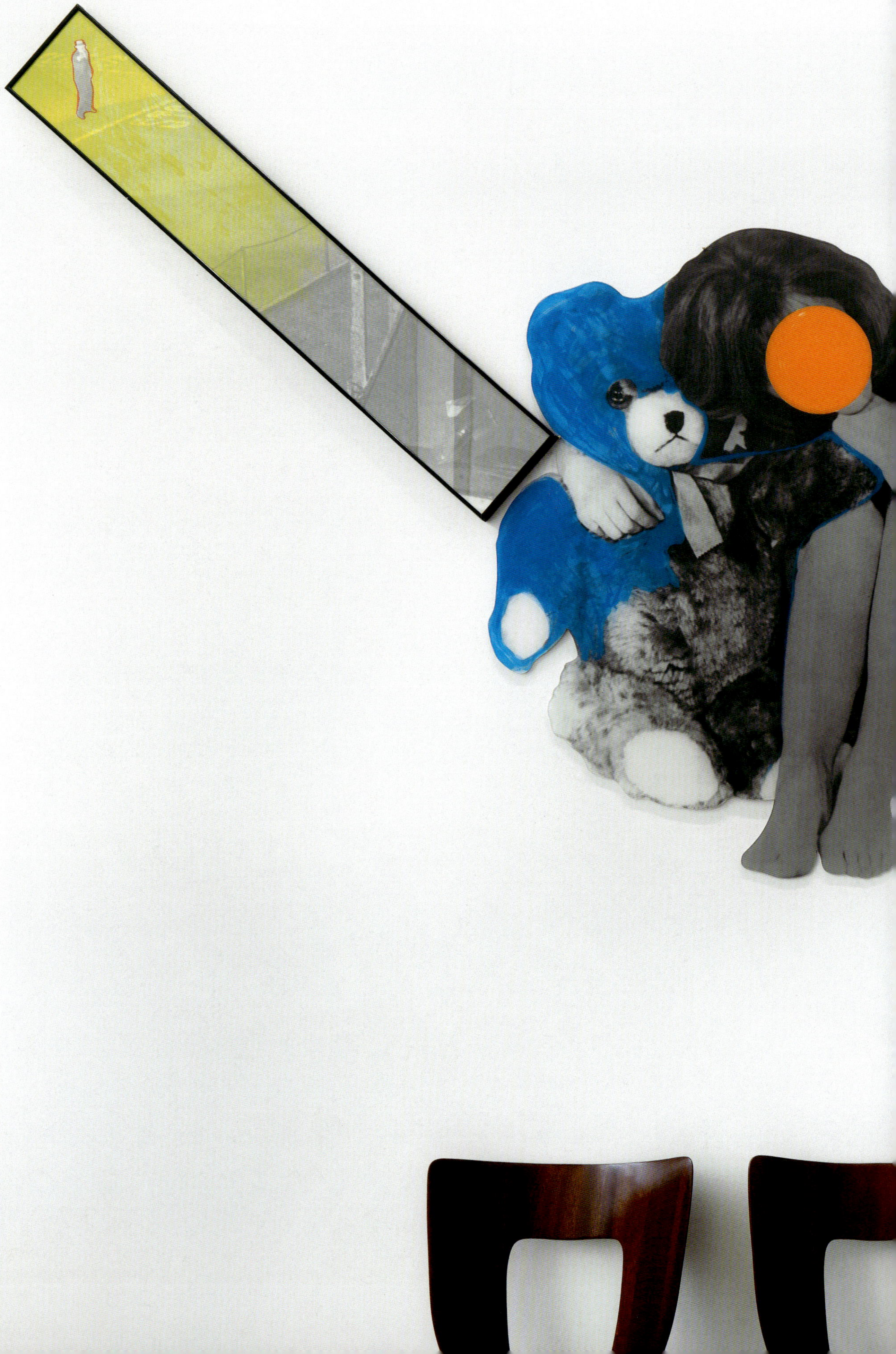

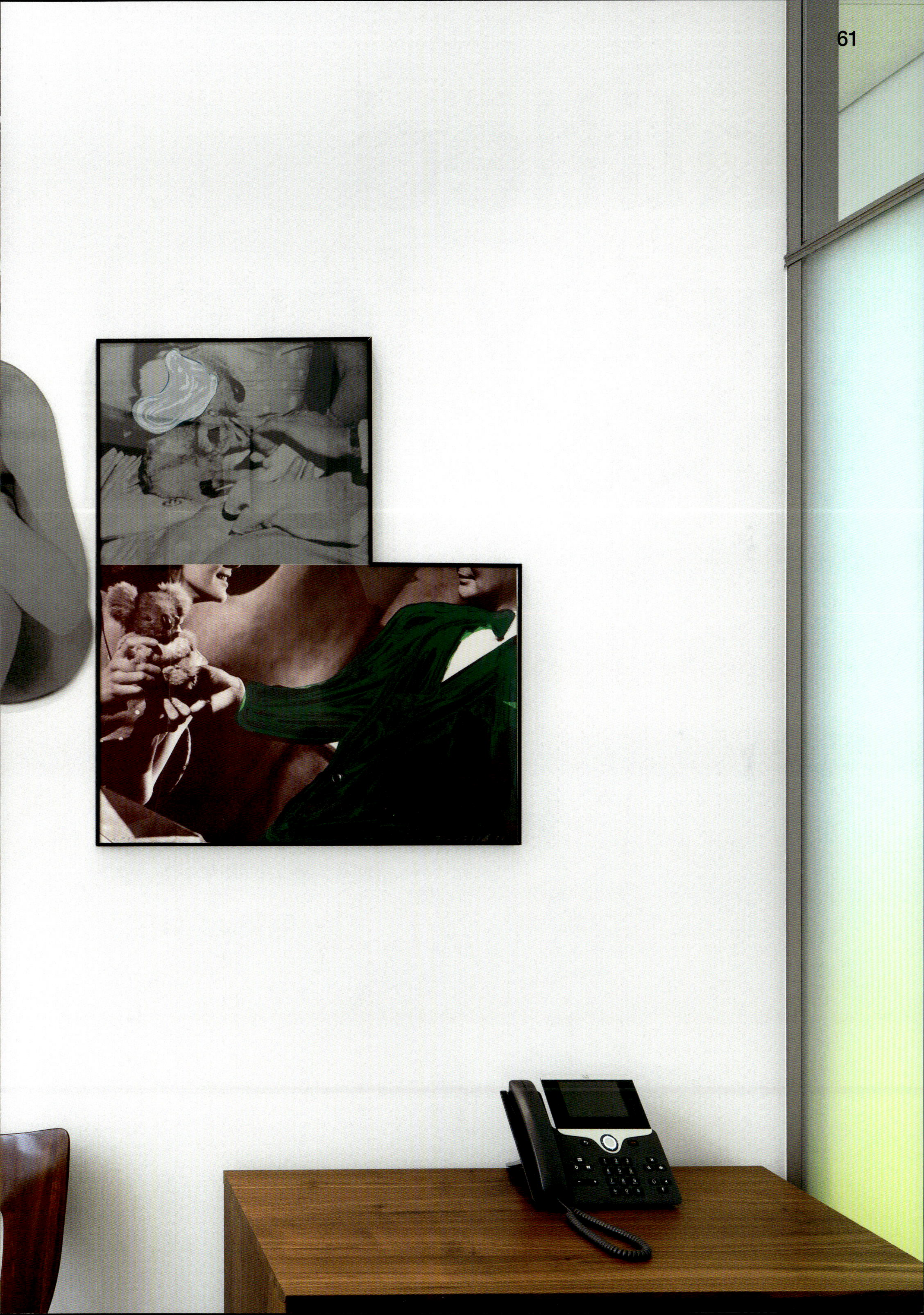

untitled (betty ford), 1989–2015

Ektacolor photograph
207 × 156.2 cm

Case Manager Timothy Poole does not mince words.

"In the next hour and a half you are going to do something which could change your lives," says Poole. "It is called Risk Taking."

All eighty patients have to write down their darkest secrets on small pieces of paper and throw them into the center of the room. The secrets are then shuffled so no one might pick his or her own and the patients are asked to weave a story around the one picked.

A burly naval officer picks the secret of a gay gigolo in the group and begins to act out the role as if it is his own. He confesses his shame at taking money from wealthy men and wants to reform. By an ironic twist of fate, the gigolo chooses the navy man's secret from the pile. It turns out the sailor is actually a closet gay.

Can it be real? There is relief in the air. People are glad to come out in the open.

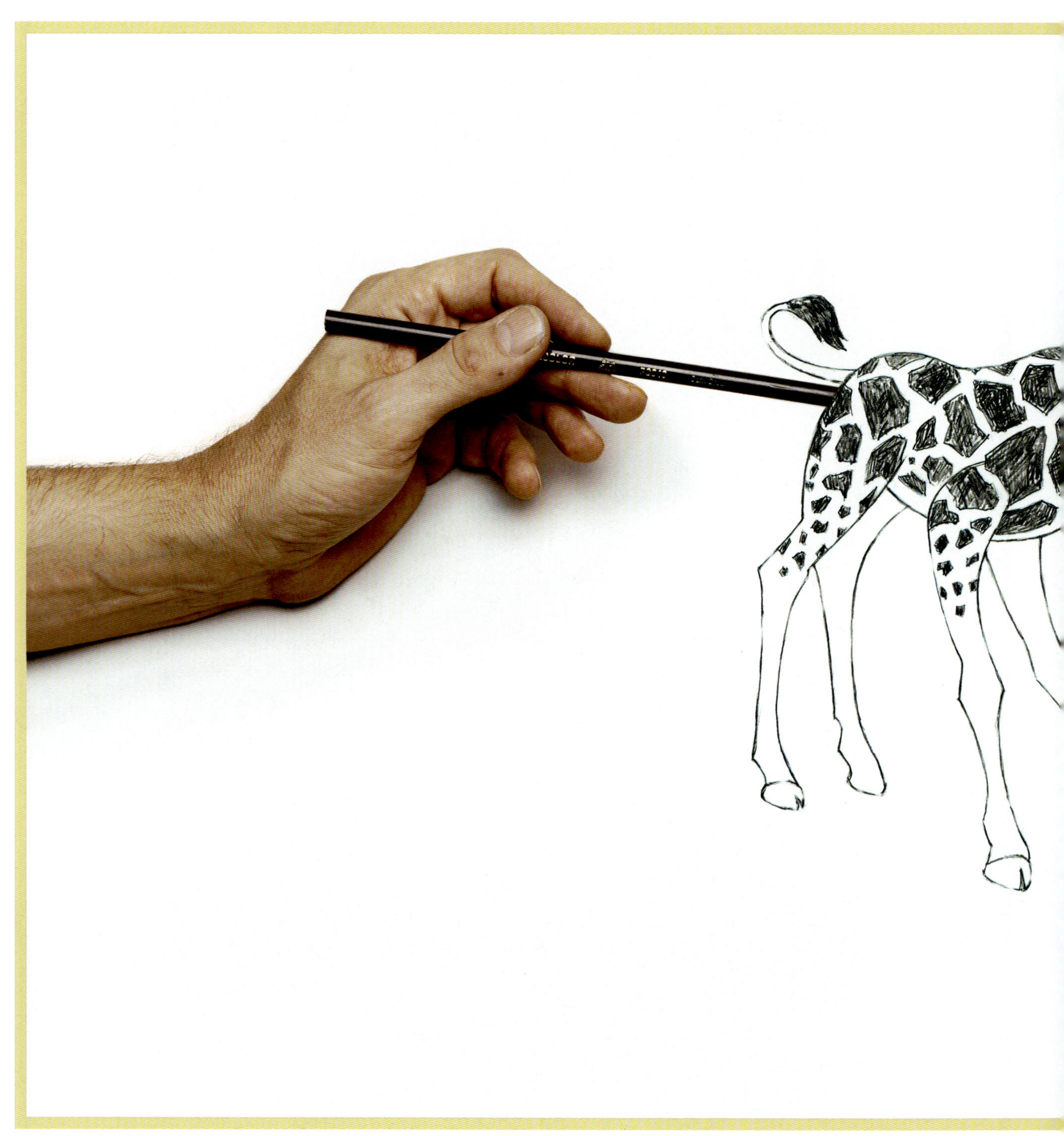

Untitled (Raven Row Giraffe), 2007–2015
Pigment print
165 × 327 cm

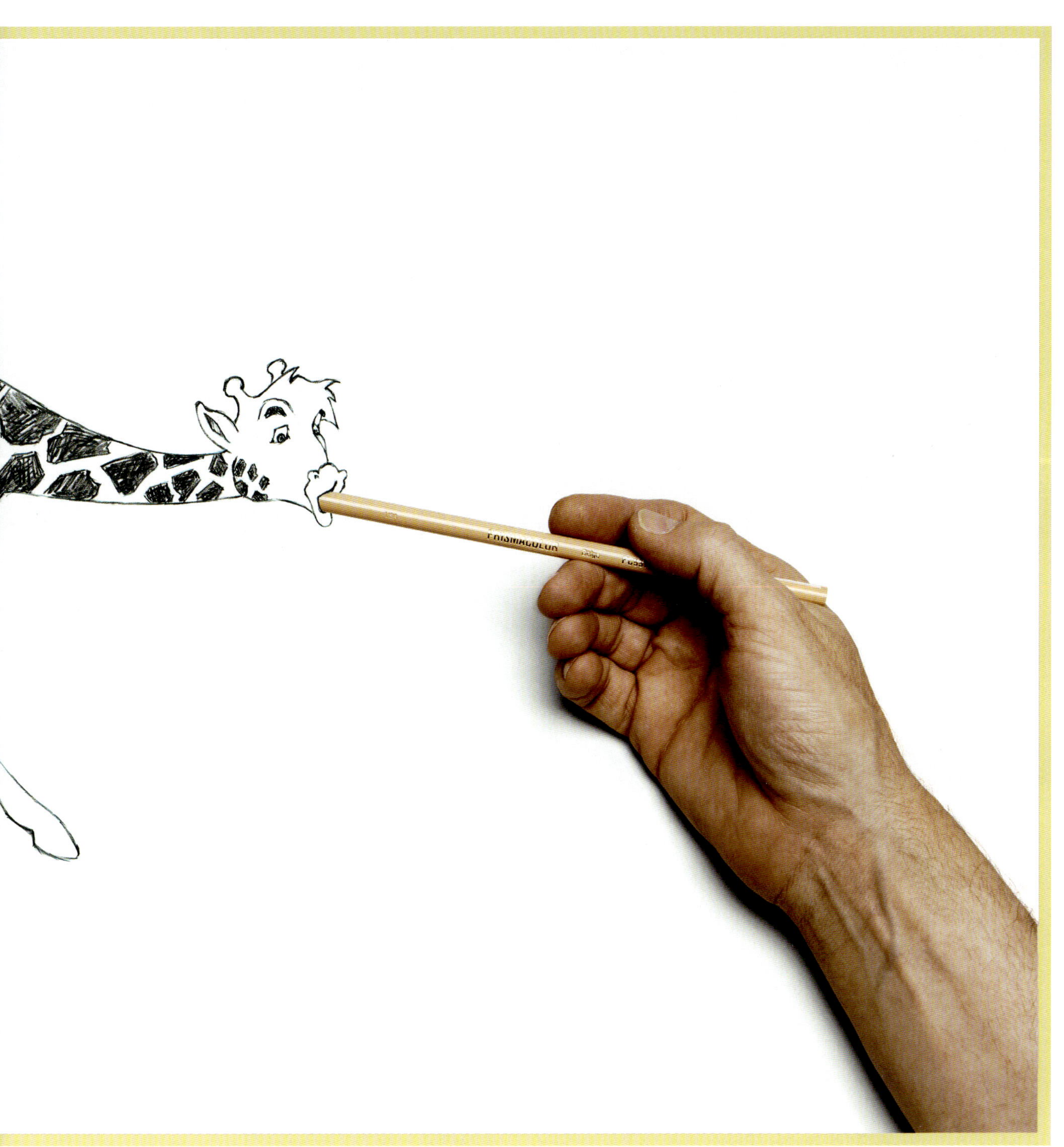
PRISMACOLOR

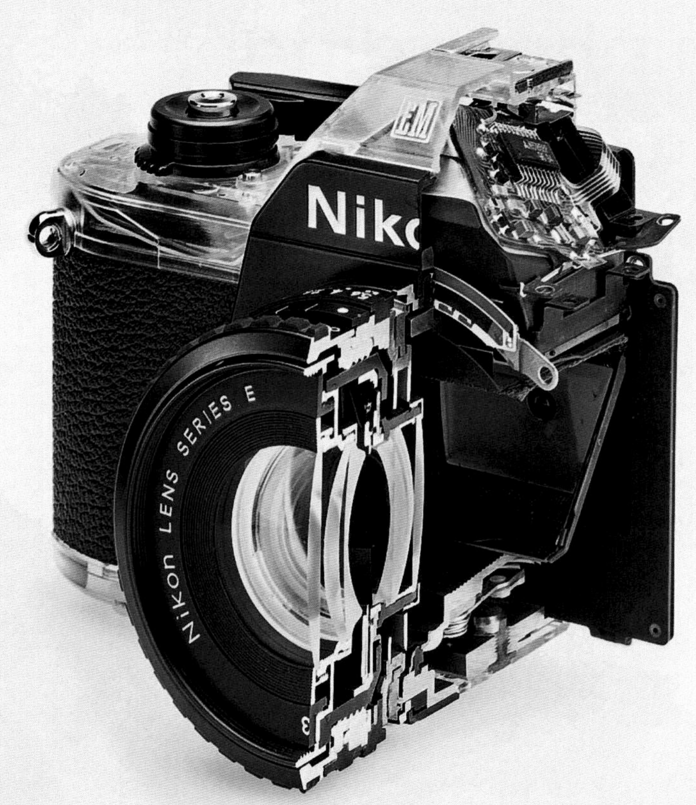

Silver gelatin print
85 × 94.5 cm

cutaway model nikon em. shutter: electronically governed seiko metal blade shutter, vertical travel with speeds from 1/1000 to 1 second, with a manual speed of 1/90th. meter: center-weighted silicon photo diode, asa 25-1600, ev 2-18 (with asa film and 1.8 lens). aperture priority automatic exposure. lens mount: nikon f mount, ai coupling (and later) only. flash: synchronization at 1/90 via hot shoe. flash automation with nikon sb-e or sb-10 flash units. focusing: k type focusing screen, not user interchangeable, with 3mm diagonal split image rangefinder. batteries: two px-76 or equivalent. dimensions: 5.3" × 3.38" × 2.13" (135 mm × 86 mm × 54 mm), 16.2 oz (460g). fotostudio axel gnad, düsseldorf, october 17, 2008, 2009

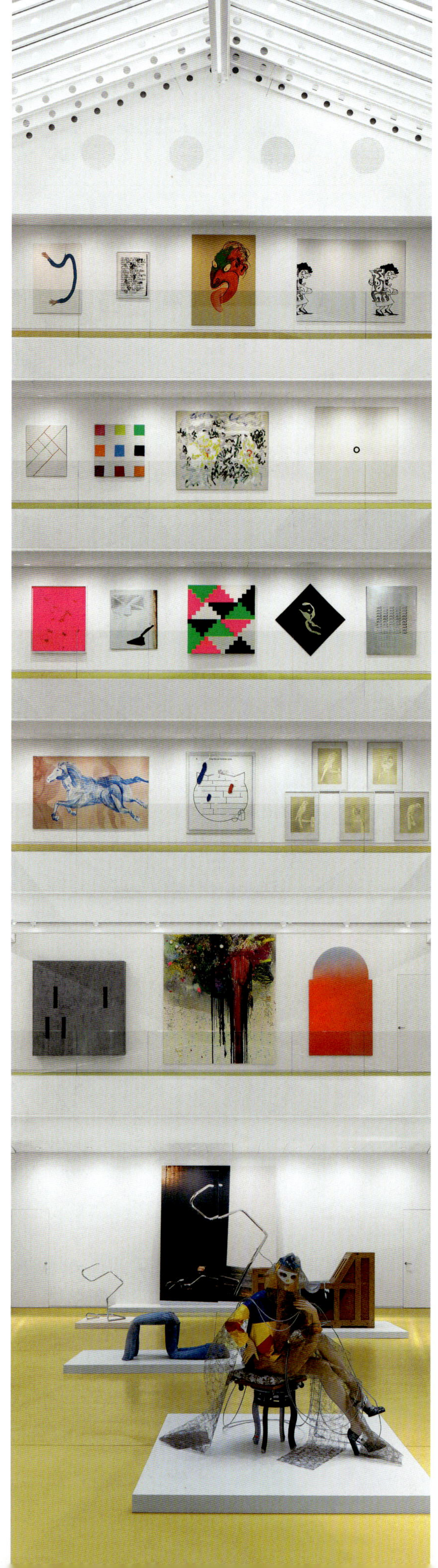

Upon entering the bank, the visitors are shown by a mannequin by Isa Genzken (*Schauspieler*, 2013) into the sculpture garden on the ground floor, where they find two pairs of jeans filled with concrete by Rob Pruitt (*Esprit de Corps: Bench*, 2006–2010) and a packing case by Richard Artschwager (*Table Prepared in the Presence of Enemies II*, 1992).

Near the reception, a plaster stewardess by Fischli Weiss (*Stewardess I*, 1989) welcomes the visitors into a space reminiscent of an airport lounge, which features two of the famous images of airports by the Swiss duo, as well as a *Furniture Sculpture* (*Untitled*, 1998) by John Armleder made up of a trunk reminiscent of a suitcase.

The ground floor installation is conceived around the notions of recovery, recycling, and sustainability. In the large inkjet painting installed against the wall (*Untitled*, 2015), Wade Guyton questions his own work by reusing one of his *Black Paintings*, photographed in his studio next to a chair by Marcel Breuer transformed by the artist into a sculpture (*Untitled*, 2014), itself exhibited next to the painting. Tobias Madison recovered the hand towels used by visitors to his exhibition at the Kunsthalle Zürich to use as material for his spherical sculpture hanging from the ceiling (*0*, 2013). Lutz Bacher's found objects—her Chinese New Year dragon's head (*Dragon*, 2012) and her camel (*Camel*, 2016)—explore the ambivalent character of symbols, while referring to the new economic and artistic territories of China and the Middle East. A waste bin (*Untitled [Trashcan]*, 2015) extracted by Klara Lidén from its urban environment—Berlin, in this case—is installed near a Fischli Weiss fake polyurethane pallet (*Untitled*, 2010), part of their series of works based on the re-creation of objects in their studio.

Around this reception area, a lounge presents works by Trisha Donnelly, characteristic of her cryptic approach, and another one photographs by Paul McCarthy, including a diptych of images of models in a shop window (*Fear of Mannequin [2]*, 1971–2002), as well as an image from his "Propo" series featuring the glasses used in one of his performances.

Visible from the reception and almost all the open spaces, the large wall of the atrium is organized by floor, each one exploring a contemporary approach to painting.

The three paintings on the first floor blur the line between painting and sculpture. In the center, John Armleder's work (*Of a Fisherman's Arrow*, 2014) follows the principle of his famous *Puddle Paintings*, but here the artist also added all sorts of material and objects, including glitter and decorative balls. Next to this piece are two paintings both referring to the idea of a window: *Bleue bleue brune infâme, infâme* (2009) by Valentin Carron—a former student of Armleder's—is inspired by the openings in the walls of shelters used for the storage of grain, like those found in the vernacular architecture of his native Valais. Alex Israel's *Untitled (Flat)* (2011), whose colors recall those of a Californian sunset, evokes filmsets inspired by Spanish Revival architecture from the Golden Age of Hollywood; the shape of the painting also echoes the windows of the building's ground floor.

On the second floor the paintings are all about animal figuration: a horse by Matthew

Lutz-Kinoy, a cat by Laura Owens, and various genetically modified canary species from Carsten Höller.

At the center of the third floor, a *Ziggurat* (1986) by General Idea, inspired by the religious buildings of ancient Mesopotamia, is installed between two works by Seth Price: on the left, a silkscreen on wood featuring an envelope, a recurring pattern in his oeuvre; on the right, one of his *Silhouettes*, showing an exchange of keys, made using UV printing on a diamond-shaped piece of metal. At each end, is a silkscreen of banknotes by Antek Walczak, also on metal, and a painting by Mathieu Malouf, onto which the artist applied mushrooms and fluorescent pink pigment, reminiscent of the technique used by Yves Klein for his blue monochromes.

Dedicated to abstraction, the fourth floor presents a *Cartouche Painting* by Michael Krebber, which diverts Mondrian's principles of composition, and Olivier Mosset's characteristic circular motif, in a famous painting exhibited at the 1967 Biennale de Paris, one of the founding moments of the BMPT group. In-between these paintings a piece by Mary Heilmann, whose soft abstraction is inspired by the world of surfing and the West Coast from which she originates, is hung next to a large painting (*Gelbe Blume 4*, 1980) by Christian Lindow, whose work explores an unstable territory between figuration and abstraction.

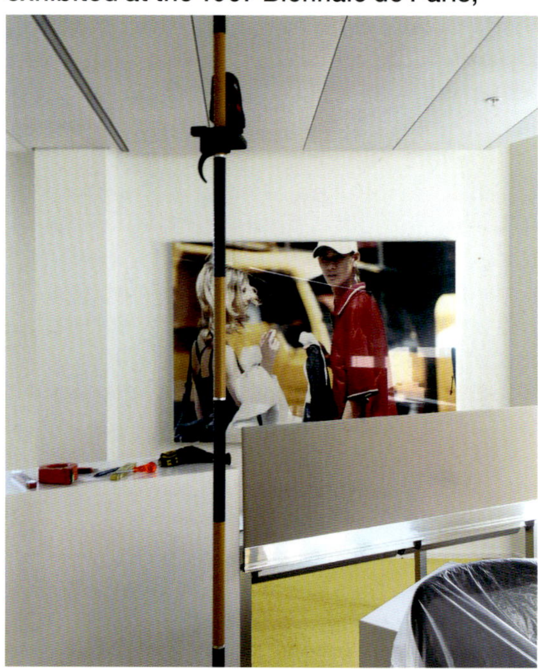

Installing the Syz Collection
Beat Streuli
Sydney/Melbourne 97/98
(36/01a), 1998
C-print, Plexiglas frame
137 × 201 cm

The fifth floor is in complete contrast to the fourth, as it is centered on figuration, notably around the reactivation of the aesthetics of comics (Michael Krebber, Oliver Osborne), associated with more gestural techniques (Eliza Douglas, Calvin Marcus).

On the building's different floors the hanging of the pieces within the work spaces is organized according to formal or conceptual combinations.

The first floor houses the bank's various reception rooms, all named after an artist present in the collection. In those devoted to photography, the conceptual approach of Californian artists such as John Baldessari, Larry Johnson, and Christopher Williams rubs shoulders with the staging games Cindy Sherman plays in her portraits. Next to a room dedicated to Wolfgang Tillmans, Juergen Teller is paired with Rosemarie Trockel to offer an ensemble devoted to fashion and the female body. On the other side of the atrium, a lobby combines several ways of using fabric in painting: from a monochrome by Günther Förg, in which the frame is covered with green fabric, to a painting for which Michael Krebber stitched together two pieces of gingham, and a pink piece by Willem de Rooij, created by delegation at a weaving factory. Further on, a ceramic piece by Rosemarie Trockel is juxtaposed with two artists who, like her, were active on the Cologne scene: Merlin Carpenter and David Ostrowski, who here both adopt a gestural and performative approach to painting. Another reception room positions two paintings by young artists Mathieu Malouf and David Hominal with a work by Carol Rama from the 1960s. A last room is devoted to Sturtevant, whose methodology of repeating works by other artists is applied here to Frank Stella's *Black Paintings*.

The second floor explores different specific approaches to contemporary photography, notably through a series of works evoking the funfair (Anri Sala, Fischli Weiss, Carsten Höller), and a meeting room dedicated to Louise Lawler, whose photographic appropriations—which question the links between artworks and the context in which they are inscribed—have the specificity of being associated here with texts inscribed on their passe-partout. Several women artists (Roni Horn, Sturtevant, Linder) are gathered on one side of this floor while, on the other side, ensembles by Wolfgang Tillmans and Elad Lassry are presented, as well as a space organized around the links between photography, fashion, and advertising (Sylvie Fleury, Roe Ethridge).

On the third floor, a series of paintings dominated by abstraction (Blair Thurman, Heimo Zobernig, Tom Burr, Josef Strau, Jason Loebs) is installed throughout the work spaces. On the other side, a set of silkscreens by Thomas Bayrle based on repetitions of motifs can be seen, as well as a more conceptual approach, notably in one of the versions of Stephen Prina's *Exquisite Corpse*, a series based on Édouard Manet's catalogue raisonné.

The fourth floor houses a set of six series of photographs documenting Roman Signer's "actions" as well as a set of drawings by three artists who have often been exhibited together: Guy de Cointet and Channa Horwitz, artists active in California, who were both interested in writing and the rigor of logic as a principle of creation; and Henri Chopin, a legendary figure associated with concrete poetry.

Under the patronage of Paul McCarthy, who takes a drawing by Buck Brown (*Artist's Studio (From Playboy Comics)*, 1976–1980/2004) as a starting point, the fifth floor brings together several groups of drawings with a deliberately childish and playful aesthetic, such as those by Lily van der Stokker, Sam Pulitzer, and Joe Bradley. A sculpture of two eyes in leather by Stefan Tcherepnin alludes to Elmo, the *Sesame Street* character.

On the sixth floor, the boardroom is centered on appropriationist approaches and themes related to exoticism and

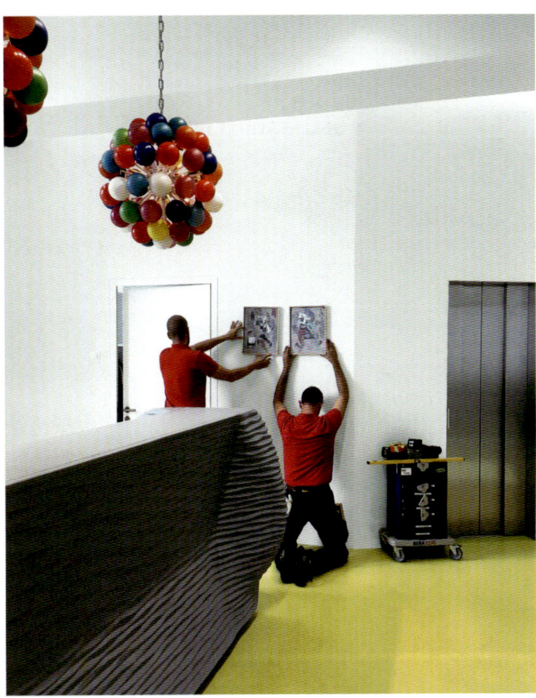

Installing the Syz Collection
Murano glass lamps
Design by Suzanne Syz

postcolonialism, and includes a series by Sherrie Levine (*After Edward Curtis*, 2005), to which a cloth piece by Vincent Vulsma based on images by Walker Evans documenting an exhibition of African art organized at the Museum of Modern Art in New York in the 1930s appears as a counterpoint. Matthew Lutz-Kinoy diverts a utilitarian ceramic pot into a mask inspired by Okinawa culture. Finally, a sculpture by Alex Israel reproduces the glass egg in *Risky Business*, the cult film that made Tom Cruise famous in the early 1980s.

In the basement of the building, near the vault, there are photographs by Candida Höfer related to storage issues, and two imposing sculptures: a black fiberglass cross by Valentin Carron, and the entrance to a scanning machine covered with red car paint by Yngve Holen.

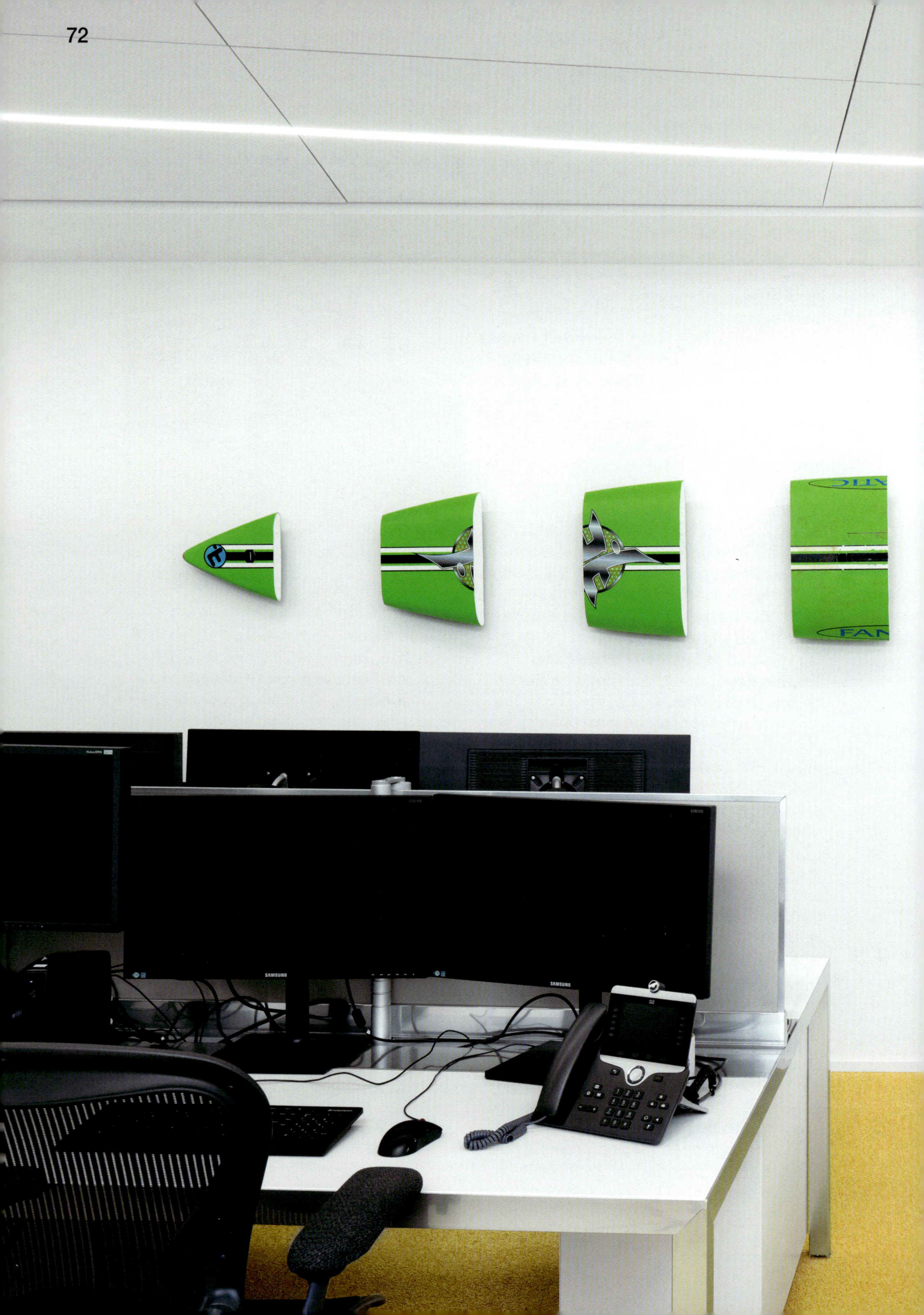

NATIC

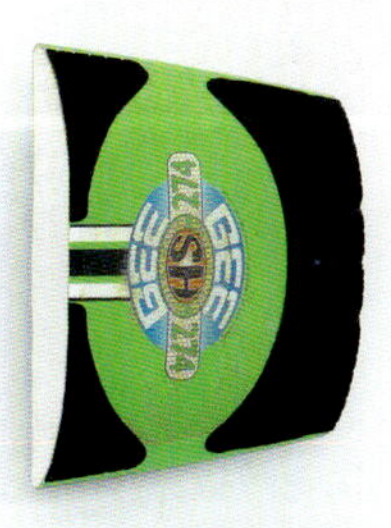

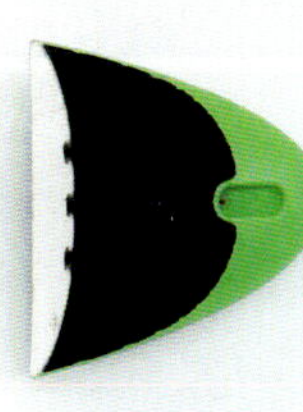

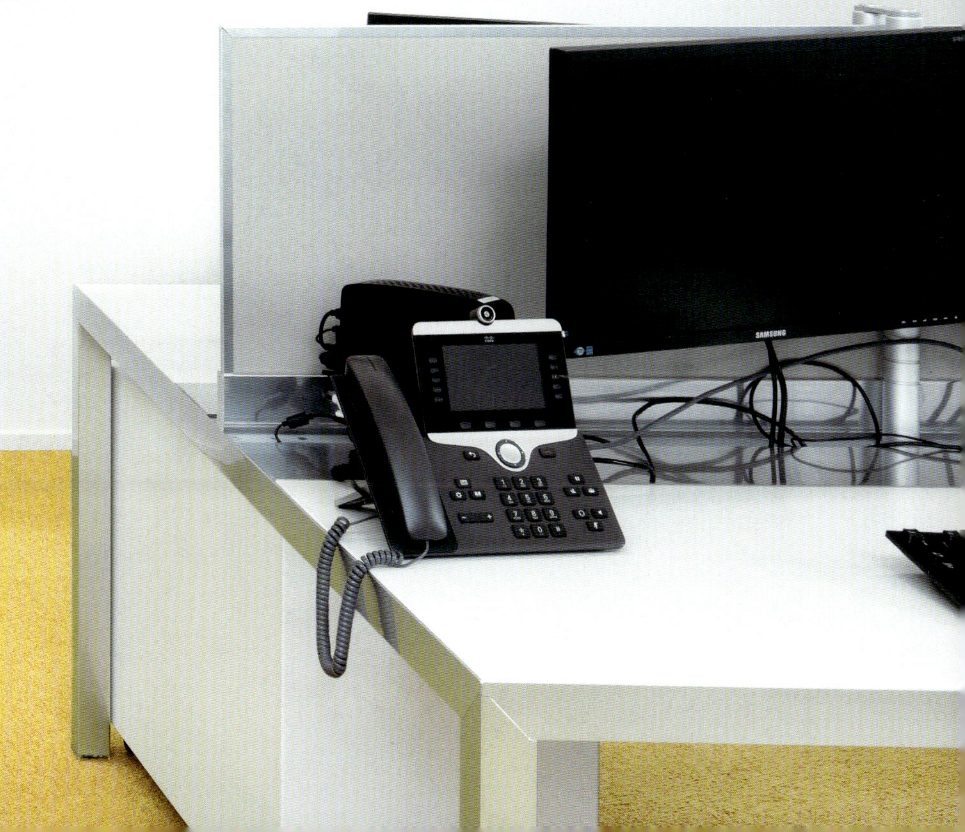

C-A-N-V-A-S 26.09.11 22:07

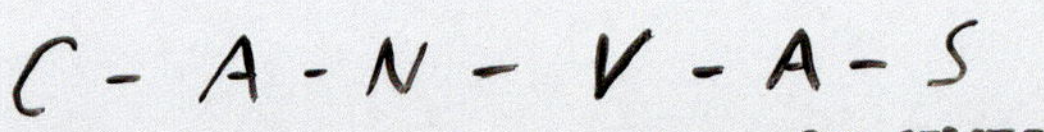

C-A-N-V-A-S

CORPSE AFTER NEGATING VISUAL ART STRATEGIES

Wednesday, 17 August 2011

At home I realized that whilst reaching over for Chris Kraus' Video Green I picked up the book Coma by Pierre Guyotat by mistake 'cause they look exactly the same. I was so bored these days that I just read it anyway.

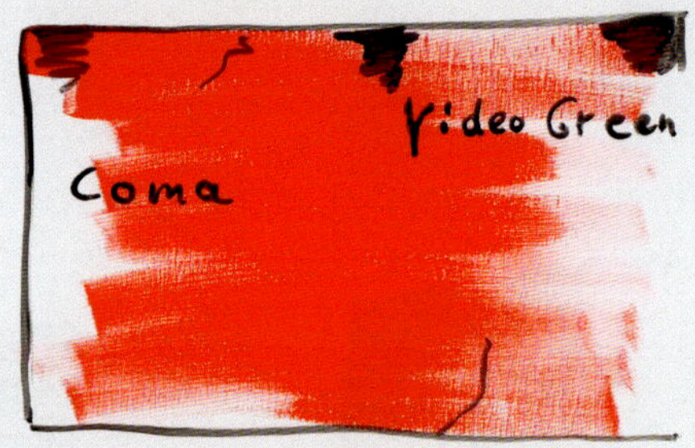

Pierre Guyotat likes Ravel and Debussy. He likes to use phrases such as "I can finally look at the world and forget myself" or "my existence, as a humble plowman of language" or "my human senses ... are what allow me to see and feel the absolute".

He describes his interests: "scrap school notebooks in public dumps, the gaze of children, the dribble of idiots..."

Gary Indiana says that the book is a "a voice that tears off its bandages."

The only interesting thing that really happens in this book is when he gets walked in on whilst using a stick to spoon out the shit out of his asshole whilst having severe constipation in someone's bathroom.

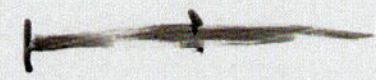

C-A-N-V-A-S Painting 7, 2011
Acrylic on linen
139.7 × 106.7 cm

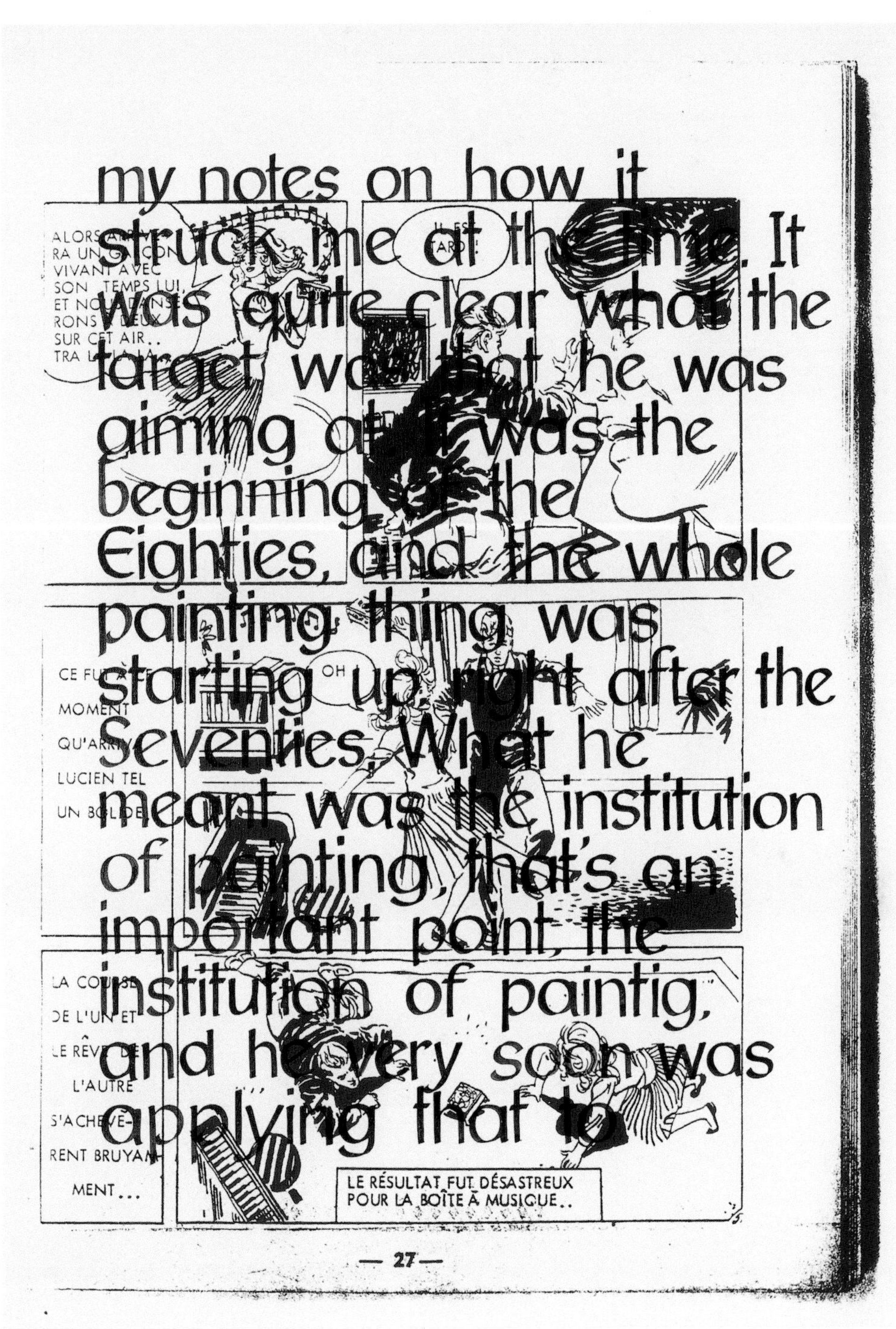

Untitled (52), 2007
Acrylic and lacquer on canvas
105 × 75 cm

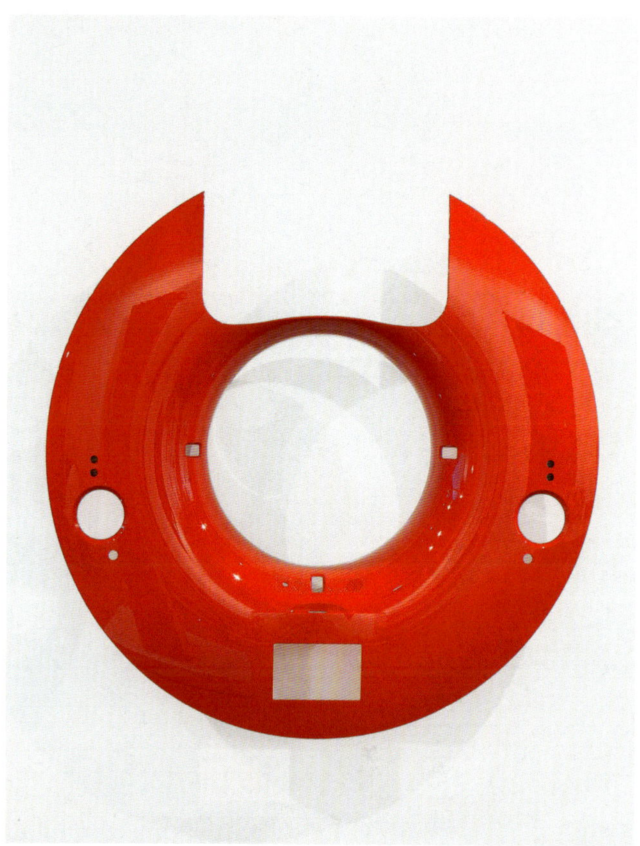

You believe in discipline, 2015
Plastic, car paint, steel
177 × 185 × 36.5 cm

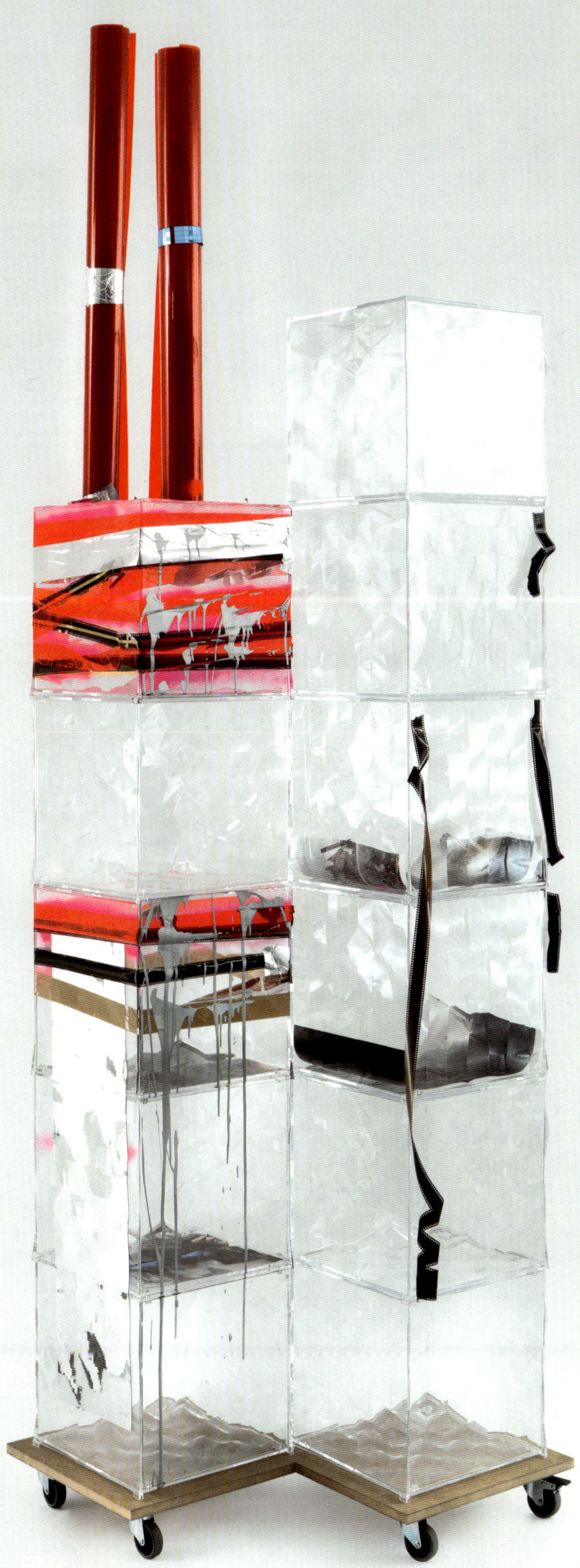

Memorial Tower
(Ground Zero), 2008
Plastic, tape,
spraypaint, acrylic,
mirror foil, film strip,
color print on paper,
MDF, casters
316 × 80.5 × 90 cm

first spaceship on venus (22), 2015

Fiberglass, glitter paint
340 × 120 × 120 cm

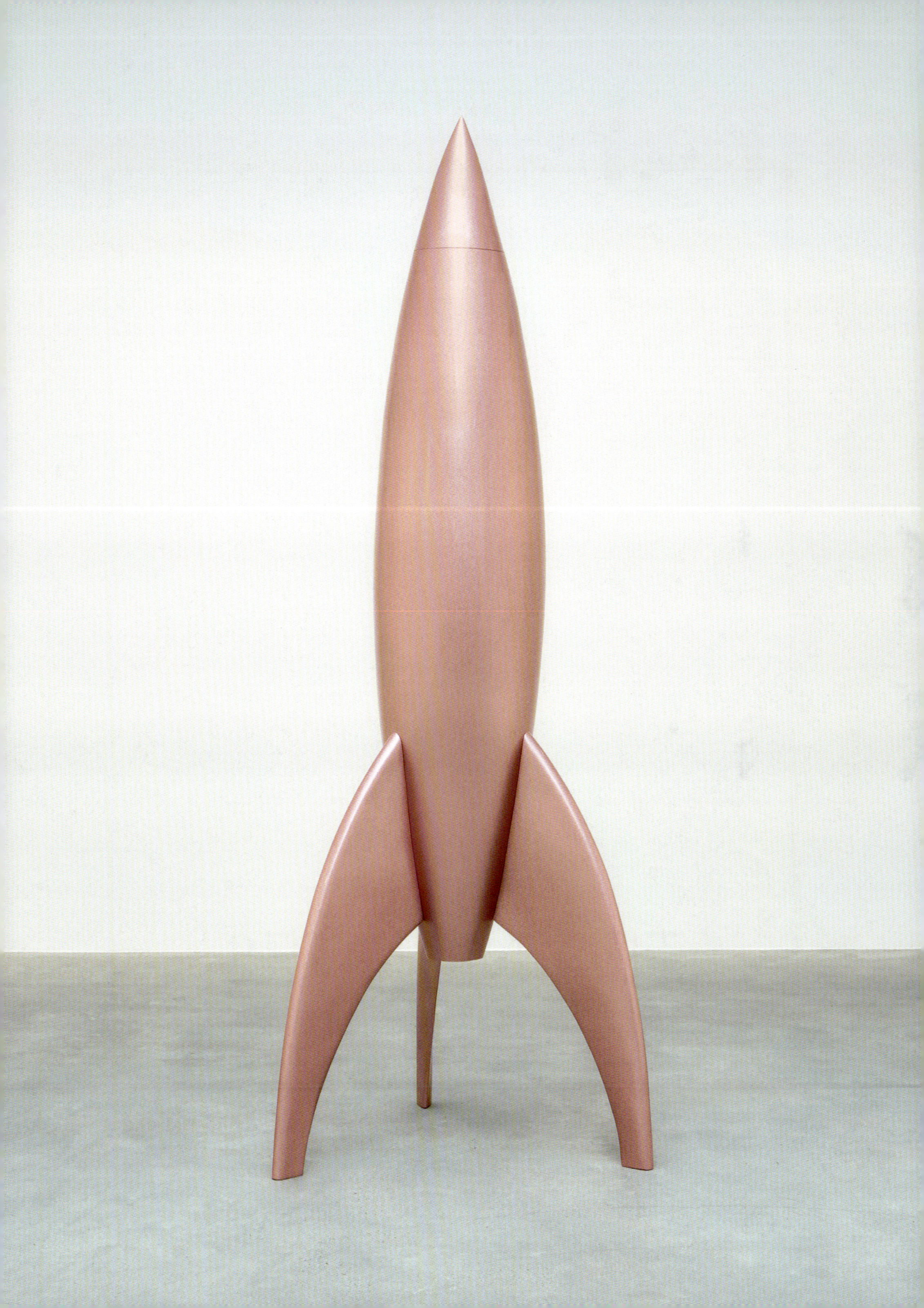

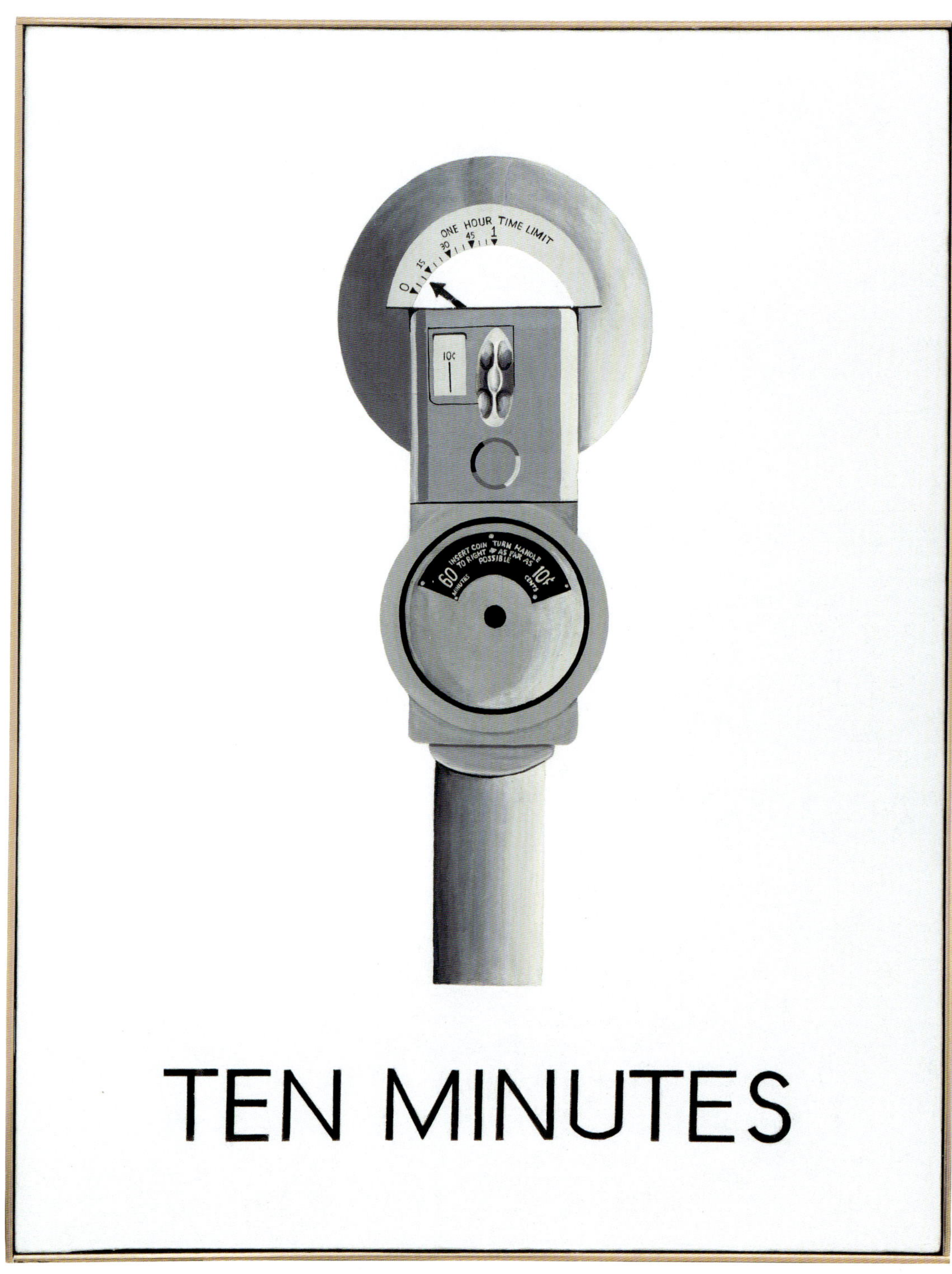

Ten Minutes, 1962
Oil on canvas
92.7 × 71.8 cm

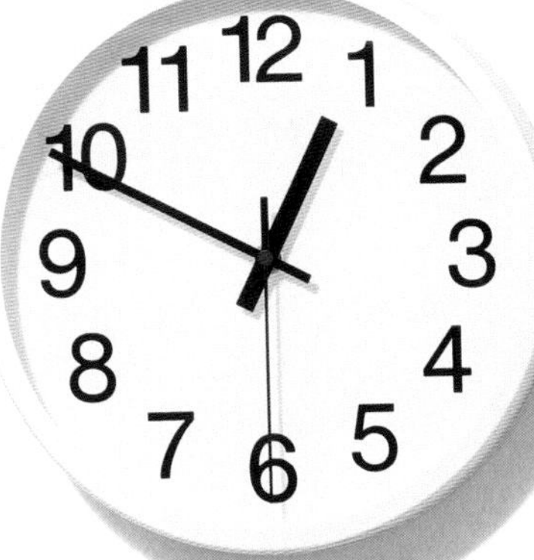
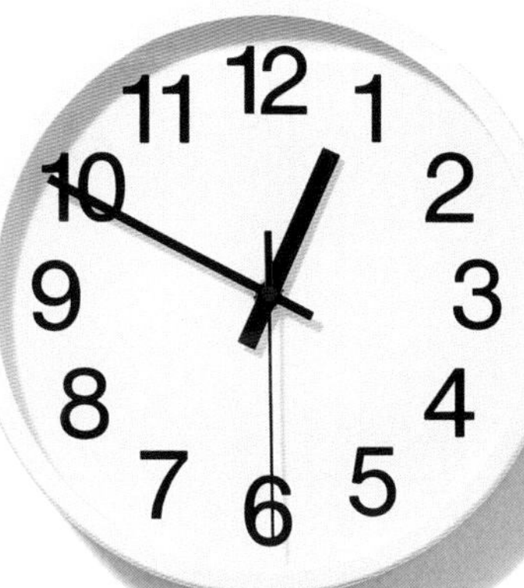
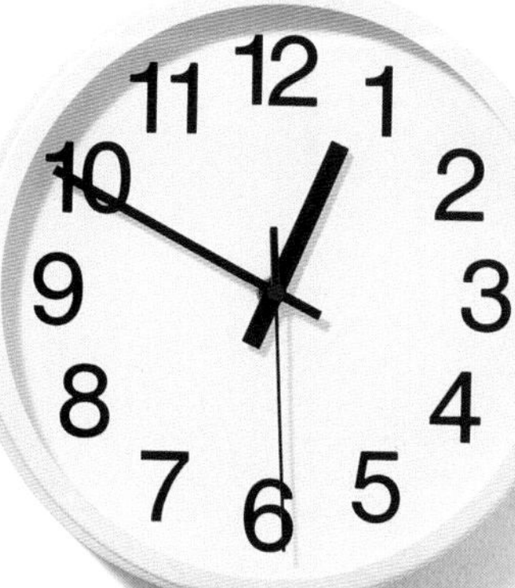

Untitled (Perfect Lovers +1), 2008
Wall clocks
23.8 × 76.5 × 4.1 cm

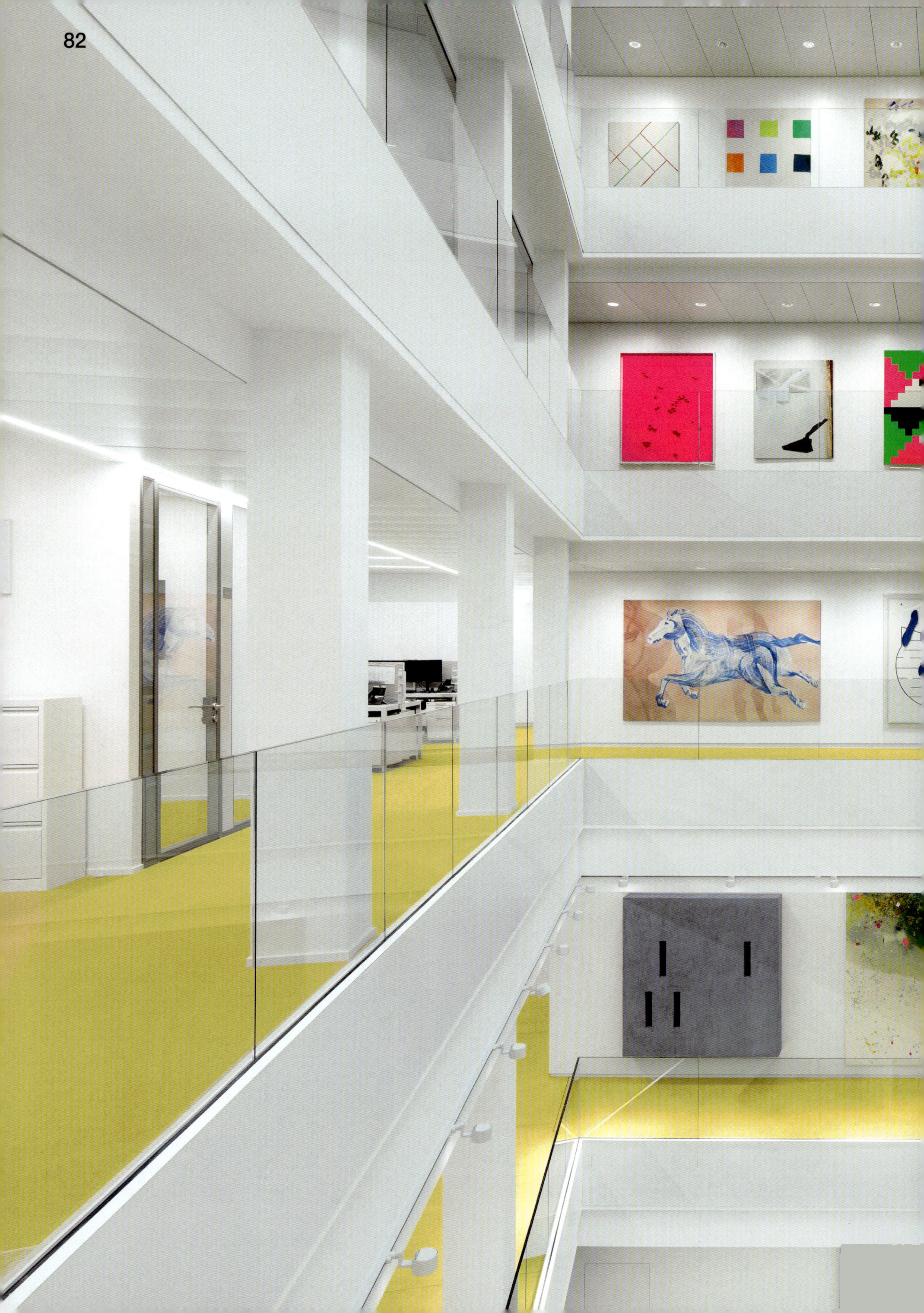

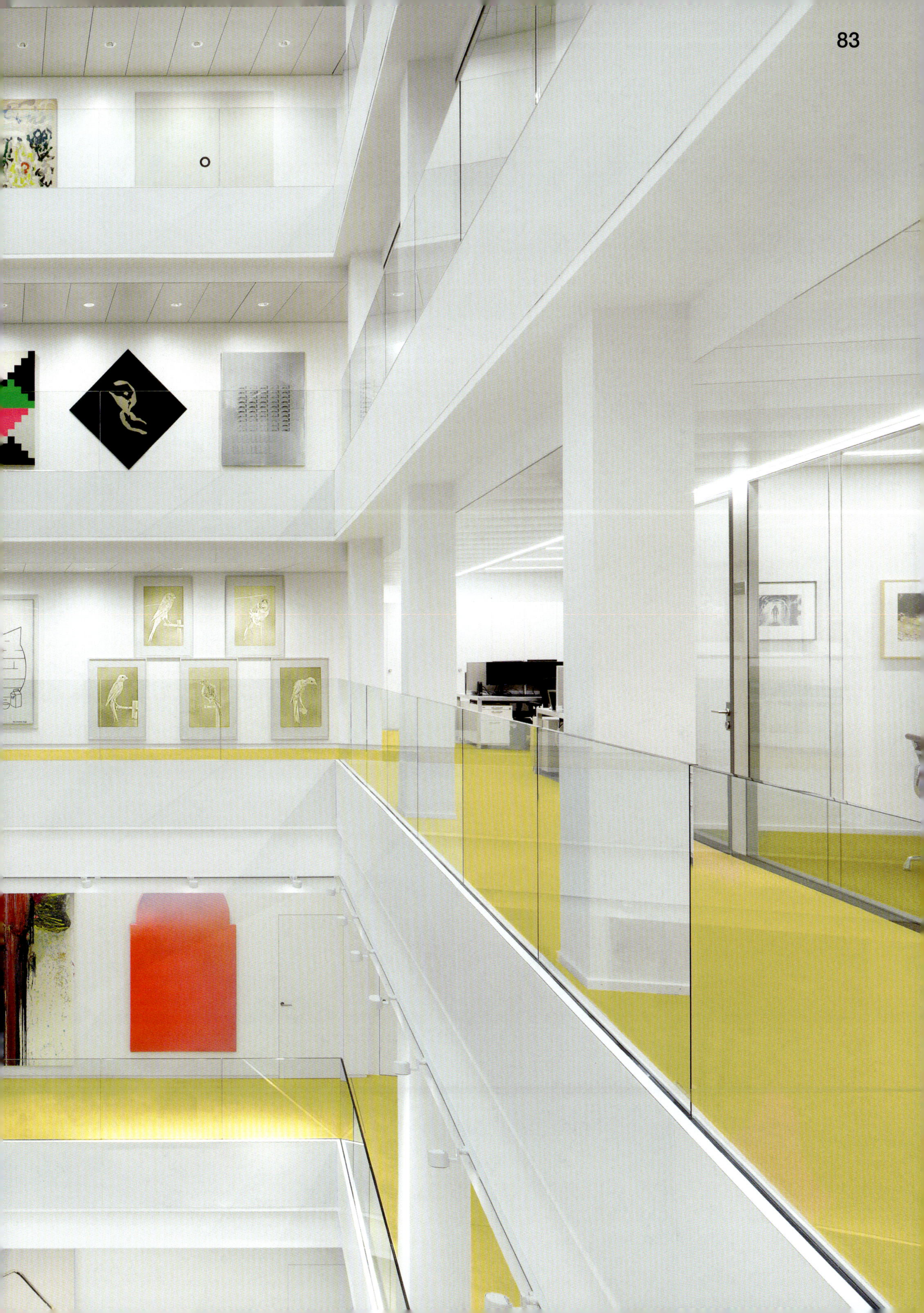

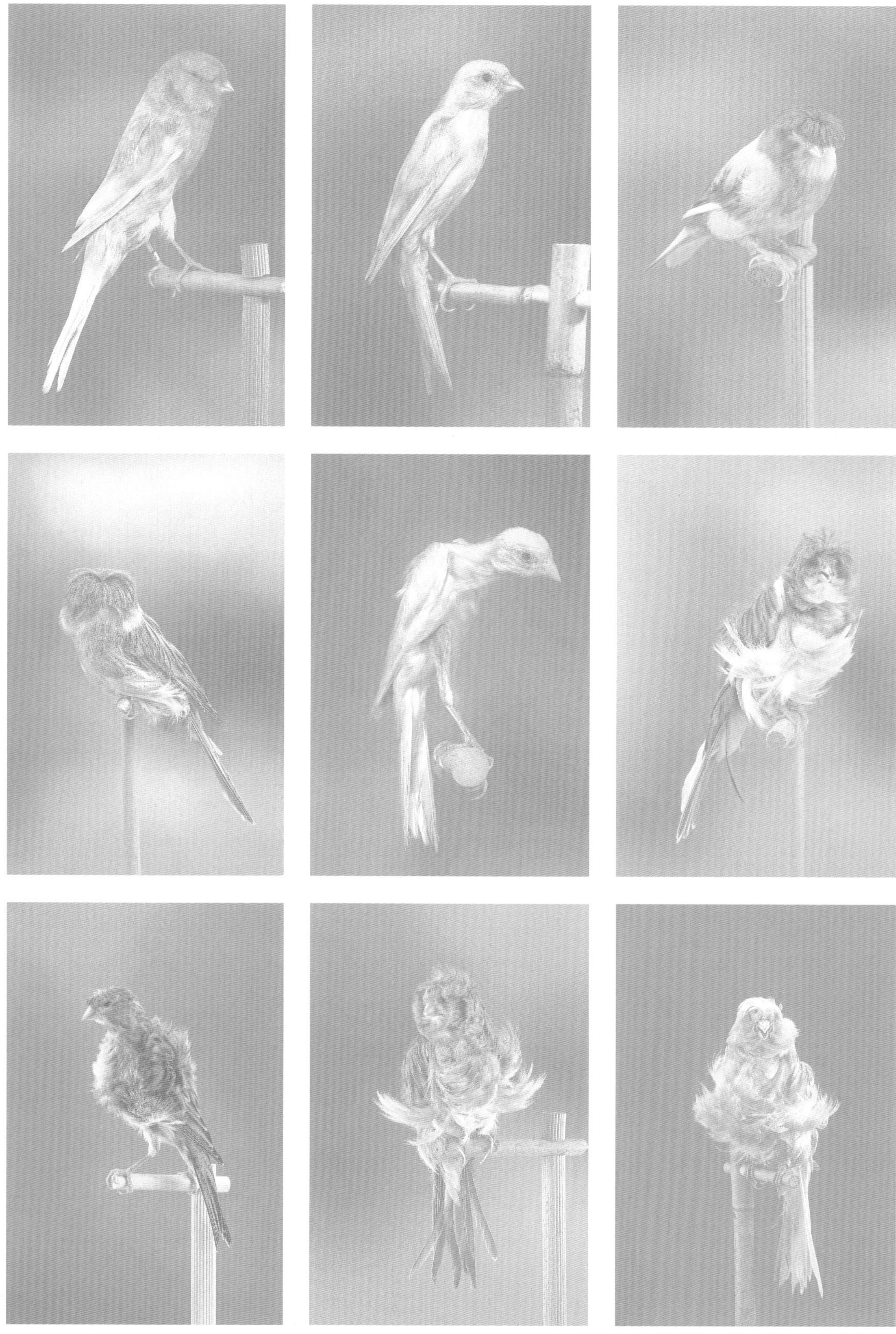

Canary (1), (2), (3), (4), (5), (6), (7), (8), (9), 2009
Engraving in gold on paper
108 × 78 cm each

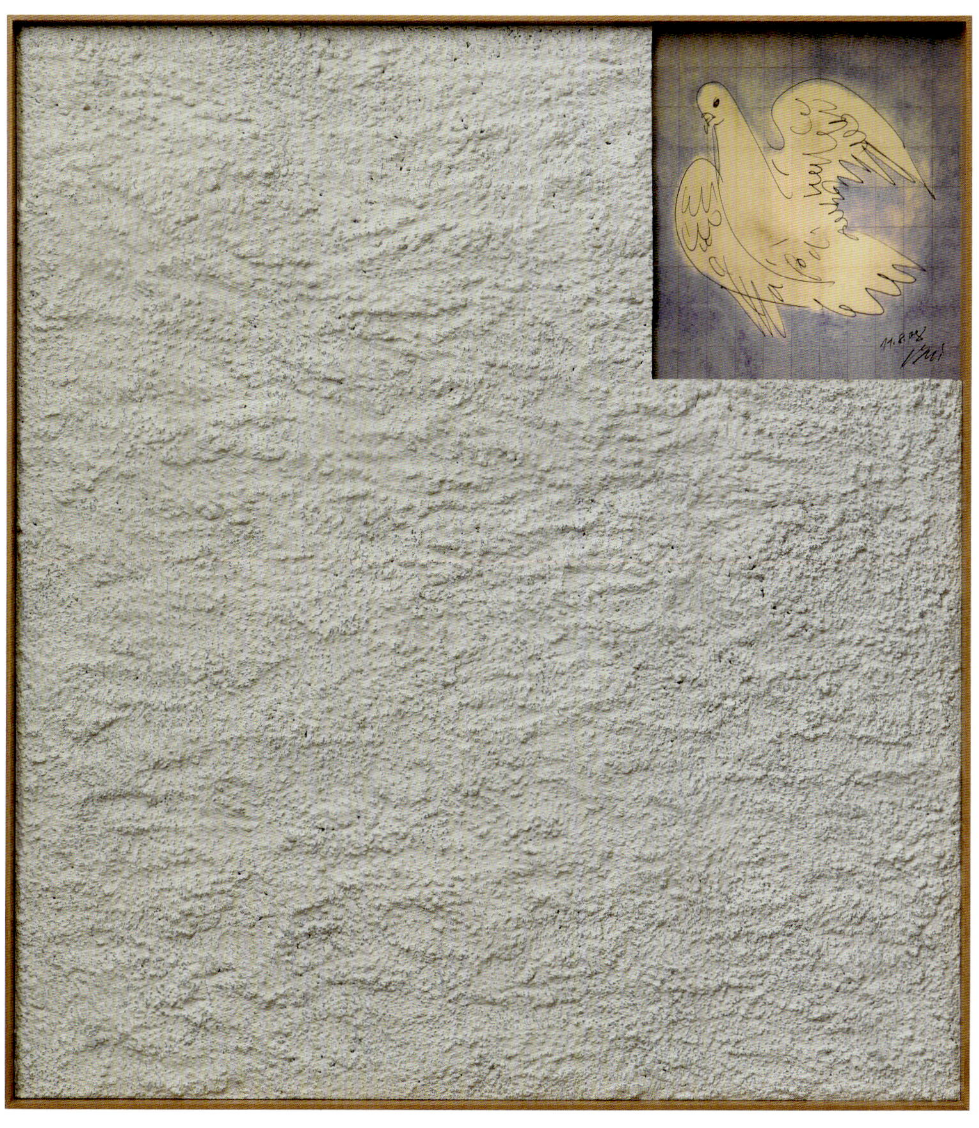

La colombe, 2017
MDF, inkjet print on adhesive paper,
acrylic resin, acrylic enamel paint
132 × 120 × 6 cm

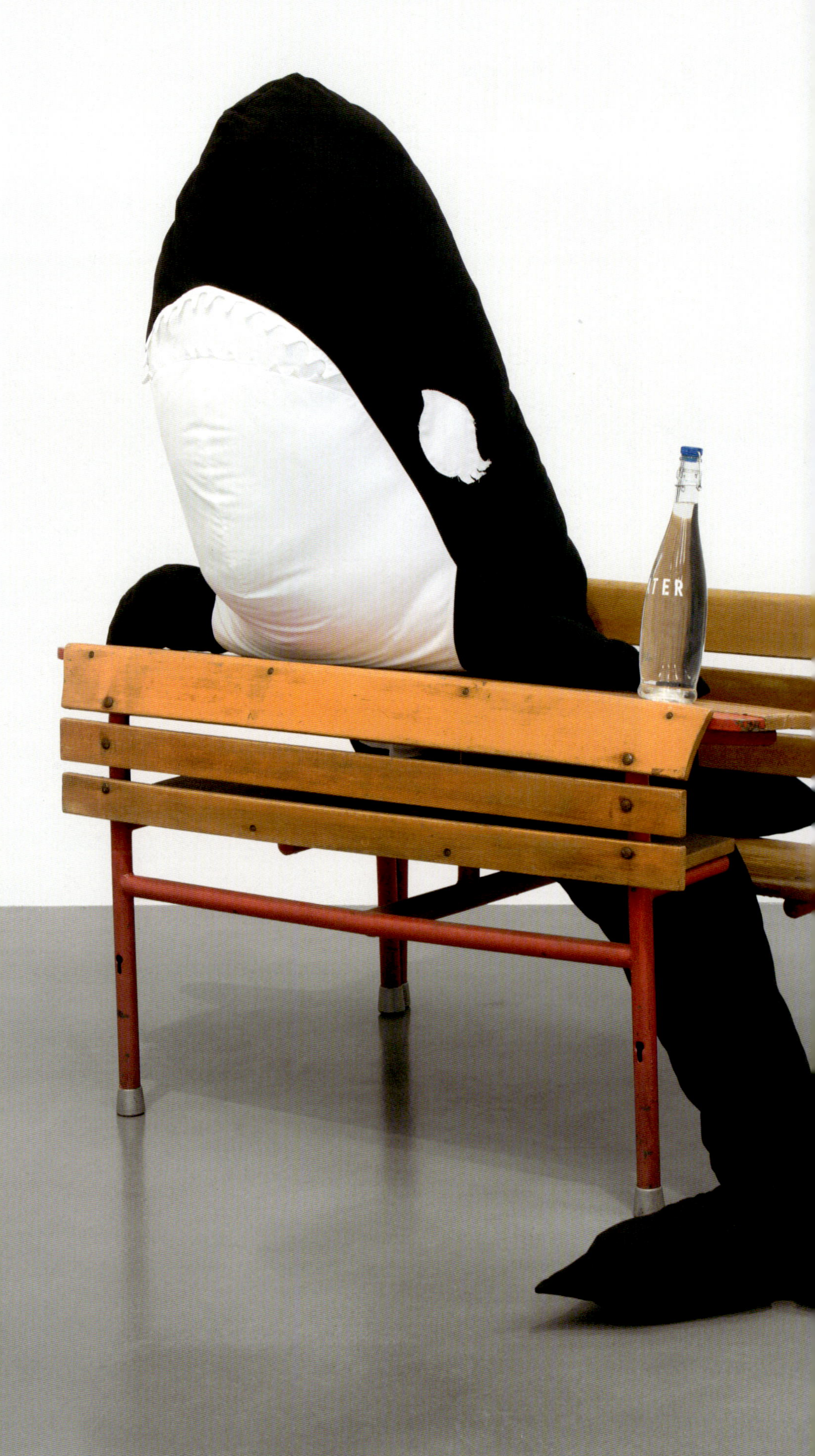

killer whale with long eyelashes 2 (school desk version), 2018

Wood, metal, glass bottle, fabric
149.9 × 119.4 × 119.4 cm

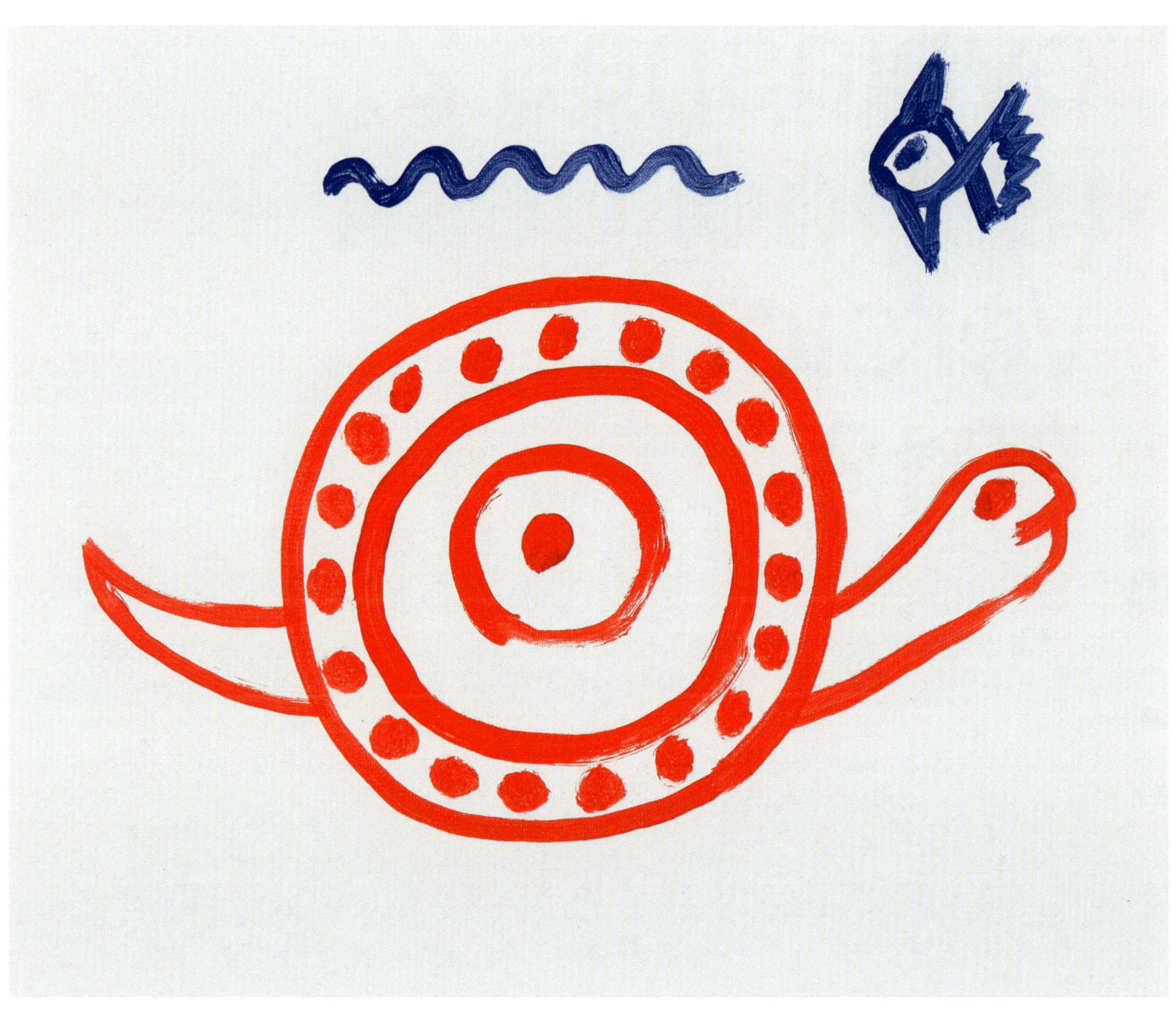

Untitled, 2014
Acrylic on canvas
40 × 50 cm

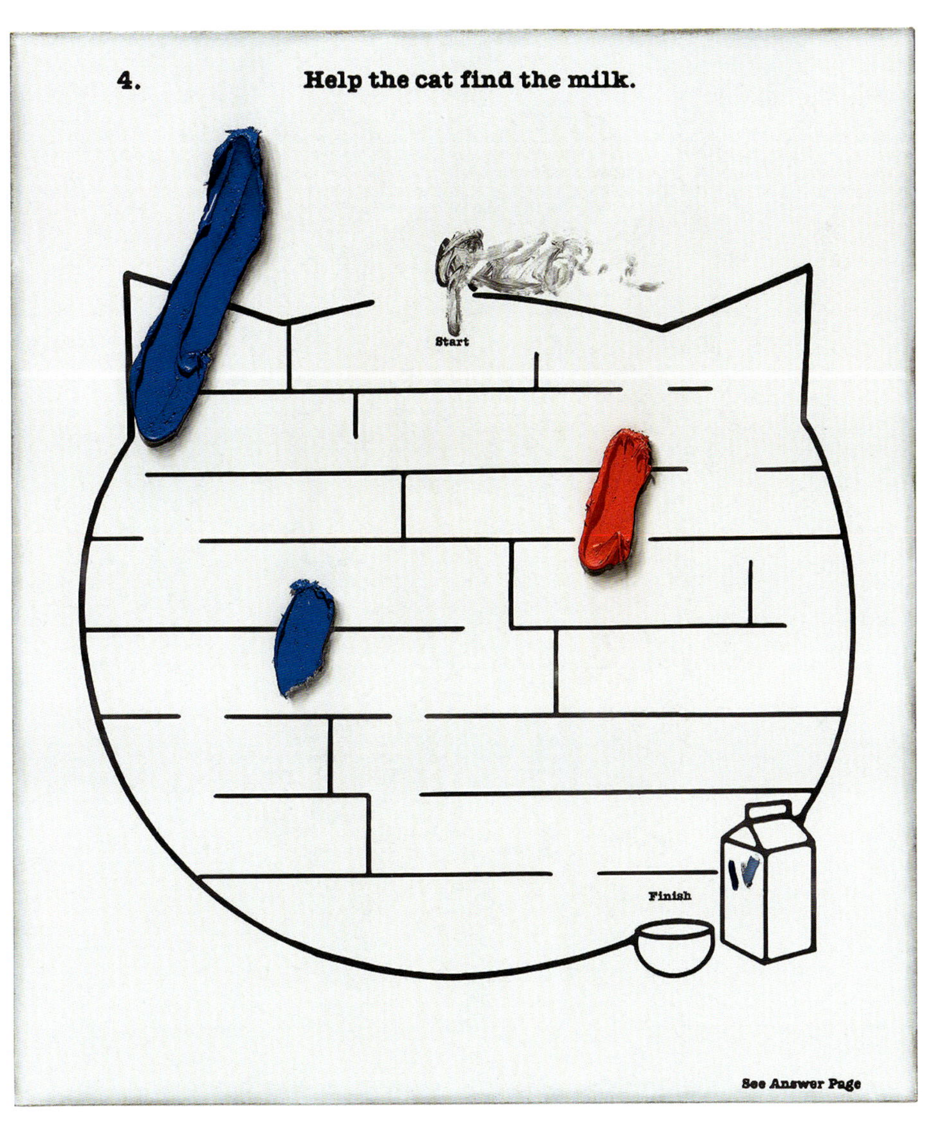

Untitled, 2014
Oil, charcoal, and gesso on linen
175.3 × 152.4 cm

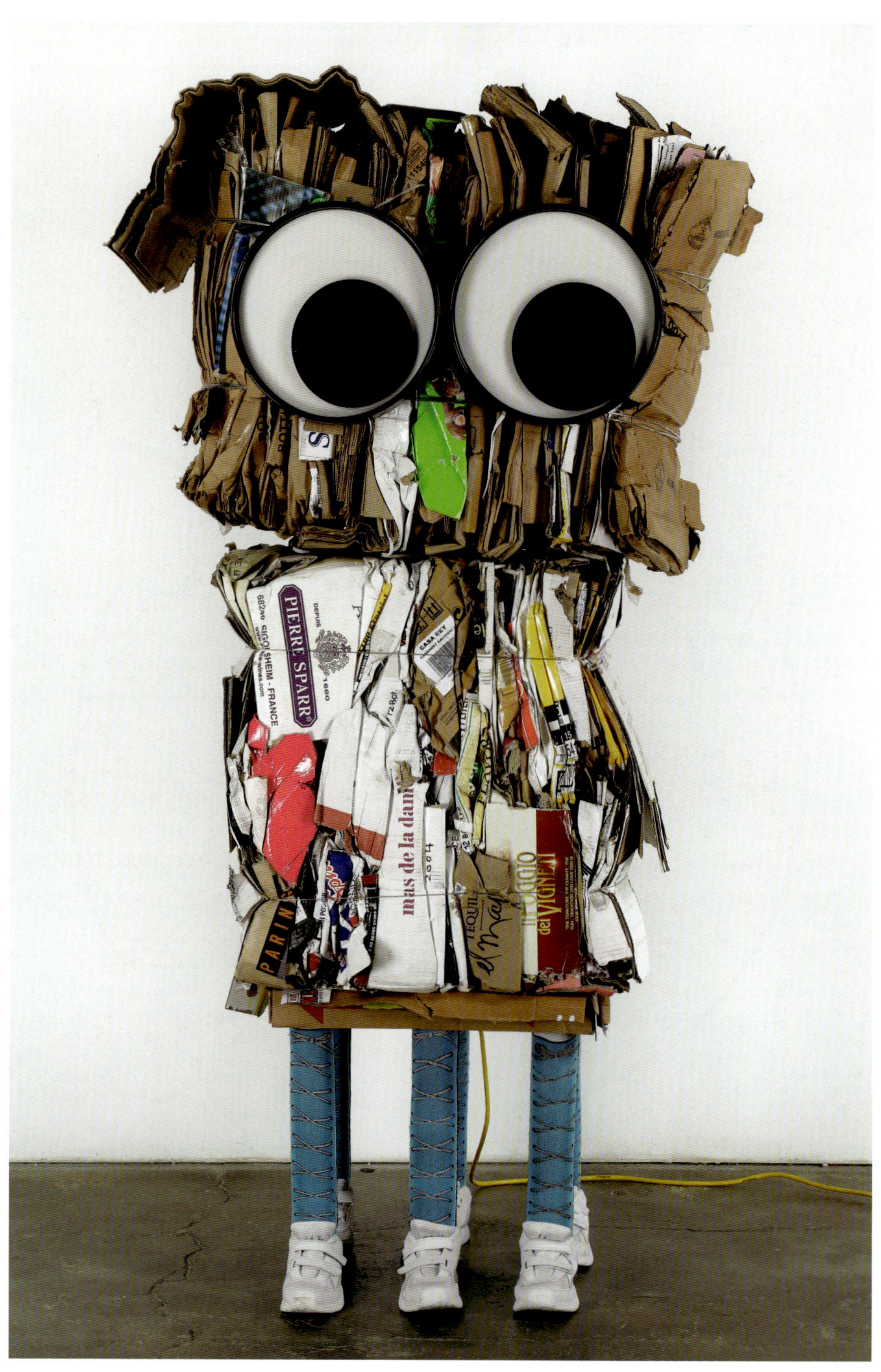

Cardboard Monster: Alison, 2010
Baled cardboard, socks, shoes, refitted electric clocks, wood, Comme des Garçons Odeur 53, wood, extension cord
213.4 × 91.4 × 71.1 cm

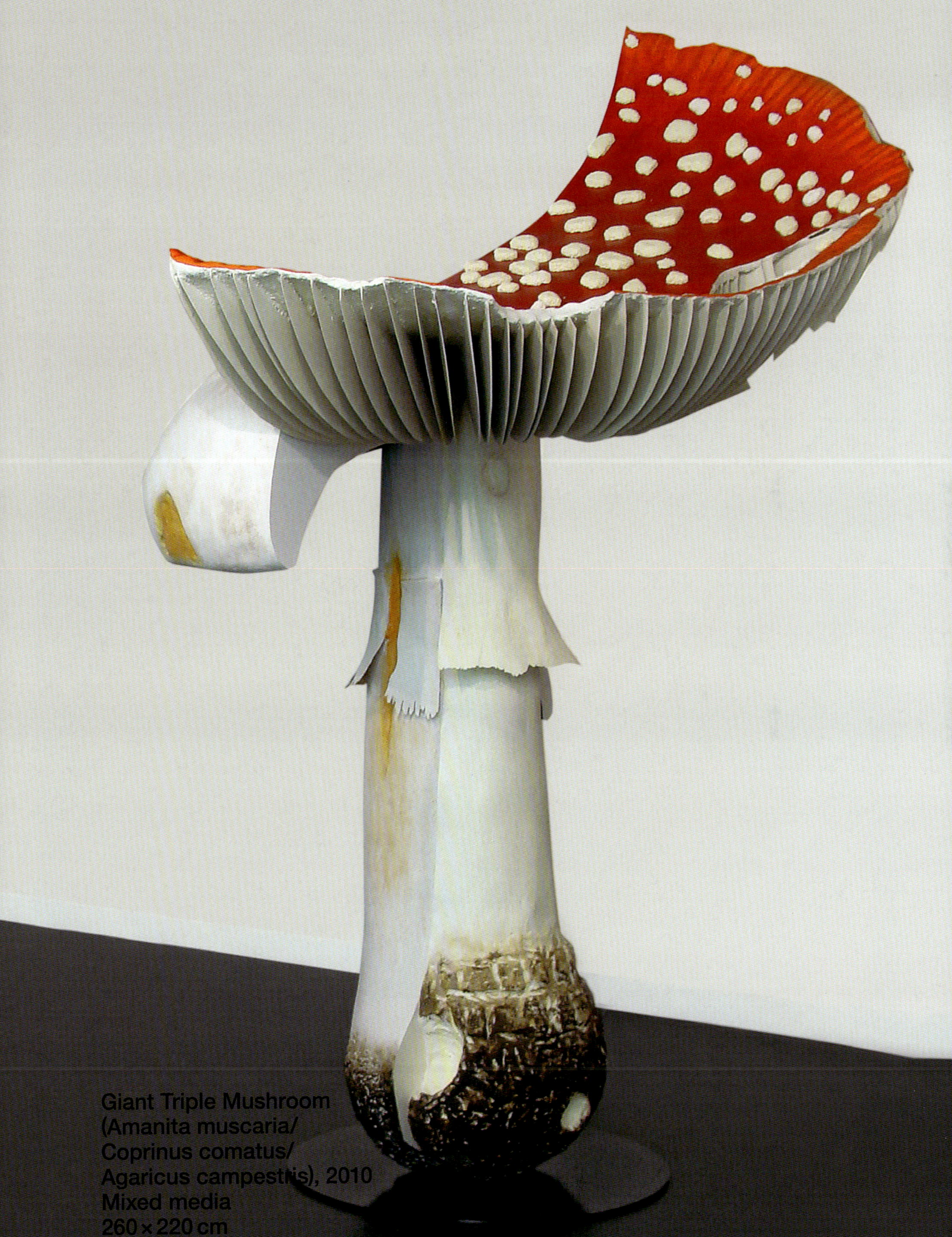

Giant Triple Mushroom
(Amanita muscaria/
Coprinus comatus/
Agaricus campestris), 2010
Mixed media
260 × 220 cm

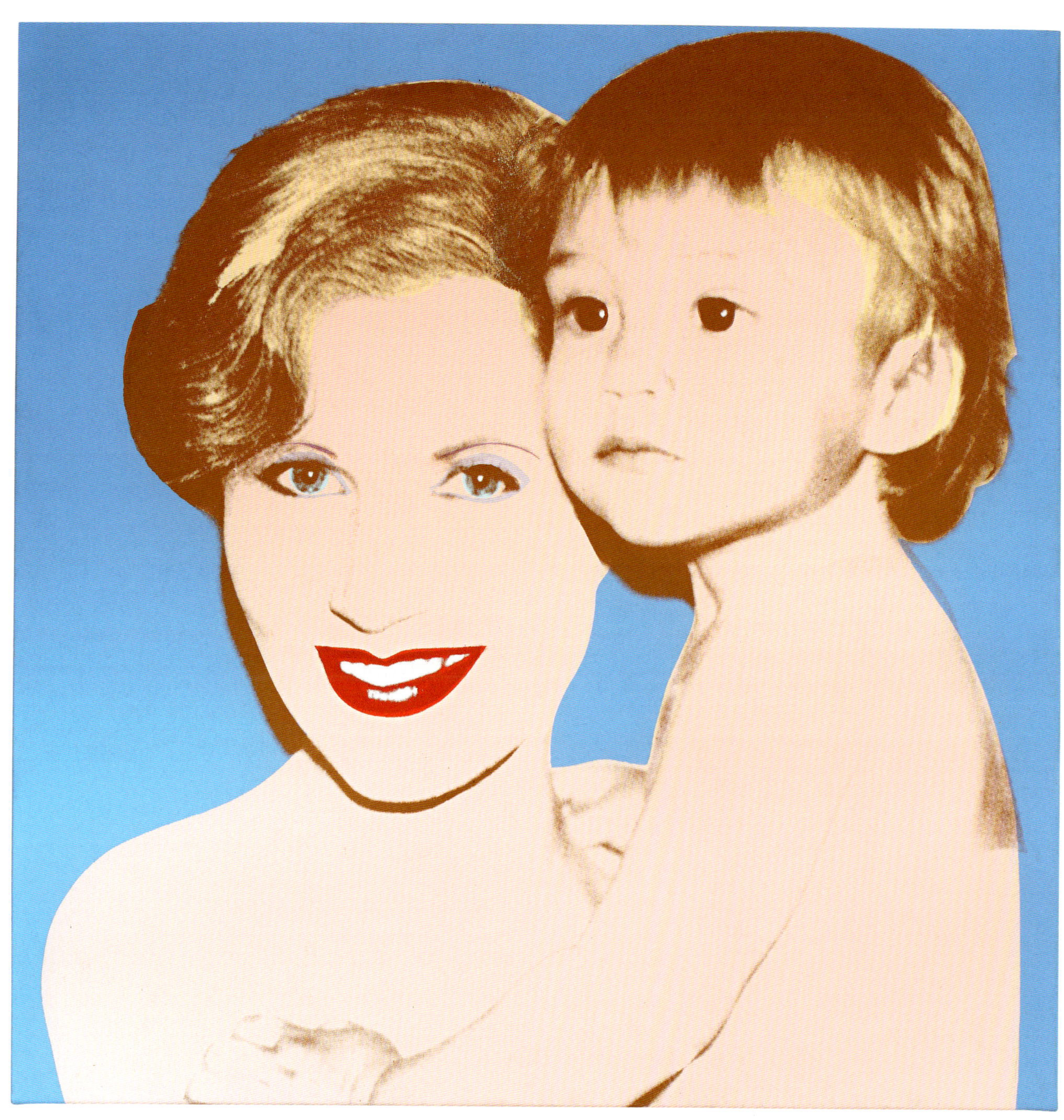

Suzanne and Marc Syz, 1982
Silkscreen on linen
102 × 102 cm

Conversation with Suzanne & Eric Syz, and Nicolas Trembley

Emmanuel Grandjean
Geneva, April 16, 2018

How did your collection start?

Suzanne Syz Between 1982 and 1985, when we were living in New York, we were hanging out a lot downtown with our friends. That is when we made contact with the gallery owners and the artists of the New York art scene. Eric and I thought it would be great to start a collection with these people.

Did you ever collect before settling in New York?

S We acquired vases, Art Nouveau objects, drawings by Italian masters. We were collectors at heart, but were not yet interested in contemporary art. Our first contemporary work is a painting by Sandro Chia that Eric's mother gave us as a wedding gift in 1981, just before we moved to the United States.

What did you like about contemporary art?

Eric Syz In the 1970s and early 1980s, the United States experienced a major recession that had a significant impact on the global economy. Inflation was controlled after that and the economy picked up again. In art, this was reflected in the fact that the great artists of the 1970s—Carl Andre, Sol LeWitt, Robert Ryman—all worked in a minimal and cold abstraction. When the economy regained some color, art also became more colorful again. The return to expression and figuration, in Germany, France, Italy, and the United States, owes nothing to chance. To realize that art was such a mirror of the present time fascinated me completely.

S In New York we used to frequent artists all the time. We lived with them, so to speak, and understood them. We also felt that what we were experiencing was a key moment. In the 1980s, in New York, you only found the best in all areas. It was prolific and very exciting.

Who were the first artists in your collection?

S Thanks to Bruno Bischofberger, who was our friend, we were introduced to Andy Warhol, and younger artists like Jeff Koons, Julian Schnabel, and Jean-Michel Basquiat, with whom we became close because he spent some winters in Saint-Moritz. It was also the time when the public did not know him at all, when he was still doing well. It was also at this time, in 1982, that he did his best paintings. We bought our first Basquiat for a few thousand dollars—which represented a sum for us. I remember having dinner with him in a trendy brasserie: Jean-Michel told us that before becoming famous, he had never

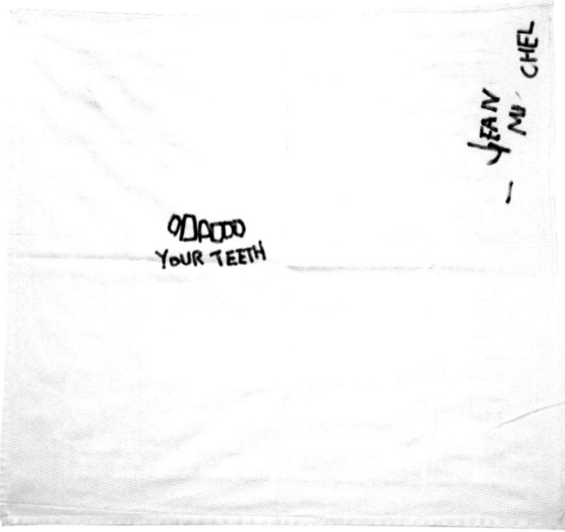

Jean-Michel Basquiat
Your Teeth, 1982
Pen on linen
40 × 60 cm

been allowed in. Now, in the 1980s, he was the king of New York! He drew my teeth on a towel that night; I still have that drawing. We continued collecting European and American Neo-Expressionists.

Then you became close friends with Andy Warhol. What was he like?

S On his good days, he was adorable. At first he was a little cold, and even though we became very close afterward, he always impressed me a lot.

You posed for him.

S Eric wanted to offer me a painting where I would pose with Marc, our one-year-old son, a portrait that Marc could then keep. At Warhol's studio he cried a lot because they had covered my face with some kind of white foundation to take the photograph Andy was going to work from. The session went rather well and, two months later, the Factory called me to tell me that I could come and get my painting. Andy asked me what I thought of it. I am naturally good tempered and of a sunny disposition, but I saw myself looking sinister, in chromatic hues that did not fit at all. I told him that I did not recognize myself in this portrait. Andy didn't take offense. He was even willing to do it again. A month later, the Factory called me again: my new painting was ready. I went back telling myself that this time, whether I liked it or not, I would have to take it. When I arrived, there were three different portraits, each as beautiful as the other. "So, how do you like them?" asked Andy. I gave him a huge hug and said that they were absolutely wonderful, that it was me, absolutely. He then said, "Then take all three." Three Warhols for the price of one. I was blown away.

Are there any artists you regret not having bought at the time?

S We missed Jeff Koons' *Hoovers*. They cost 20,000 dollars and were displayed in a small downstairs window in one of our friend's houses. I tried unsuccessfully to convince Eric to buy some. Years later, I went back to Jeff Koons to see if I could buy one of his *Balloon Dogs* that I love. I went to his workshop where dozens of assistants were working. The red one was already sold to the Mercedes Collection. Jeff told me I could have one in a different color, but warned me that the production costs were exorbitant. He could sell it to me for a million dollars. I left empty handed, but having spent a very pleasant afternoon.

Did Bruno Bischofberger influence the way in which you collect contemporary art?

E I wouldn't say influenced, rather he inspired us. Bruno is a real character; he gets to the bottom of things. That is fascinating. When he becomes infatuated with a topic, he exhausts it completely. If you walk with him in the Grisons, he can describe the flora and fauna like no one else. The same for art, Memphis design, Alpine furniture that he knows by heart and collects. He has a frenzied, communicative, and delirious enthusiasm. It is true that we copied that. Because to do things right, you have to do them to the full.

Why did you become interested in photography?

S It came much later, around 1996, when Eric opened his bank. We thought that hanging a Basquiat in the entrance would perhaps be a little complicated for his clients to understand. Our interest in photography began when I visited the first edition of Paris Photo. I saw interesting things, and easier to comprehend than some of our paintings.

Then I visited Kaspar M. Fleischmann from the Zur Stockeregg Gallery in Zurich a lot: really to learn everything about photography. At that time the photographic medium had finally been recognized in the field of contemporary art. We started by collecting historical photographers, the pictorial ones such as Alfred Stieglitz and Heinrich Kühn, and artists like Man Ray. Starting at the very beginning was the best way to understand the challenges of modern photography with which the creators we later bought were dealing: Bernd and Hilla Becher, Cindy Sherman, Thomas Ruff.

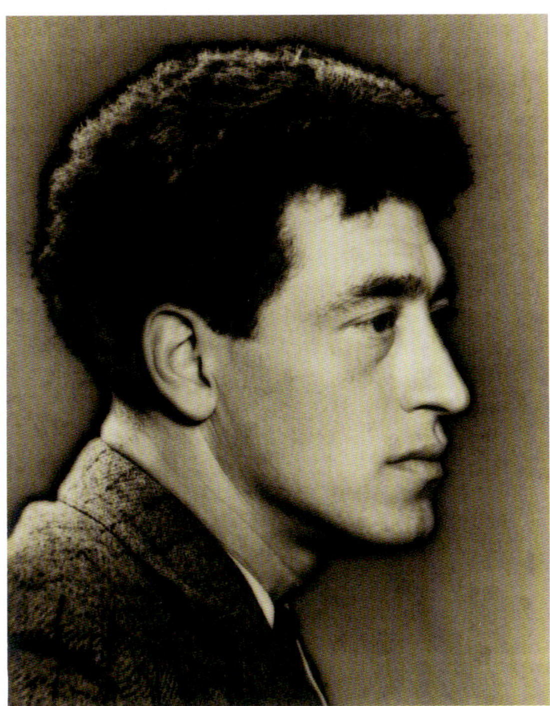

Man Ray
Alberto Giacometti, 1934
Solarized vintage gelatin silver print
29 × 22.7 cm

But you never stopped collecting painting.

S Of course we continued. Especially since photography causes both problems of exposure, when it is too large, and stability. Some color prints did not age well. Fischli Weiss have agreed to provide us with "exhibition copies," so that we can present those instead of the originals. Richard Prince refused. However, my photographs by Guy Bourdin have not changed. I have always been a huge fan of his work. He is the one who really invented fashion photography as it is practiced today.

You built this collection together, the two of you, then Nicolas Trembley joined you in 2008. How do you work together?

E Suzanne and I almost always agree. It is very rare that one of us buys an artwork without asking the other's opinion. Unless it's a gift ...

S A good example is Lutz Bacher's *Camel* exhibited in the bank's entrance. I thought it was amazing, but I knew Eric would probably be less excited. Nicolas had to think about how this work could be integrated into the collection. But I loved it too much. So I offered it to Eric for Christmas. In fact, we are very complementary. I'm in love at first sight; Eric looks, and Nicolas tries to align us.

Nicolas Trembley Suzanne goes with me to art fairs a lot. She is extremely fast. I look, I present different arguments to work out whether the artwork Suzanne likes is interesting in the collection, to ensure the cogency of the whole. If Eric is not with us, we will talk to him later.

How would you define the collection?

N It has been through different stages and, in this sense, each decade represents the art that was being created at that time very well. It is not a collection of trophies, but a collection that takes the pulse of art as it evolves. It is very important that the collection is now visible, also for the artists who helped us a lot. We thank them.

E The collection combines the tastes of my wife, who loves very expressive and sometimes slightly extravagant art, and my perhaps more cerebral approach to things. The mix of the two gives a good result.

Is it a choice to collect mainly American and European artists?

E If we do not collect Asian, Latin American, African, or Middle Eastern artists, it is because we do not know them well, and, for a long time, we were not really interested in them. Today, it would take too much time to find out about these productions. It is not possible to collect everything. If you want to do things right, you have to limit yourself. I saw how Jean Pigozzi, one of the very first to collect contemporary African art, works. Because collecting is first and foremost about making choices.

Which Swiss artists do you collect?

S We have quite complete ensembles by Fischli Weiss and Roman Signer, as well as important works by Sylvie Fleury—who recently collaborated with me on my jewelry—and John Armleder, who is one of my favorite artists. For the younger ones, I really like the work of David Hominal and Valentin Carron.

Ten years ago, Nicolas Trembley joined you to continue building your collection. When did you feel the need to hire someone?

E If we wanted to take our collection a step further, we needed someone. The collection reflected the things we loved, but was rather dispersed. In addition we no longer had time to devote to the search for young artists, and were too dependent on galleries. Around 2006–2007, Suzanne and I realized that we needed someone. We met Nicolas. At first, we had to get to know and trust each other. He showed us artists who didn't convince us right away. That's how we missed Wade Guyton's Xs that Nicolas introduced us to three months after his arrival.

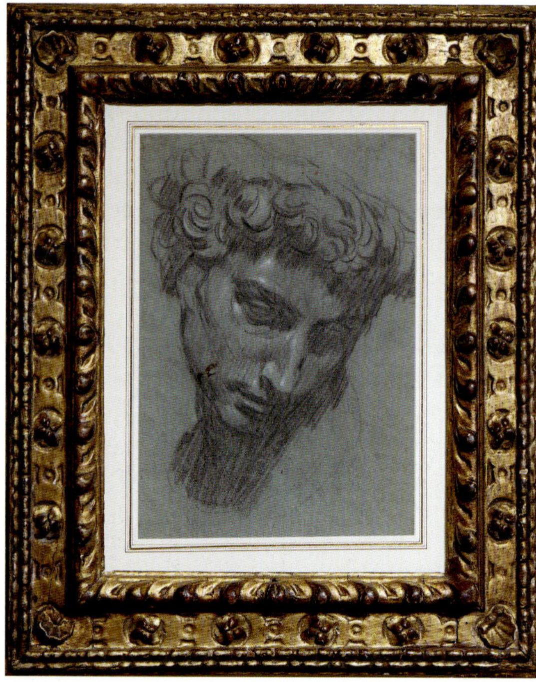

Tintoretto
Portrait of Giulio Medici
after Michelangelo, 16th century
Black chalk on blue paper
39 × 28 cm

At the time, Nicolas, you worked with large public institutions in France and Switzerland, but not in theprivate market sector. How did your conversion develop?

N I had no idea how much the works cost. In institutions, the price of a work doesn't matter; it is quality first. When I first got here, I started going through auction catalogues. As I flipped through them, I found that I didn't know half the names listed in them. Later, I realized that nobody actually knew them, except the people in the art market.

And why are you still working here ten years later?

N Whether in the private sector or in the public realm, what interests me is building a collection and taking it further. Meeting collectors like Suzanne and Eric, who decide to invest for this purpose, is quite rare. Our relationship has evolved into a friendly one.

What was the first thing you did when you arrived?

N Many works had already been acquired when I arrived. First, I conducted a rather scientific analysis of the collection, putting aside the relationships Suzanne and Eric had with the artists they were buying. I drew some ensembles and offered to complete them, or not. When that was no longer possible, but when they were really interested in an artist, I advised them that, if they wanted just one work, it should be one of the artist's seminal works.

So you gave direction to the collection.

N A collection is like an organism; it's something living that unfolds. The Syz Collection has, for example, textile works by Rosemarie Trockel and Michael Krebber, but none by Cosima von Bonin, of whose work I have just seen a remarkable exhibition in New York. We have just acquired one of her emblematic works. My job is also to fill the gaps.

S In some ways, Nicolas has given us a new direction. I especially wanted him to show me the work of young artists, because it's not very interesting to collect what everyone else collects.

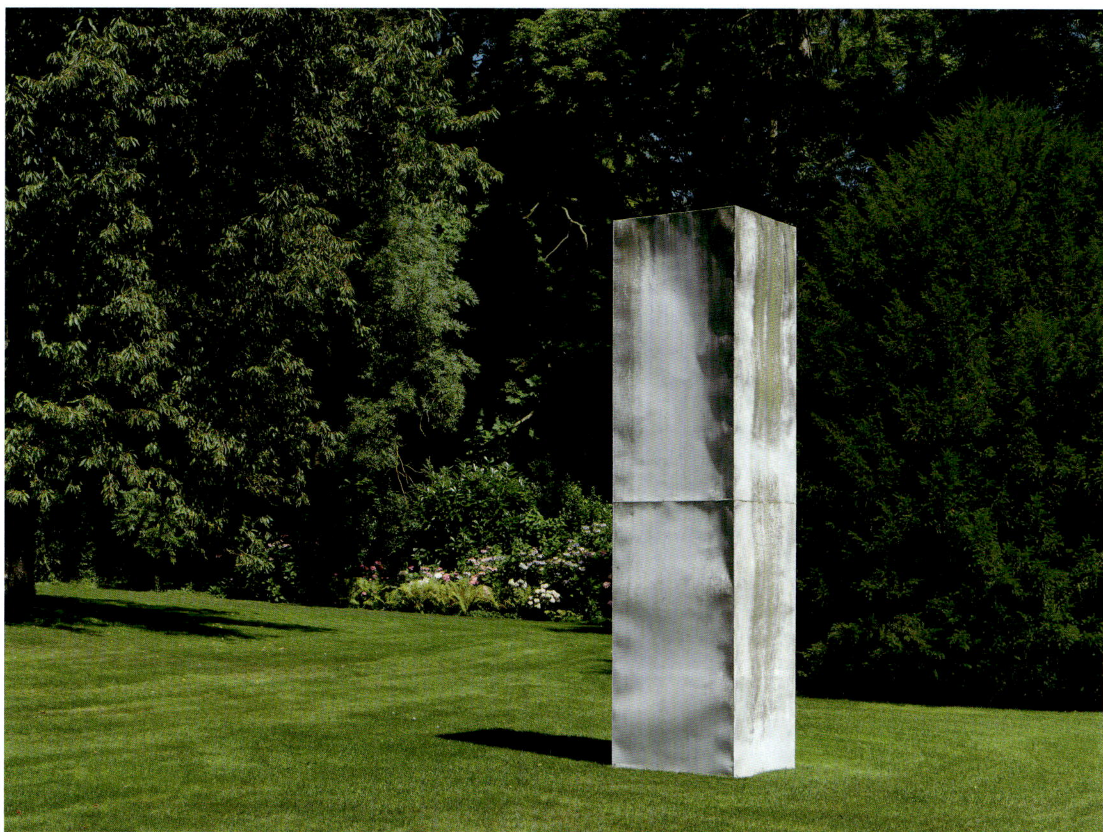

Franz West
James Lee Byars, 1997
Lacquered Nirosta steel
401 × 100 × 100 cm

In New York, artists were your friends. Are you still as close to the ones you collect today?

S Not as much as we were in New York. It must be said that that scene was of our generation. So yes of course, we regularly see artists like Wade Guyton whom we ended up loving. For us, it is important to know the artists well. But the relationships we have with today's artists are different from those of the past.

You exhibit part of your collection in the premises of the SYZ Group. What difference do you make between a corporate collection and a collection, like yours, that is private, but displayed at your company headquarters?

E For me, a corporate collection is democratic. It represents not only the image of the company, but also has a philanthropic vocation and sometimes a marketing goal. This is not the case of a private collection displayed in one's company. Such a collection reflects a certain style, a certain personal taste, which one may or may not like, but which does not necessarily have to go hand in hand with the philosophy of the company where it is shown.

N In the same spirit, we never buy a work thinking that it would do well in the bank …

S Just as we never think of purchasing a work because of the premises' architecture. Acquiring works according to the walls is decoration, which we absolutely avoid.

Did you intend to exhibit this collection in the first place?

E We were already exhibiting works in the old building. But the premises were small and unsuitable. When we rented this building and discovered the space available, we saw its potential, but without necessarily thinking about the project as it stands today. Once Suzanne had conceived of the design in the bank, some of the armchairs and all the lounges, and worked on the colors of the walls, we really realized what this place had become, and that the artworks would sit very comfortably there.

What did your employees say when they arrived?

S They think it is great to be able to work in this environment. That is the best compliment they could give us.
N It is interesting to note that in the old building there were works that people did not like. But those same people appreciate them today because they are exhibited in different conditions.

Nicolas, you were in charge of choosing the works and hanging them in the working spaces and the reception rooms. How did you proceed?

N The main challenge has been to give meaning to the whole, to make people understand why one work is displayed next to another. I conceived a hanging that unfolded on several levels, as much in terms of movement through space as in the possibility of meaning. On the second floor for example, I have brought together works featuring representations of animals. On the fourth floor, abstract works are shown, some "hard abstractions" in the guise of Olivier Mosset's paintings, some softer ones with Mary Heilmann's works—a combination of pieces intended for those who are already familiar with contemporary art. Above these, the work of a new generation that is returning to figurative art, particularly drawing within the discourse of the comic strip tradition, is presented. For this dialogue between works to exist, there are also sometimes underlying links. To combine John Armleder with Valentin Carron is to say that the former was the latter's teacher, and that the two appreciate each other very much.

How did you deal with the fact that this place is a working space and that the collaborators would live with the works daily?

N As far as possible, I have chosen works that fit into a whole, in order to avoid any atomization or dispersion.

How will the hanging evolve?

N Everything was installed before the employees arrived in the building. It would be difficult to do it again, especially since the choice and implementation processes have been colossal. The large entrance hall, on the other hand, is more modular and friendly: it is the only place to which the public has access. We are considering the possibility of organizing small solo exhibitions there.

And you, Eric, which works did you choose for your office?

E I chose them from Nicolas' proposals. I surrounded myself with a Wade Guyton, a work by Sturtevant, and another, smaller work by Henry Moore. That's all. Art is something that stimulates us all and helps create an exciting work environment. The people who work here tell me so.

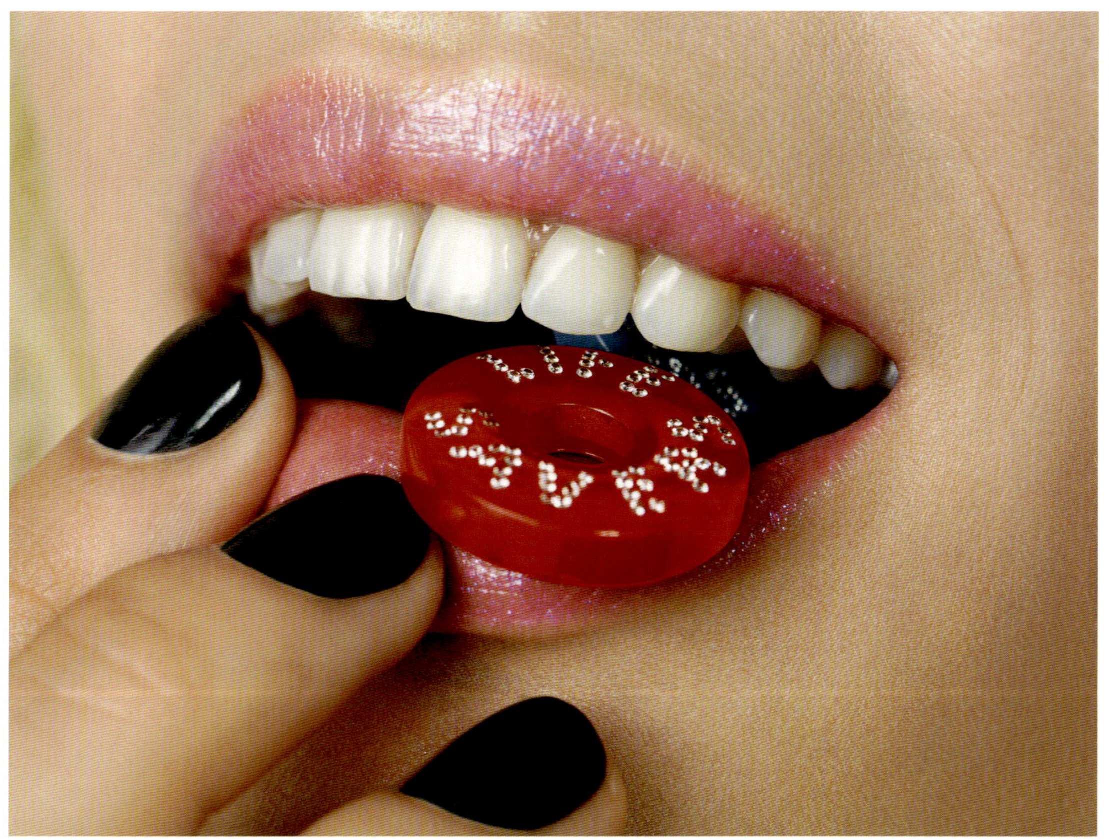

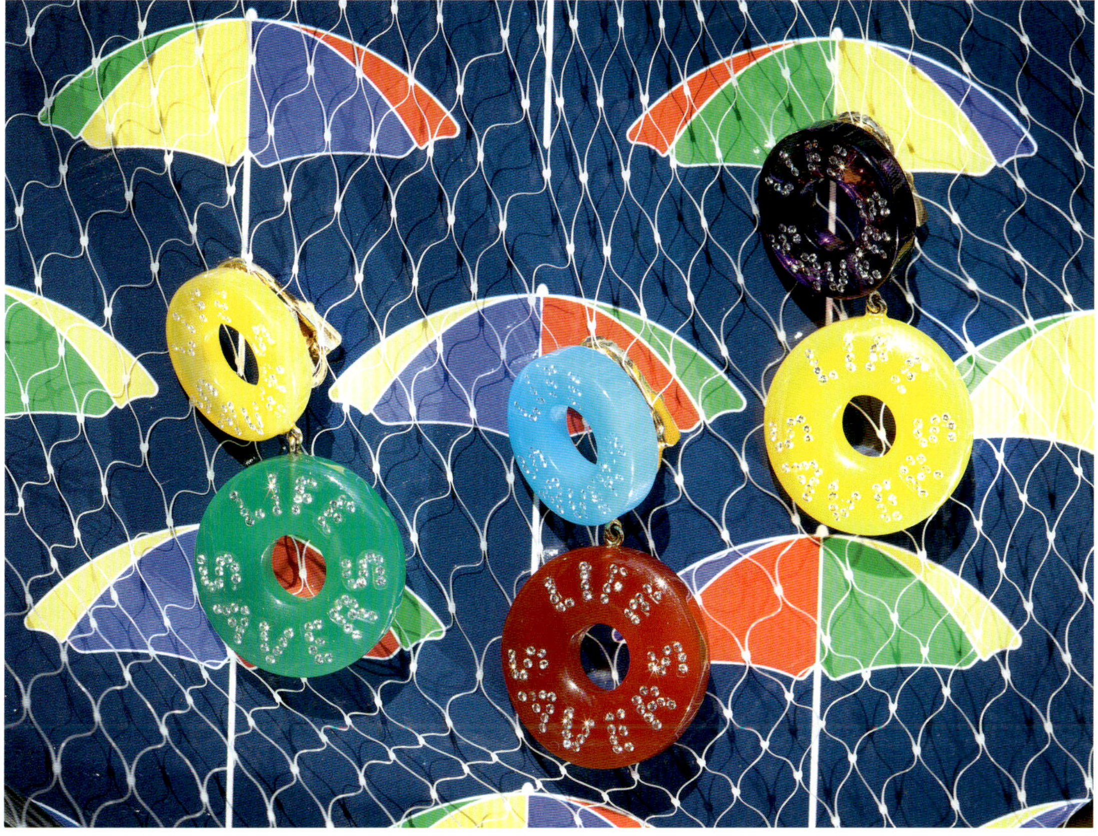

Stef with Life Savers Earrings, 2012
C-print
84 × 112 cm

Life Savers, 2012
C-print
83.8 × 110.2 cm

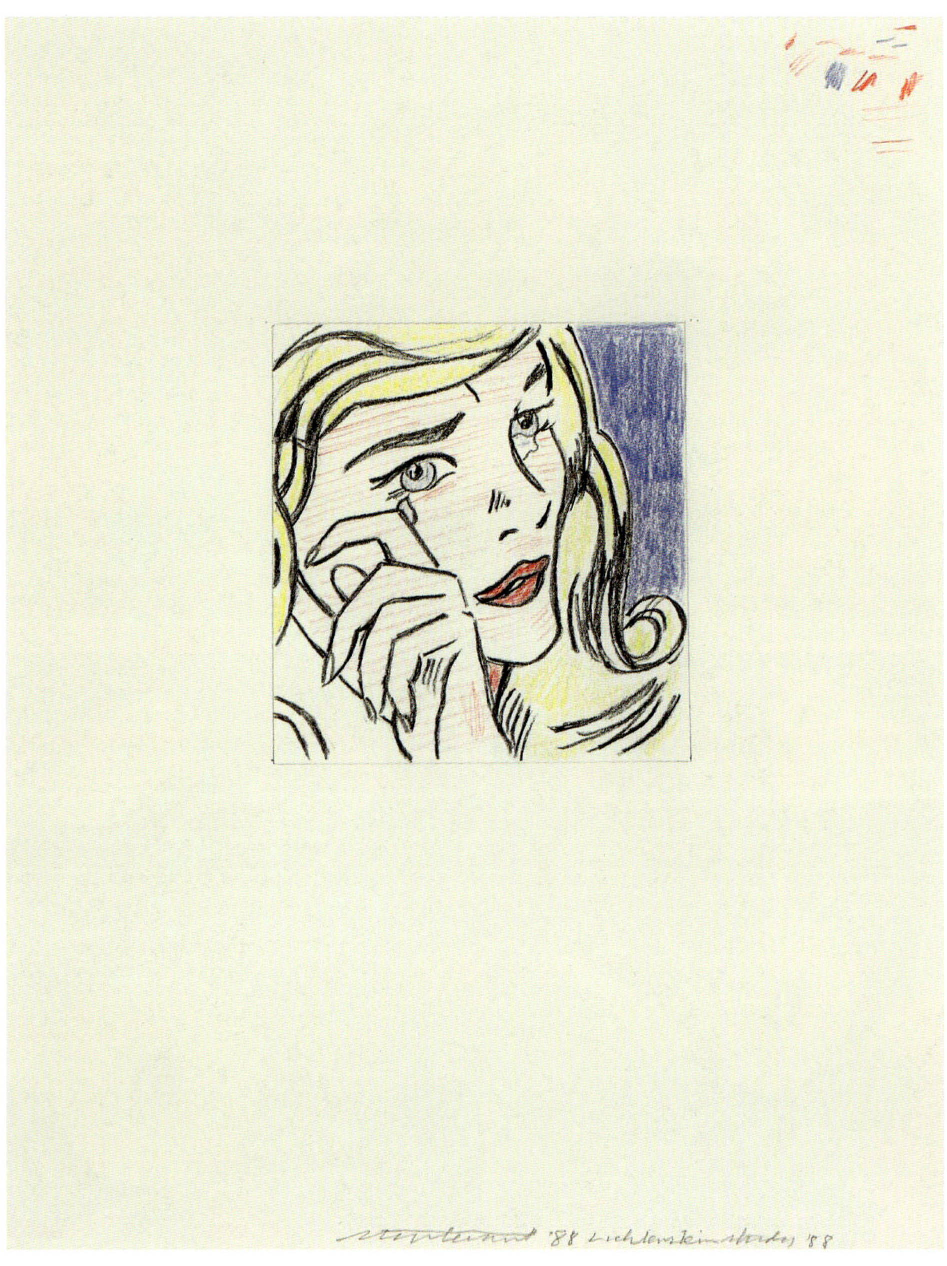

Lichtenstein Study, 1988
Color pencil and graphite pencil on paper
35.4 × 28 cm

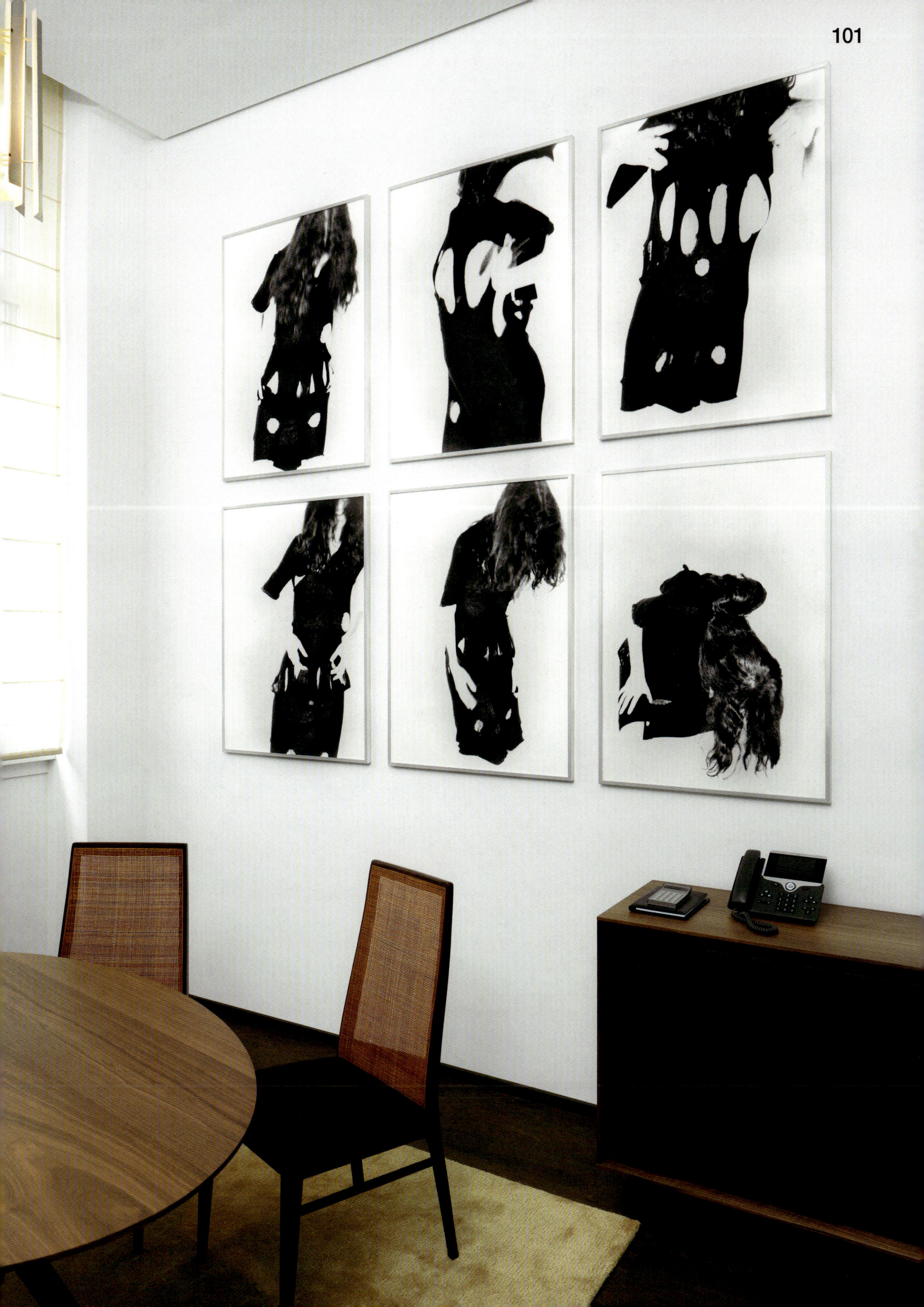

come find me when i’m hiding, 1981–2010

Digital print from original negative on photographic paper
144.8 × 106.7 cm

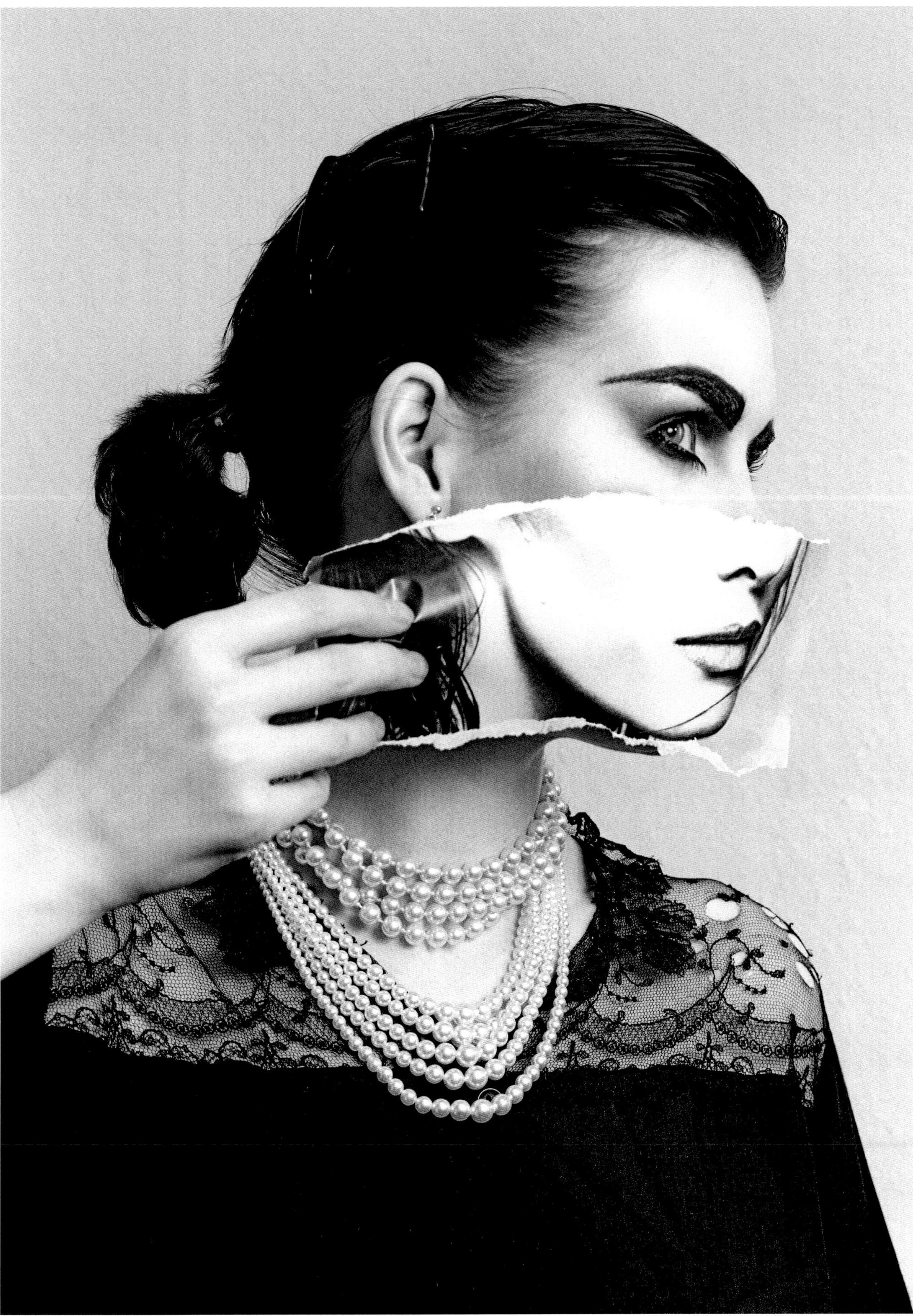

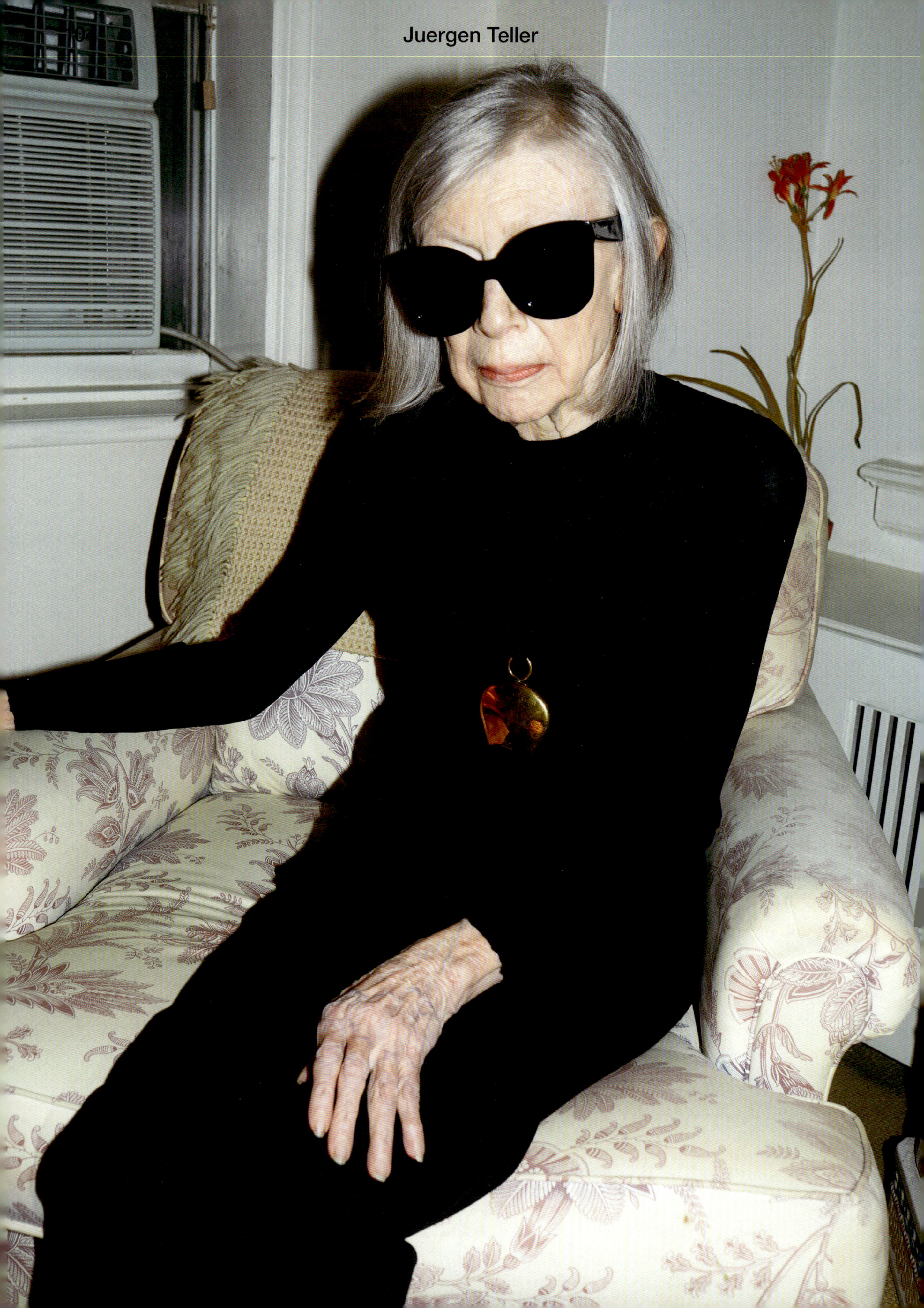

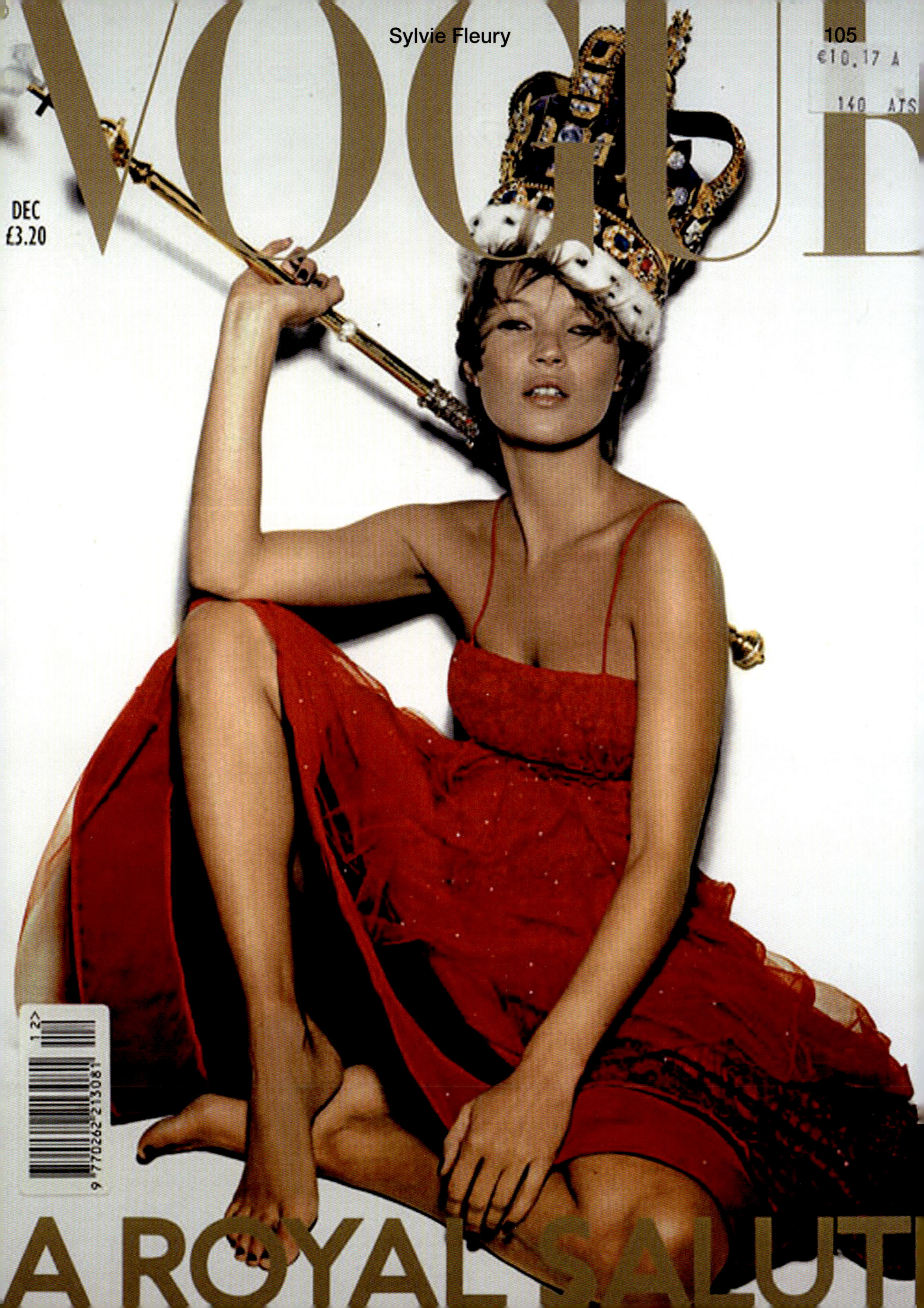
VOGUE
DEC
£3.20
€10.17 A
140 ATS
A ROYAL SALUTE
9 770262 213081 12

playboys (inflation), 1991–1993

Airbrush and silkscreen on canvas
111.8 × 91.4 cm

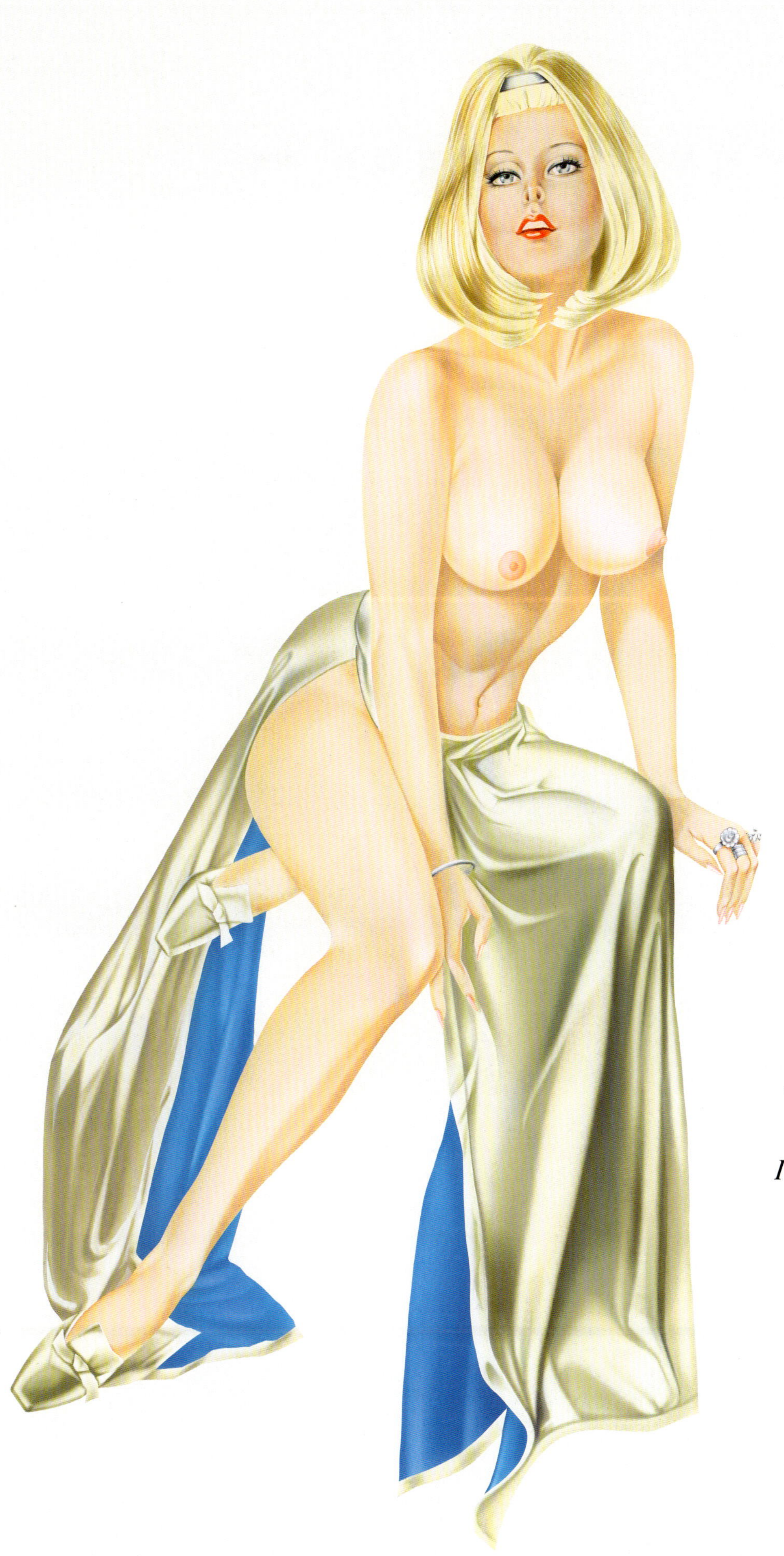

"Of course, there are certain kinds of inflation that I don't mind at all."

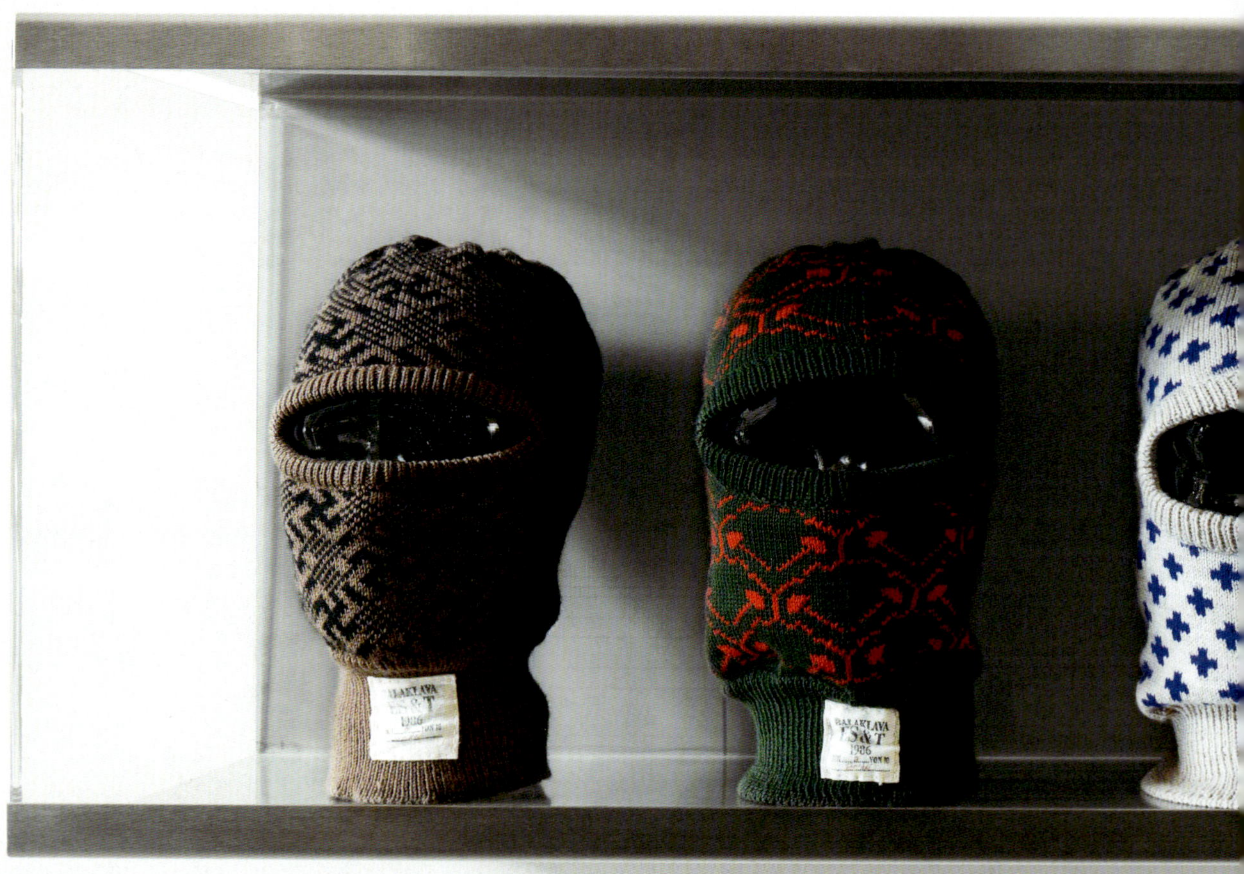

Balaklava, 1986
Wool
28 × 20 cm each

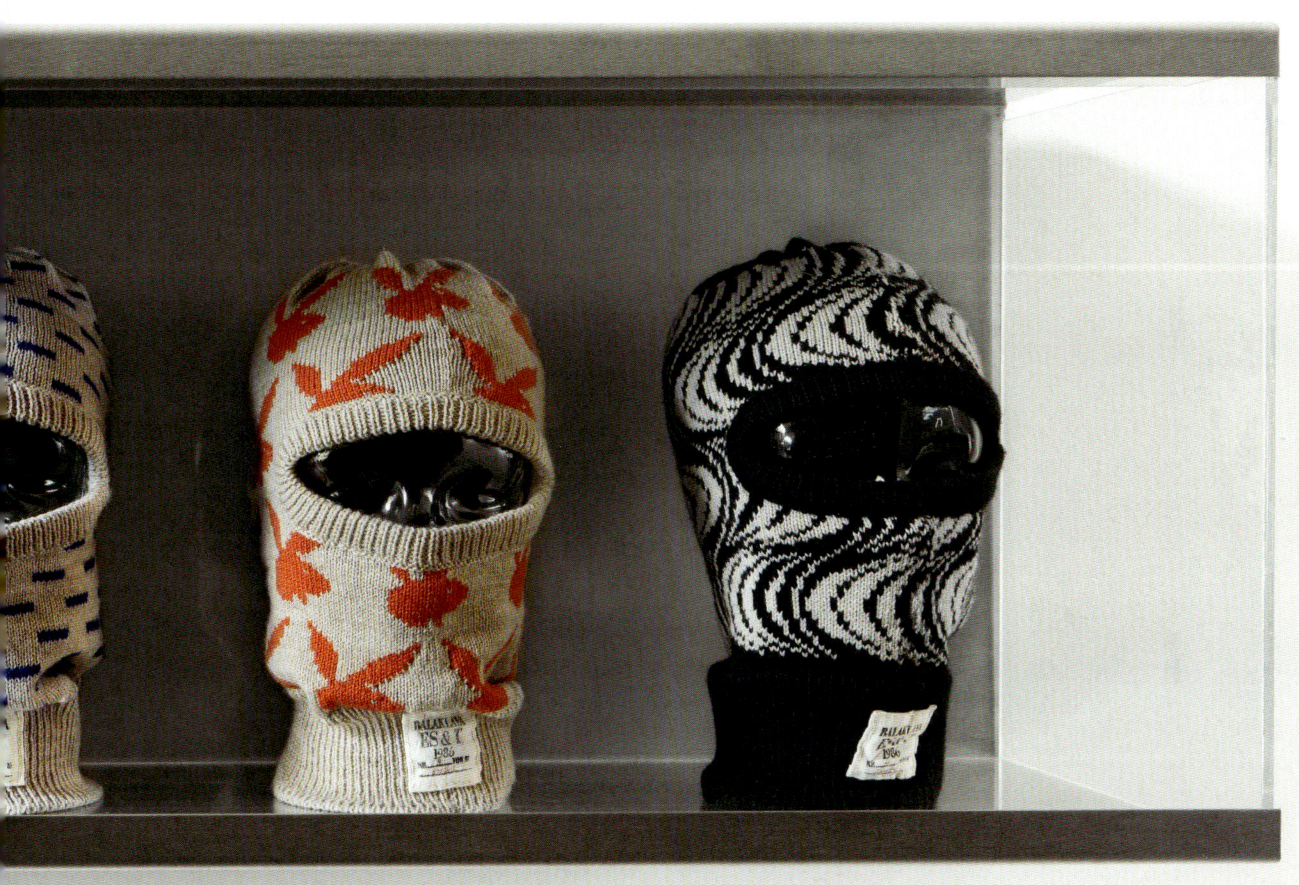
ES & T
1986
1986

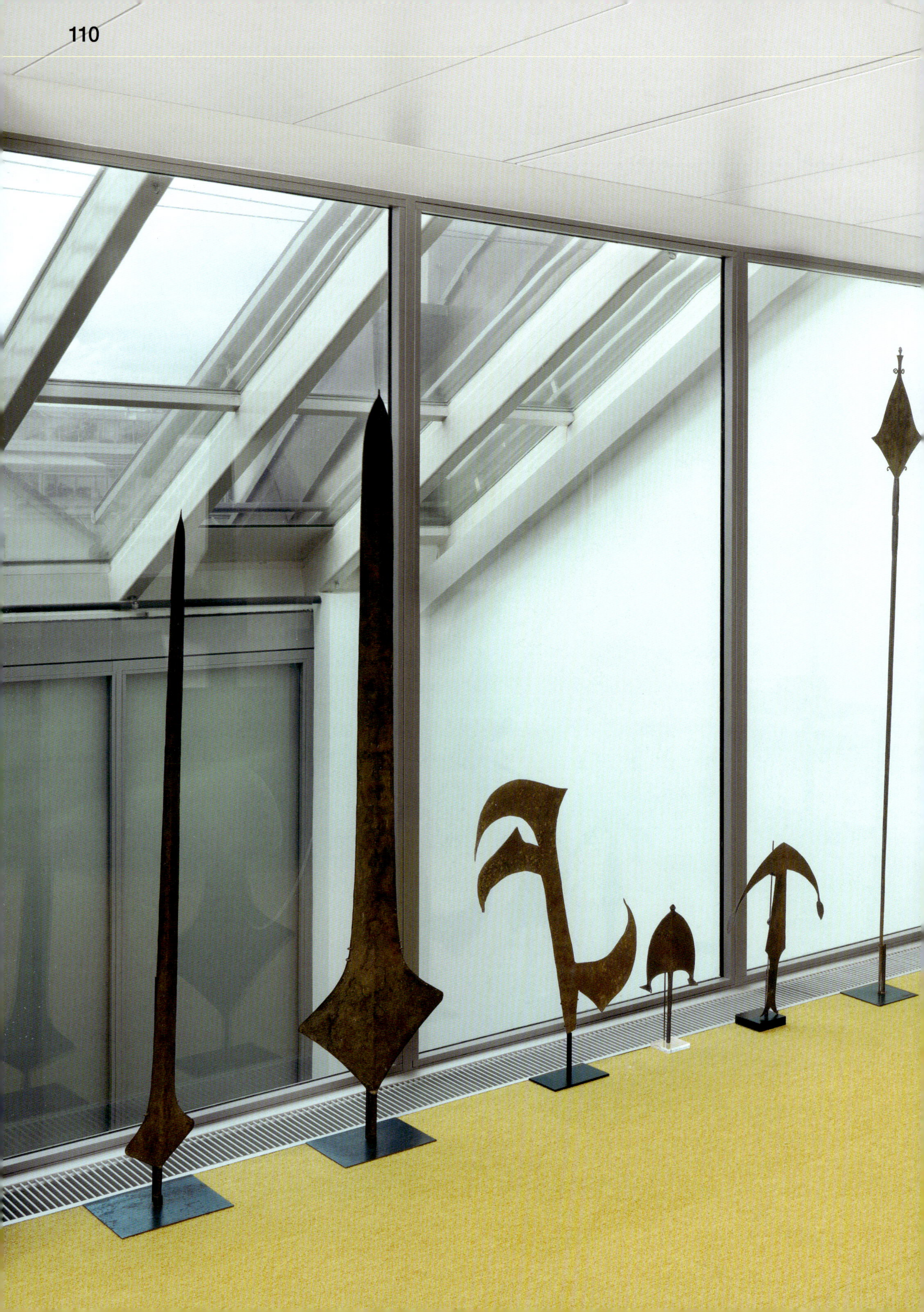

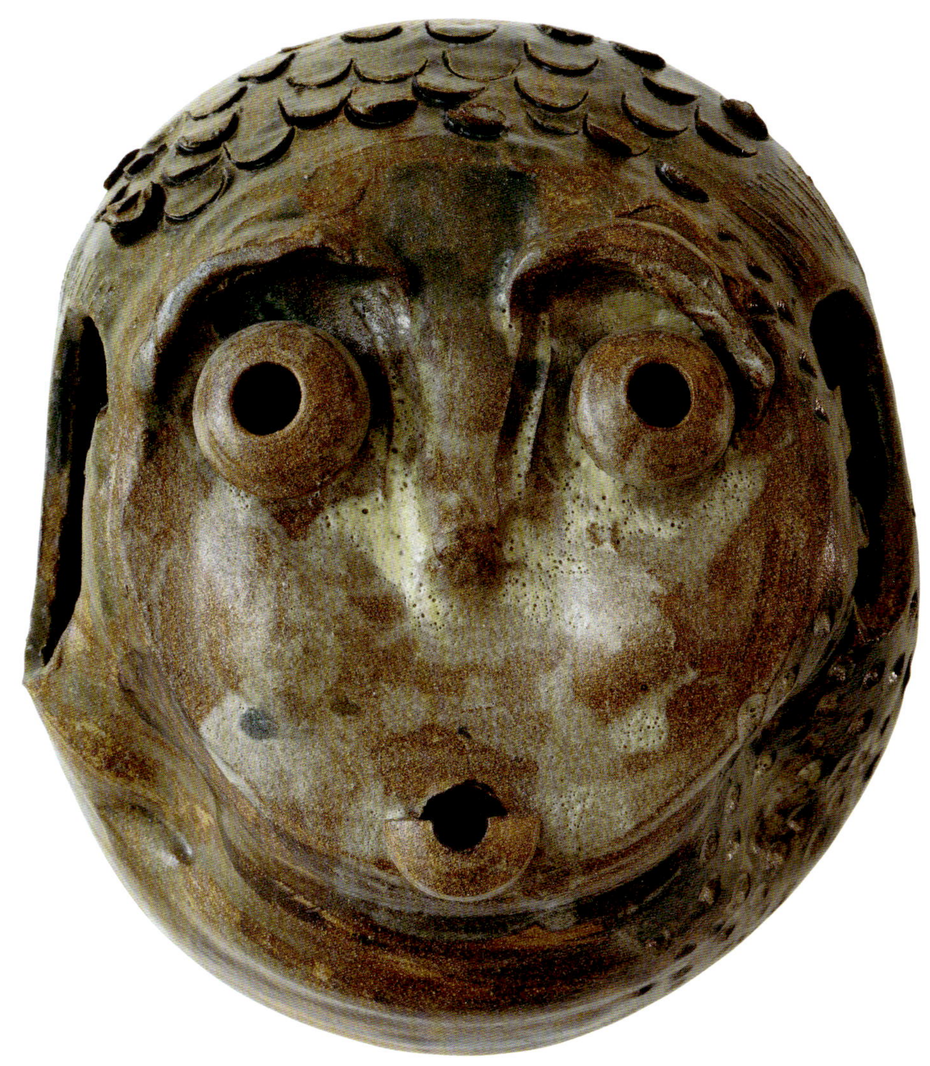

Squid Spider Octopus, 2016
Glazed ceramic
29.2 × 25.4 × 14 cm

risky business, 2014–2015

Crystal mounted on black glass base
20 × 15 × 15 cm

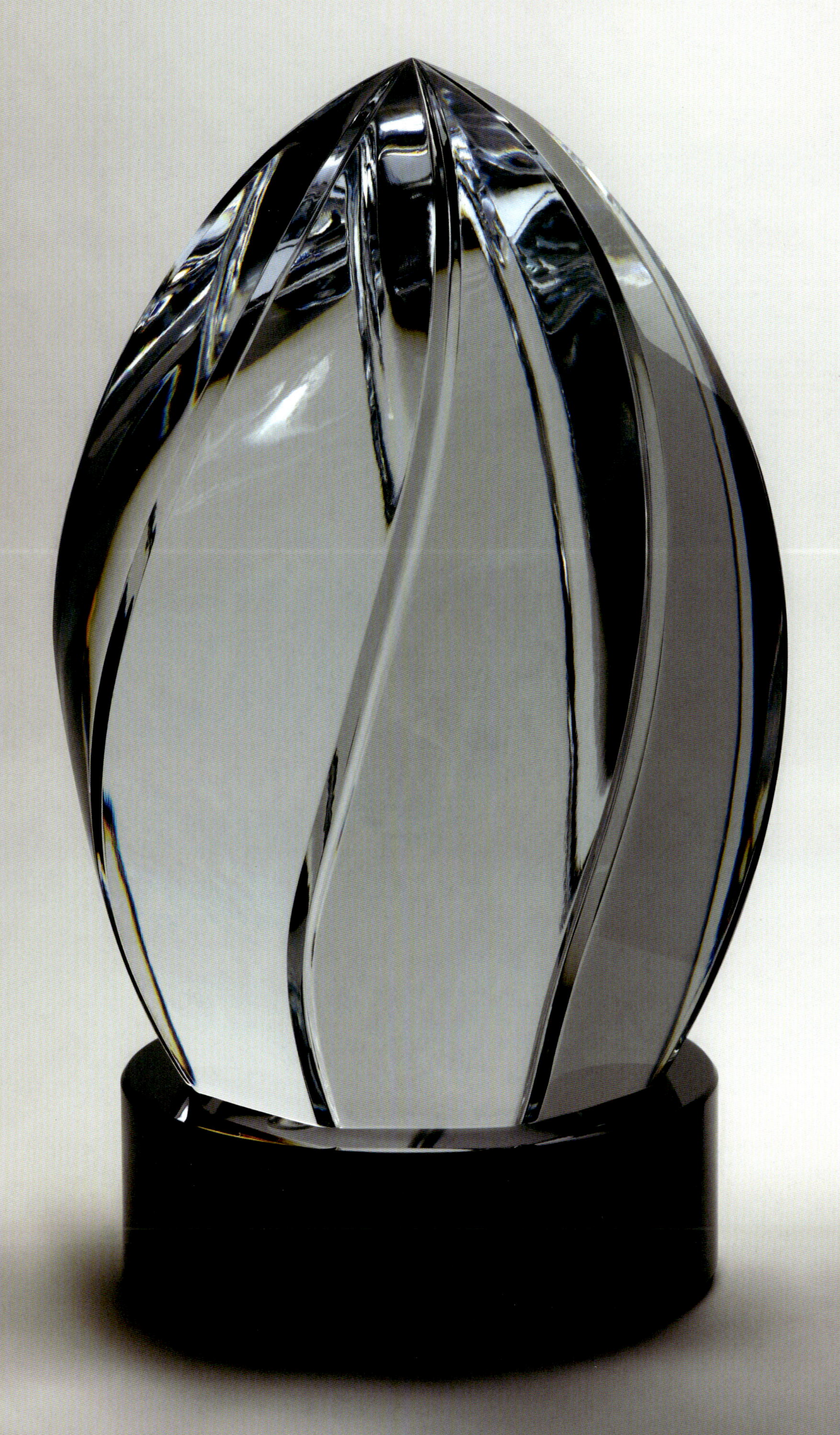

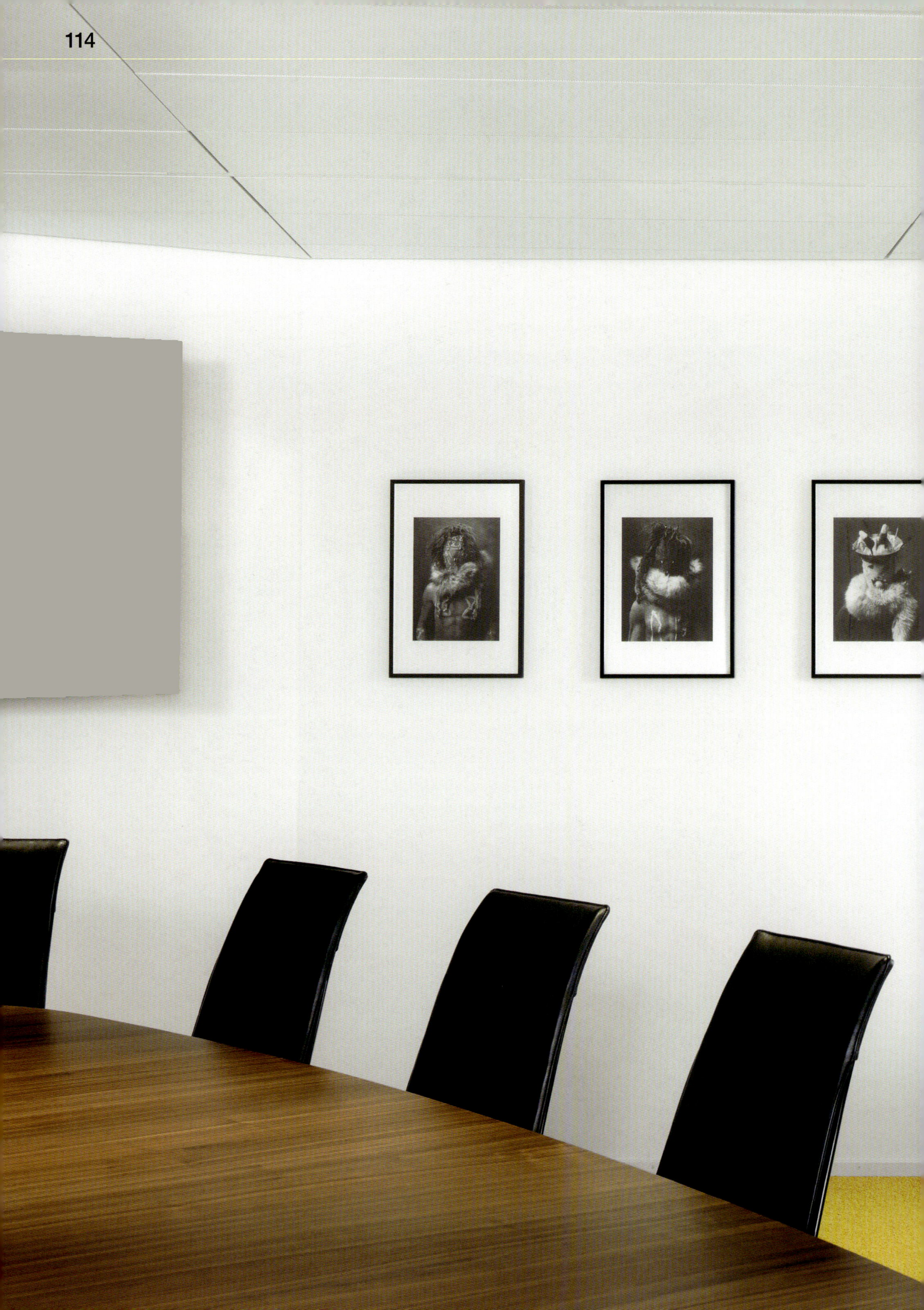

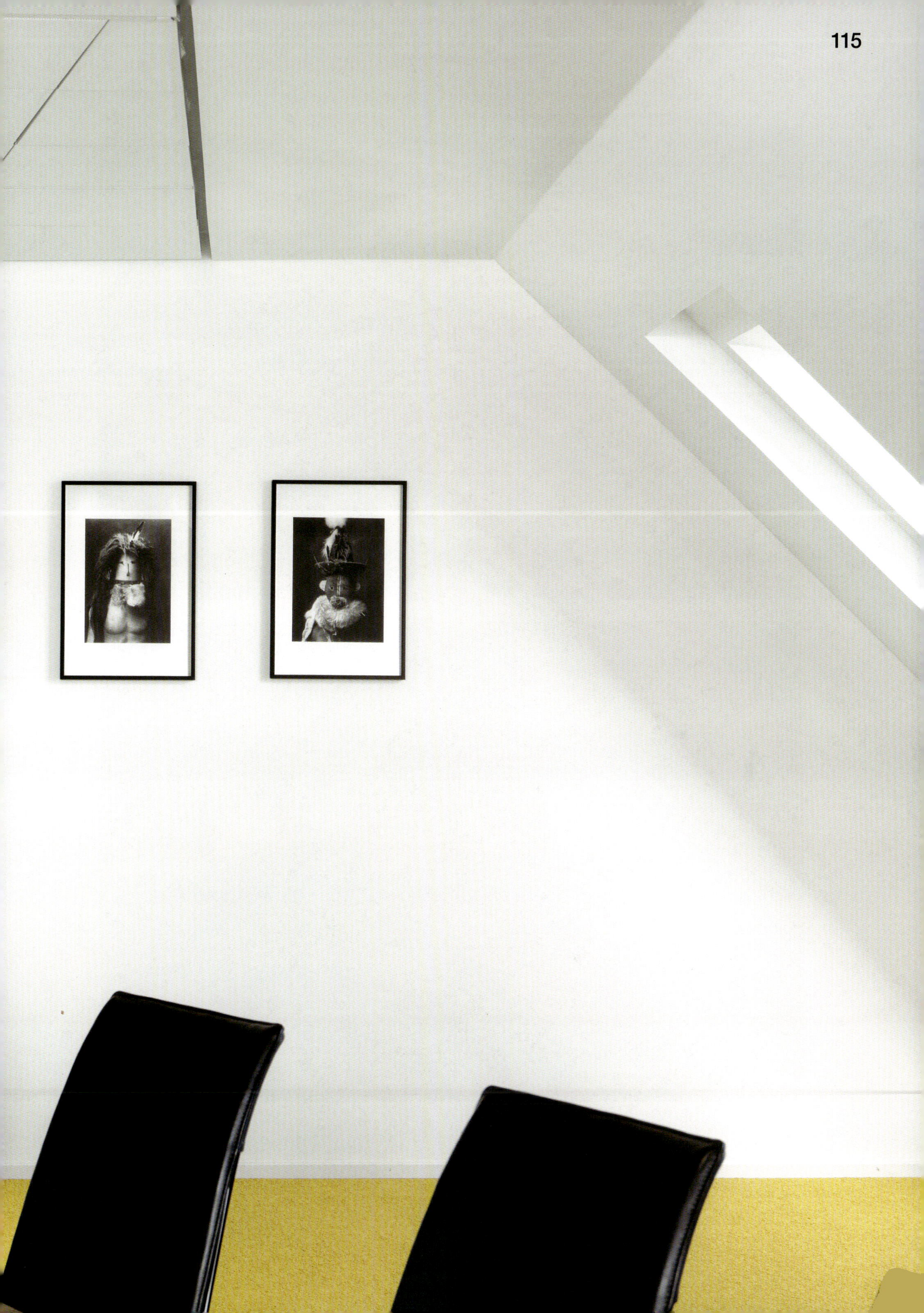

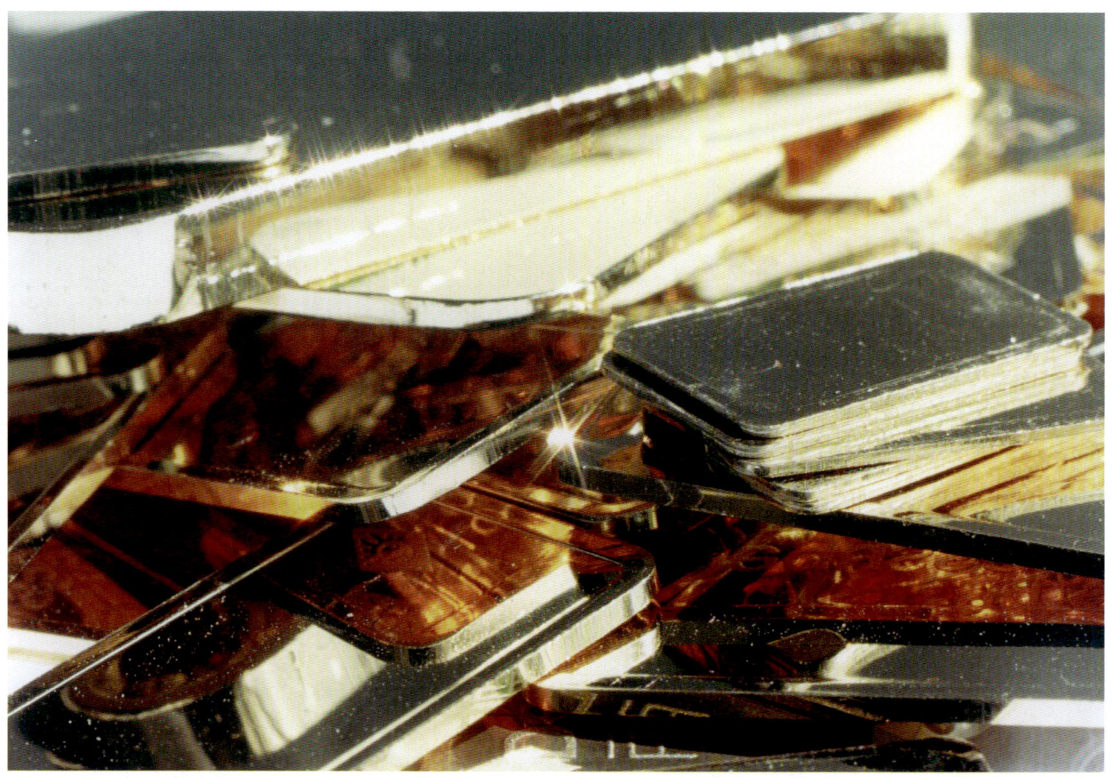

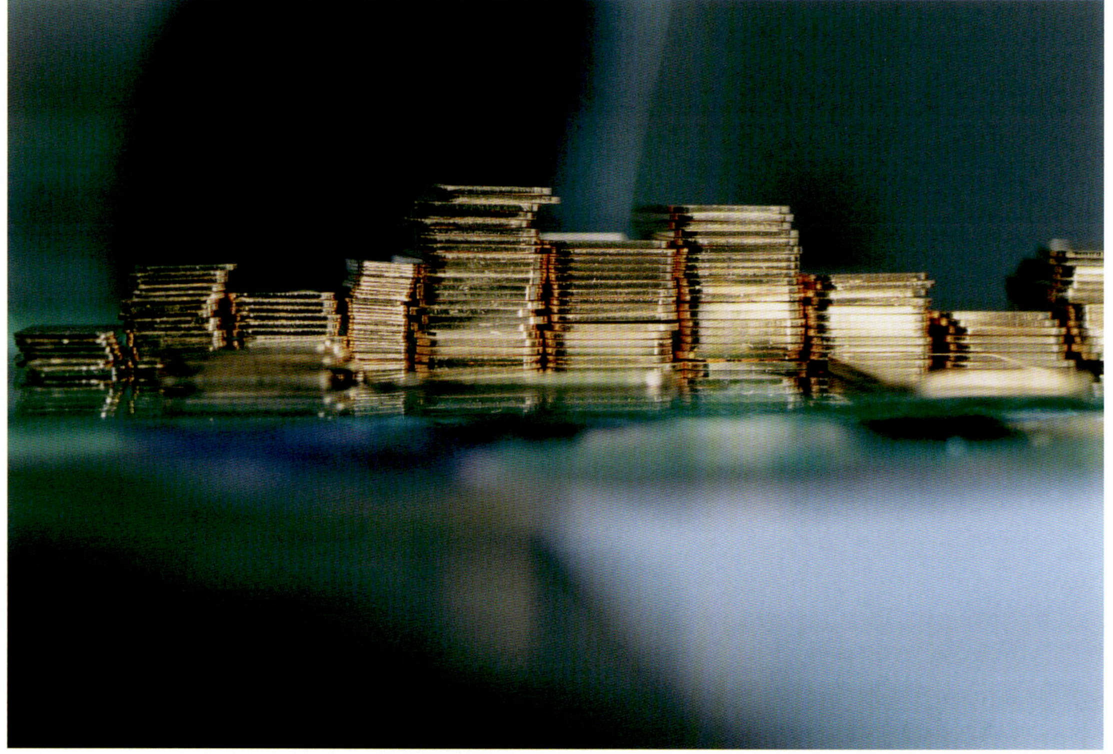

Gold (e), (c), (b), (d), 2002
C-prints
30 × 40 cm each

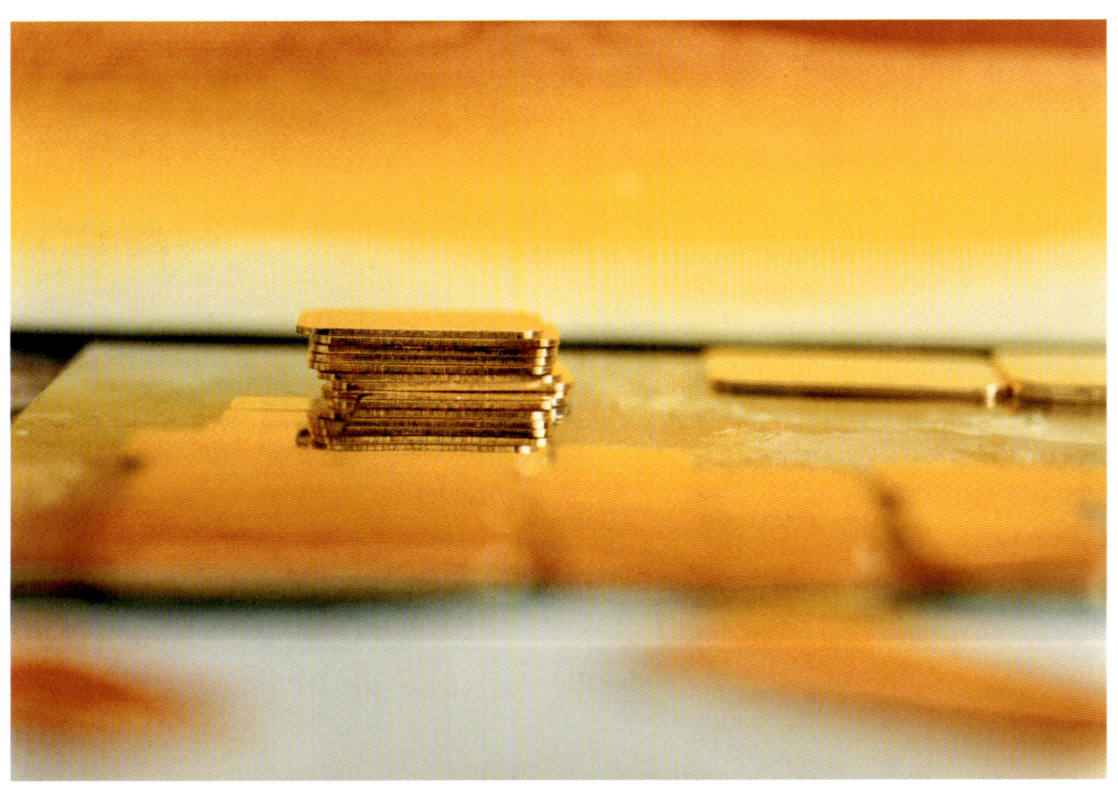

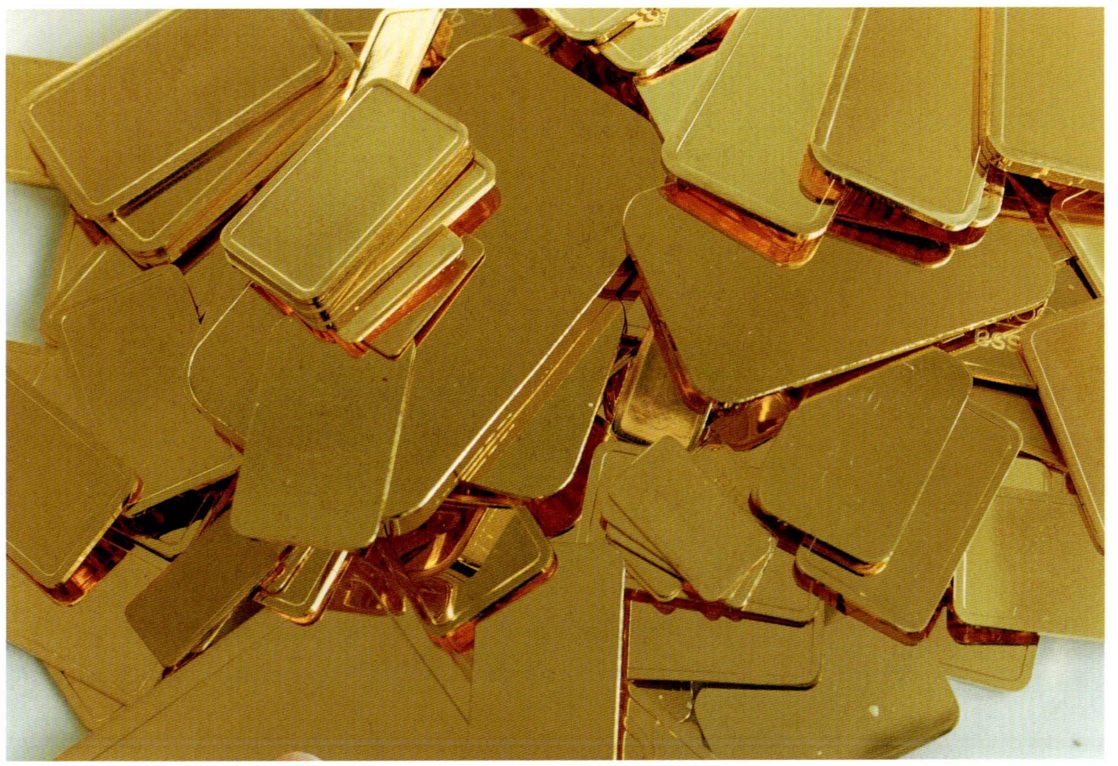

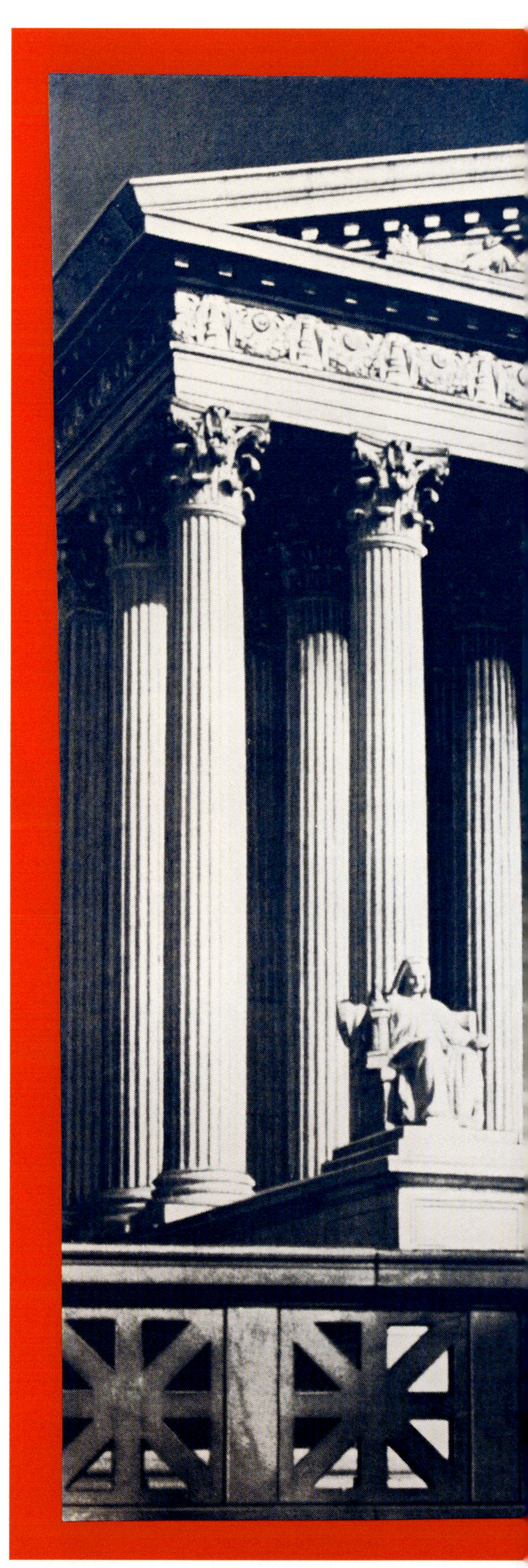

Man’s best friend, 1987
Silkscreen on canvas
242 × 287 cm

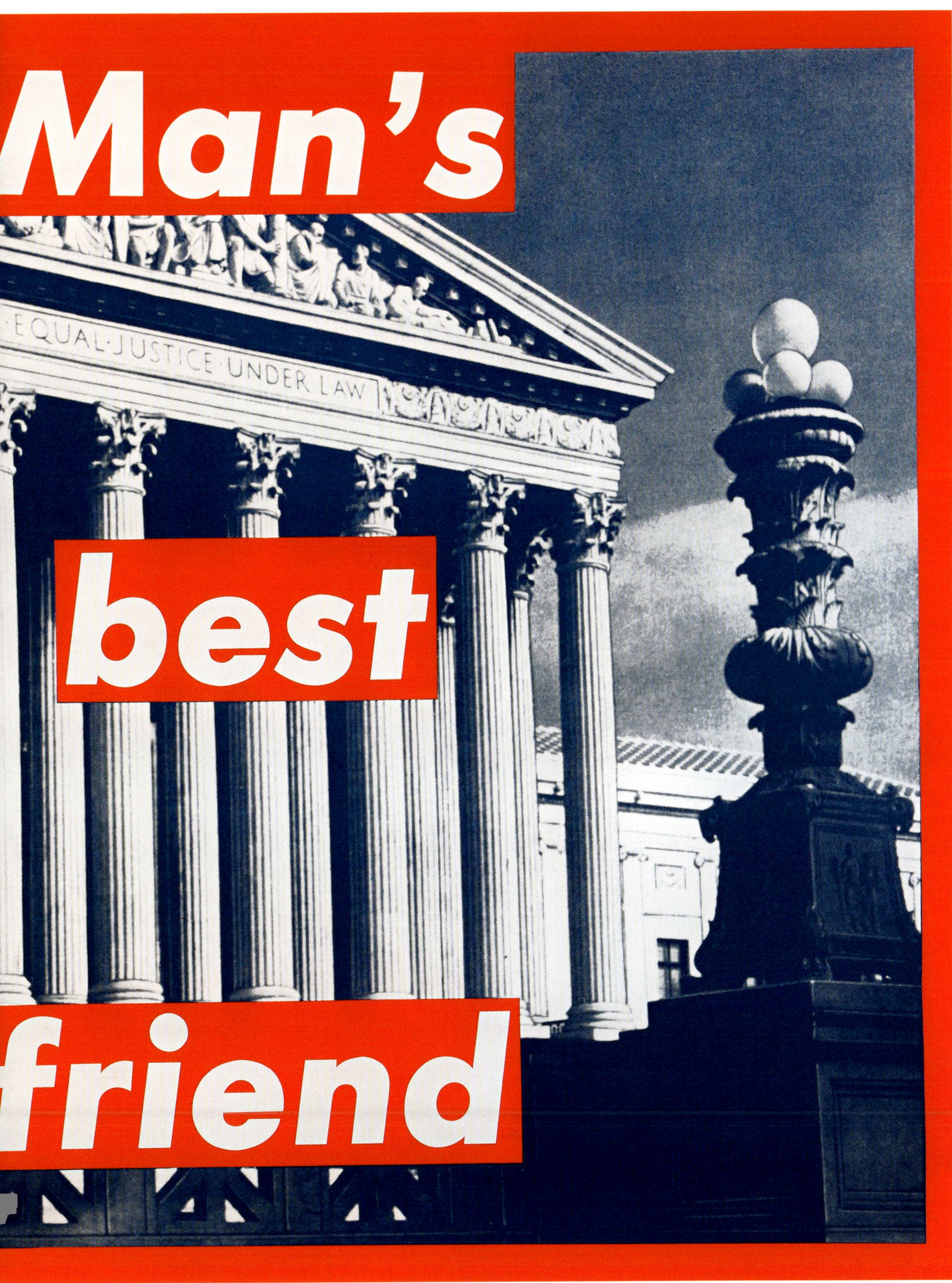
Man's
best
friend
EQUAL JUSTICE UNDER LAW

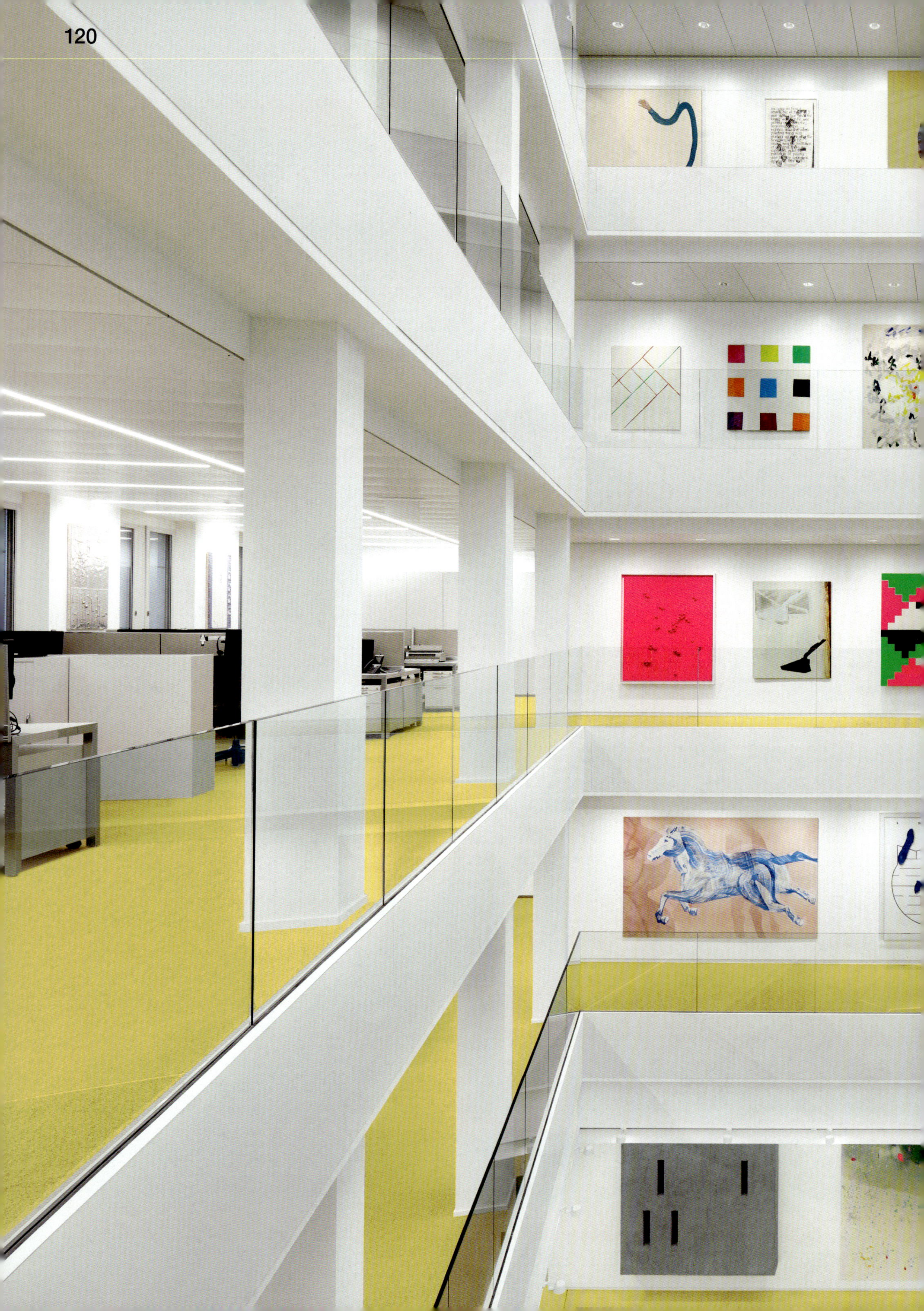

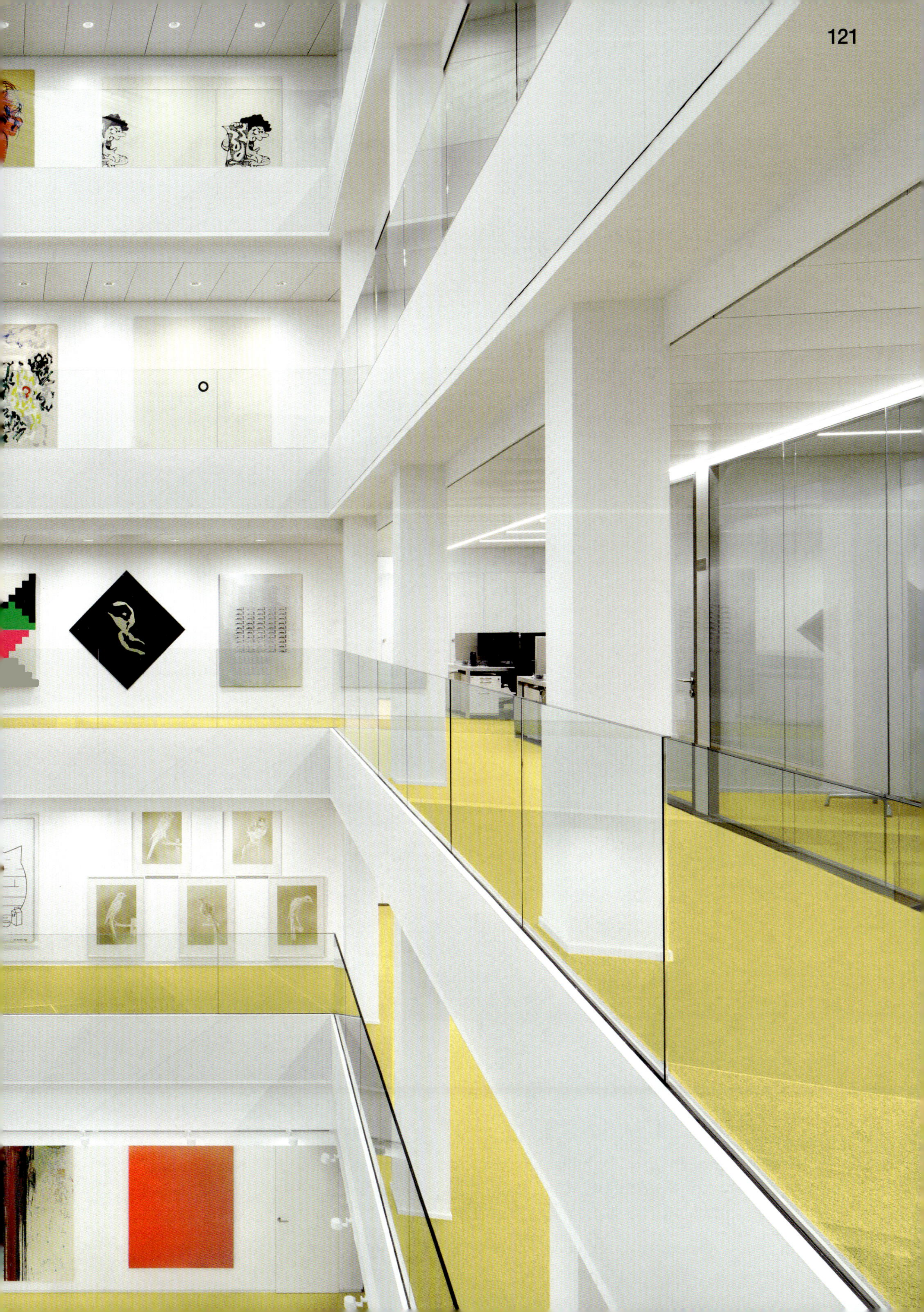

Partis 1 (répétition, recyclage,
fonds de commerce), 2016
Poster, paper, spices, acrylic, isorel
176 × 120 cm

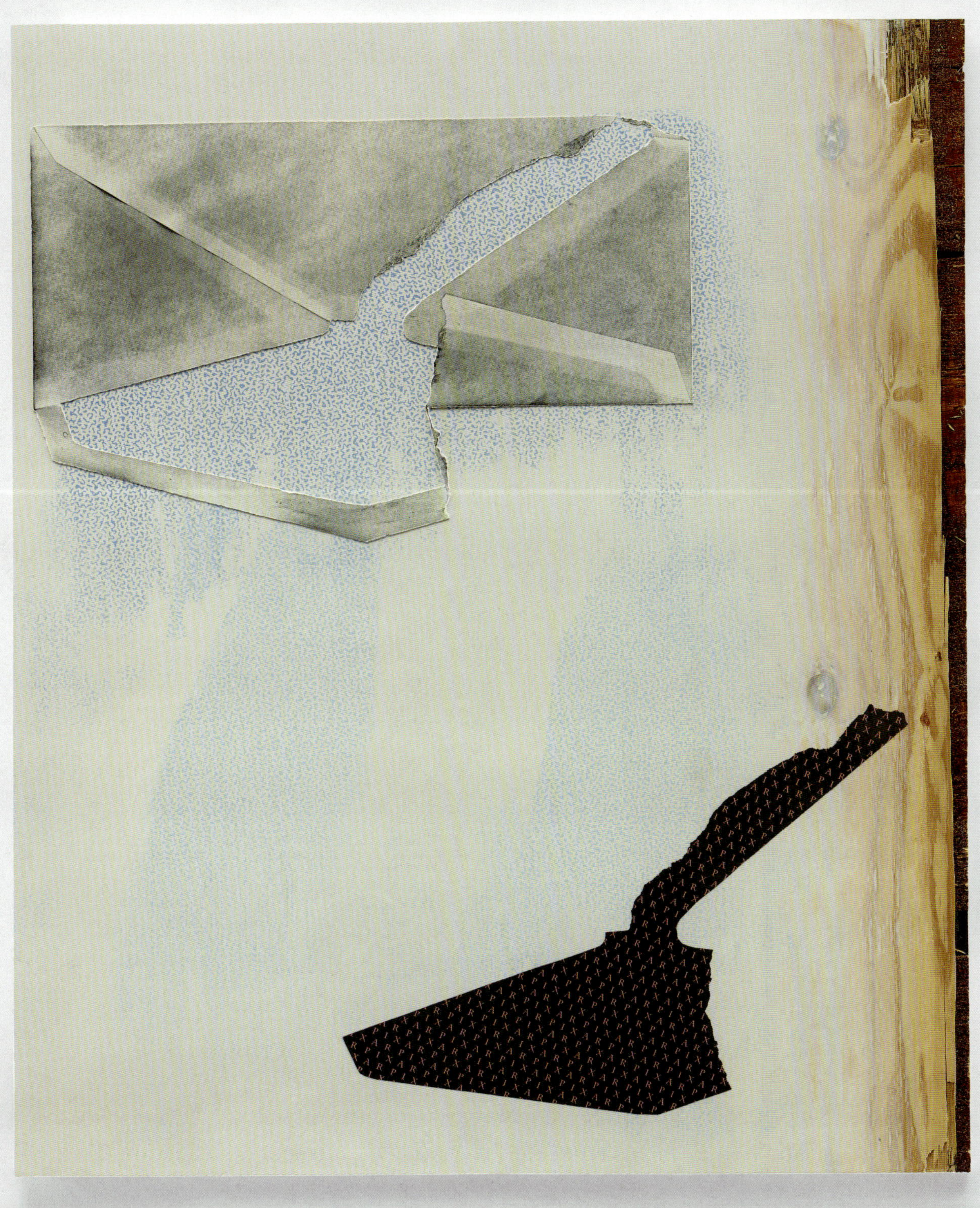

Medium, 2014
Screenprint, acrylic, pigmented
acrylic polymer, and gesso on plywood
138.4 × 114.9 × 1.3 cm

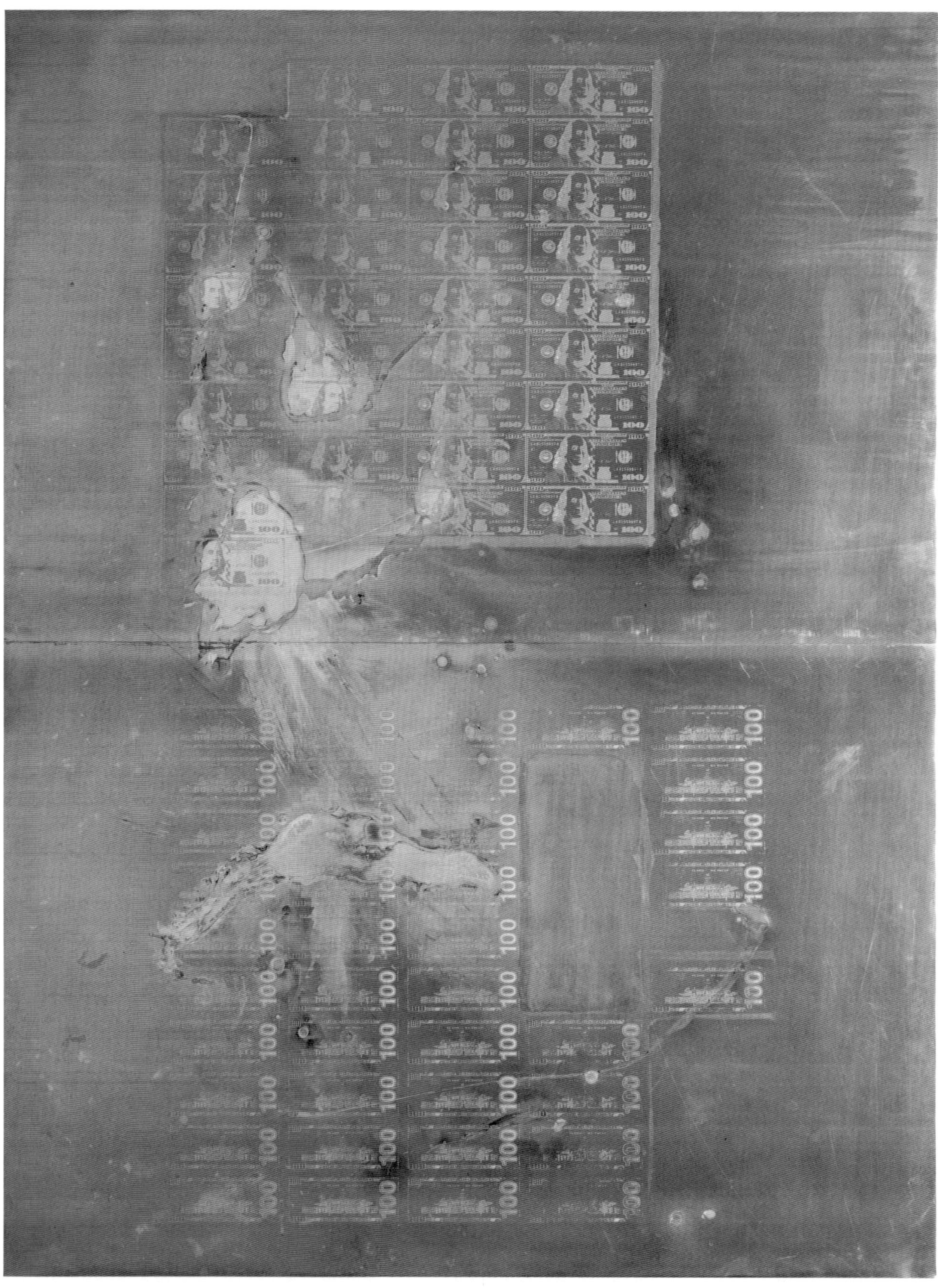

Culture XL, 2017
Silkscreen on copper sheet
160 × 120 cm

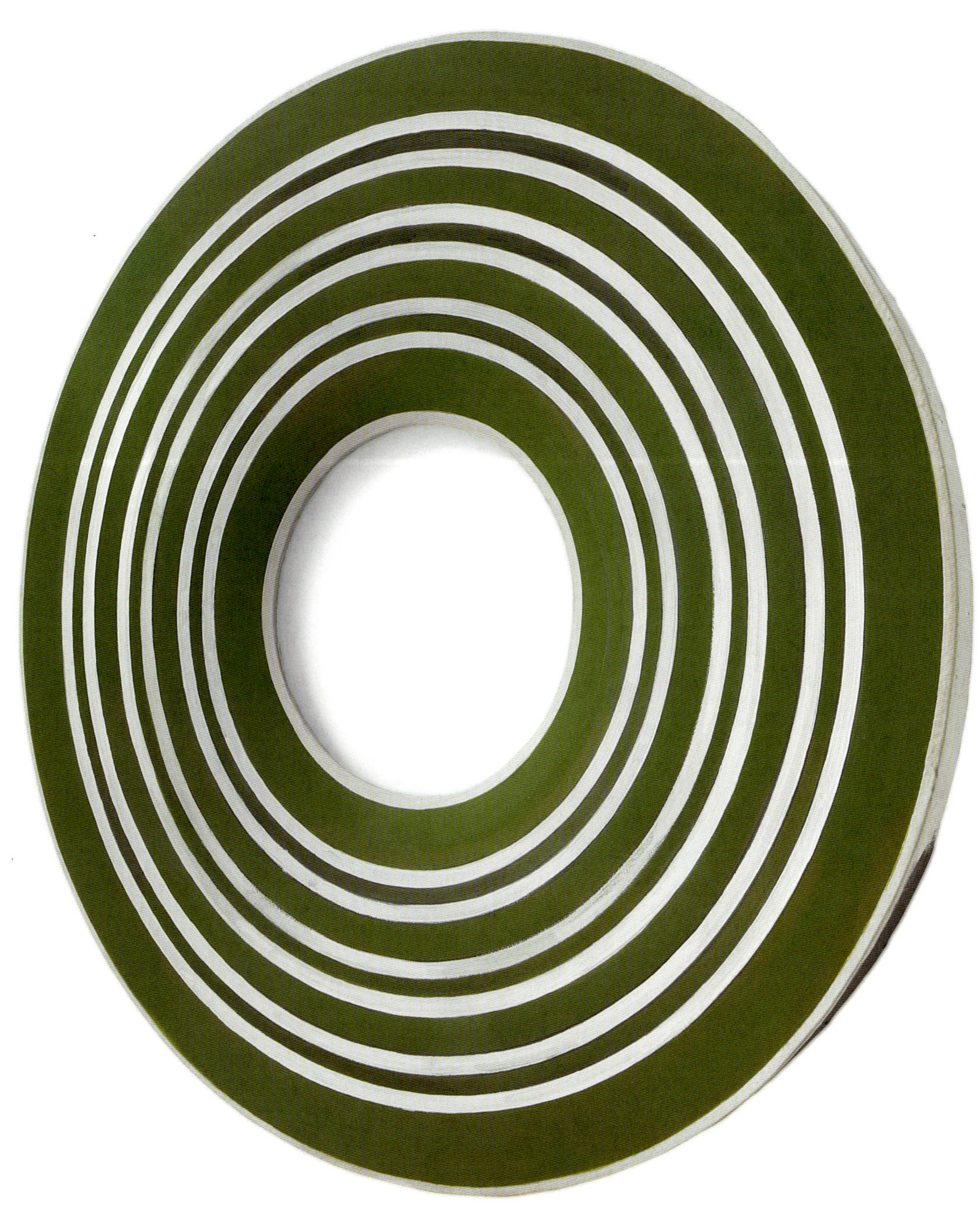

American Sluts (Super Saver), 2010
Acrylic on canvas on wood
153.7 × 14 cm

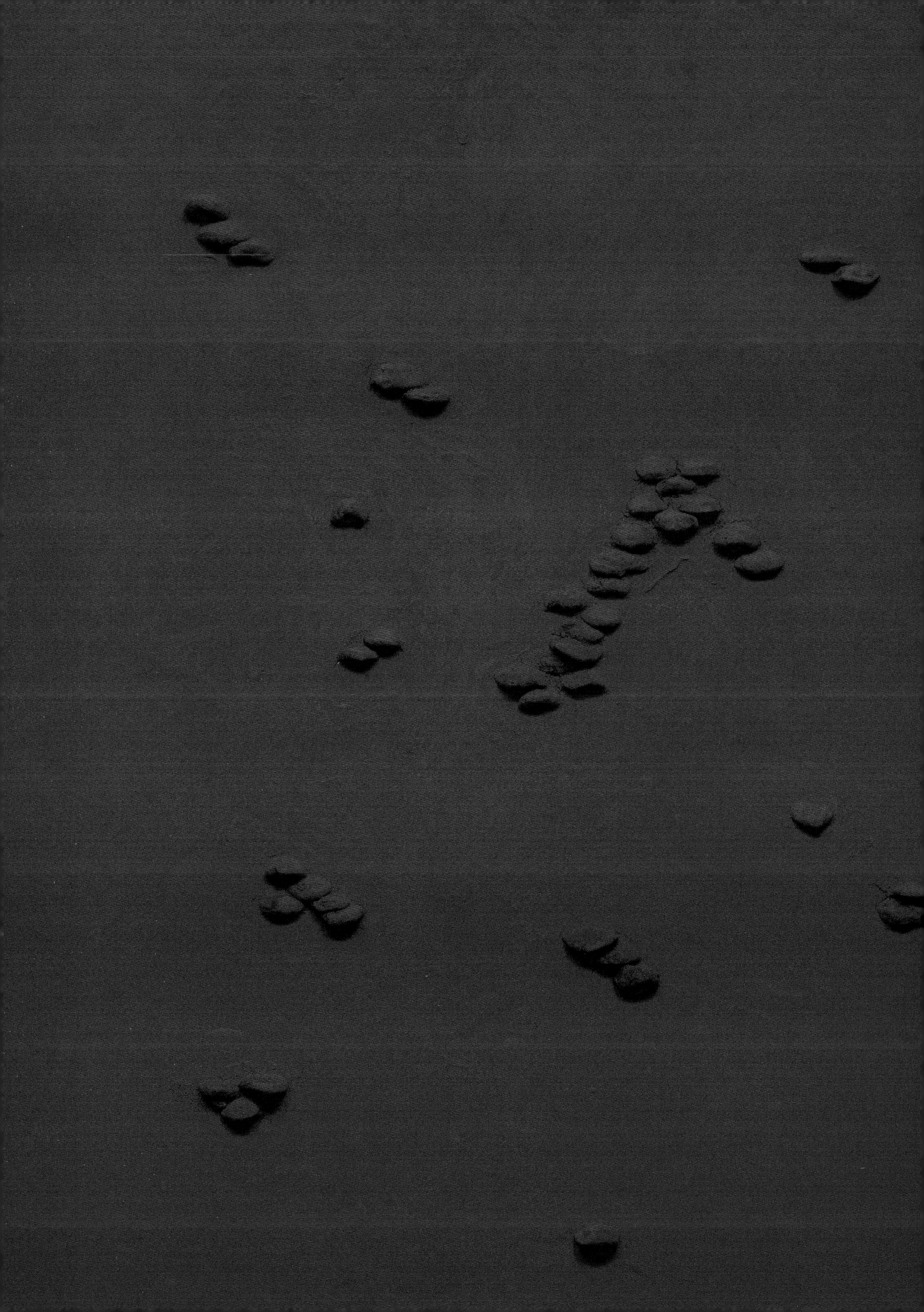

this is the night when christ broke the prison-bars of death and rose victorious from the underworld, 2017

Acrylic, pigment, mushrooms on canvas
150 × 130 cm

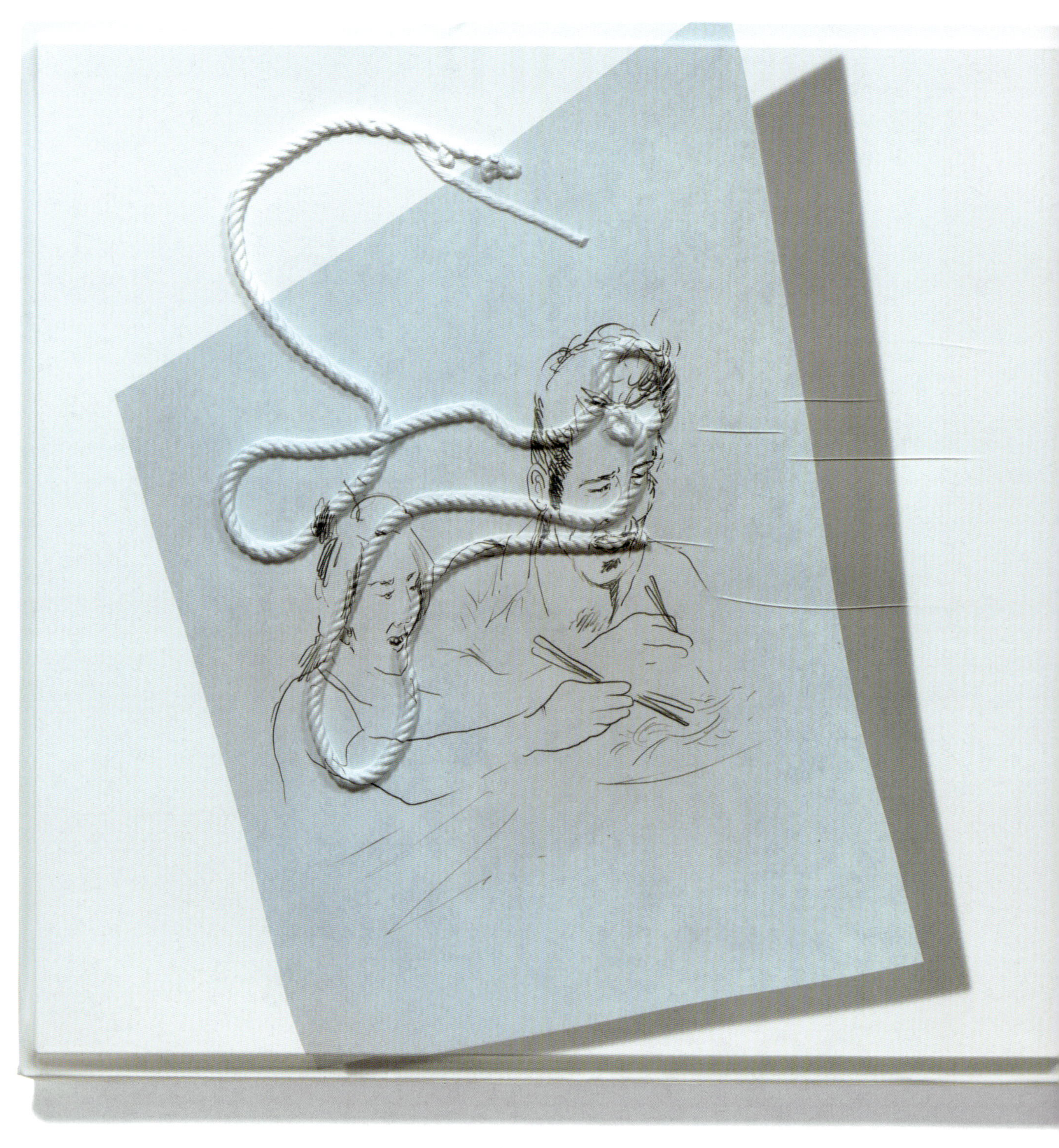

Chopsticks, 2011
UV-cured inkjet on polystyrene
vacuum-formed over knotted rope
115 × 236.5 cm

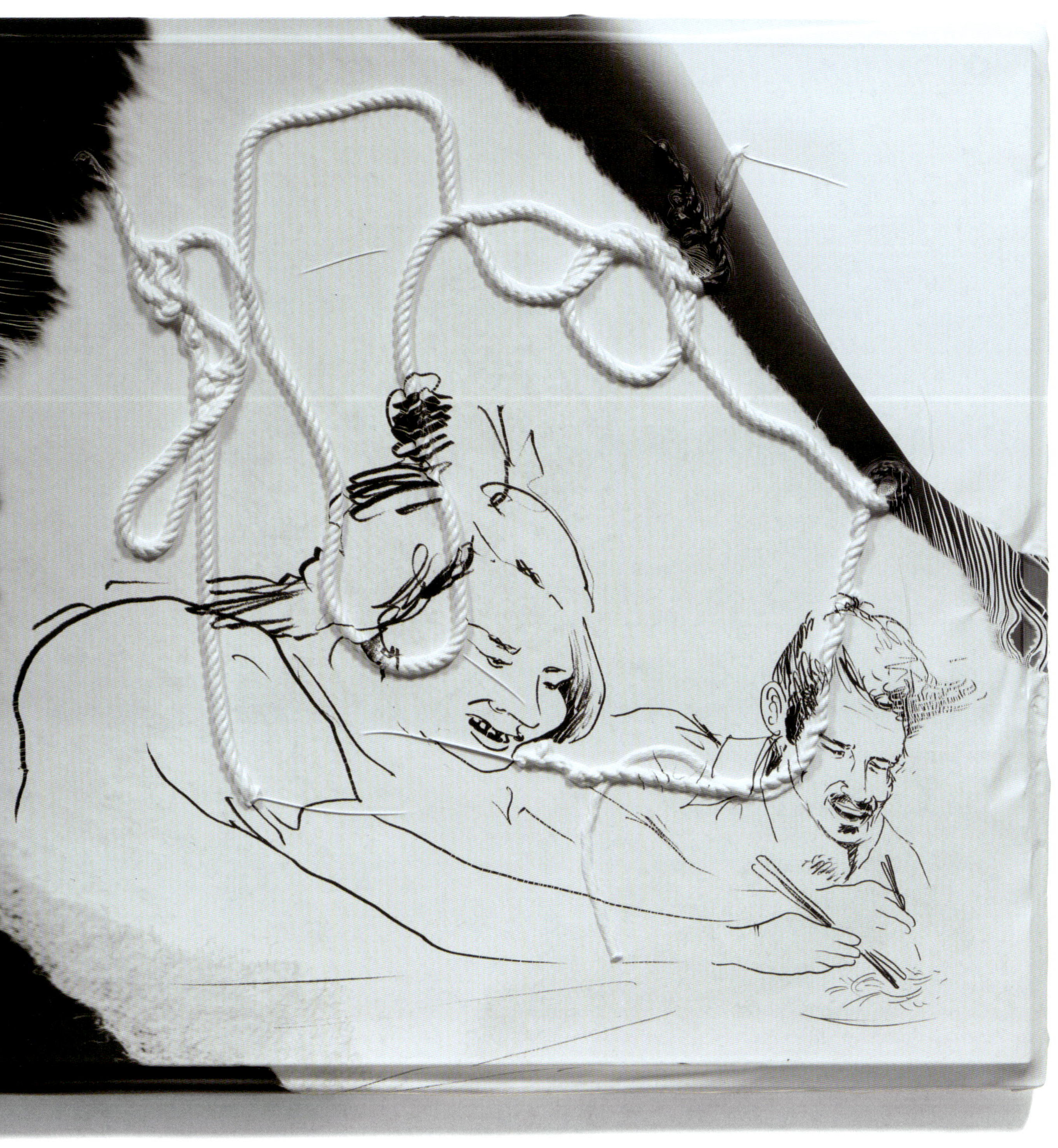

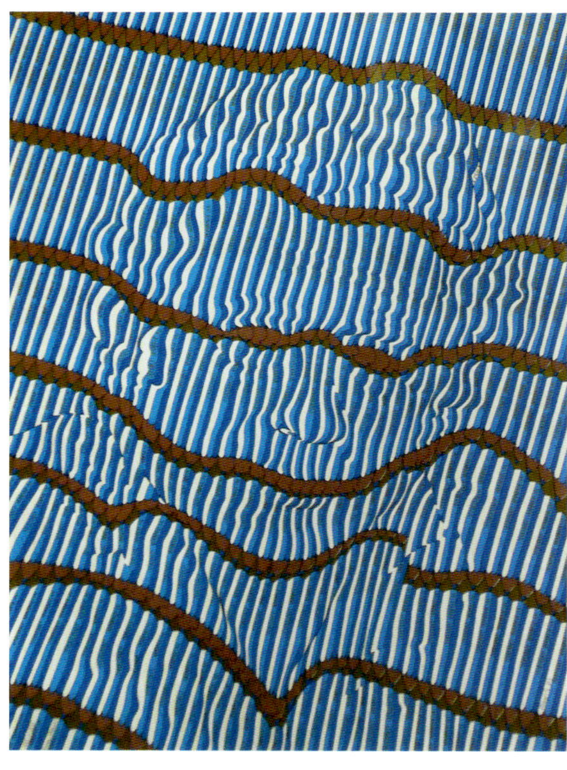

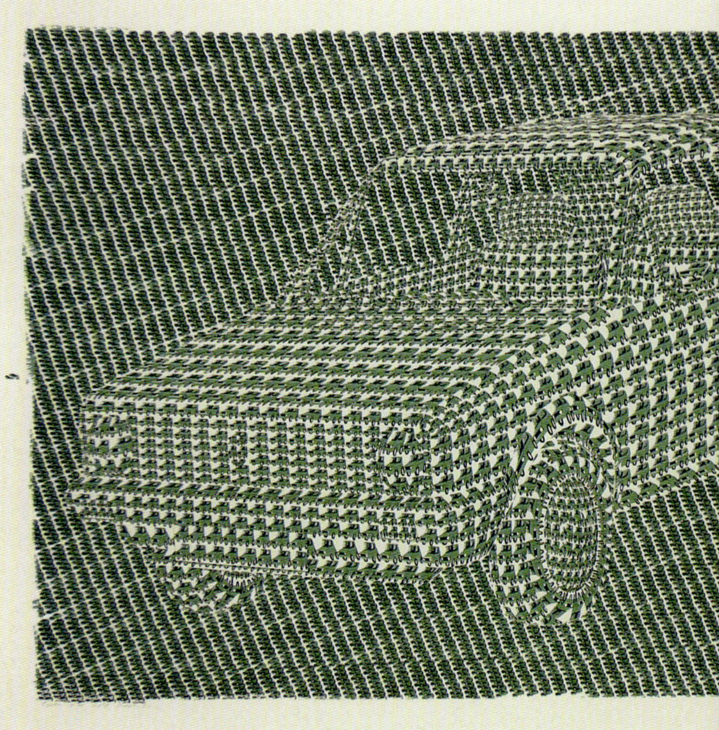

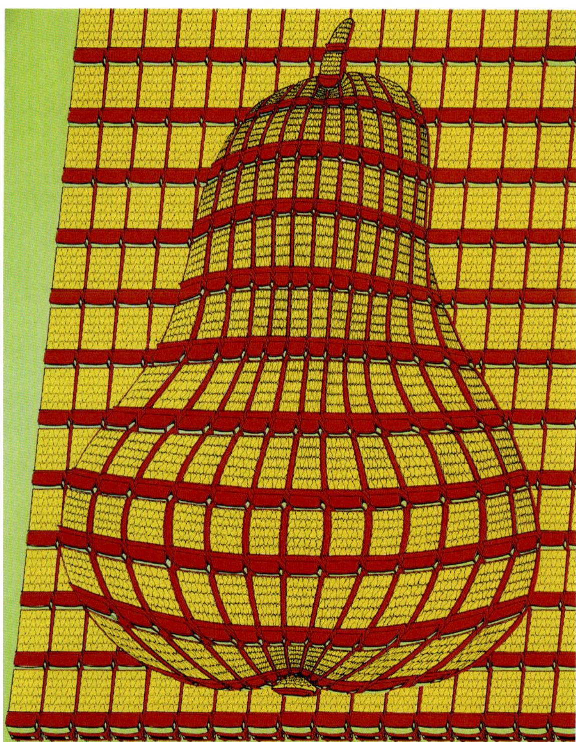

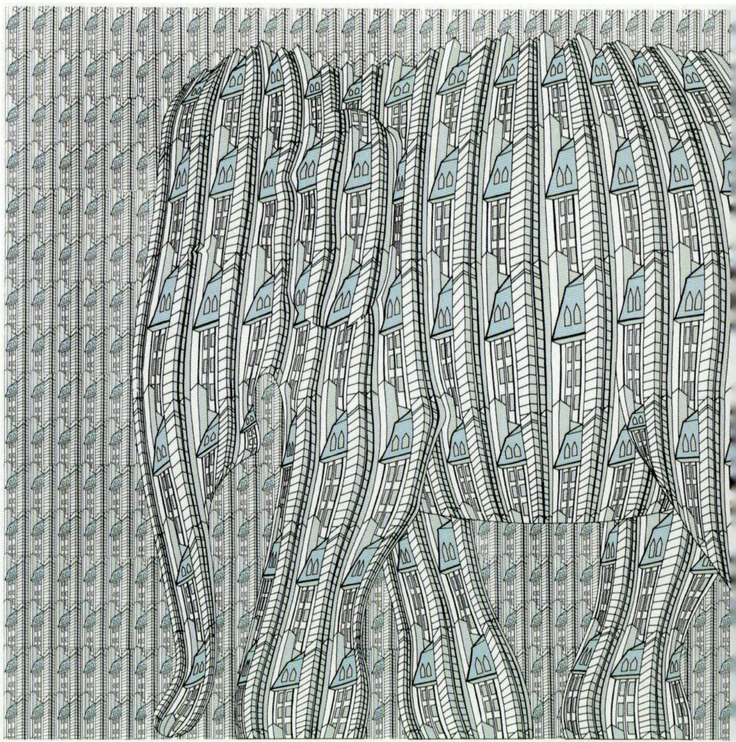

Norman Mailer (blaue Version), 1971
Silkscreen on cardboard
70 × 53.5 cm

Distribution (Birne/rote Version), 1971
Silkscreen on cardboard
77.5 × 61 cm

Golf (grüne Version), 1980
Silkscreen on cardboard
66.4 × 90.5 cm

Elefant (graue Version), 1972
Silkscreen on cardboard
50 × 70 cm

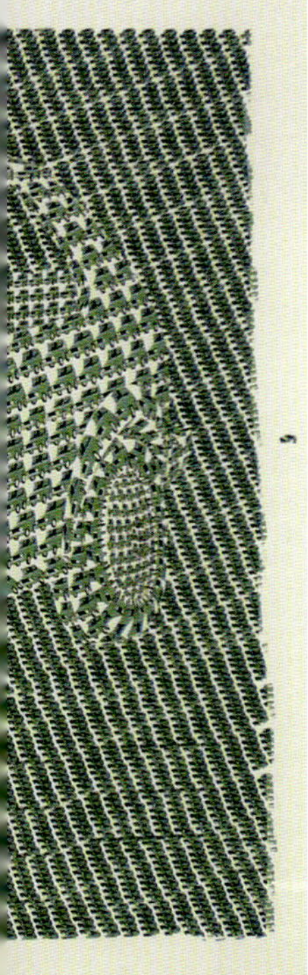

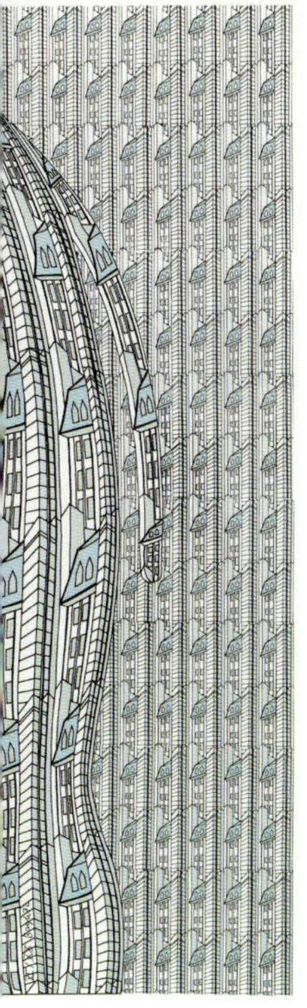

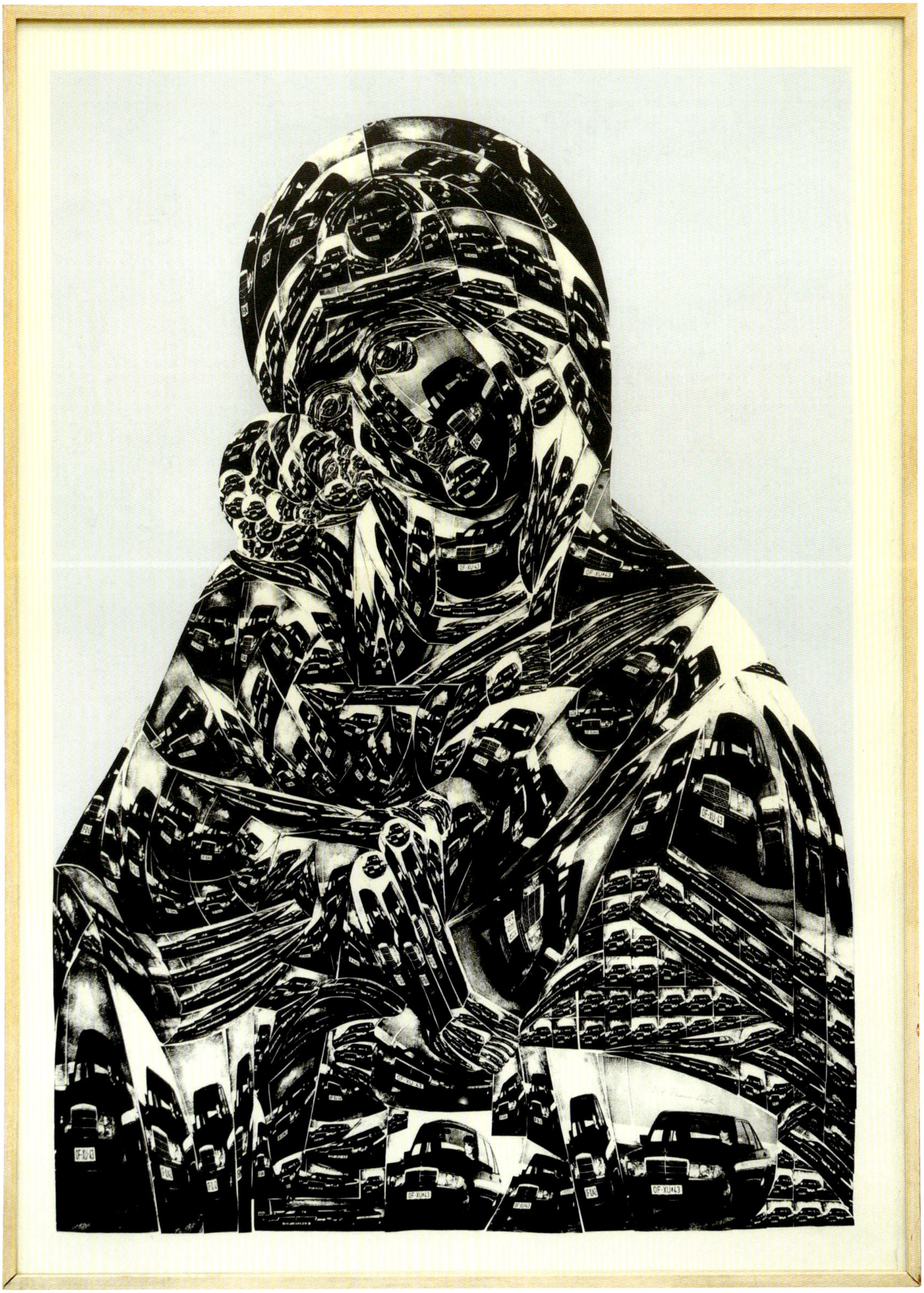

Madonna Mercedes, 1989
Silkscreen
165 × 123 cm

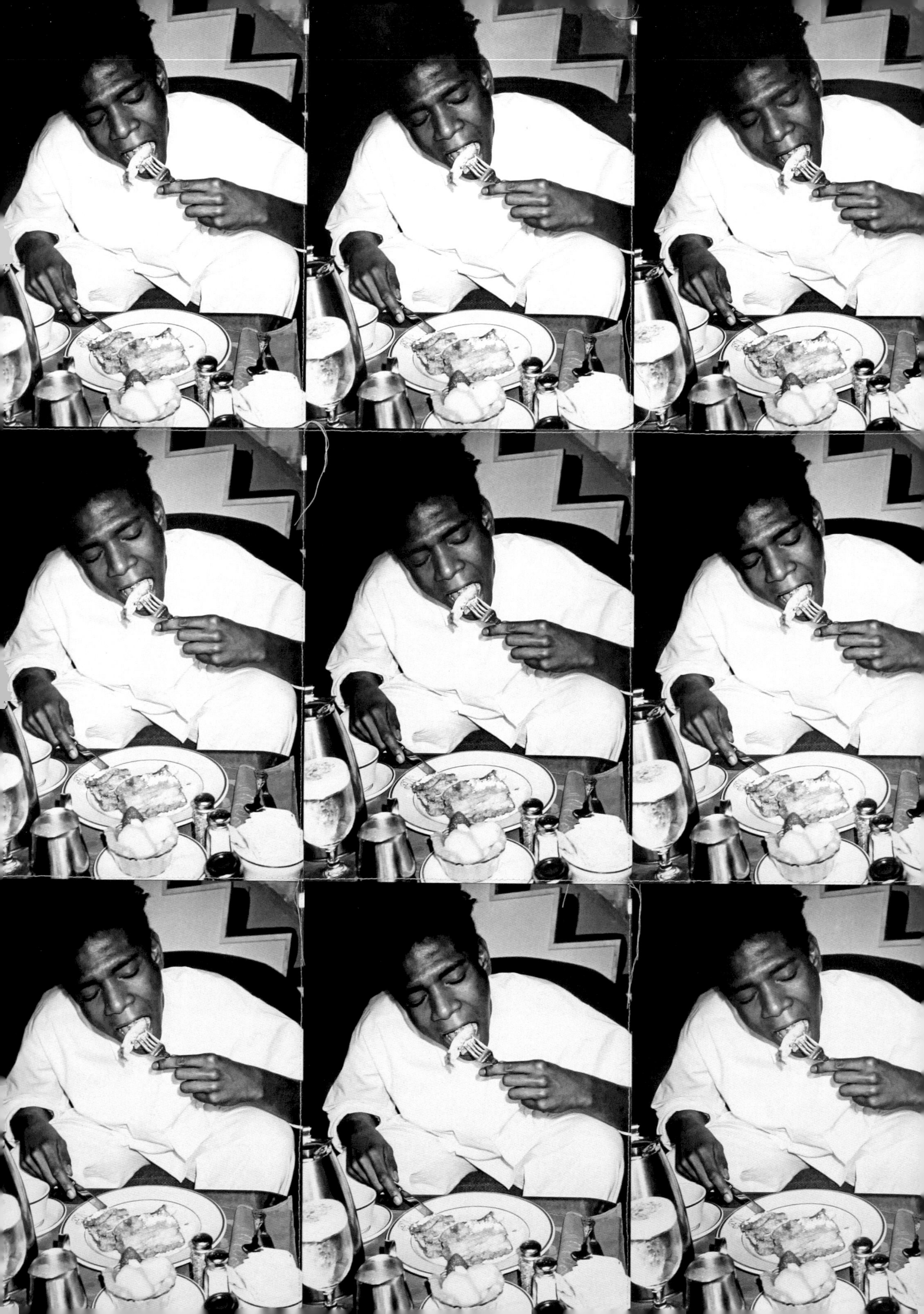

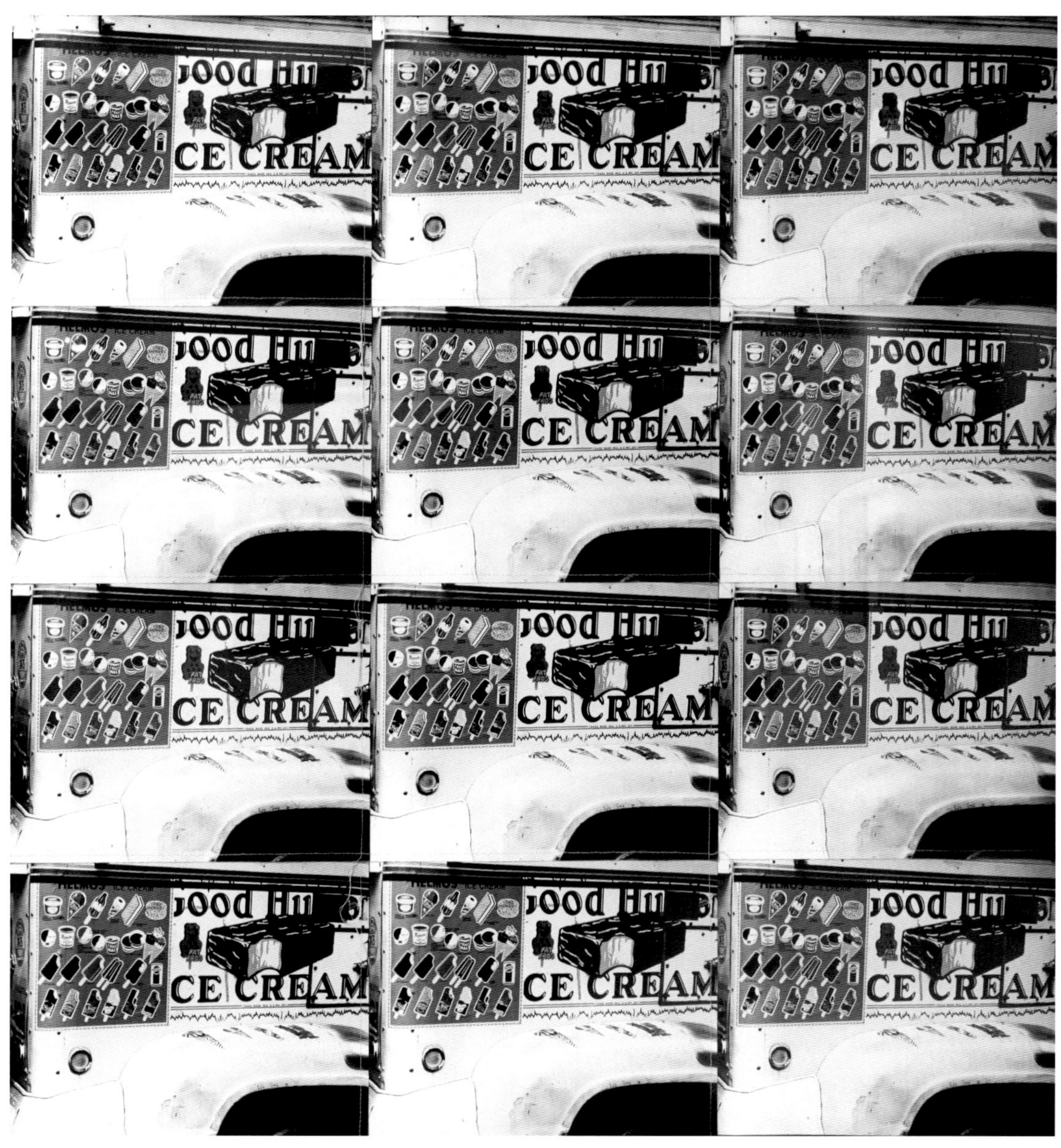

Jean-Michel Basquiat
Eating, 1976–1987
Gelatin silver prints
stitched with thread
103.4 × 80 cm

Good Humor
Ice Cream, 1976–1986
Gelatin silver prints
stitched with thread
111.8 × 106.7 cm

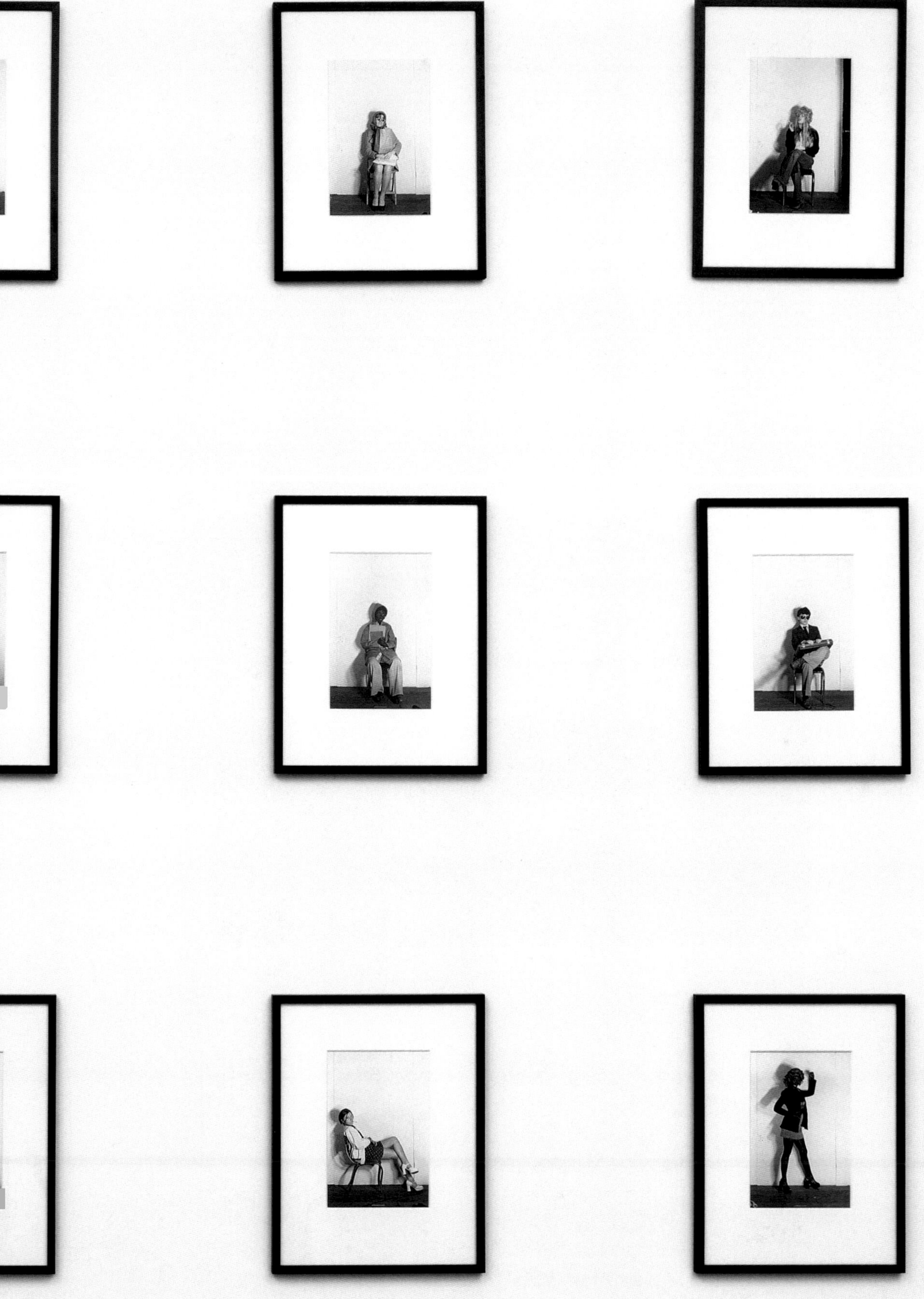

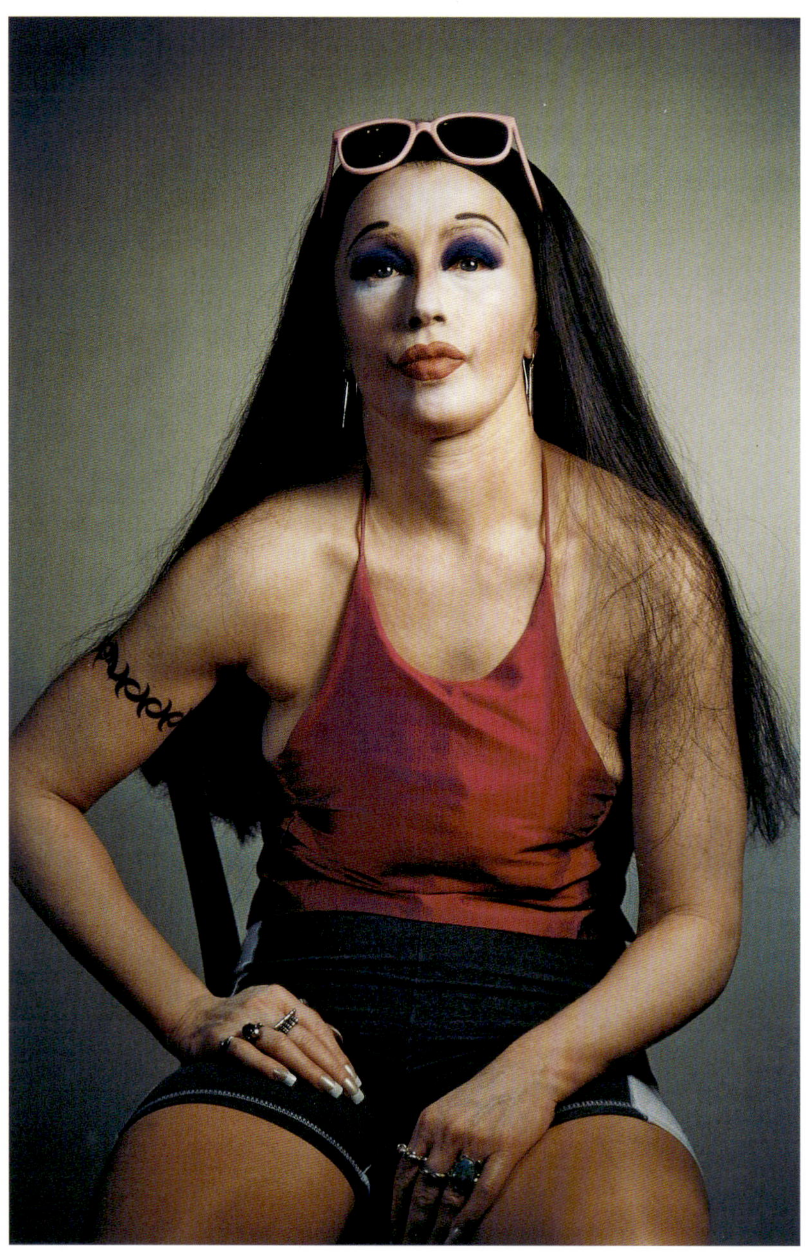

Untitled #355, 2000
Photograph
91.4 × 61 cm

Untitled #564, 2016
Dye sublimation metal print
171.6 × 114.3 cm

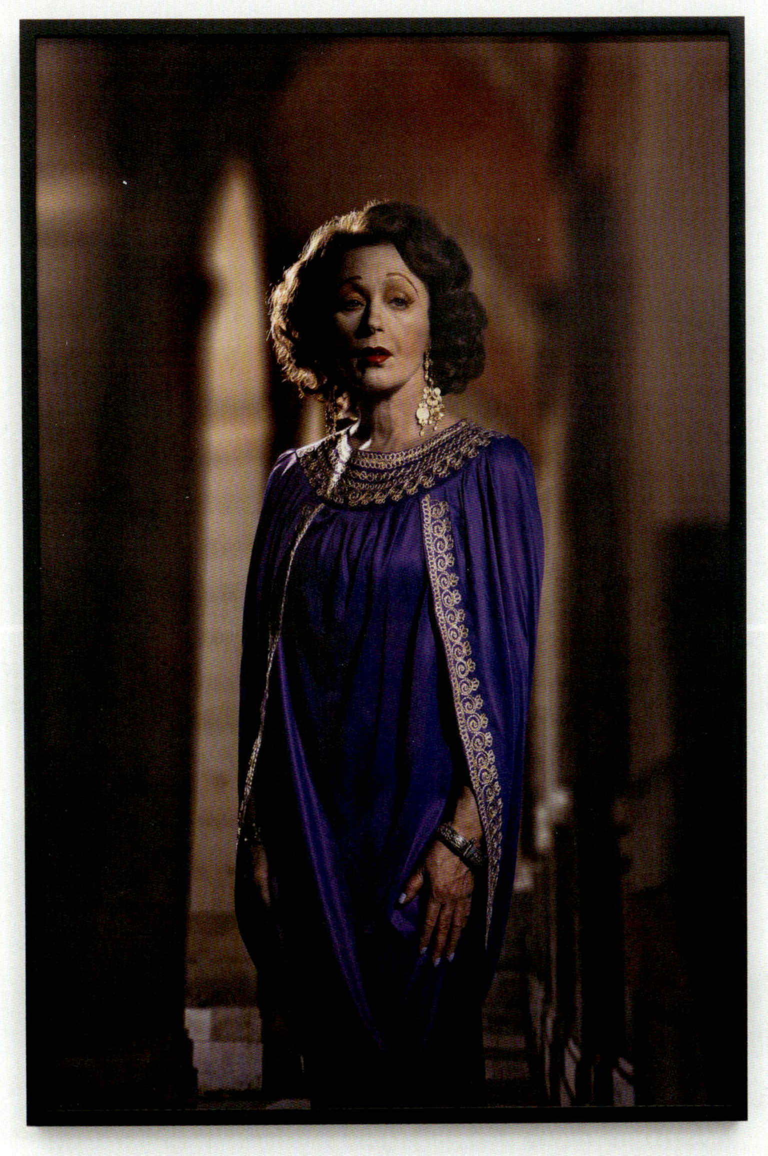

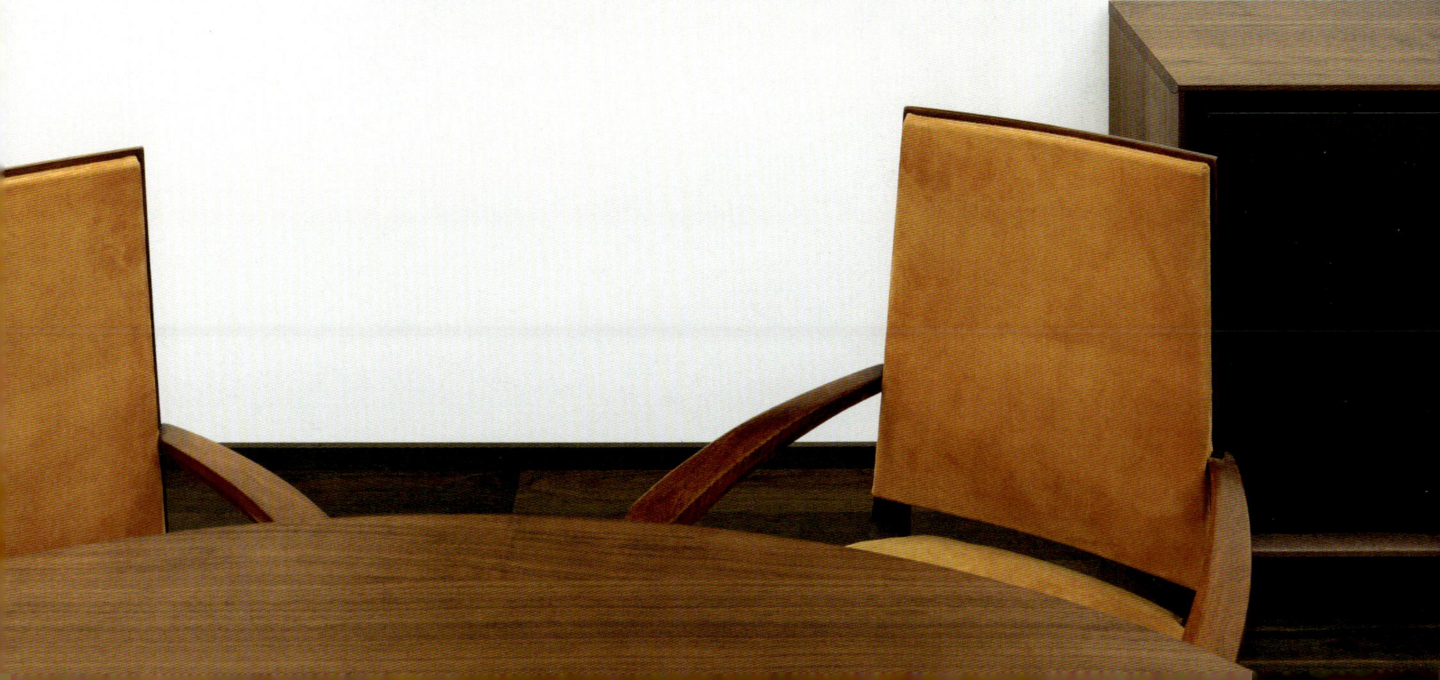

anders pulling a splinter from his foot, 2004

C-print
40 × 30 cm

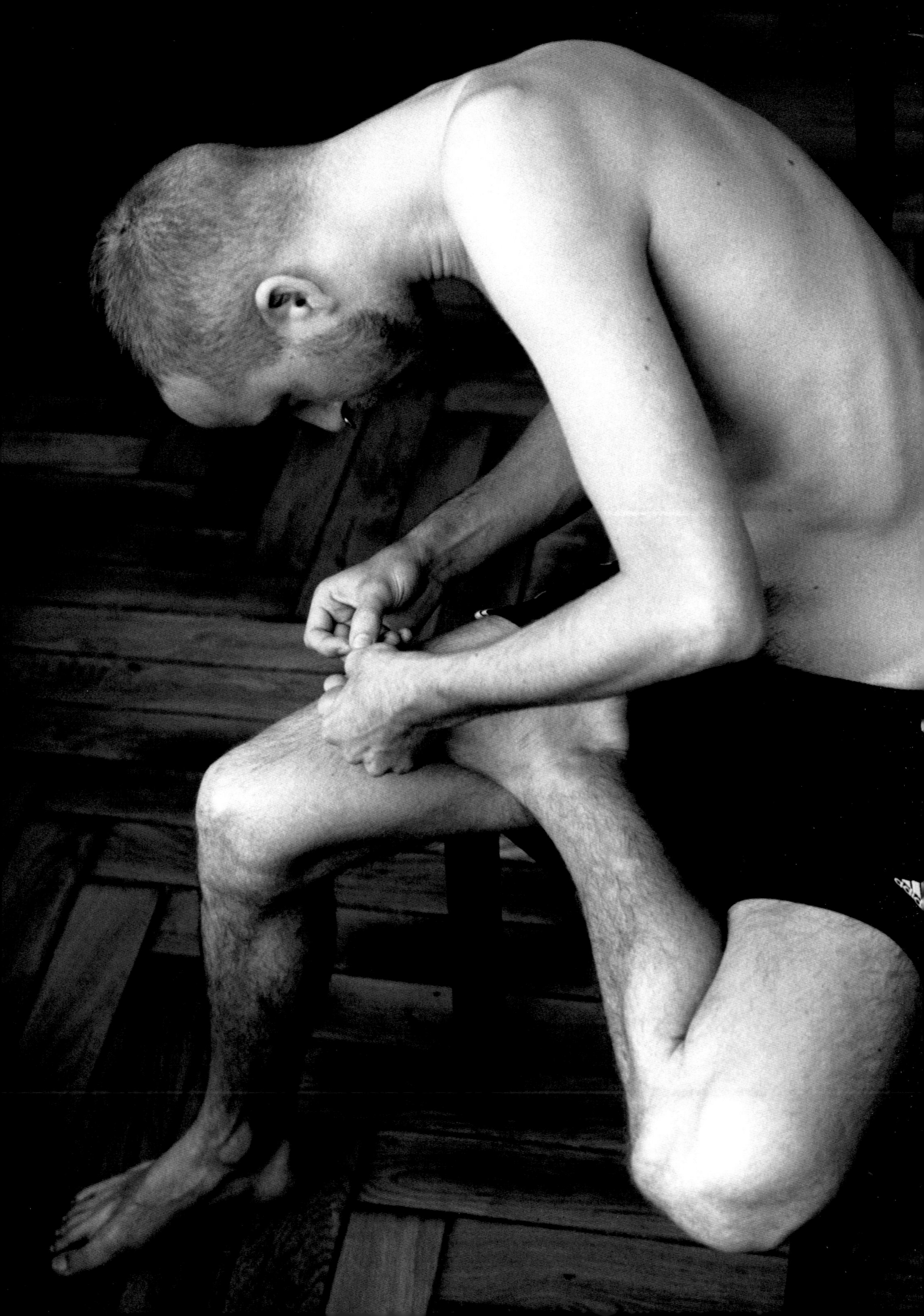

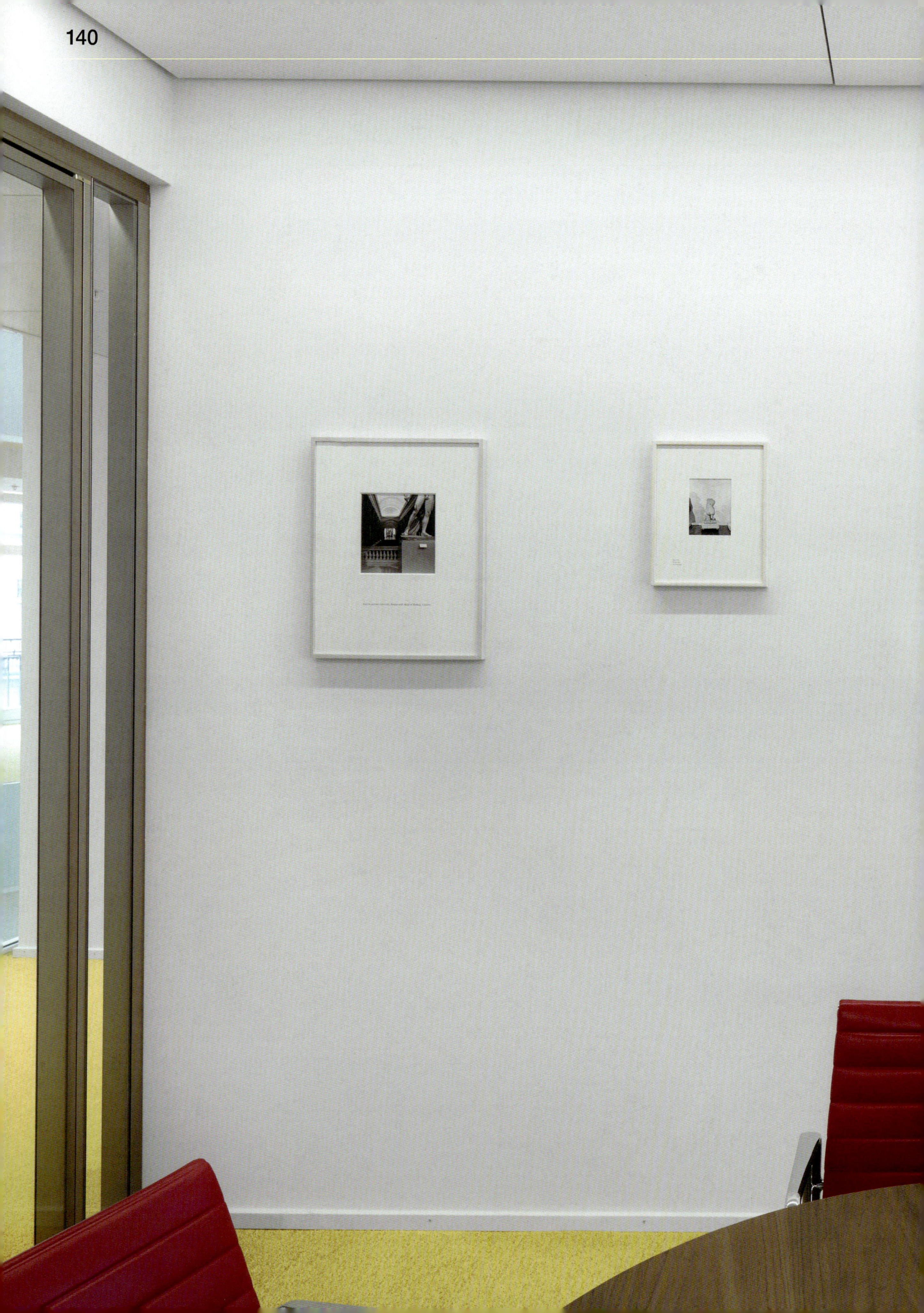

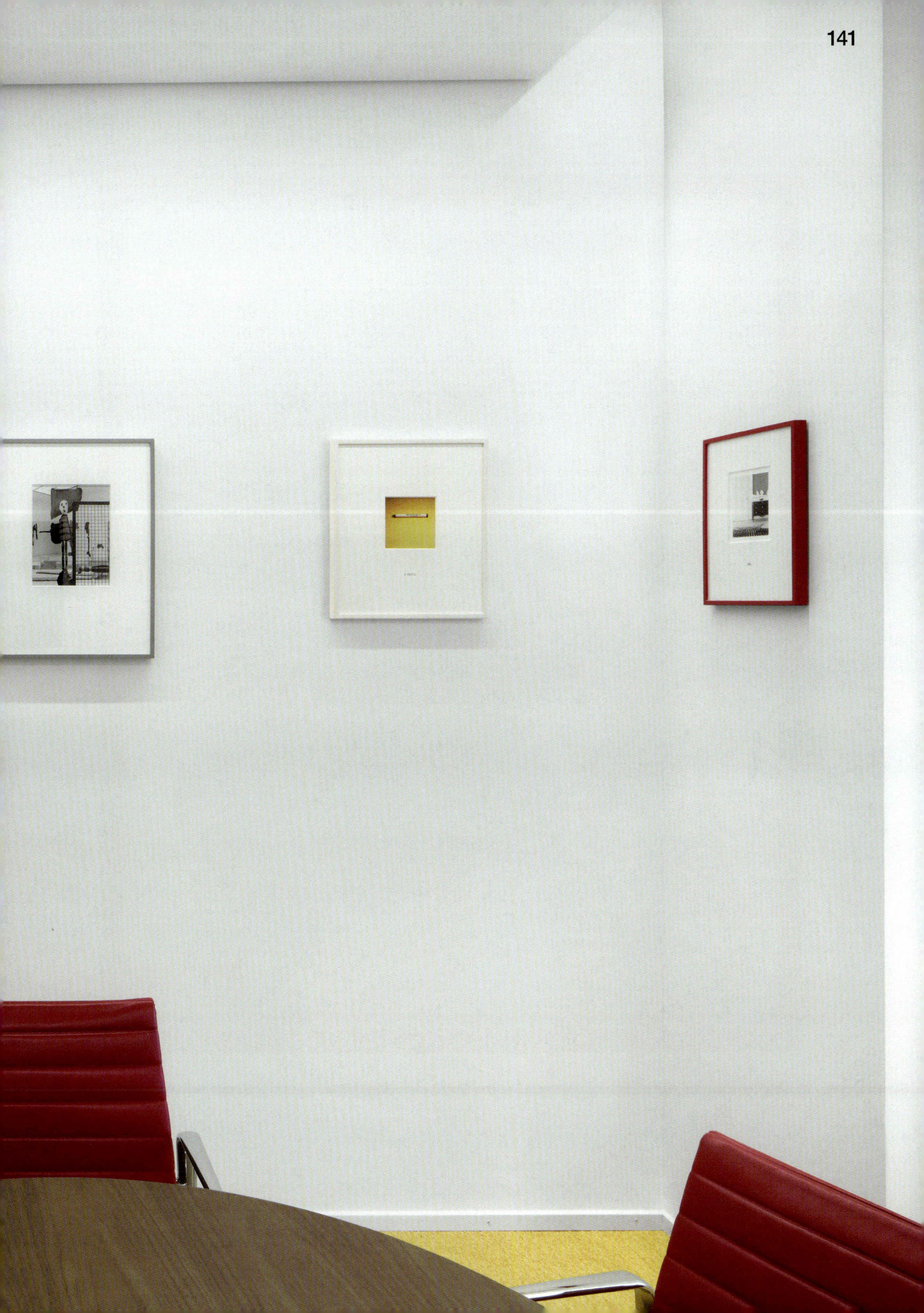

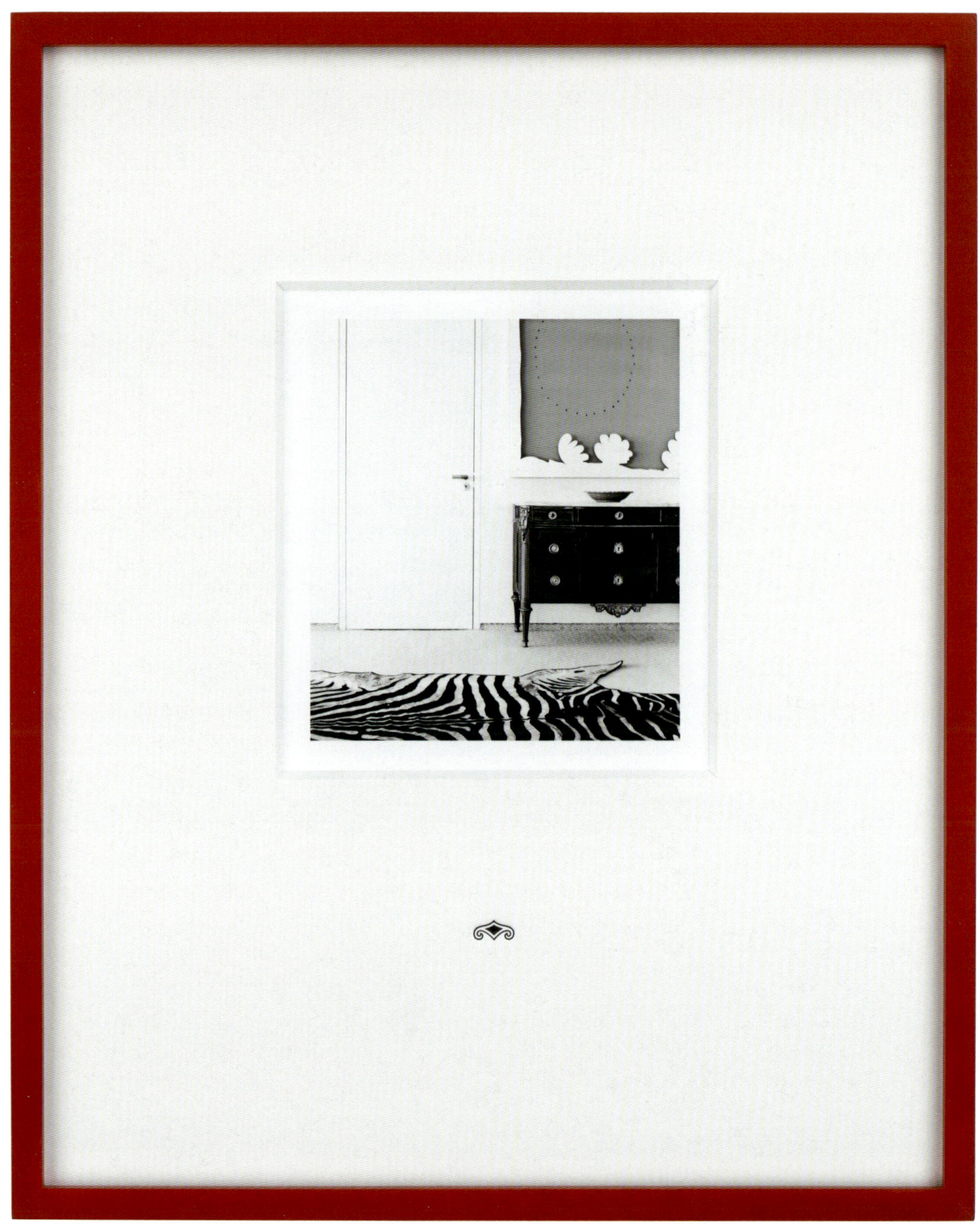

Skin from Angola, bought in Portugal, 2001–2010
Silver gelatin print with printed mat
36.2 × 29.2 cm

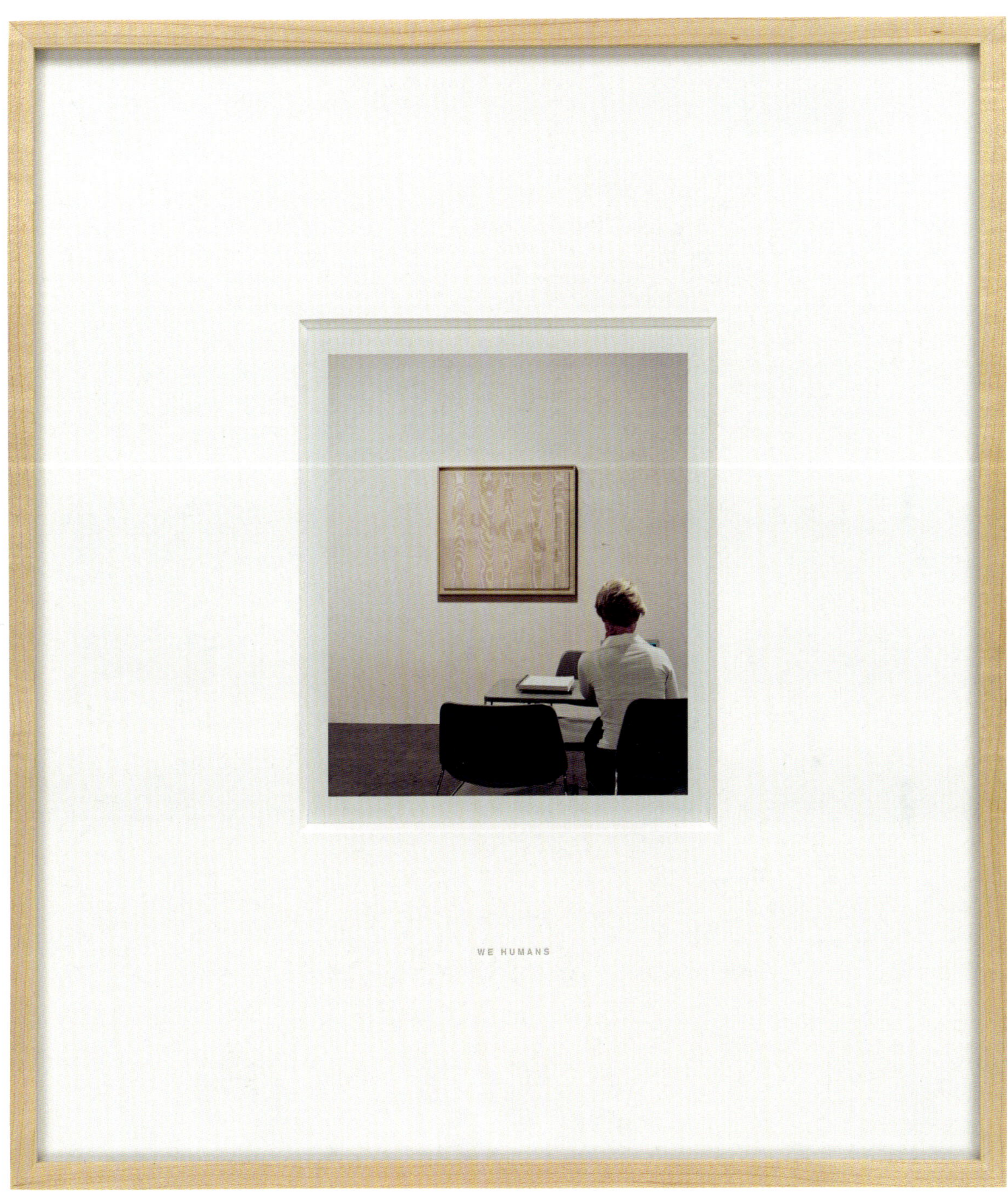

Not Cindy, 2002–2008
Digital cibachrome with text on mat
35.9 × 31.4 cm

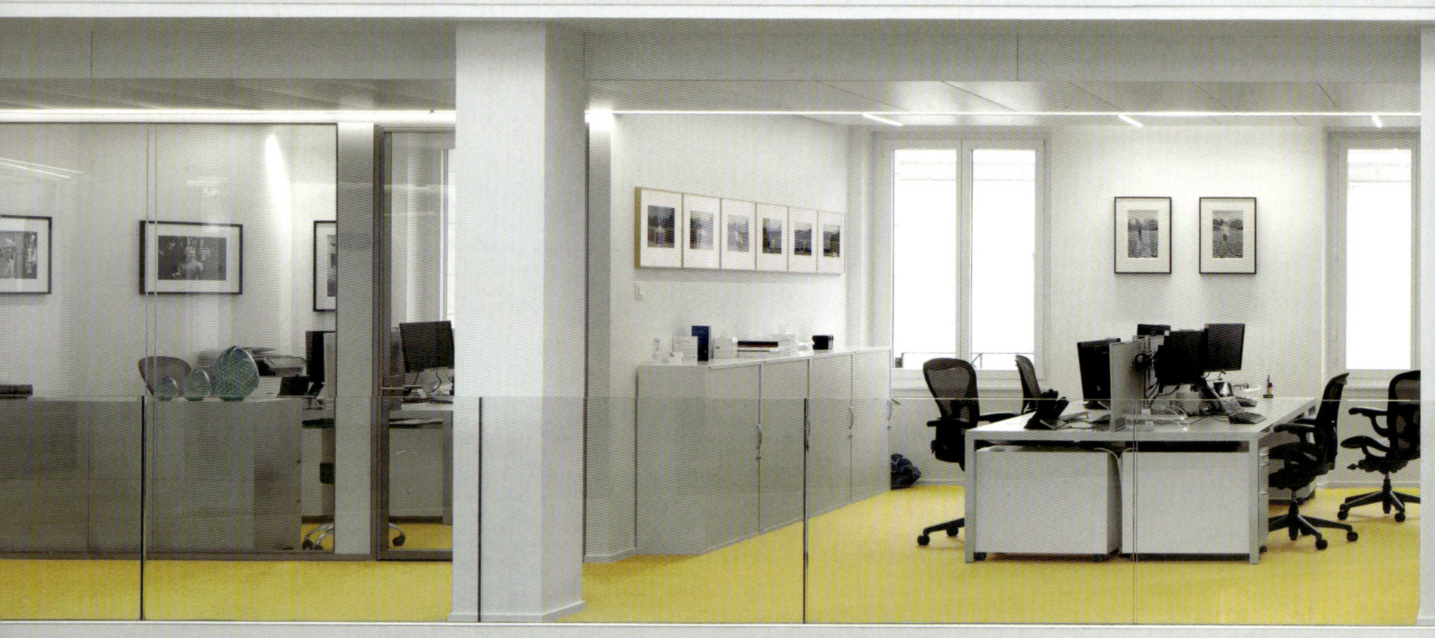

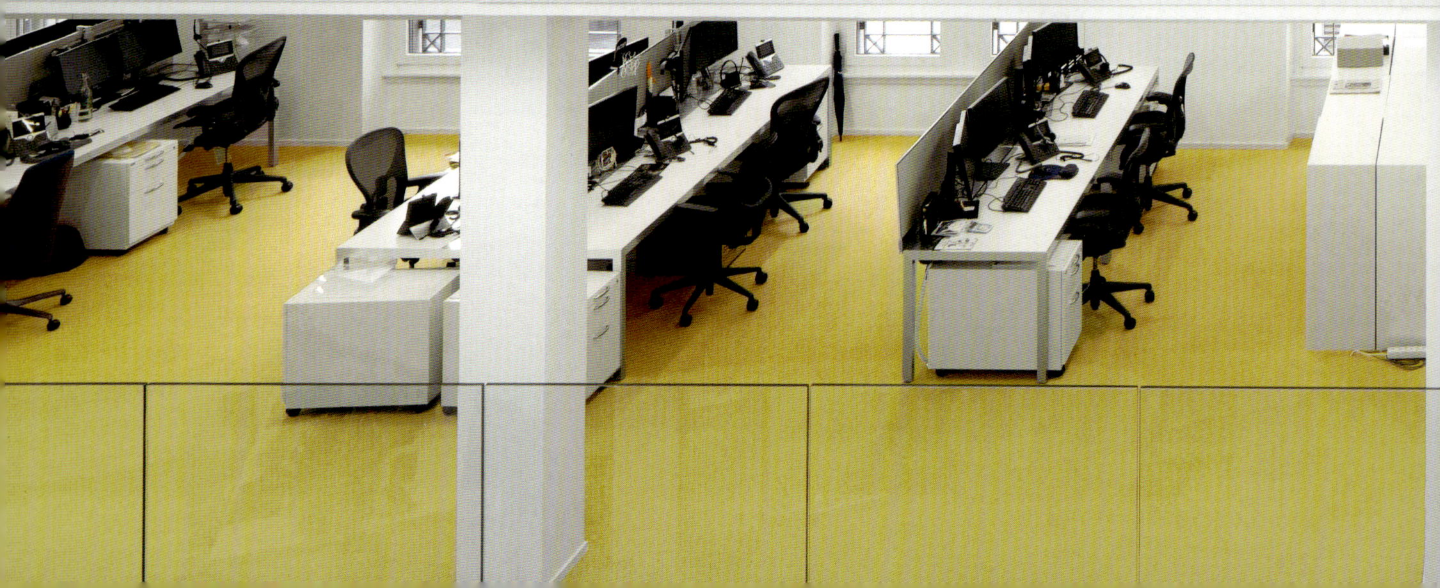

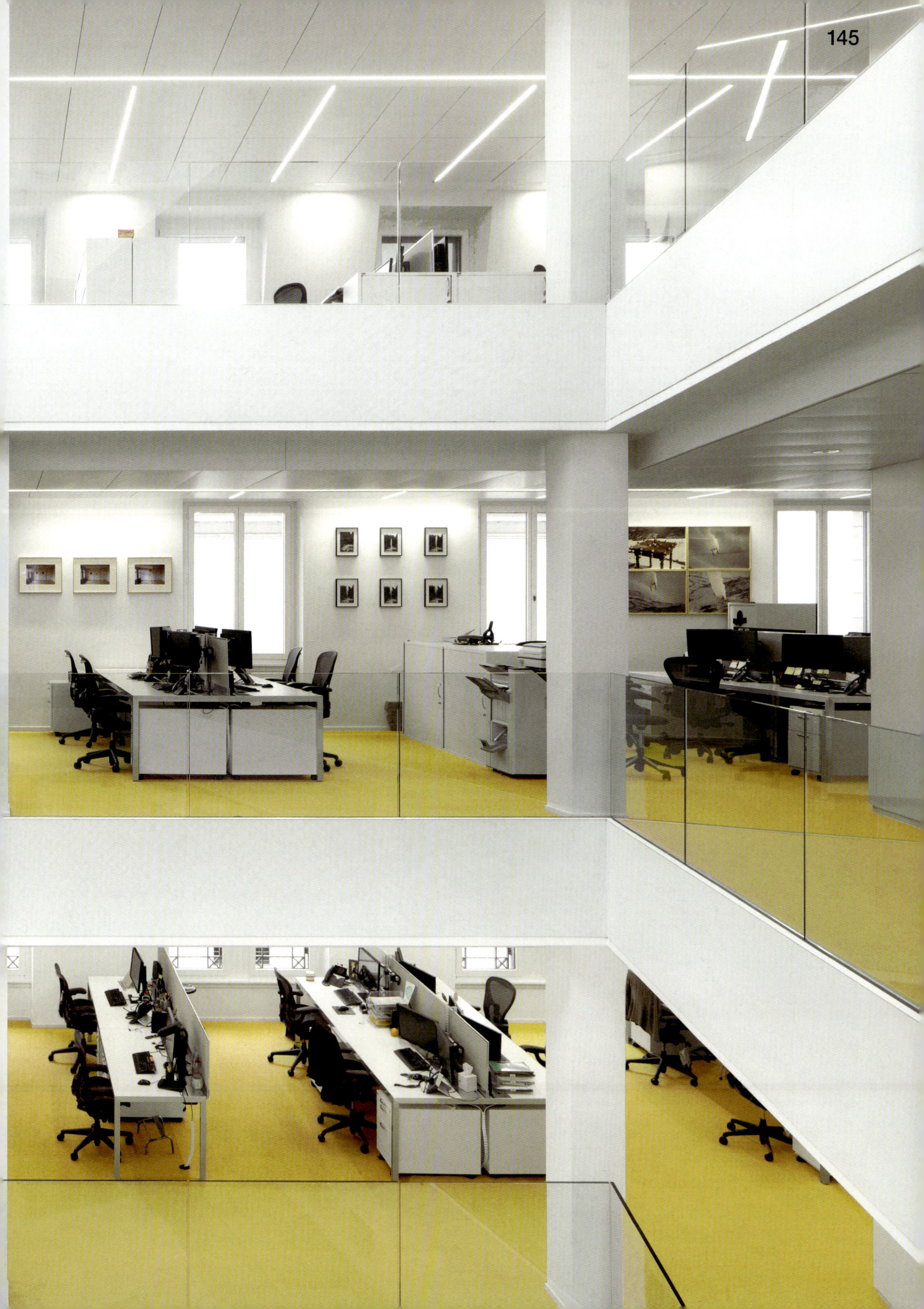

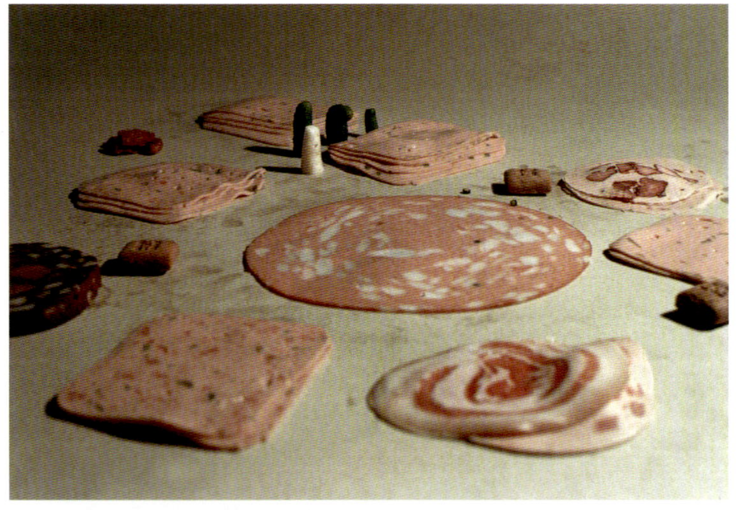

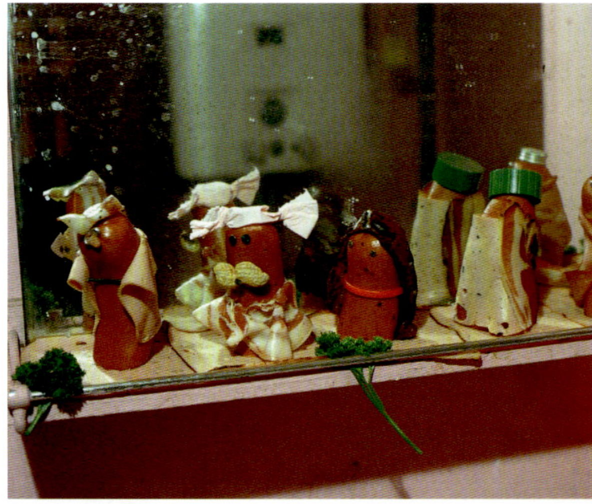

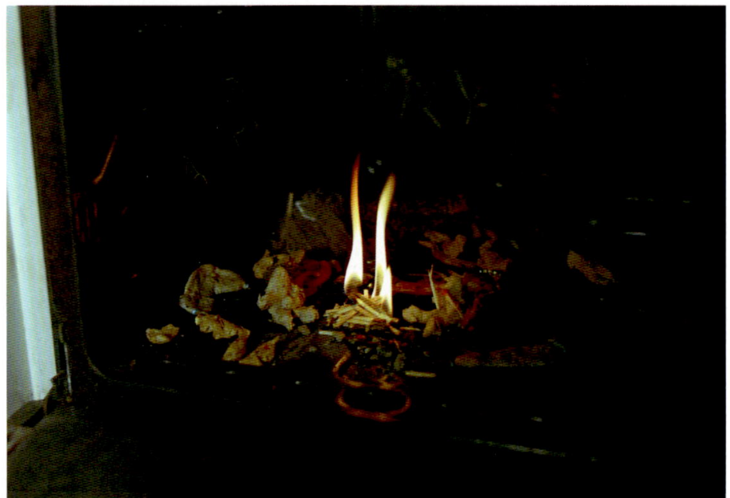

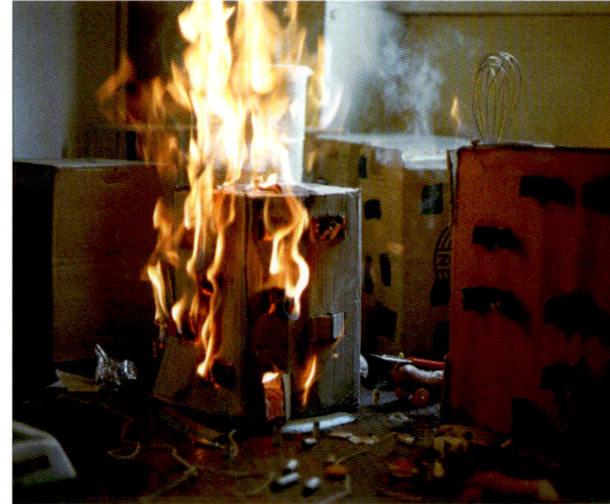

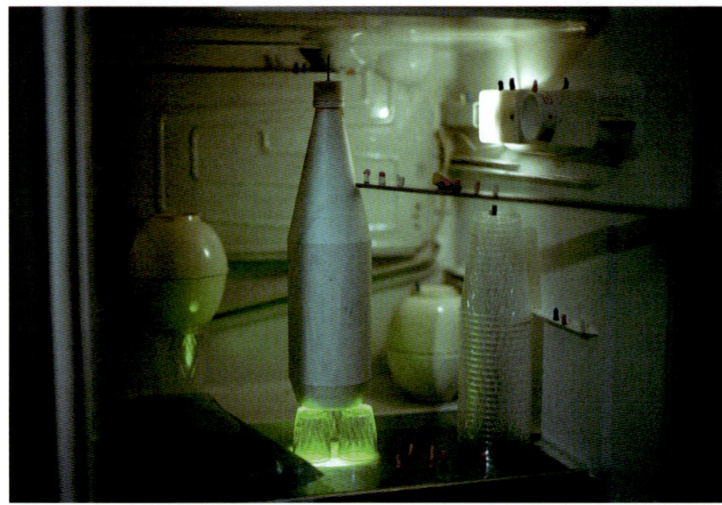

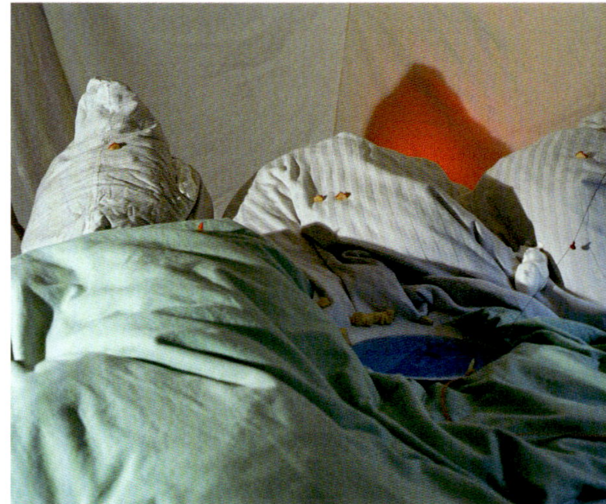

Wurstserie, 1979
C-prints
20 × 24 cm each

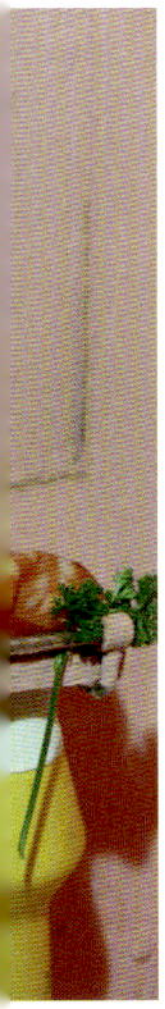

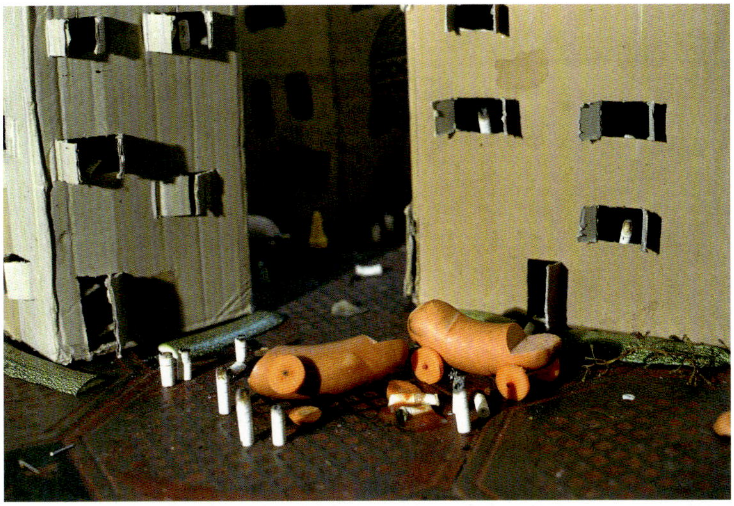

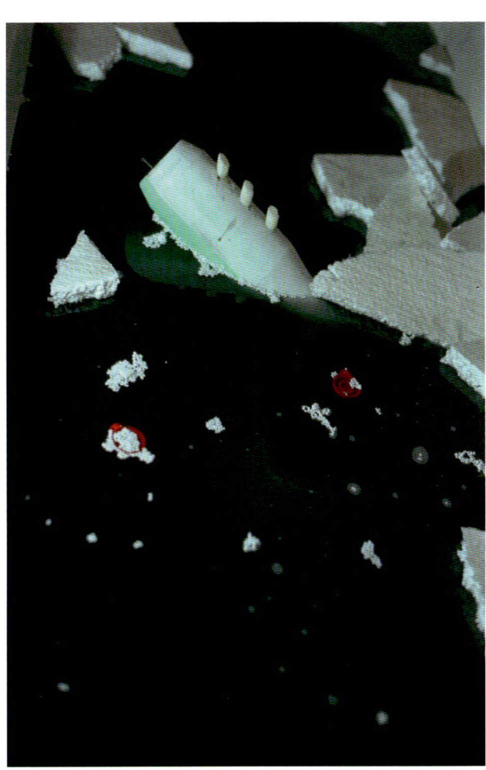

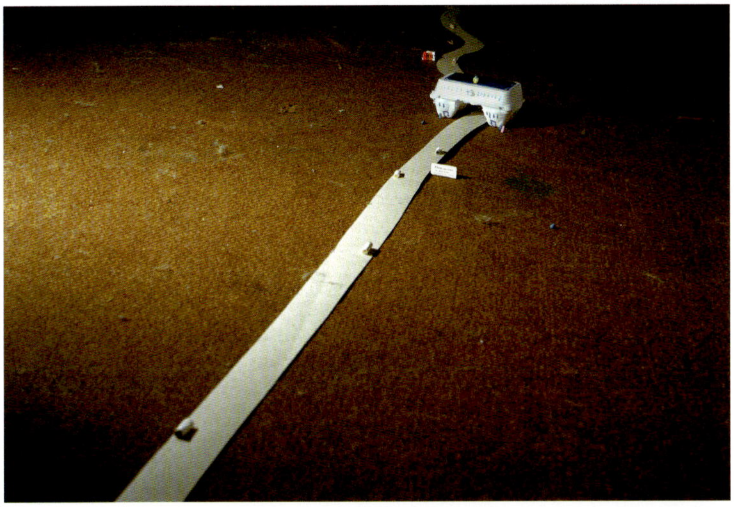

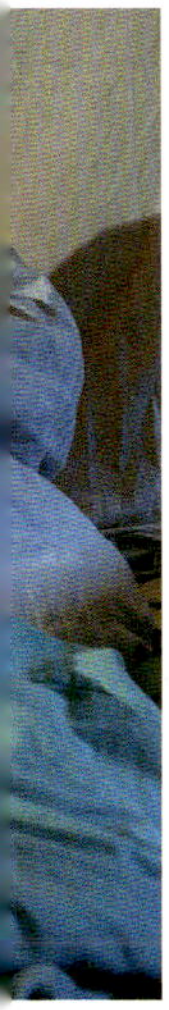

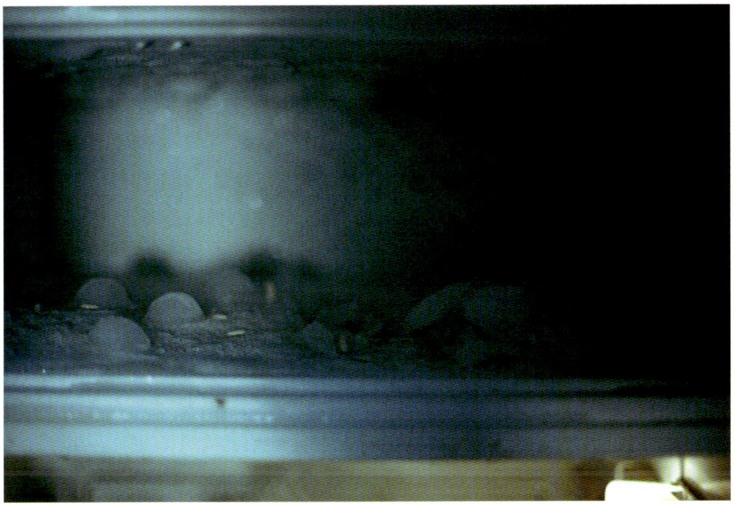

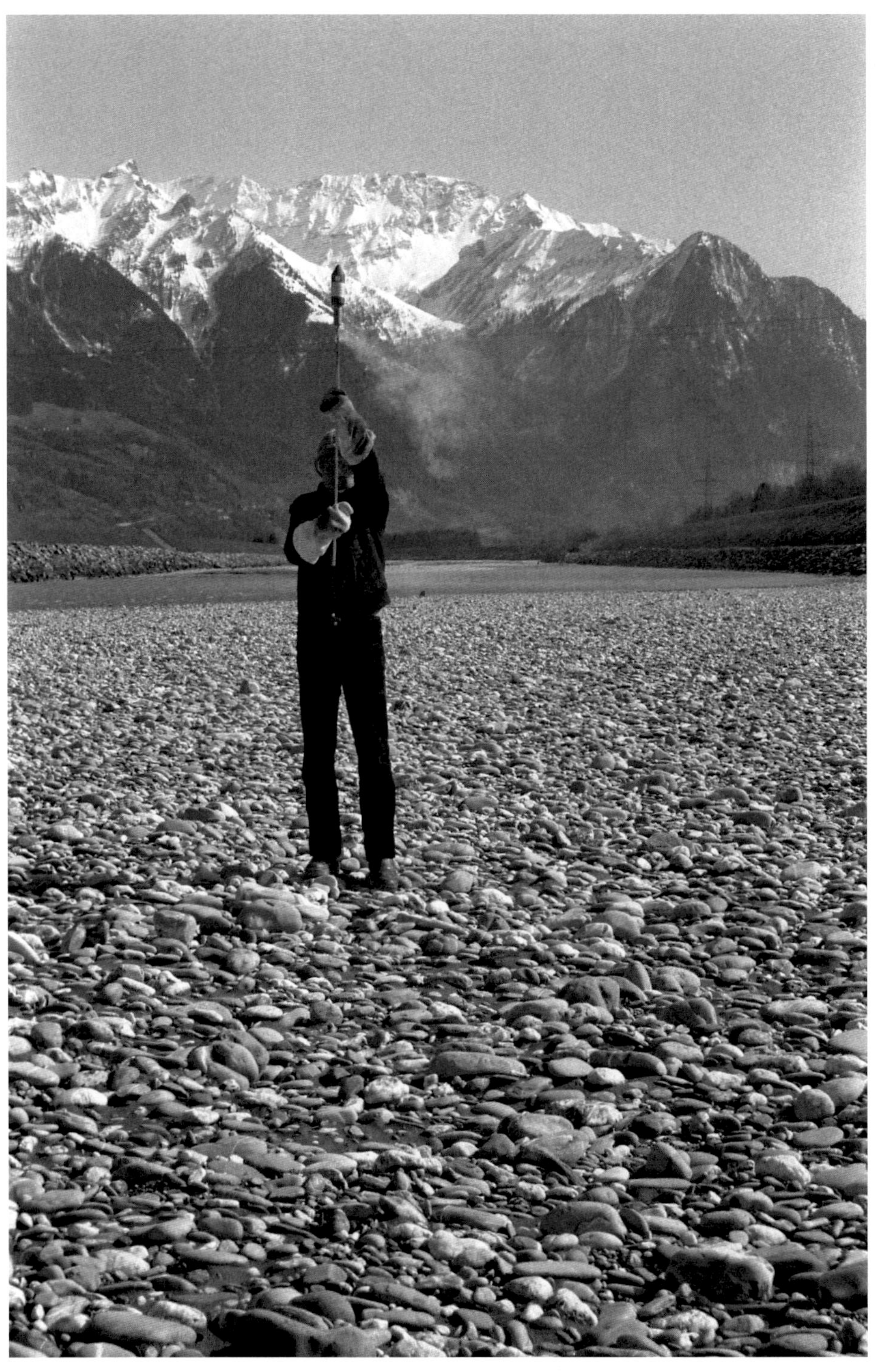

Nicht loslassen, 1983
Photographs on barrit paper
36 × 24 cm each

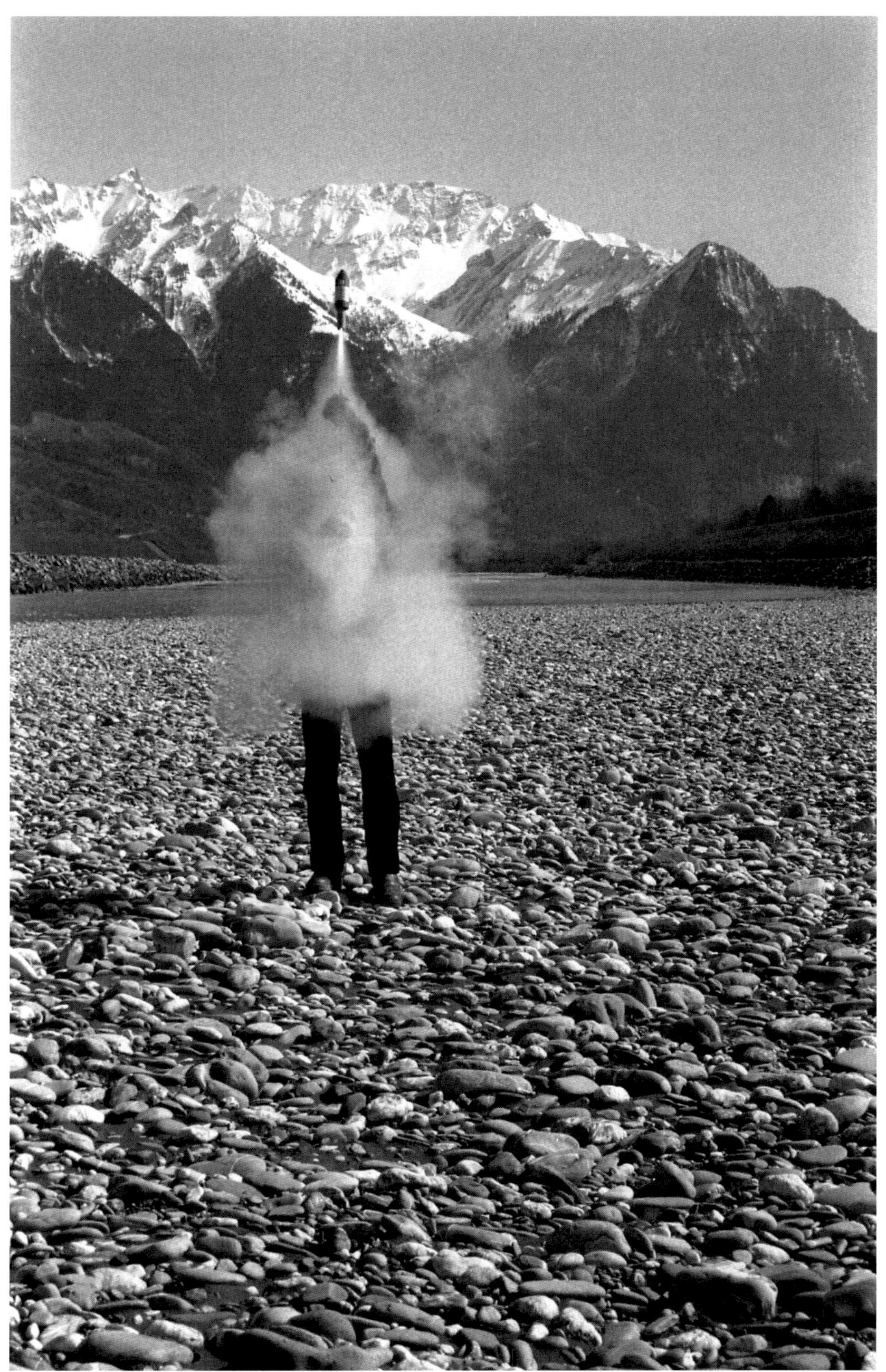

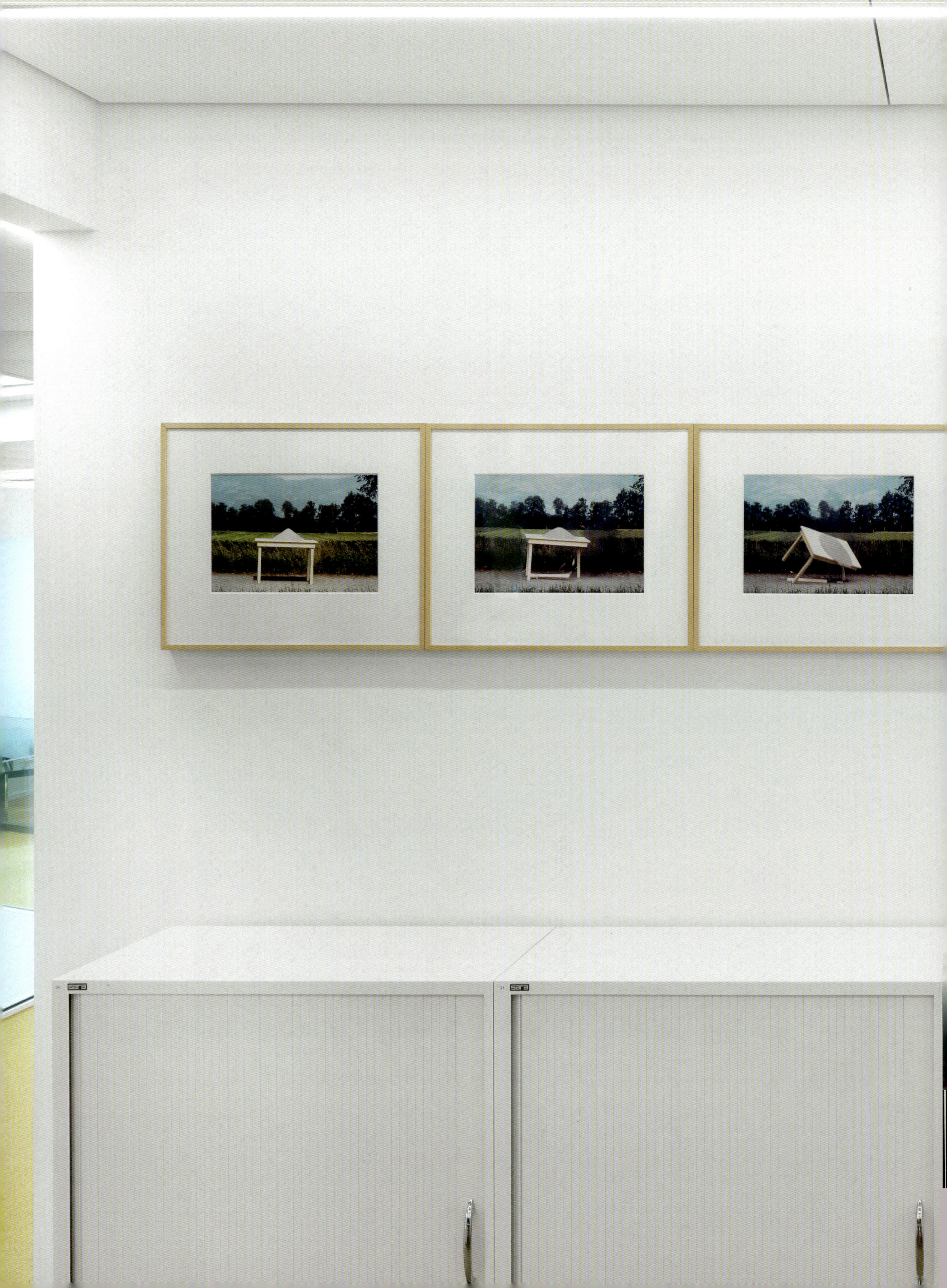

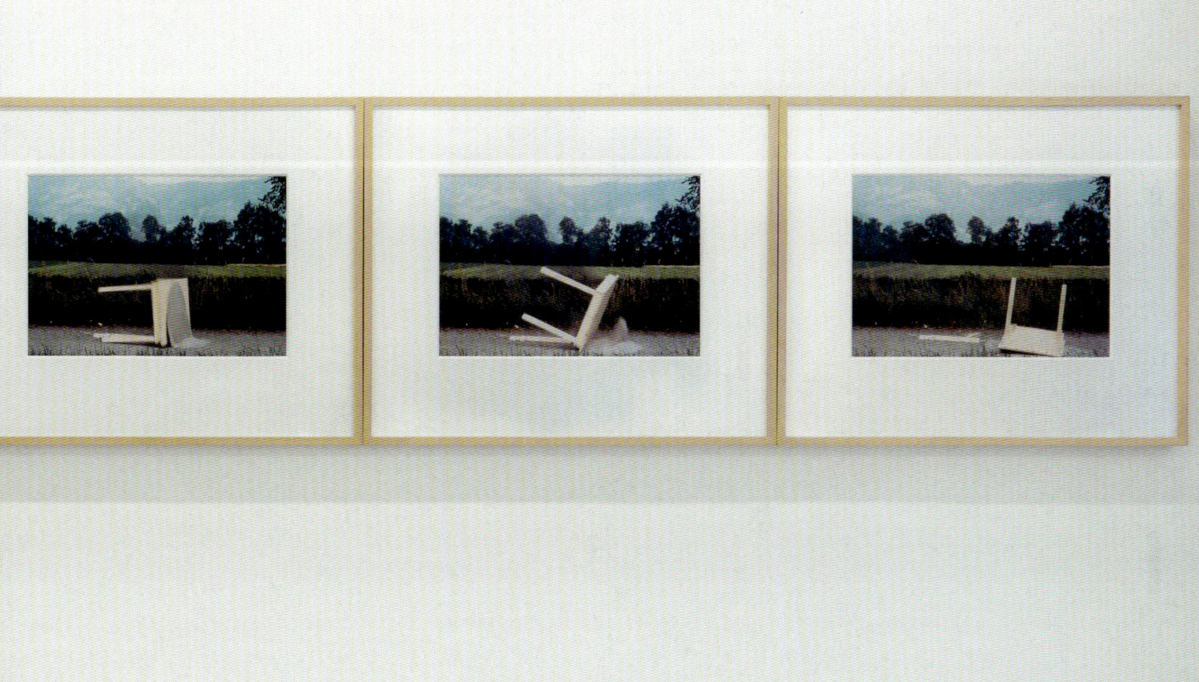

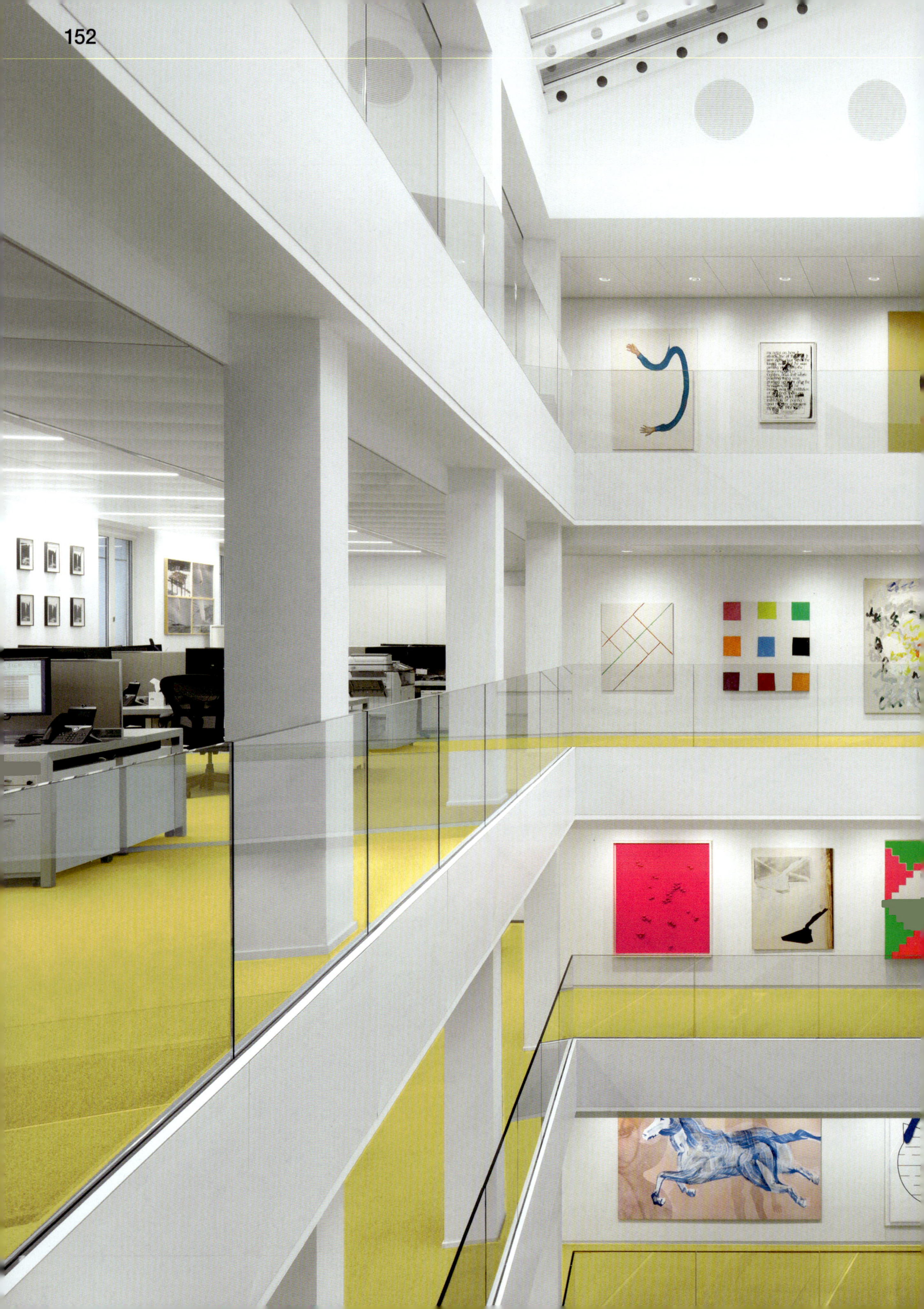

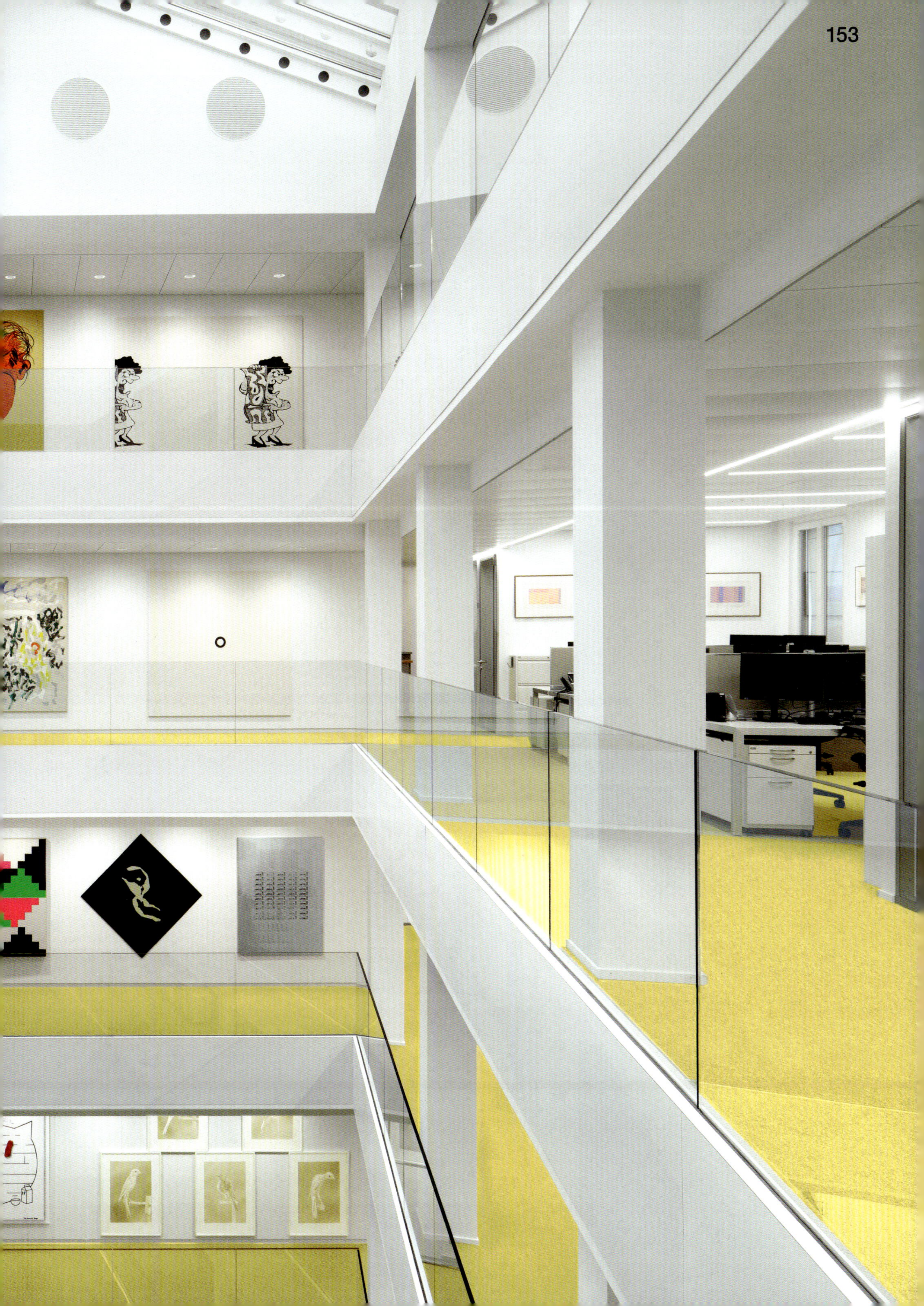

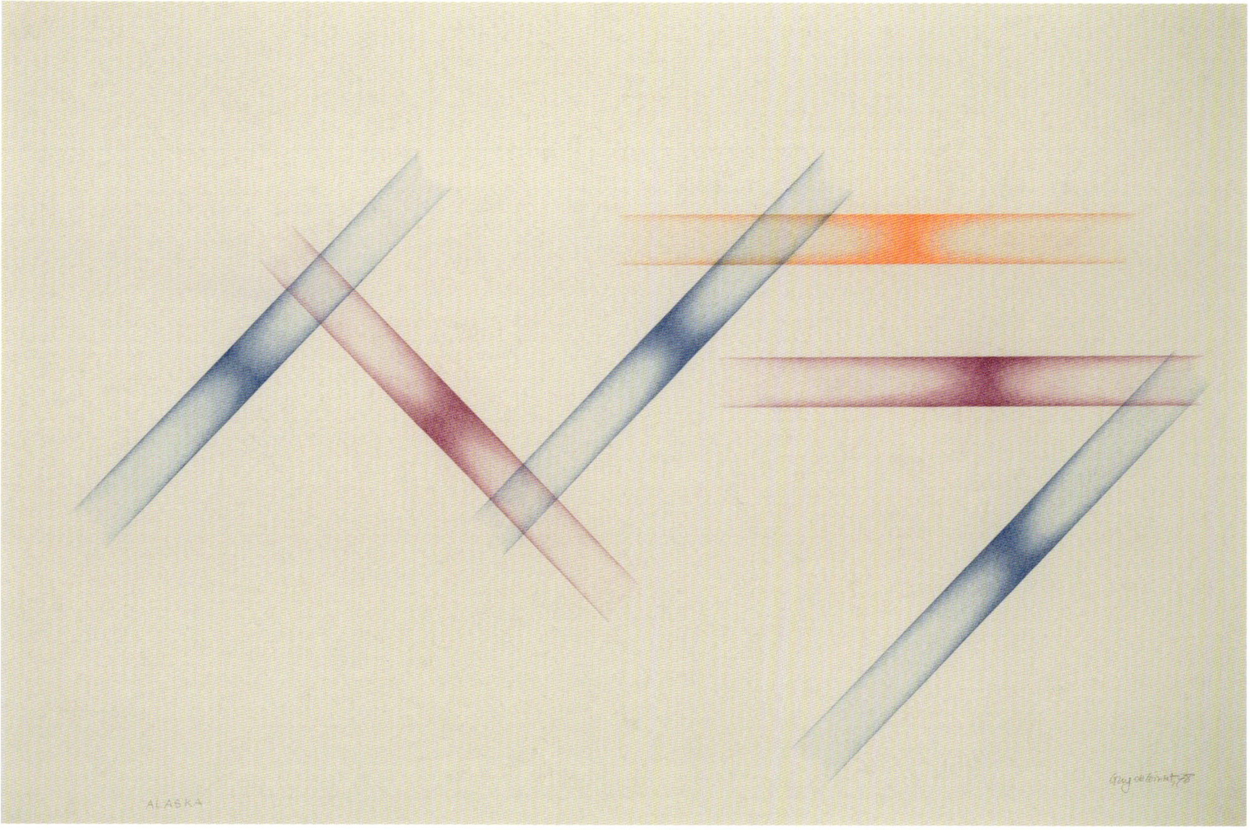

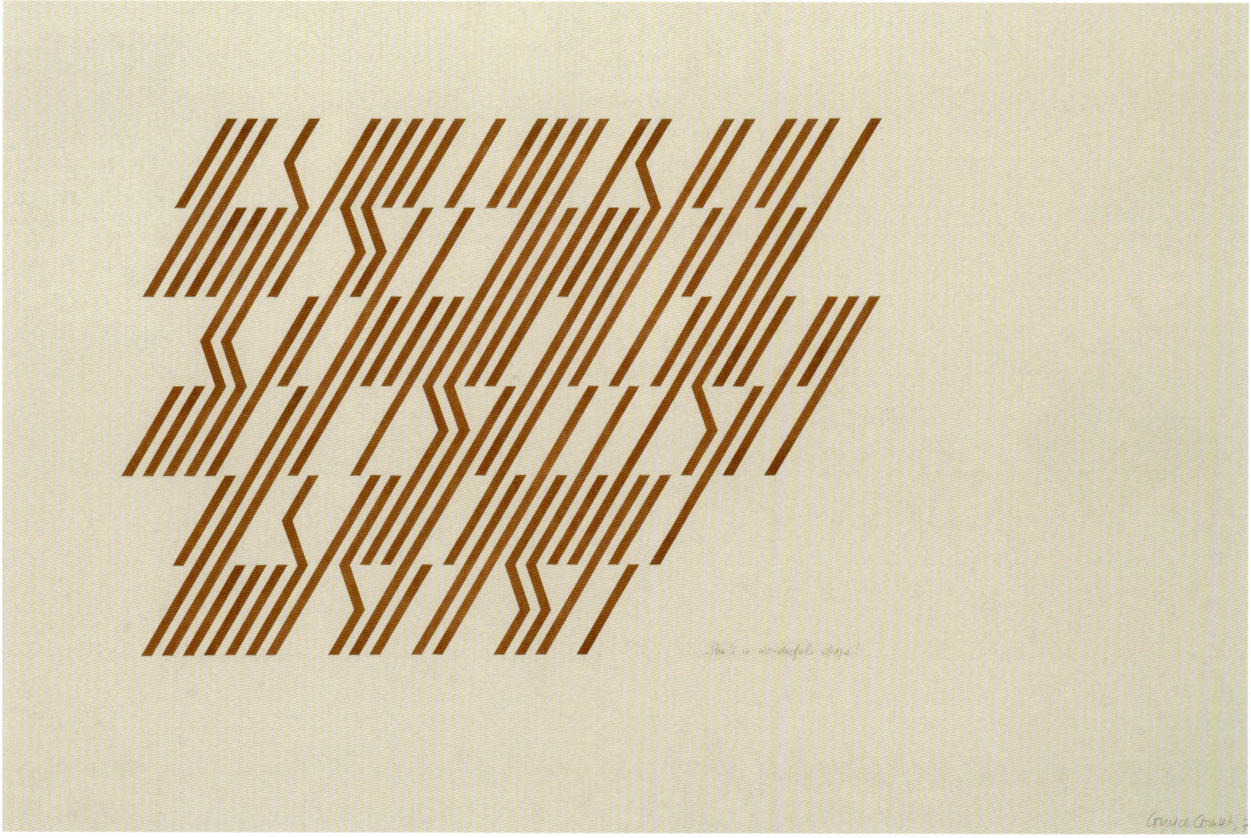

Alasaka, 1978
Color pencil on Arches paper
65 × 102 cm

She is in wonderful shape!, 1977
Ink and pencil on Arches paper
65 × 102 cm

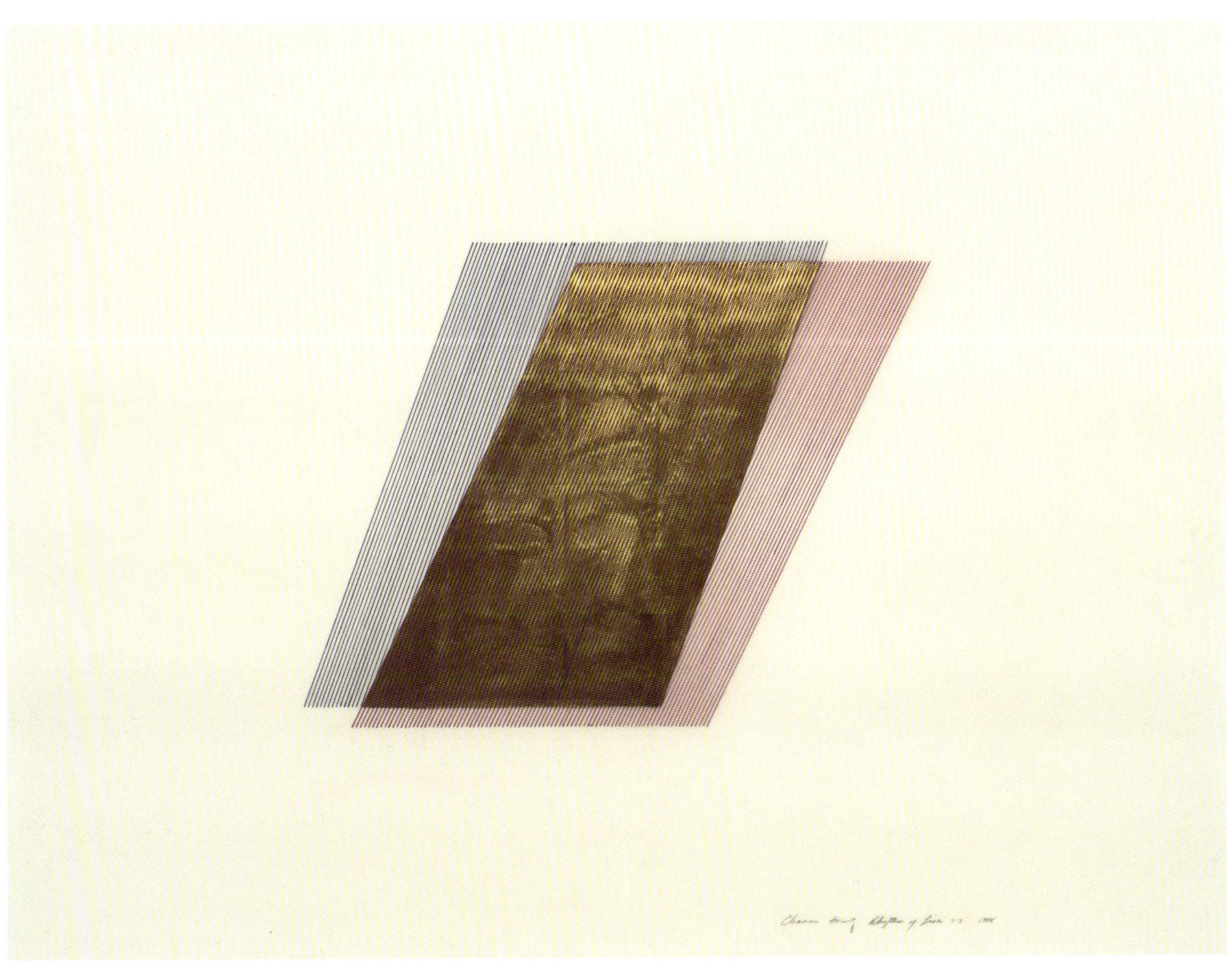

Rhythm of Lines 4–3, 1988
Plaka and gold leaf on Mylar
76.2 × 101.6 cm

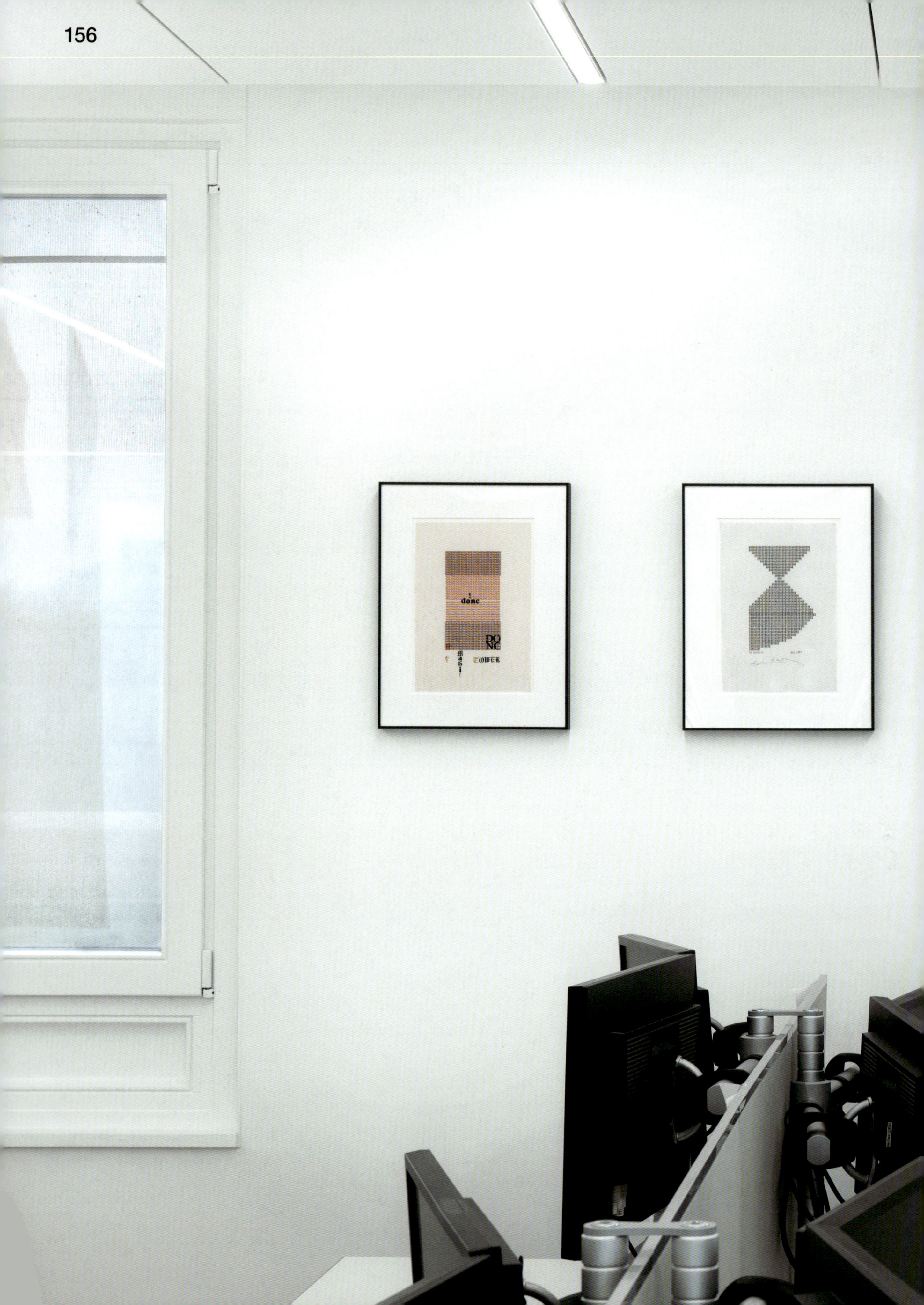

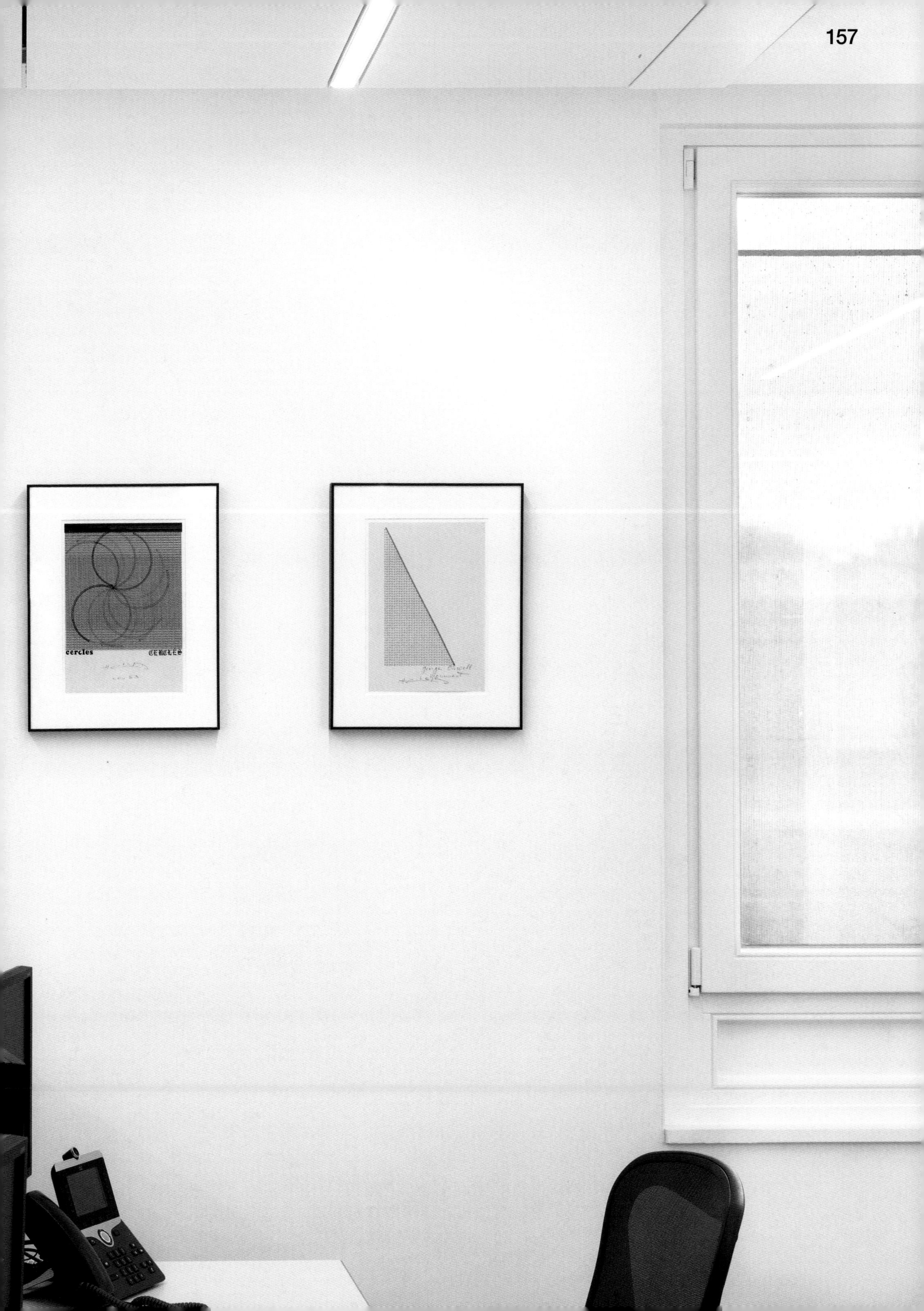
cercles

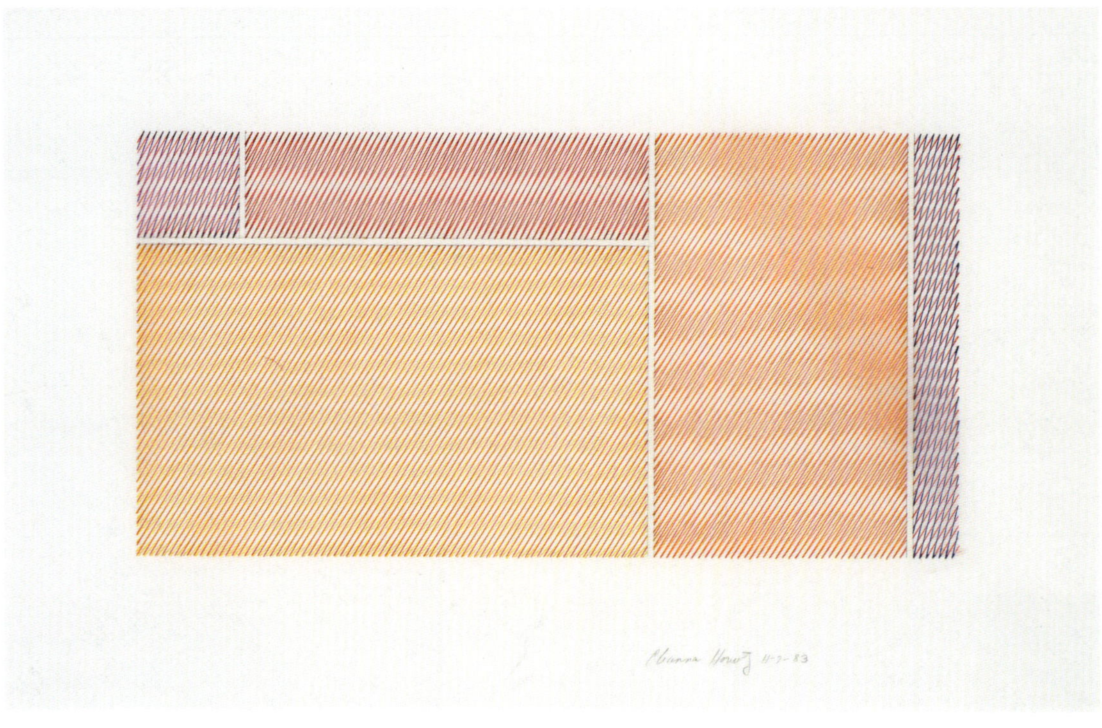

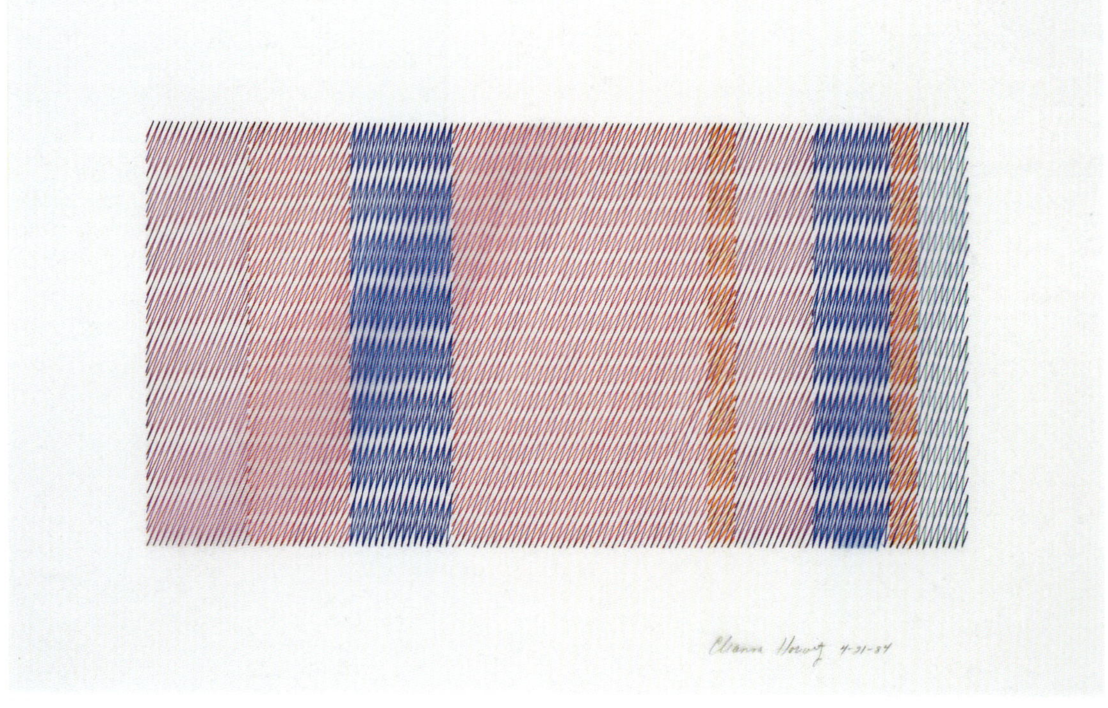

Moiré (with Angles) I, 1983
Plaka on Mylar
56.3 × 76.4 cm

Moiré (with Angles) II, 1984
Plaka on Mylar
56.4 × 76.5 cm

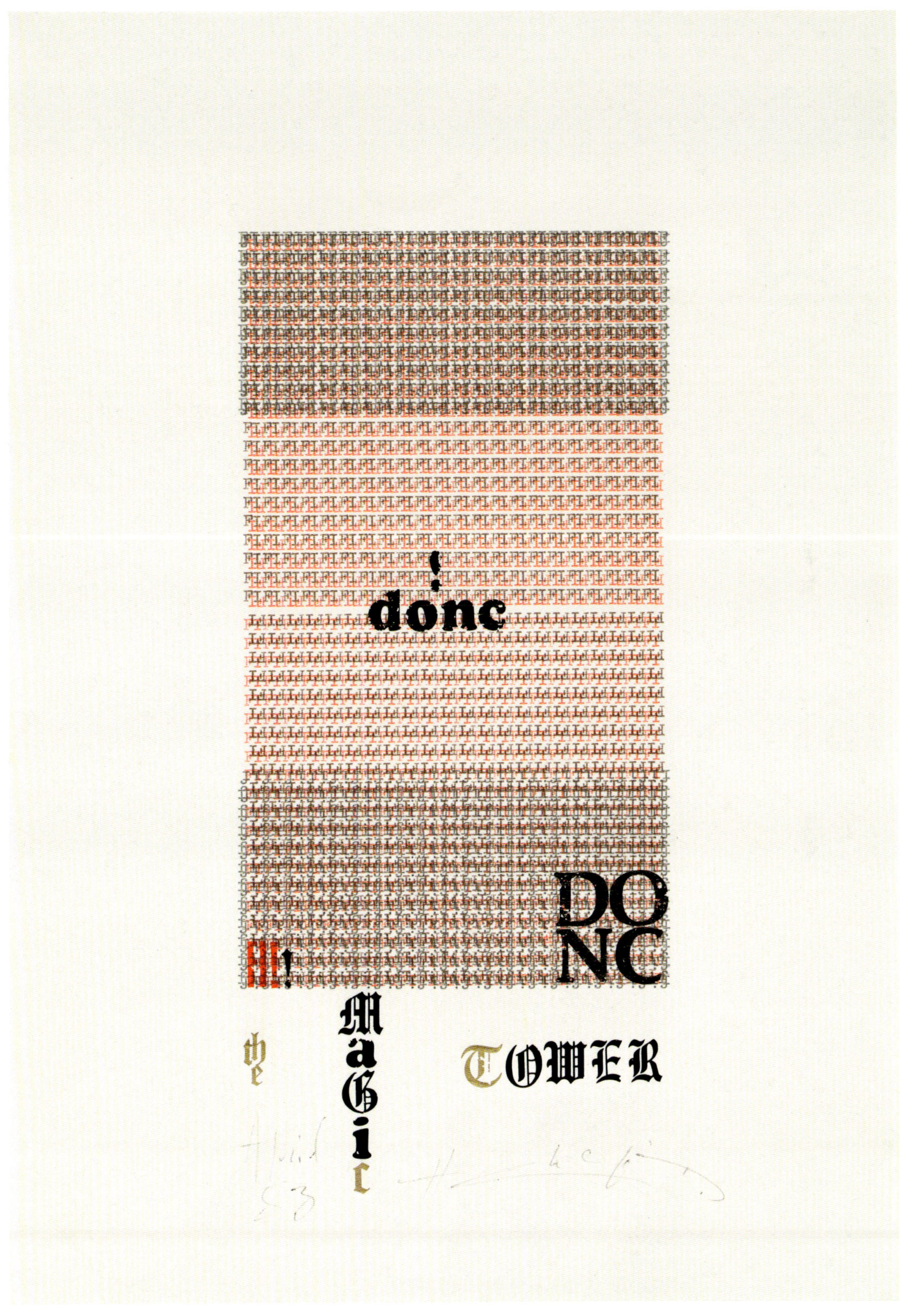

The Magic Tower, 1983
Ink on paper
29.6 × 20.7 cm

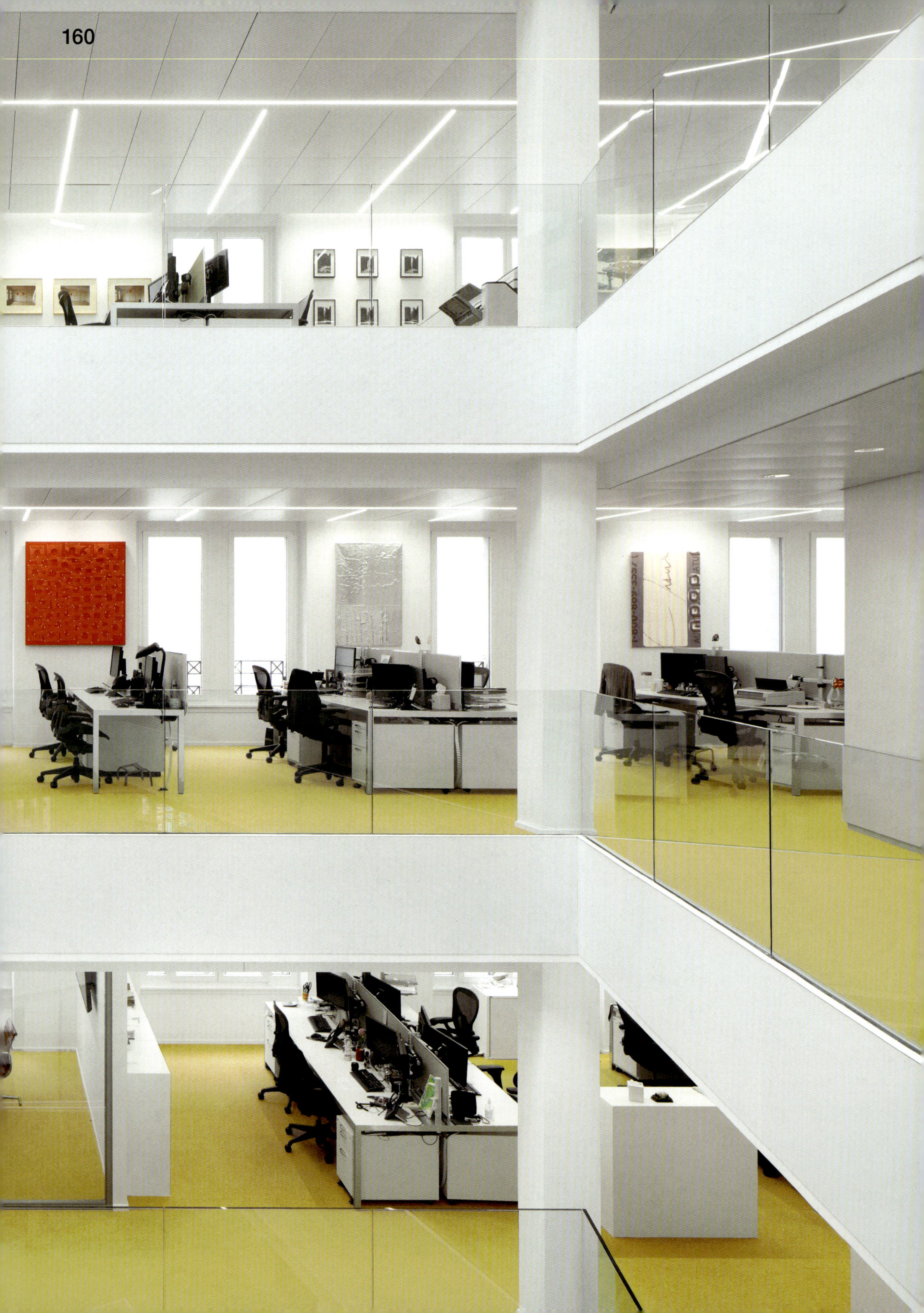

For several decades now, art lovers have clearly understood that it is the "viewer who makes the picture," and that the art experience results from a triangular relationship connecting the artist, the artwork, and the viewer. The fourth component in this relationship is taken into consideration very little, and yet is just as crucial: that is to say, the context and physical presentation of the work, namely the frame of looking.

For centuries artworks were always conceived and commissioned for specific and predefined settings and premises. The meaning of such works and the way they were looked at were interwoven in a vast network of beliefs and codes. Temples and churches, guild buildings, royal castles, city halls, and republican palaces were the artworks' ultimate settings for a long time, during periods when the relationship between the public and the private spheres were quite different from what they are today, when art was inextricably linked to religion and social order. It is only relatively recently, particularly since the 19th century, that artists began to create freely, without regard for the constraints of where and how their works would be displayed. This freedom was then shared with critics, audience, and the artworks themselves, especially in museums in which works are now gathered together from so many various provenances.

In the last third of the 20th century a new kind of site began to host and display artwork: corporate buildings like the SYZ Group headquarters in Geneva. Corporations and entrepreneurs started to collect art with the intention of showing it to and sharing it with their collaborators and partners. This is a real shift in terms of audience: being a worker (mostly white collar) and an art viewer, instead of being a worshipper/citizen/courtesan and an art viewer. How does this new audience position change the way one looks at art? And consequently change the art that is shown? These questions remain open, but it would certainly feel strange today not to encounter artworks when visiting major corporate headquarters. As the foundation of the International Association of Corporate Collections of Contemporary Art (IACCCA) in 2007 proves, the field of the corporate display of contemporary art is now a growing one, and has been professionalized. IACCCA now comprises 46 members from 17 countries and maps the diversity of the field in terms of collection owners, collection policy, and the kind of art collected.

Given the ambition and the achievement of the Syz Collection presentation at the Quai des Bergues, as well as the unique way its owners Eric & Suzanne Syz, and its curator Nicolas Trembley, reflect on it in the conversation reproduced infra, it seems most appropriate to inscribe the collection display unveiled at length in this publication in a brief history of artistic hangings in the corporate world—to frame it, so to speak. An insight into the Syz Collection can be provided by analyzing other examples from a range of different businesses, thus highlighting various methods for bridging art and the corporate world.

One of the most pioneering models in this history takes us to France at the end of the 1960s: it is a story of collecting, displaying, and producing artworks, in collaboration

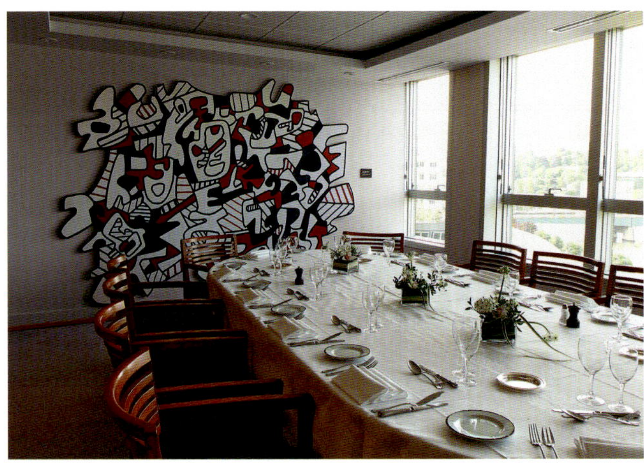

Dining room
Renault headquarters
Boulogne-Billancourt

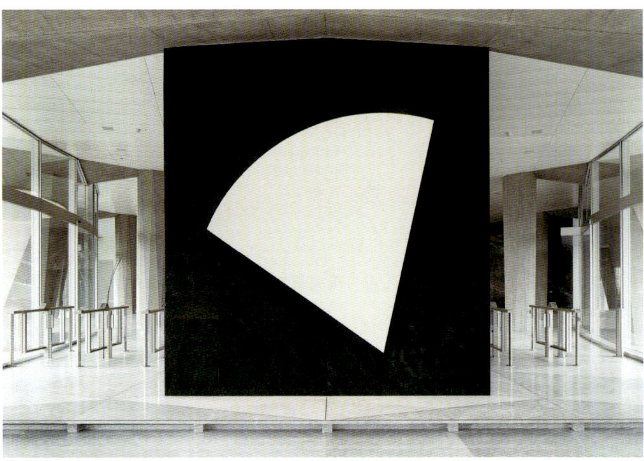

Reception foyer
Nestlé headquarters
Vevey

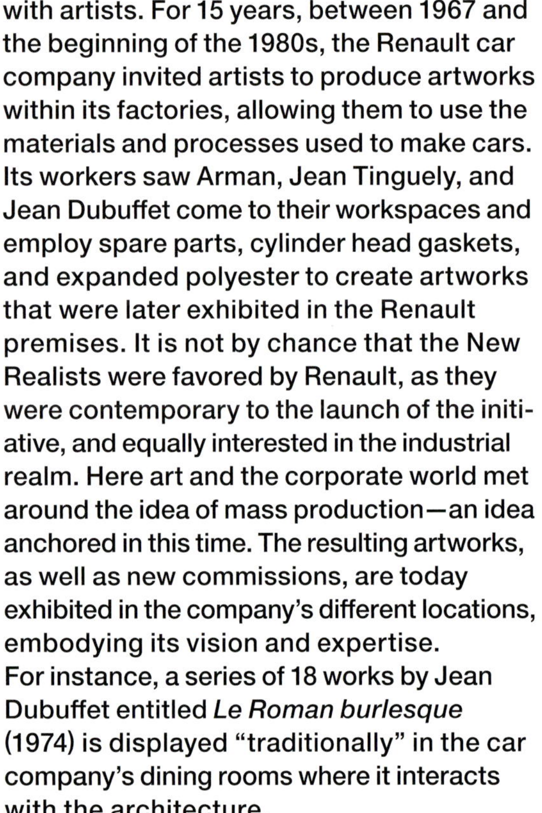

with artists. For 15 years, between 1967 and the beginning of the 1980s, the Renault car company invited artists to produce artworks within its factories, allowing them to use the materials and processes used to make cars. Its workers saw Arman, Jean Tinguely, and Jean Dubuffet come to their workspaces and employ spare parts, cylinder head gaskets, and expanded polyester to create artworks that were later exhibited in the Renault premises. It is not by chance that the New Realists were favored by Renault, as they were contemporary to the launch of the initiative, and equally interested in the industrial realm. Here art and the corporate world met around the idea of mass production—an idea anchored in this time. The resulting artworks, as well as new commissions, are today exhibited in the company's different locations, embodying its vision and expertise. For instance, a series of 18 works by Jean Dubuffet entitled *Le Roman burlesque* (1974) is displayed "traditionally" in the car company's dining rooms where it interacts with the architecture.

In Switzerland, one of the most striking examples of a corporate site-specific contemporary art collection is Nestlé. When the company's new headquarters were designed in Vevey by Jean Tschumi in the late 1950s, one of its guiding principles was that "art and architecture should work together in harmony." From the very beginning it was clear that the building should display works of art, including pieces that Tschumi specifically commissioned. The buildings feature artworks acquired from artists and galleries (from Ferdinand Hodler and Alexander Calder to Olivier Mosset and Fischli Weiss), but also specific commissions by Per Kirkeby and Ulrich Rückriem placed in the park. Inside the main building, Ellsworth Kelly conceived his *White Curve* derived from his renowned shaped canvases, and came to Vevey to hang it against the black marble of the reception foyer. Tschumi and Nestlé thus considered artworks as a way to enhance working conditions, as well as to underline the expertise of a global company commissioning and collecting artworks from internationally acclaimed artists.

A more modest but more contemporary case is that of Eurogroup Consulting, an independent consultancy group. Being a company without any physical production—except paperboard presentations, Powerpoints, and commercial offers—Eurogroup Consulting draw a parallel between the activities of the nomadic consultant paid for his/her ideas and the contemporary artists whose computer is for many their one and only studio. This gave birth to a series of residencies offered to upcoming artists to nurture the mutual understanding of the corporate and the artistic spheres.

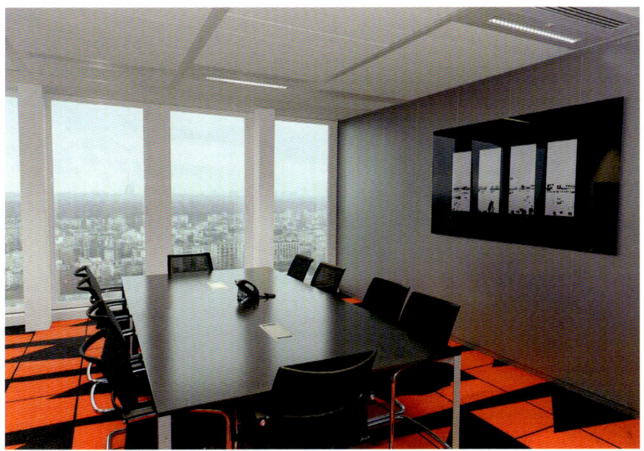

Meeting room
Eurogroup Consulting headquarters
La Défense, Paris

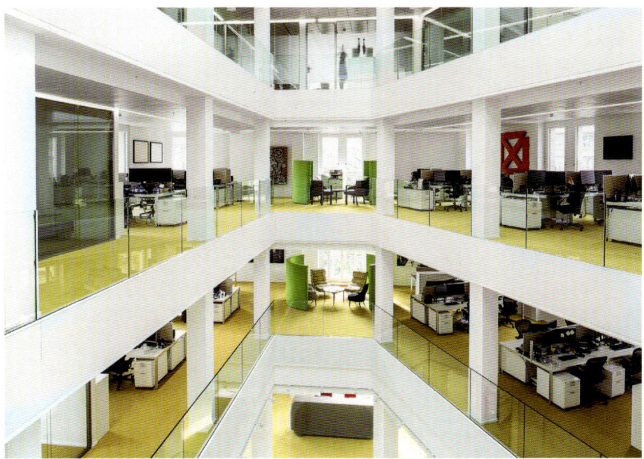

Atrium
The SYZ Group headquarters
Geneva

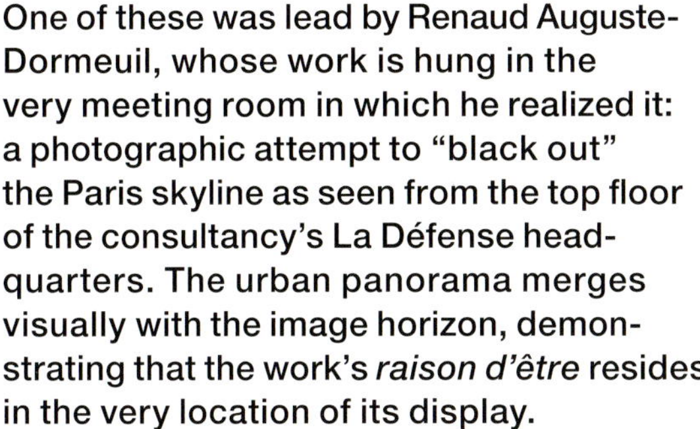

One of these was lead by Renaud Auguste-Dormeuil, whose work is hung in the very meeting room in which he realized it: a photographic attempt to "black out" the Paris skyline as seen from the top floor of the consultancy's La Défense headquarters. The urban panorama merges visually with the image horizon, demonstrating that the work's *raison d'être* resides in the very location of its display.

Of course, there is also a strong tradition of companies collecting art without organizing residencies, commissioning artists, or establishing a dialogue between art and architecture. In this case, they might decide to focus on a specific area of collecting, as is the case of the French-Dutch banking group Neuflize ABN AMRO, which, since 1997, has dedicated its Collection Neuflize Vie to portraits and human representation.

In this context, the Syz Collection has its own way of operating. Thanks to its spectacular atrium, the Syz Collection clearly belongs to a group of initiatives that emphasize architecture—but it takes this model a little further. First of all, it should be remembered that the Syz Collection does not belong to the SYZ Group, but to Eric & Suzanne Syz who have decided to exhibit it at the bank's headquarters. Thus, it is not a corporate collection per se, but a private collection displayed in a corporate environment.

Most importantly, the interplay of the display of the collection—curated by Nicolas Trembley—with its back and forth between artists, themes, generations, and media, and its subtle play with the ongoing history of contemporary art, paired with the interior architecture and design conceived by Suzanne Syz, contribute to a sense of a consistent whole, a kind of *Gesamtkunstwerk*. This global museum-like gesture allows us to consider simultaneously the artworks themselves, the way they encounter and complement each other, and the way they inhabit the space. By transforming the building's architecture into a curatorial device whose centerpiece is the six-floor atrium wall conceived as an all-at-once vertical exhibition, a multitude of perspectives are offered on the display, which constantly changes according to one's progress through the offices—in other words, the Syz Collection proposes a unique and energetic frame for looking at art, an approach to collecting and displaying which is very contemporary, open, and generous to the artworks, the artists, and the audience.

Note: To learn more about the examples quoted in this text, see www.iaccca.com; *Renault and Art. A Modern Aventure*, Ann Hindry (ed.), Hazan, Paris 2000; *Nestlé Art Collection*, Julie Enckell Julliard (ed.), JRP|Ringier, Zurich 2016; and www.eurogroupconsulting.com/vous-et-nous/nos-engagements/notre-residence-dartistes.

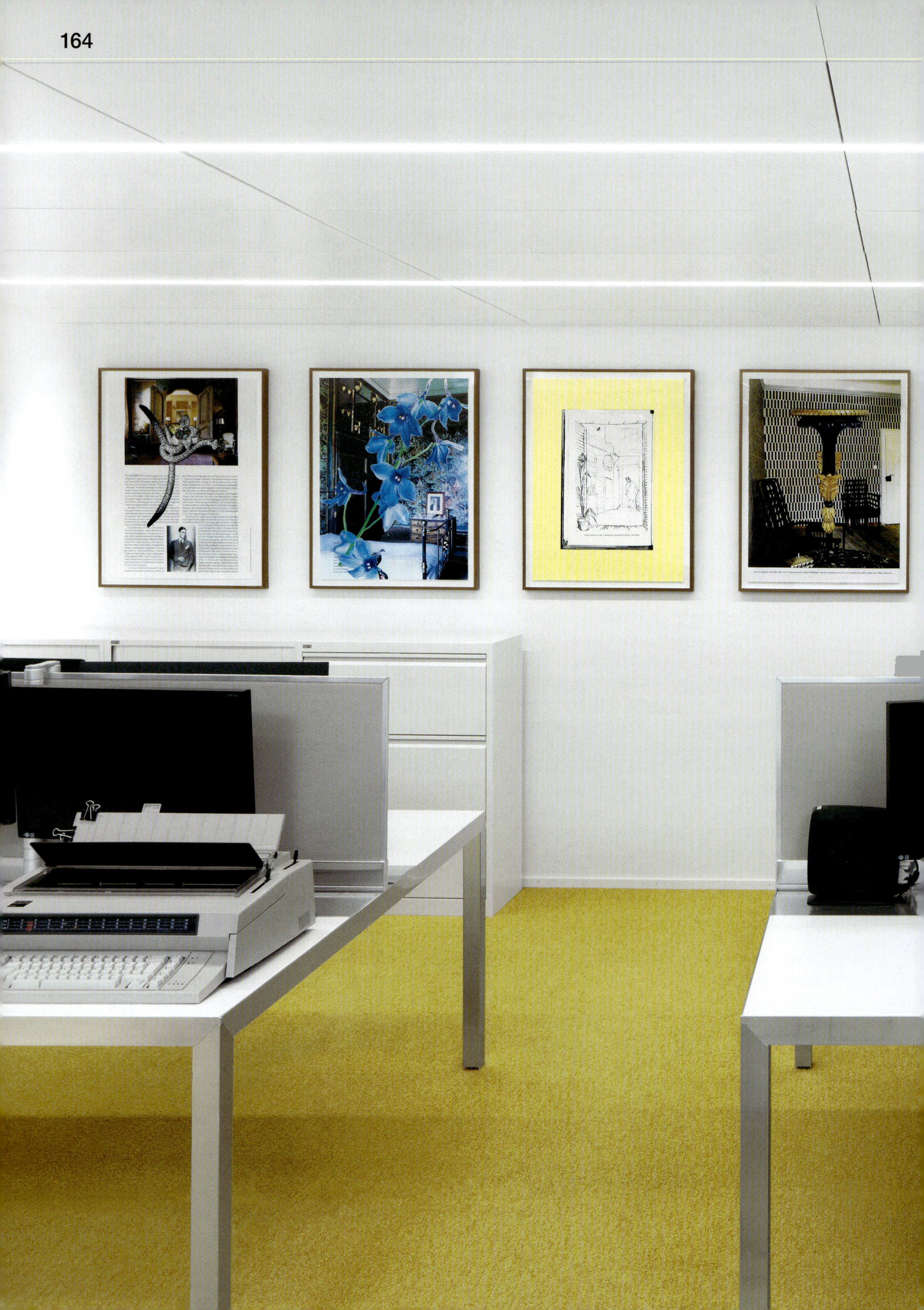

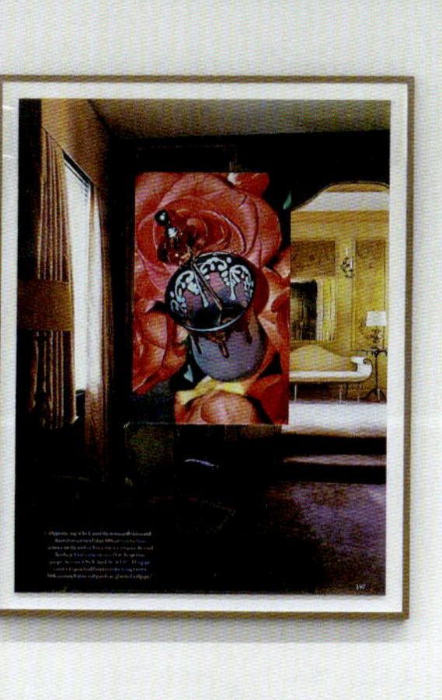

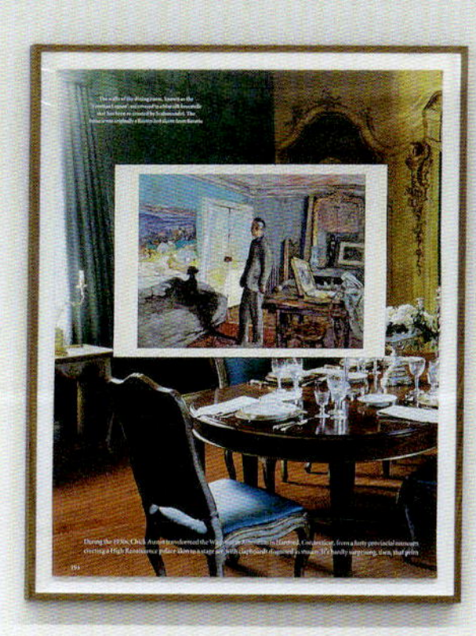

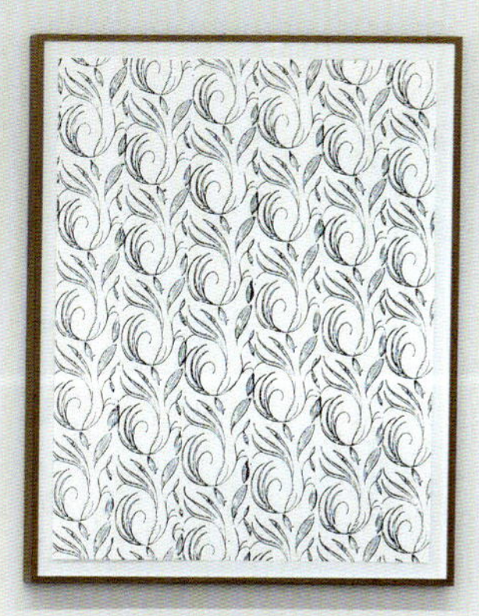

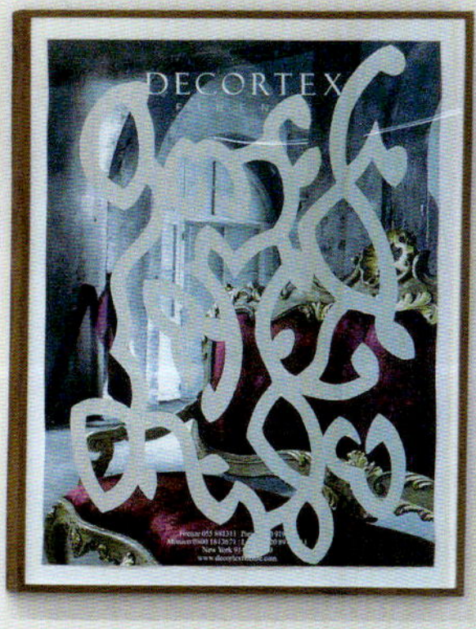
DECORTEX

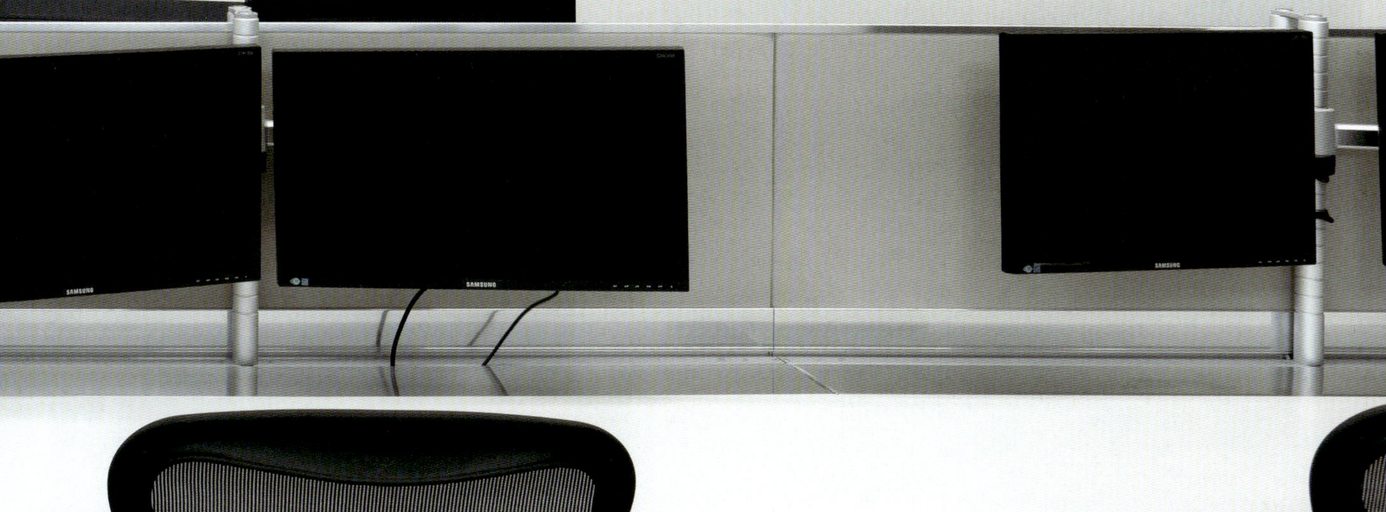

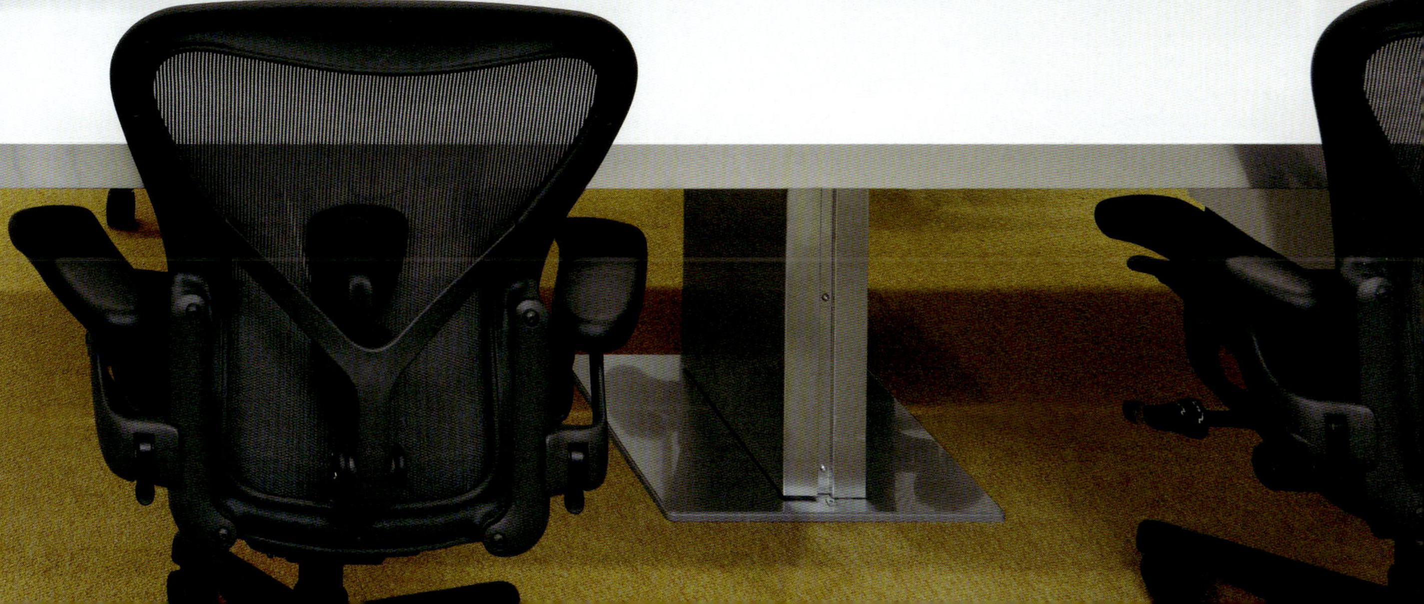

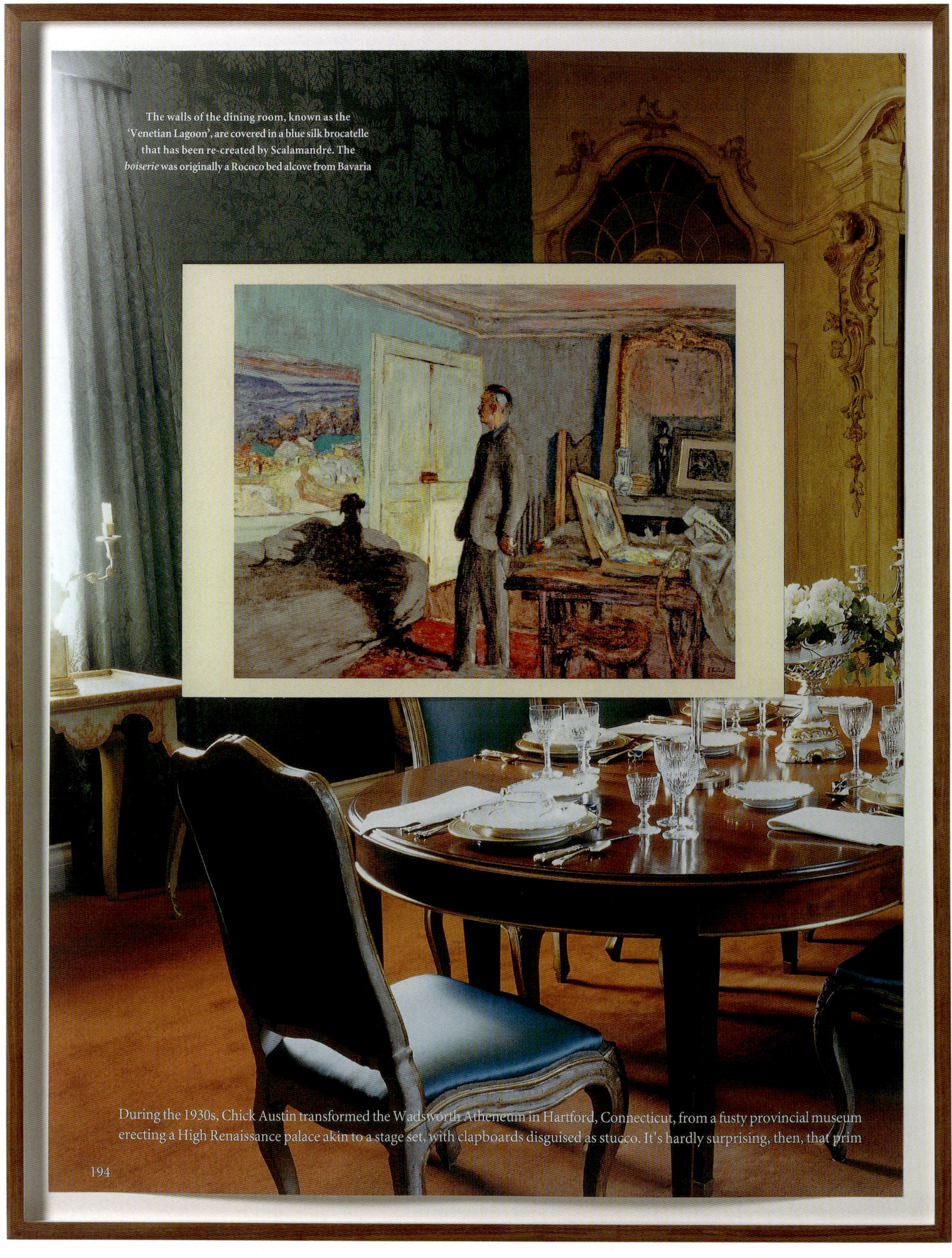

Chapter One, V (World of Interiors), 2008
Hand-printed screen print, offset silkscreen, varnish
89 × 69 cm

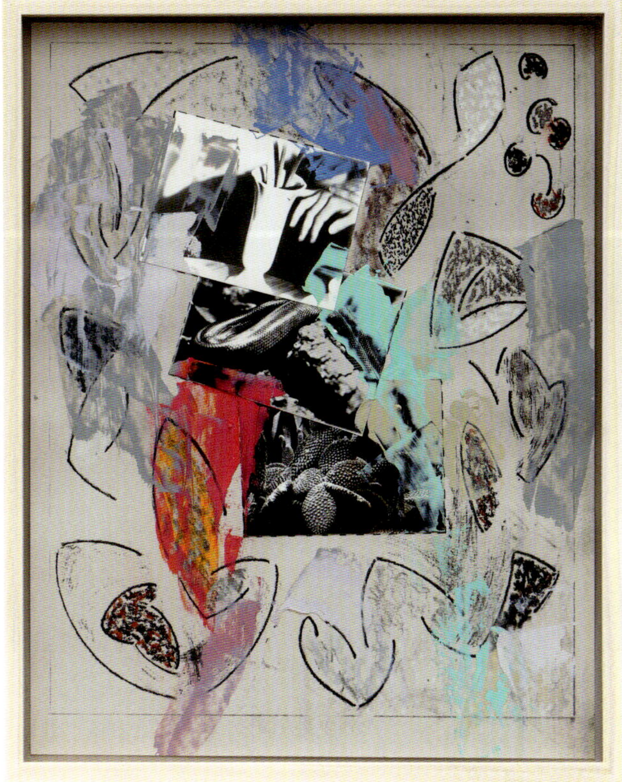

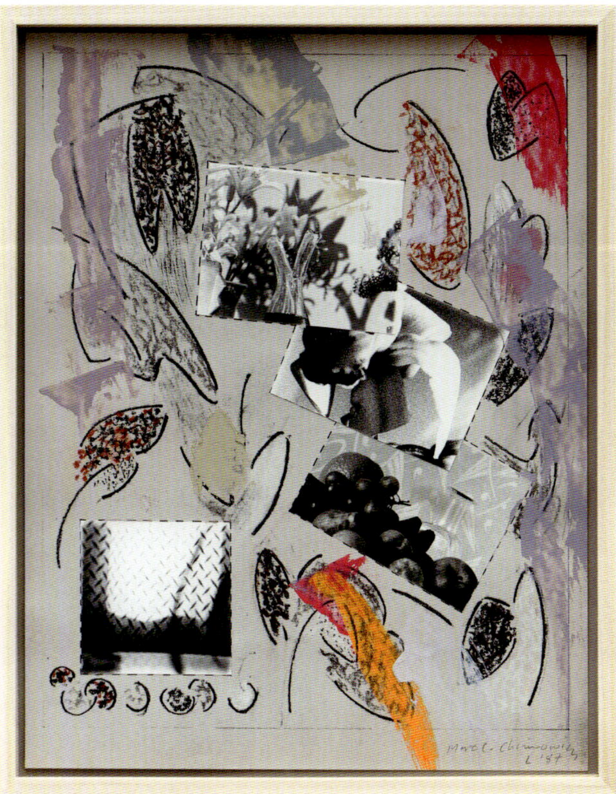

Untitled, 1987
Mixed media on paper
36.2 × 28.6 cm each

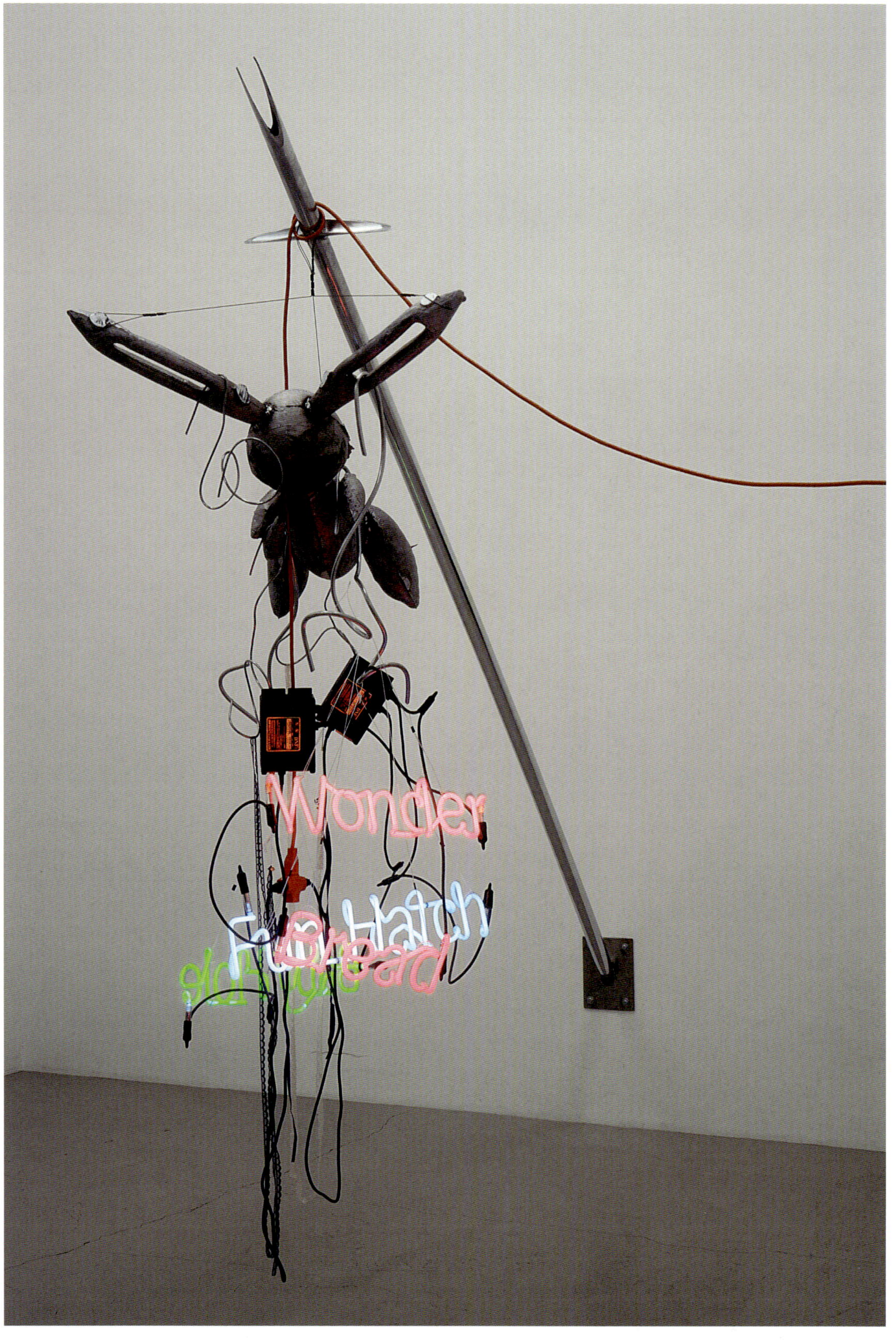

CHANDELIER #8 (Baby Hole, Fun Hatch, Wonder Bread), 2005
Stainless steel spear, mounting board, colored elastic laces,
neon, transformers, metal hooks, aluminum
100 × 64 × 35 cm

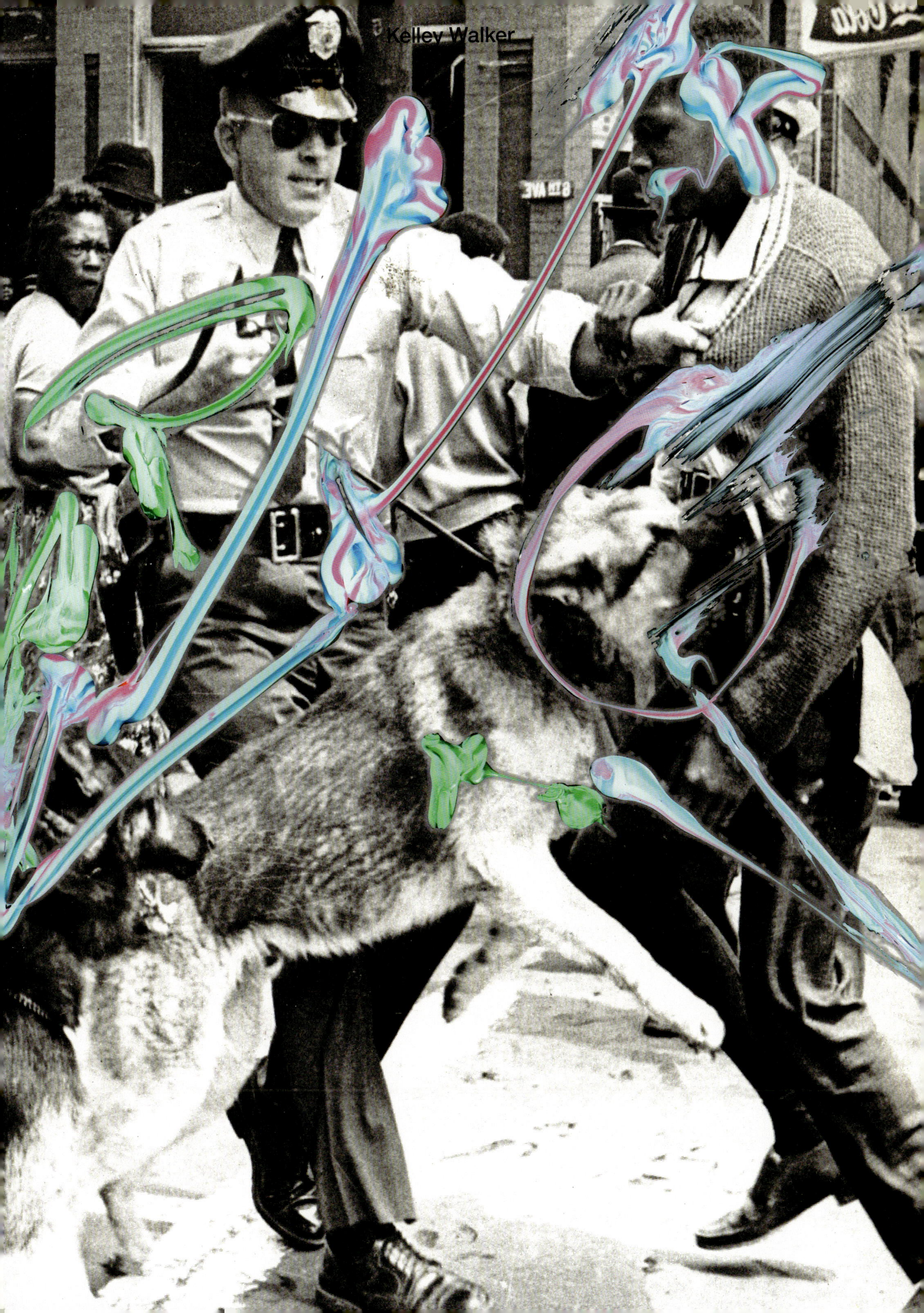
Kelley Walker

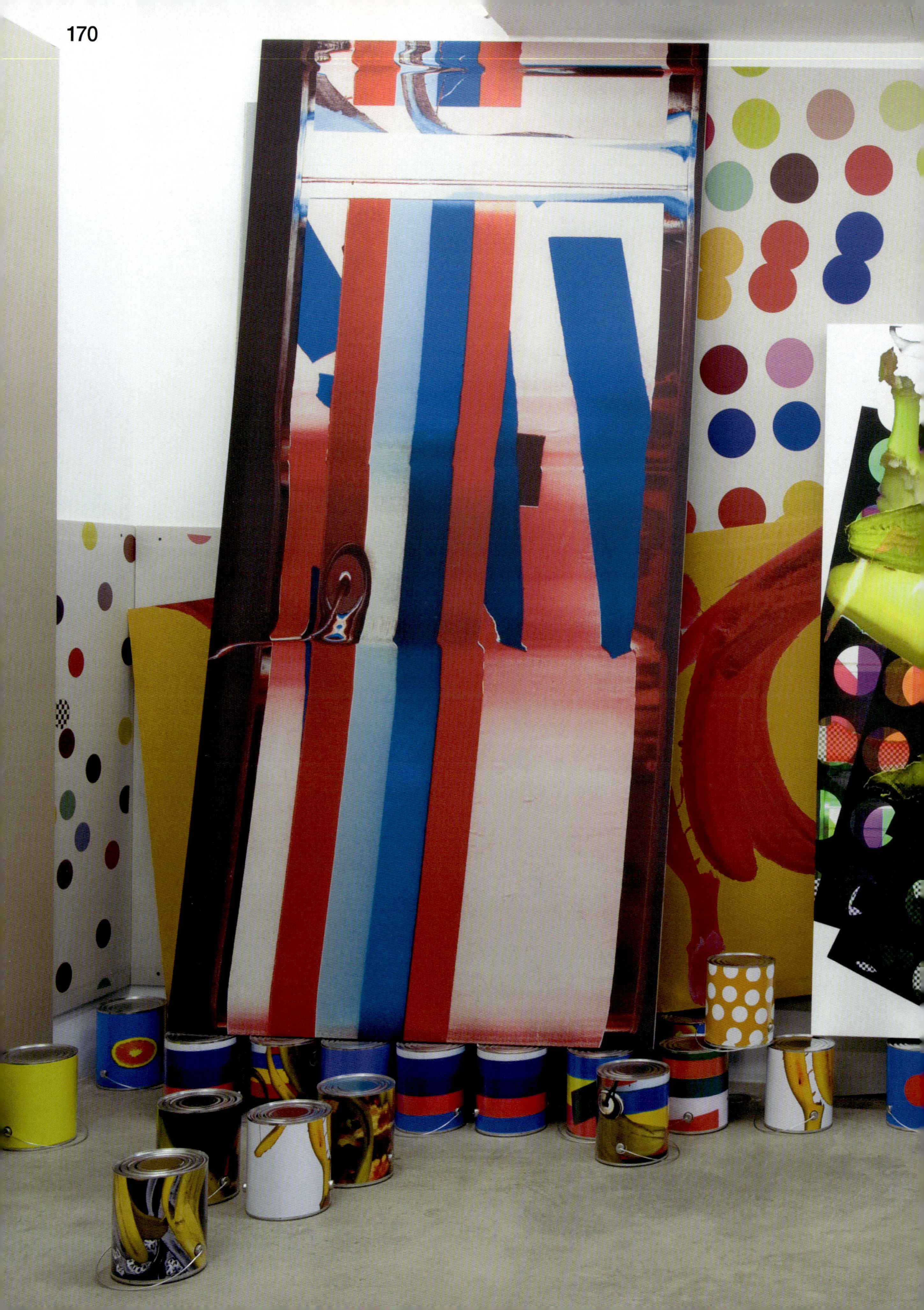

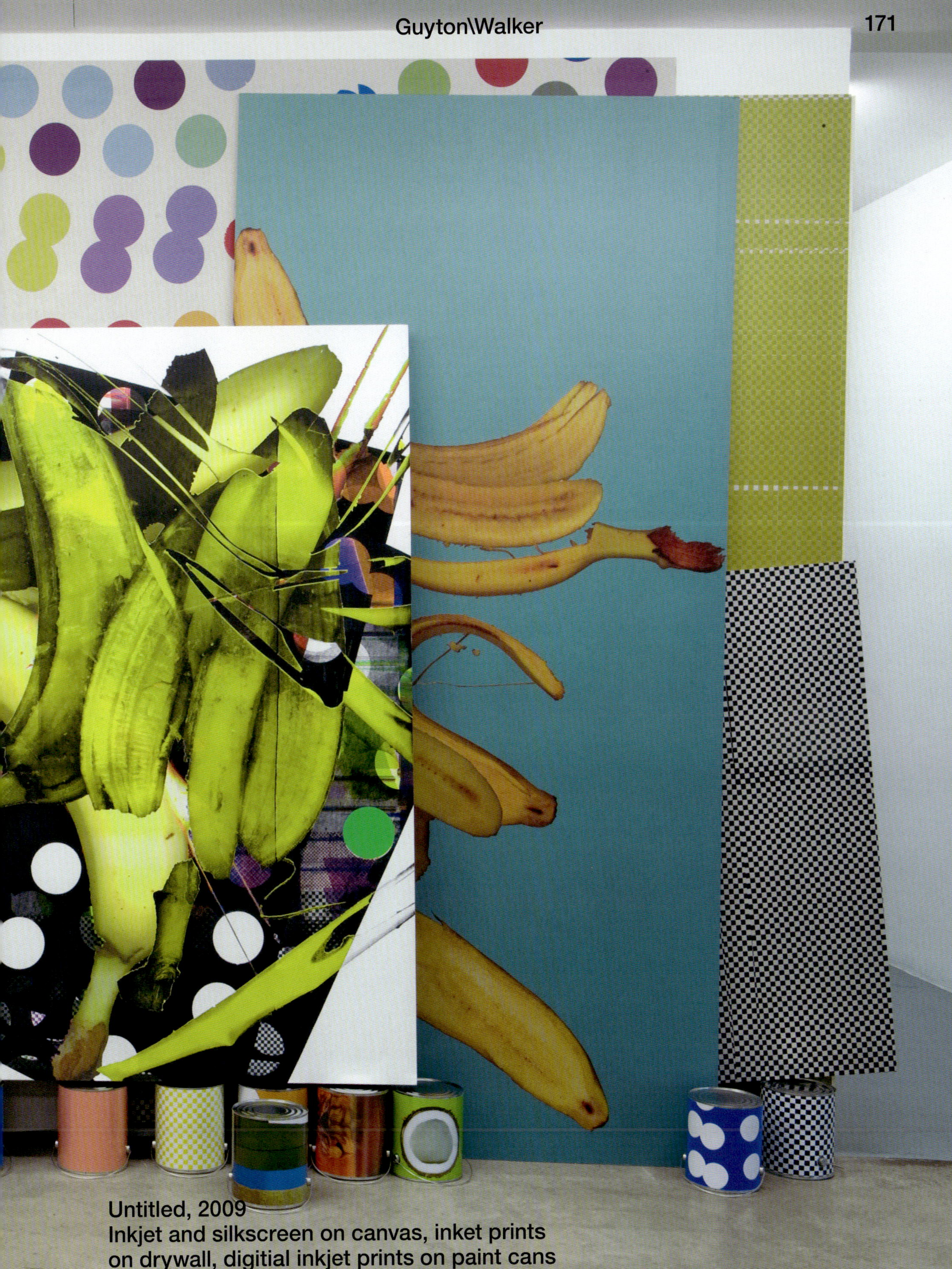

Untitled, 2009
Inkjet and silkscreen on canvas, inket prints on drywall, digitial inkjet prints on paint cans
265 × 538 × 60 cm

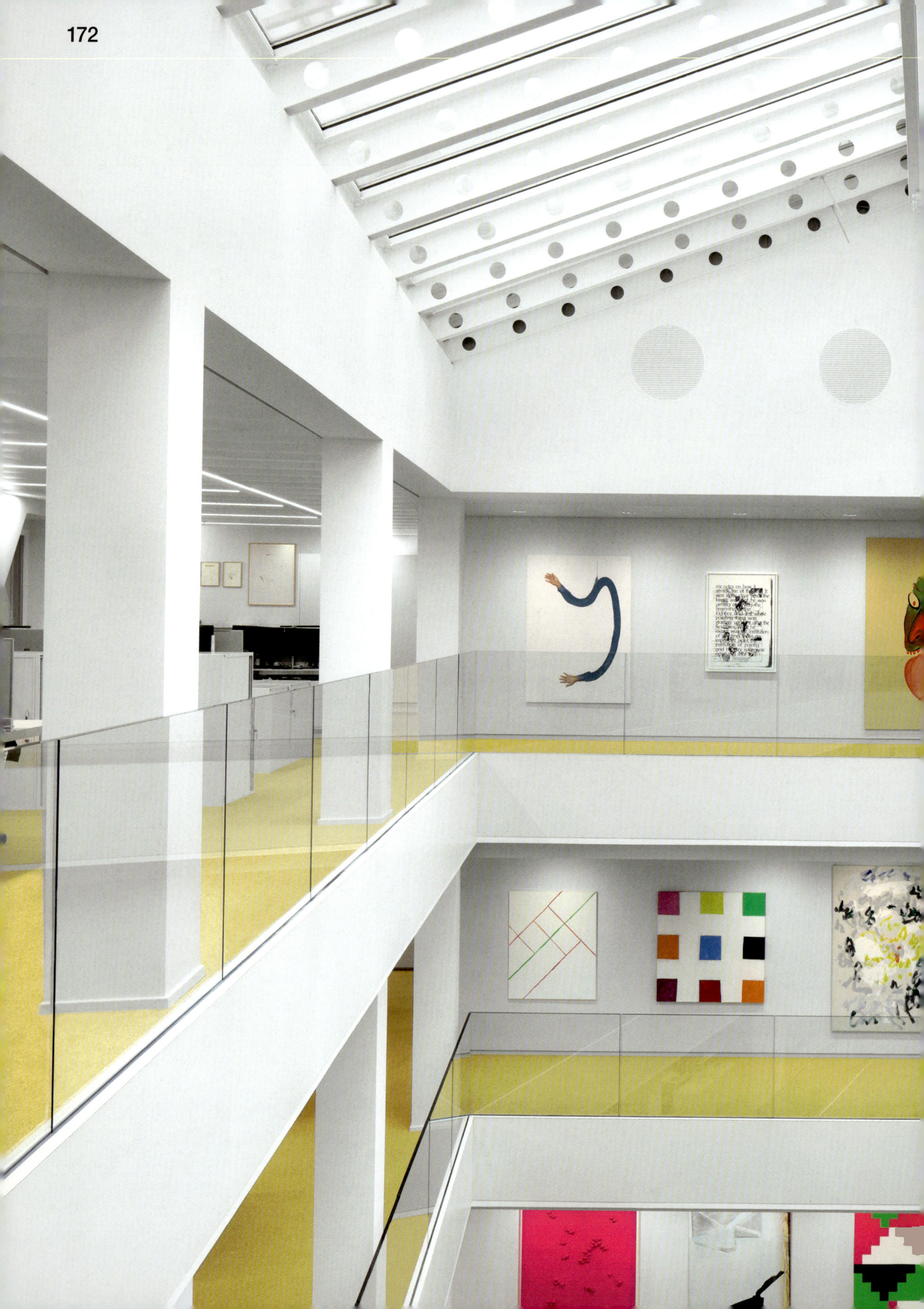

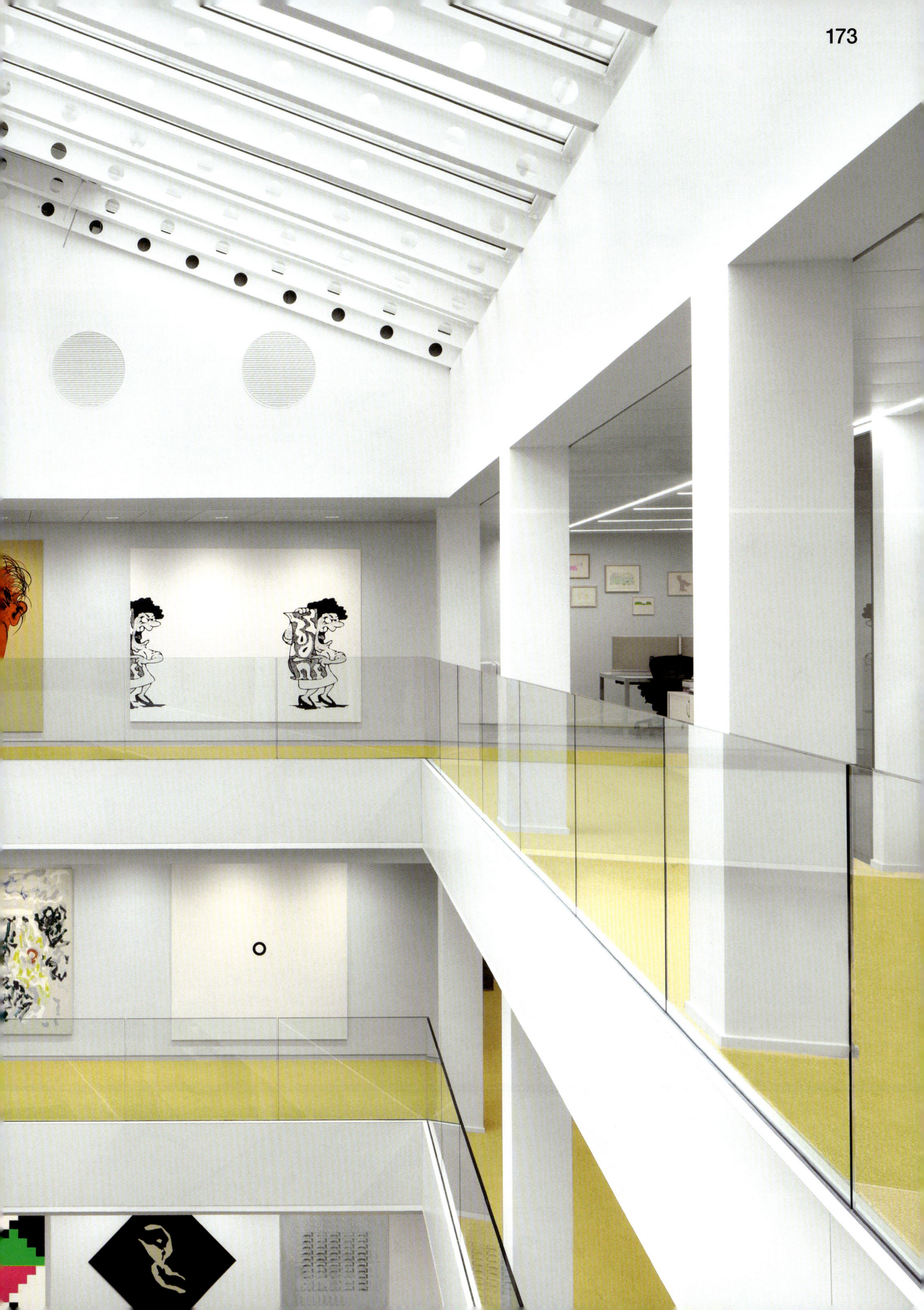

a dream

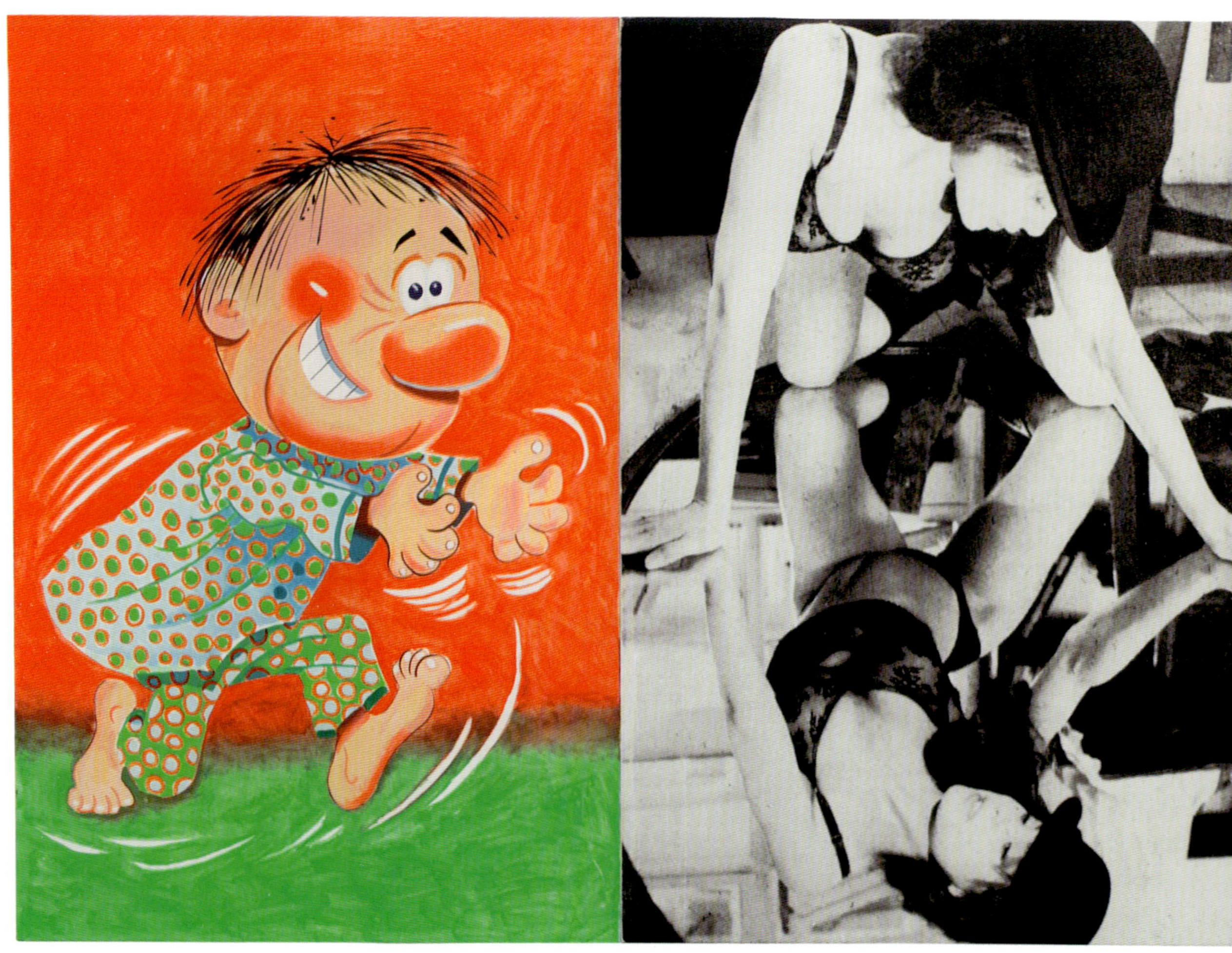

Oil, flash, and lacquer ink on canvas
127 × 355.6 cm

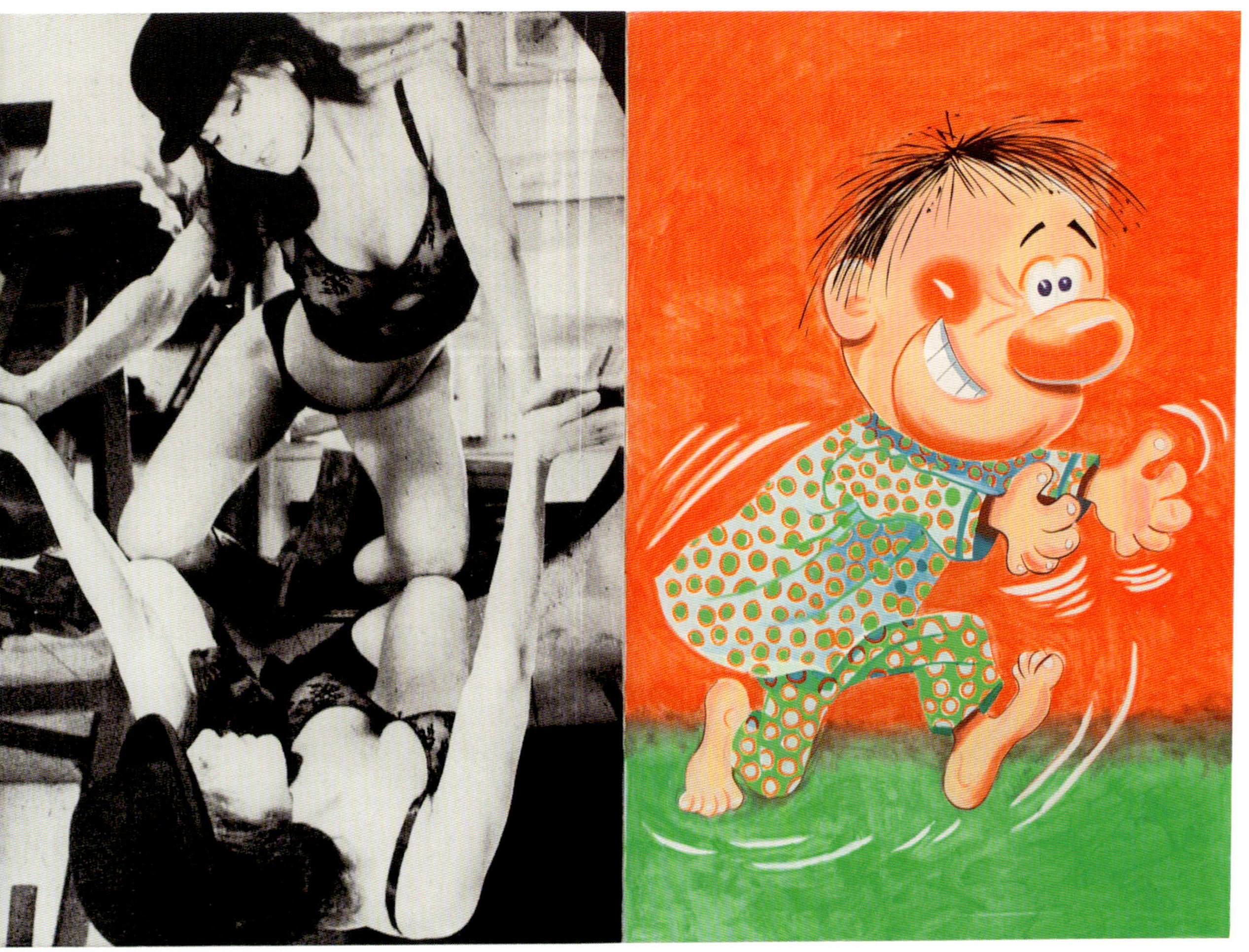

# of symmetry, 1988

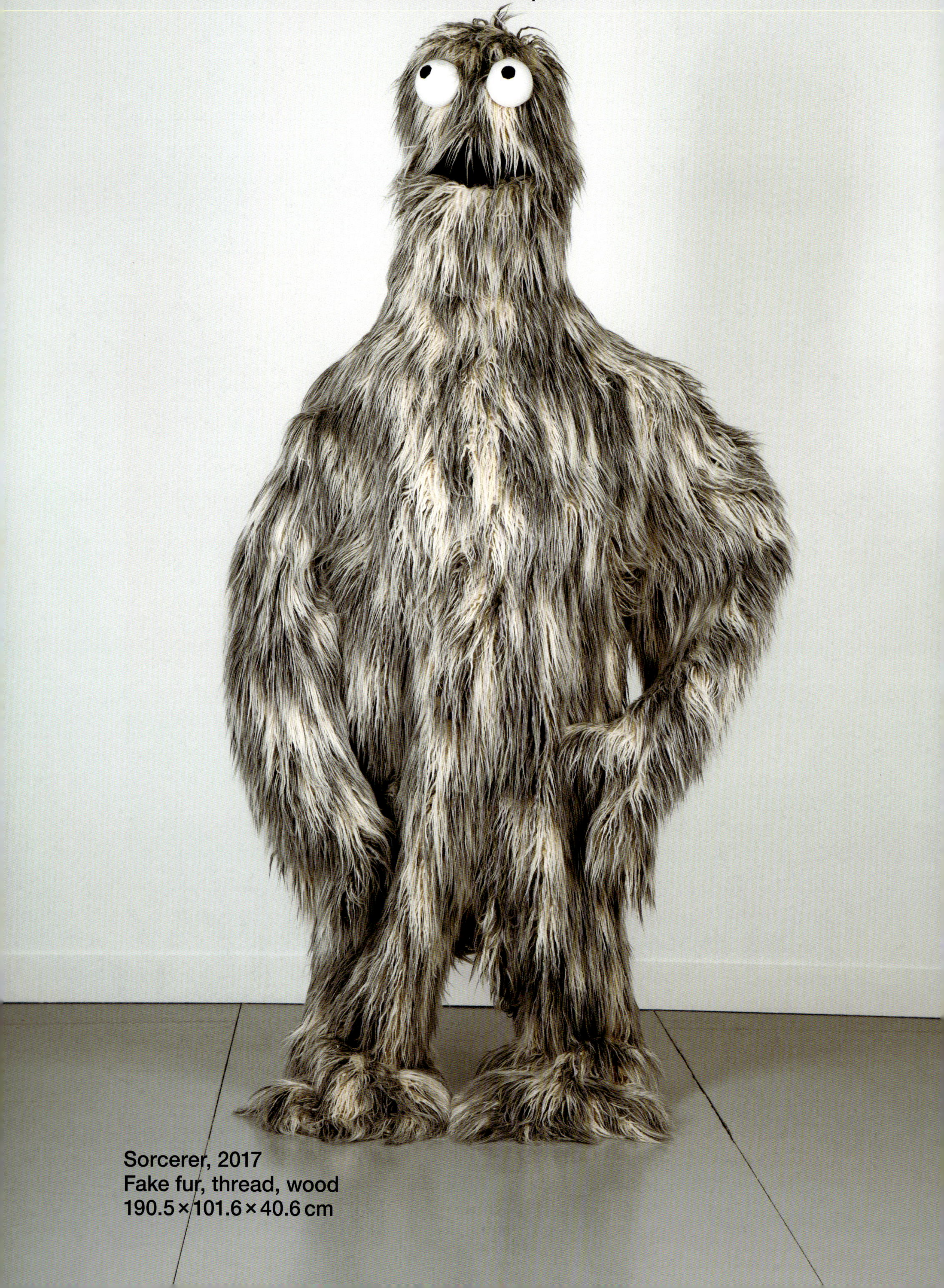

Sorcerer, 2017
Fake fur, thread, wood
190.5 × 101.6 × 40.6 cm

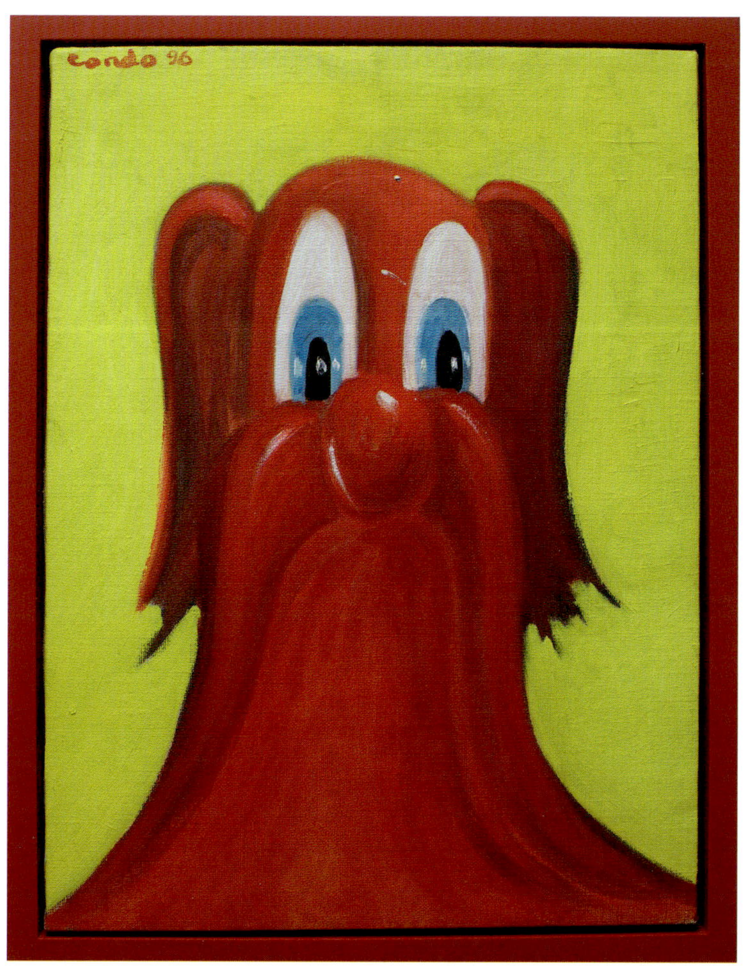

Big Red, 1996
Oil on canvas
40 × 30.5 cm

fred the frog rings the bell, 1990

Wood, nails
130 × 110 × 25 cm

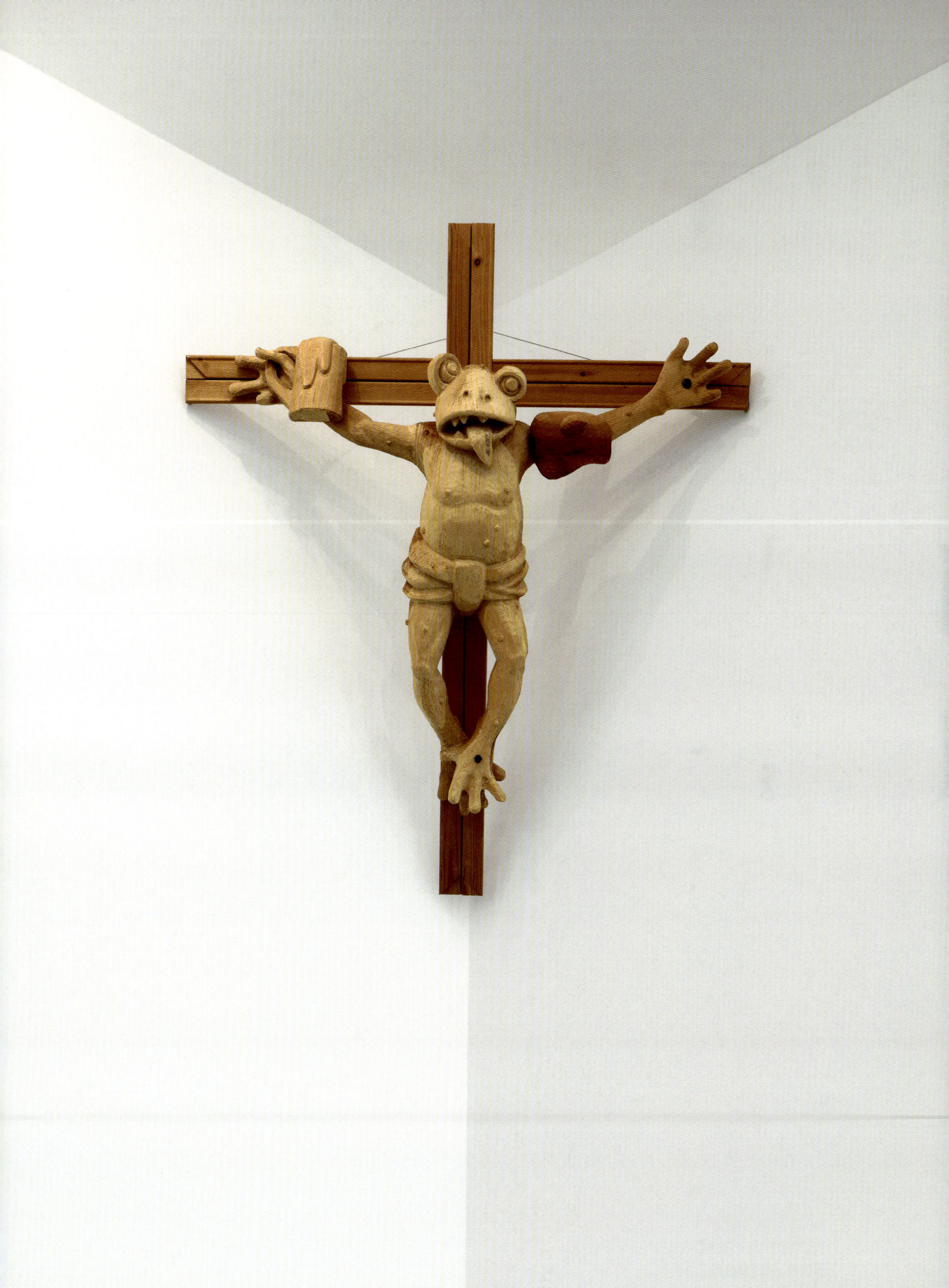

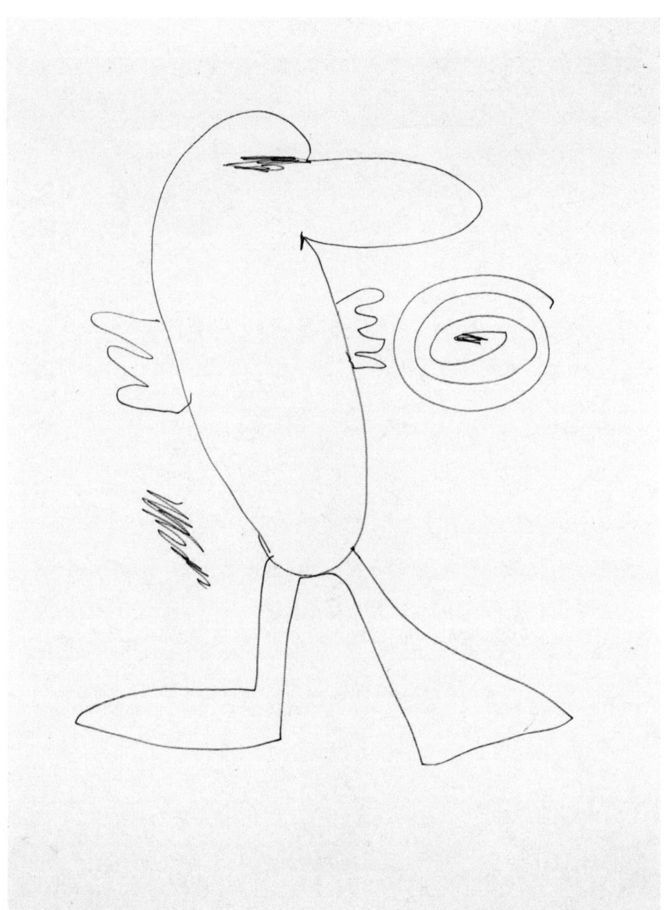

Untitled, 2011
Graphite on paper
80 × 60 cm

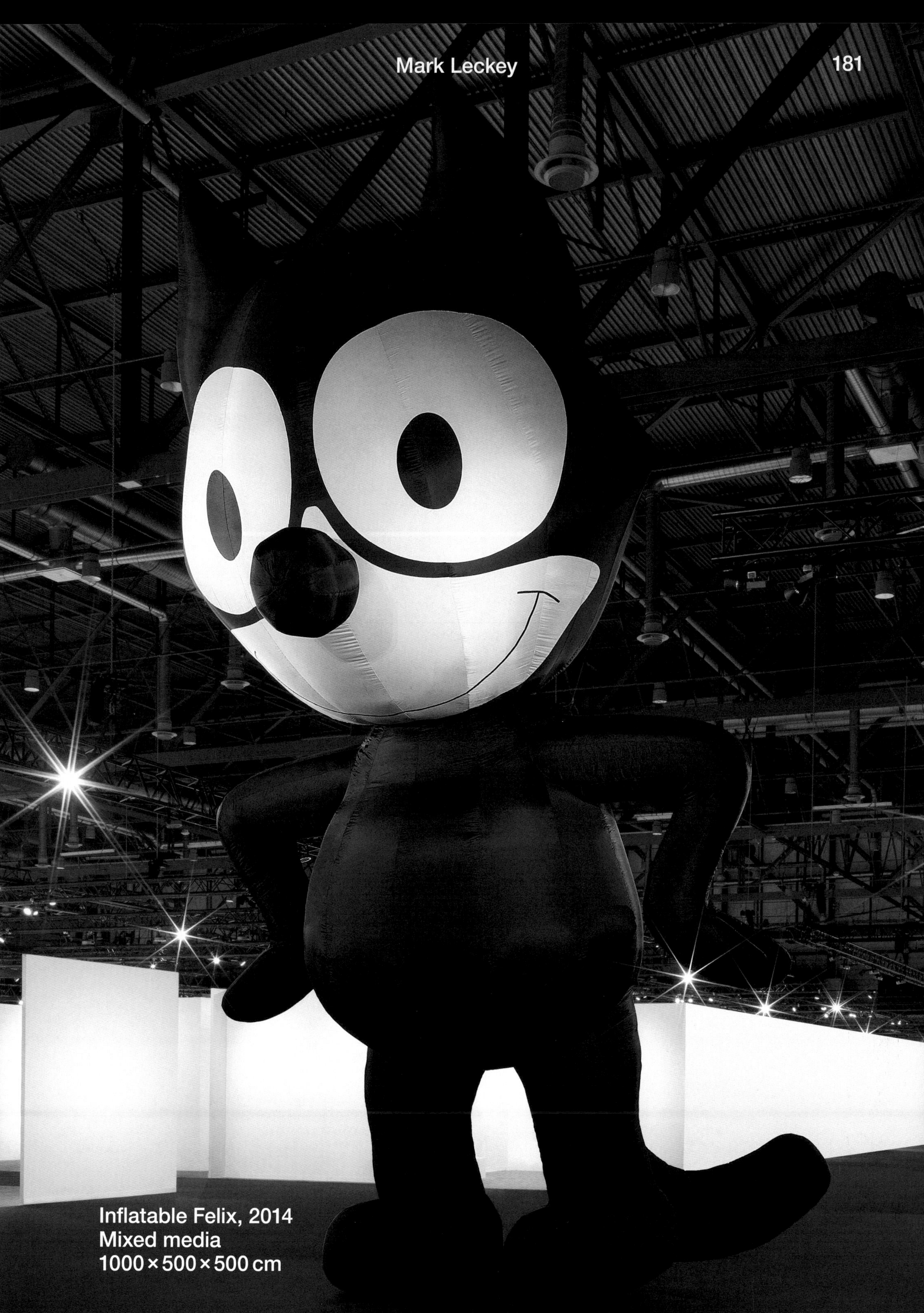

Inflatable Felix, 2014
Mixed media
1000 × 500 × 500 cm

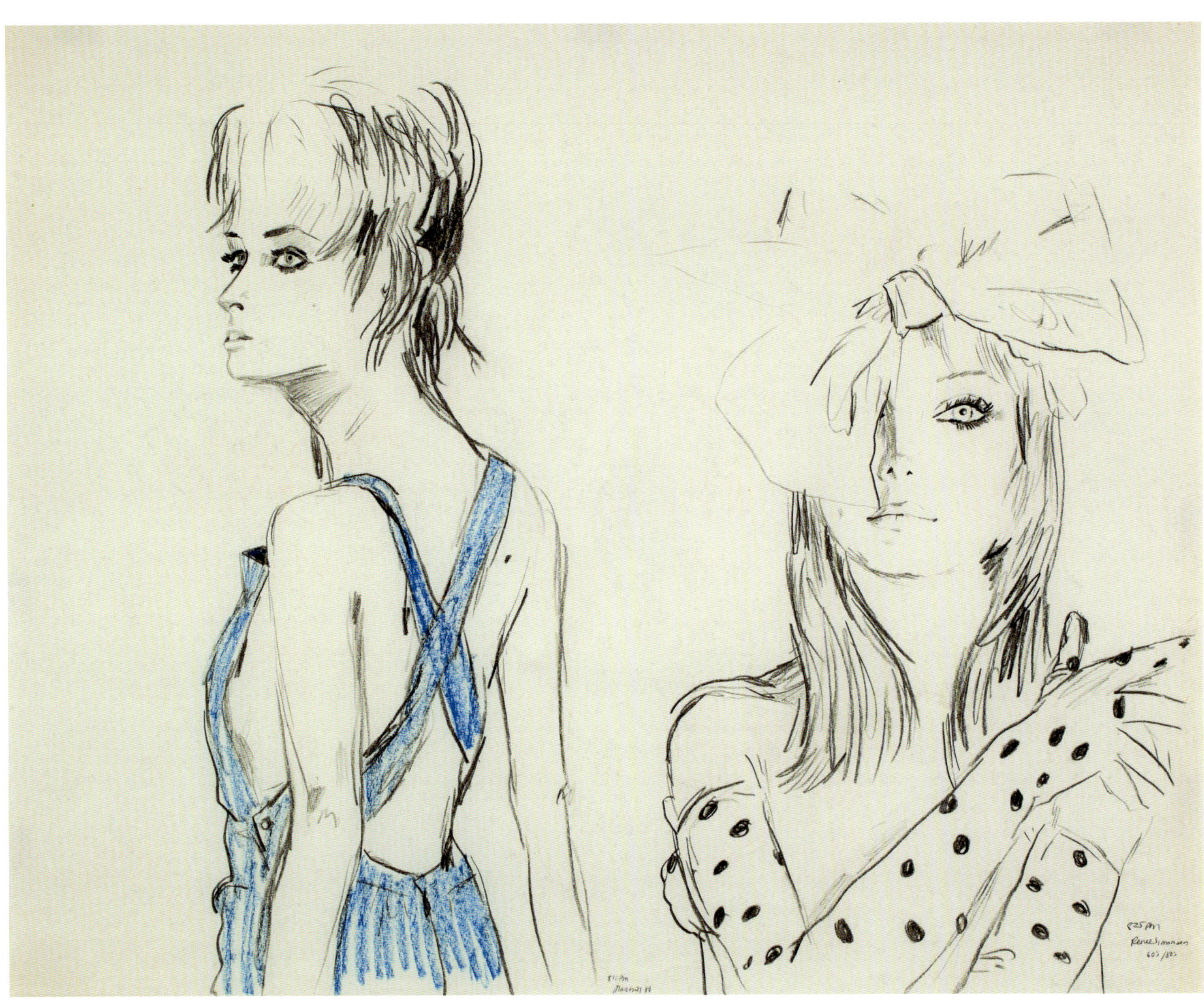

My blue pinafore sundress, 1986
Pencil on paper
58.4 × 73.7 cm

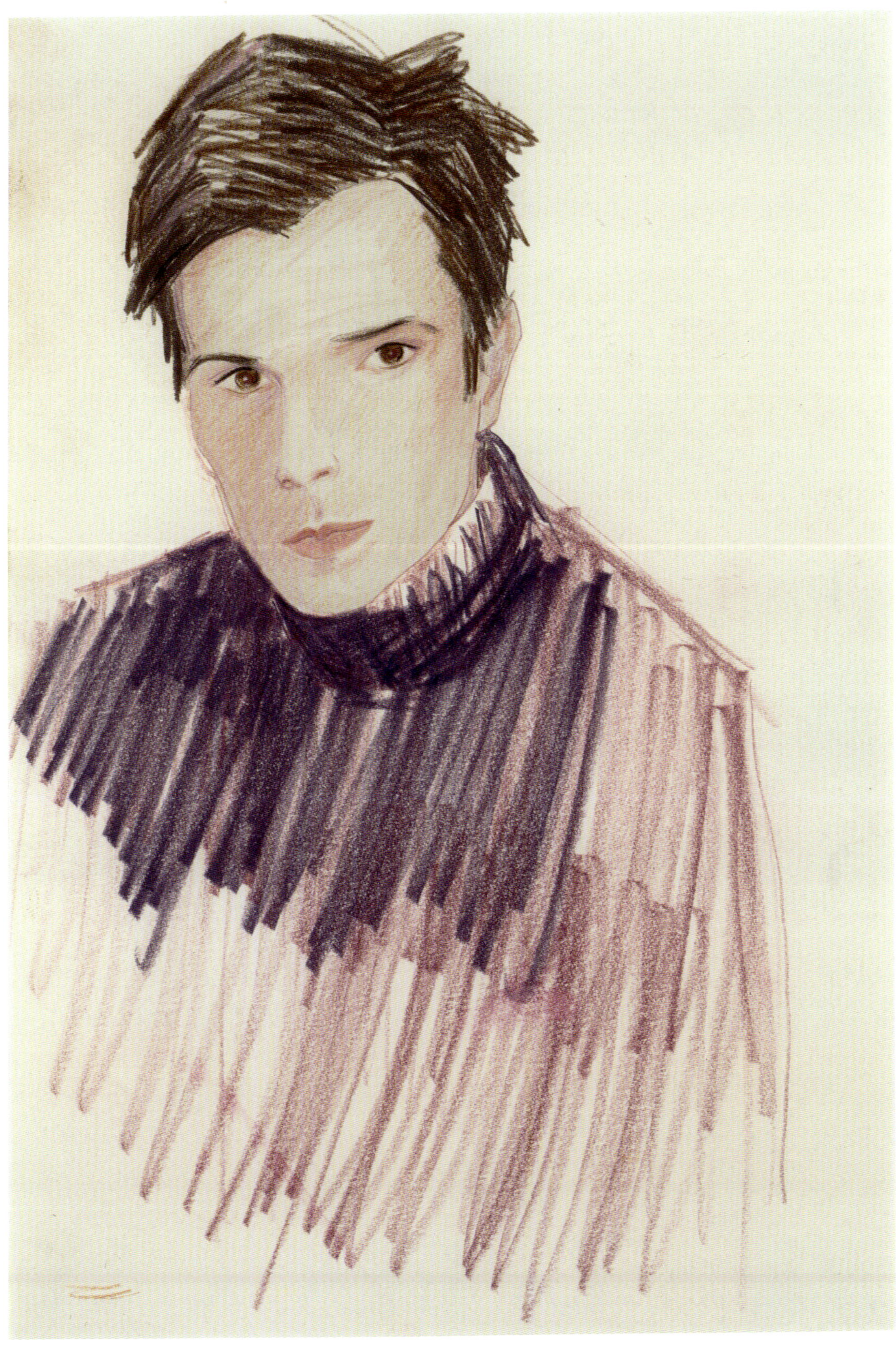

Rob, 1999
Colored pencil on paper
22.3 × 25.3 cm

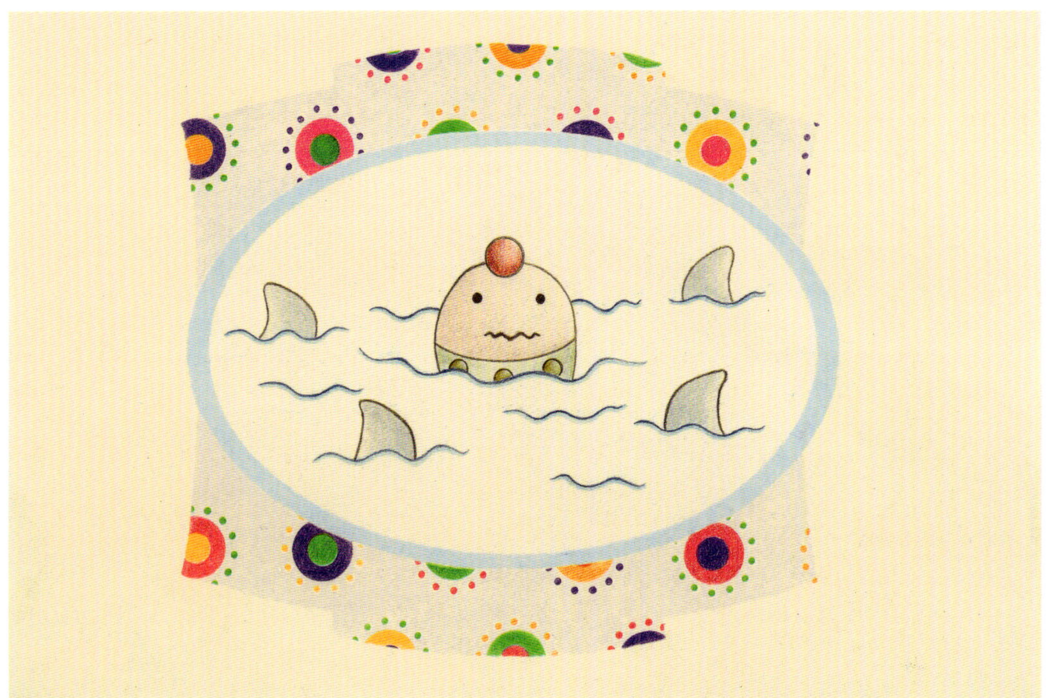

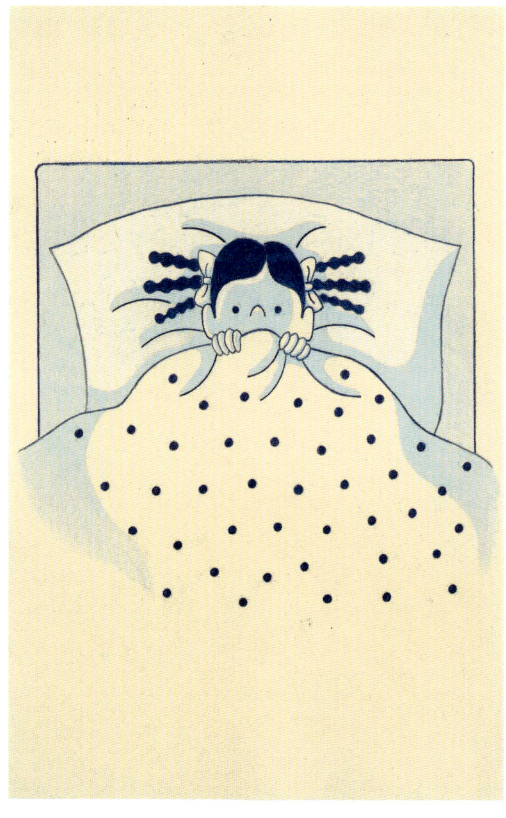

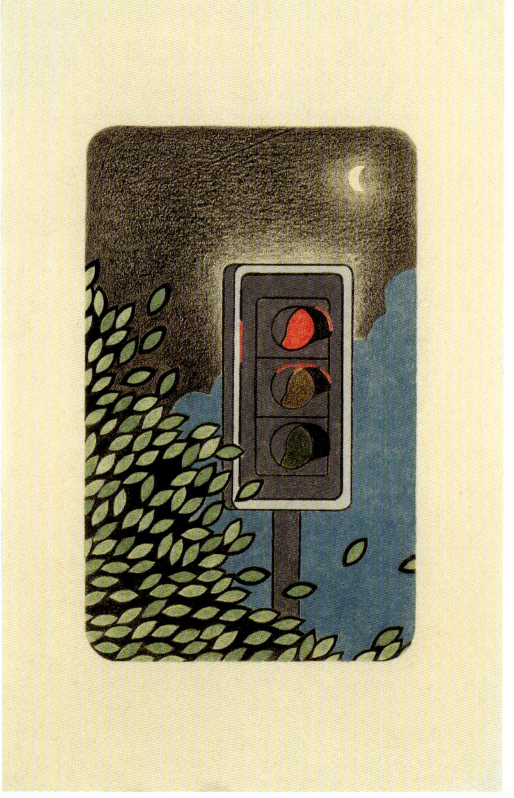

Buddy, you look like you could use a hand, 2016
Colored pencil on paper
27.9 × 43.2 cm

Does fear sleep?, 2016
Colored pencil on paper
43.2 × 27.9 cm

Moonlight, 2016
Colored pencil on paper
43.2 × 27.9 cm

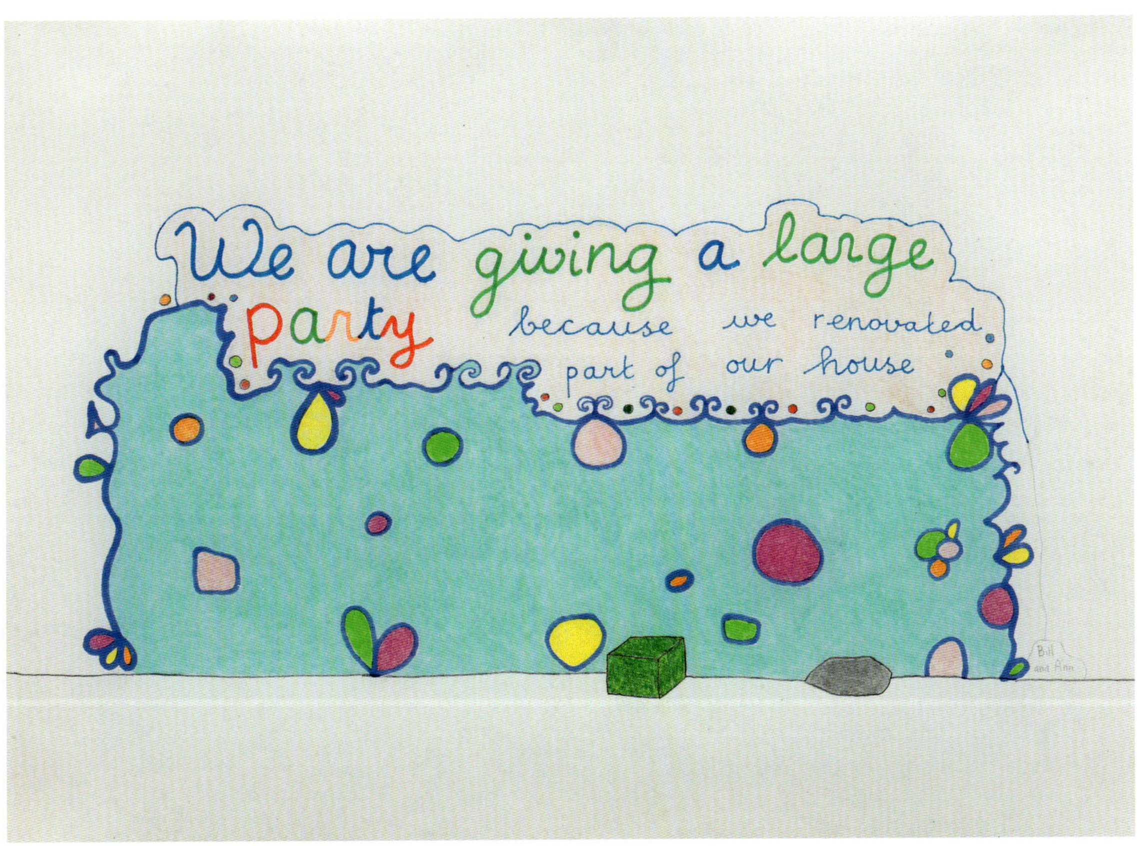

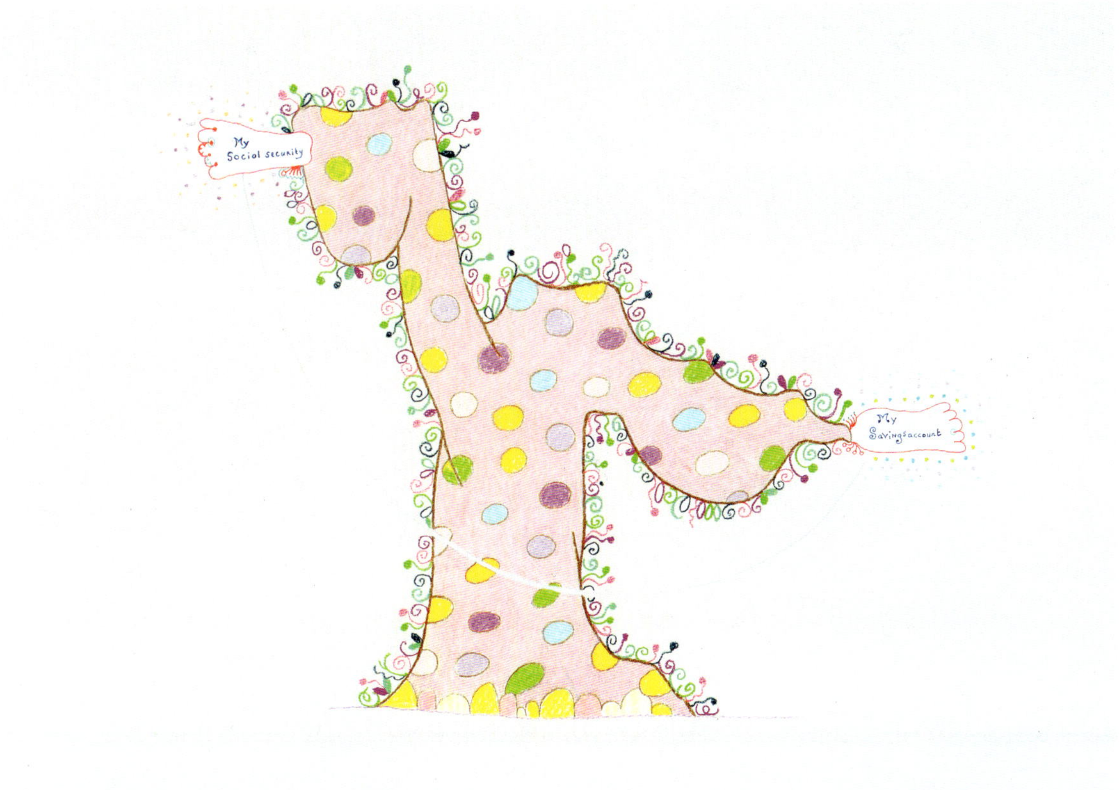

Renovation Party, 2003–2006
Marker and colored pencil on paper
29 × 41.5 cm

Social security saving's account, 2008
Marker and colored pencil on paper
29 × 41.5 cm

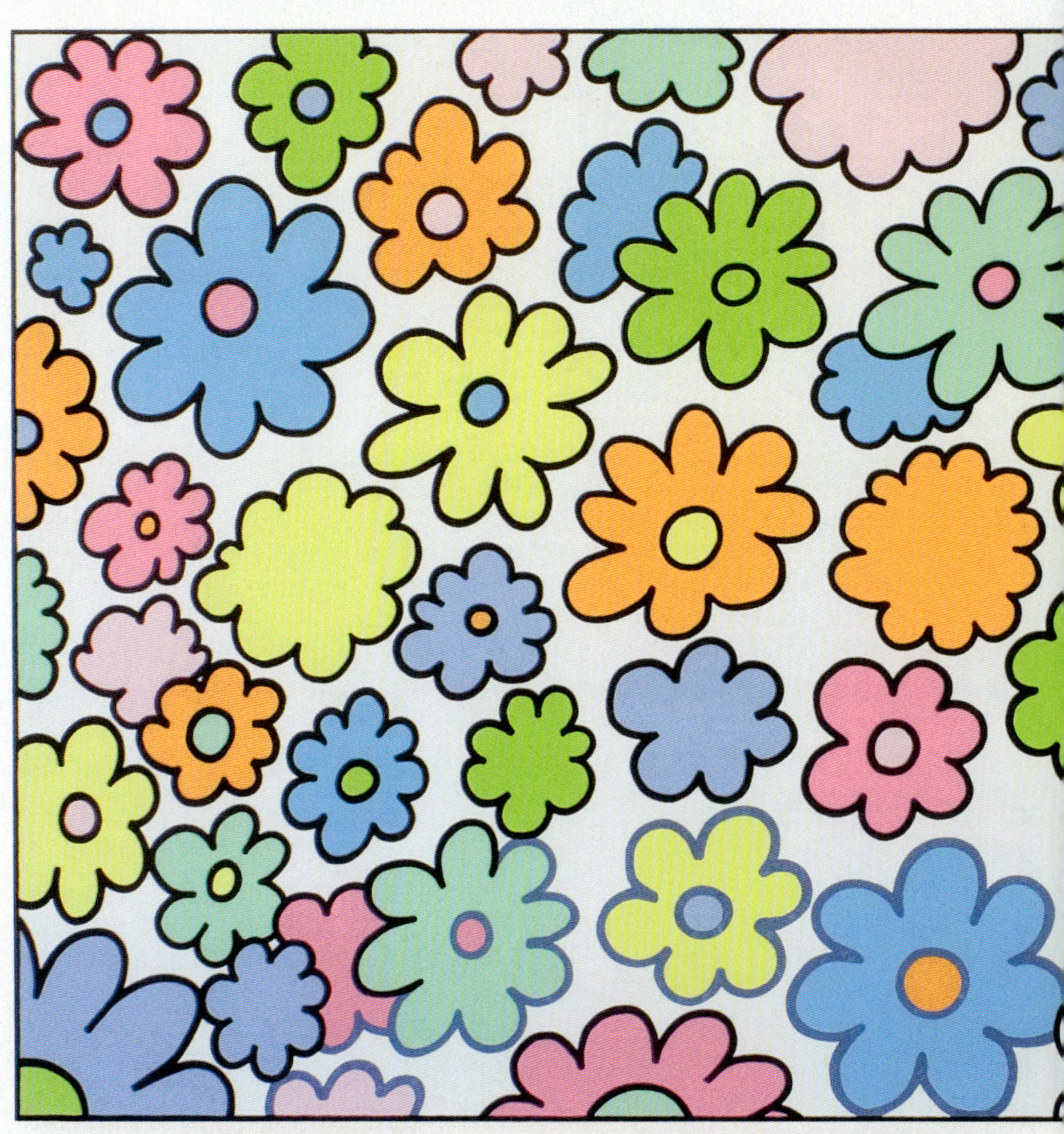

Nothing Really, 2016
Acrylic on canvas
187 × 393 cm

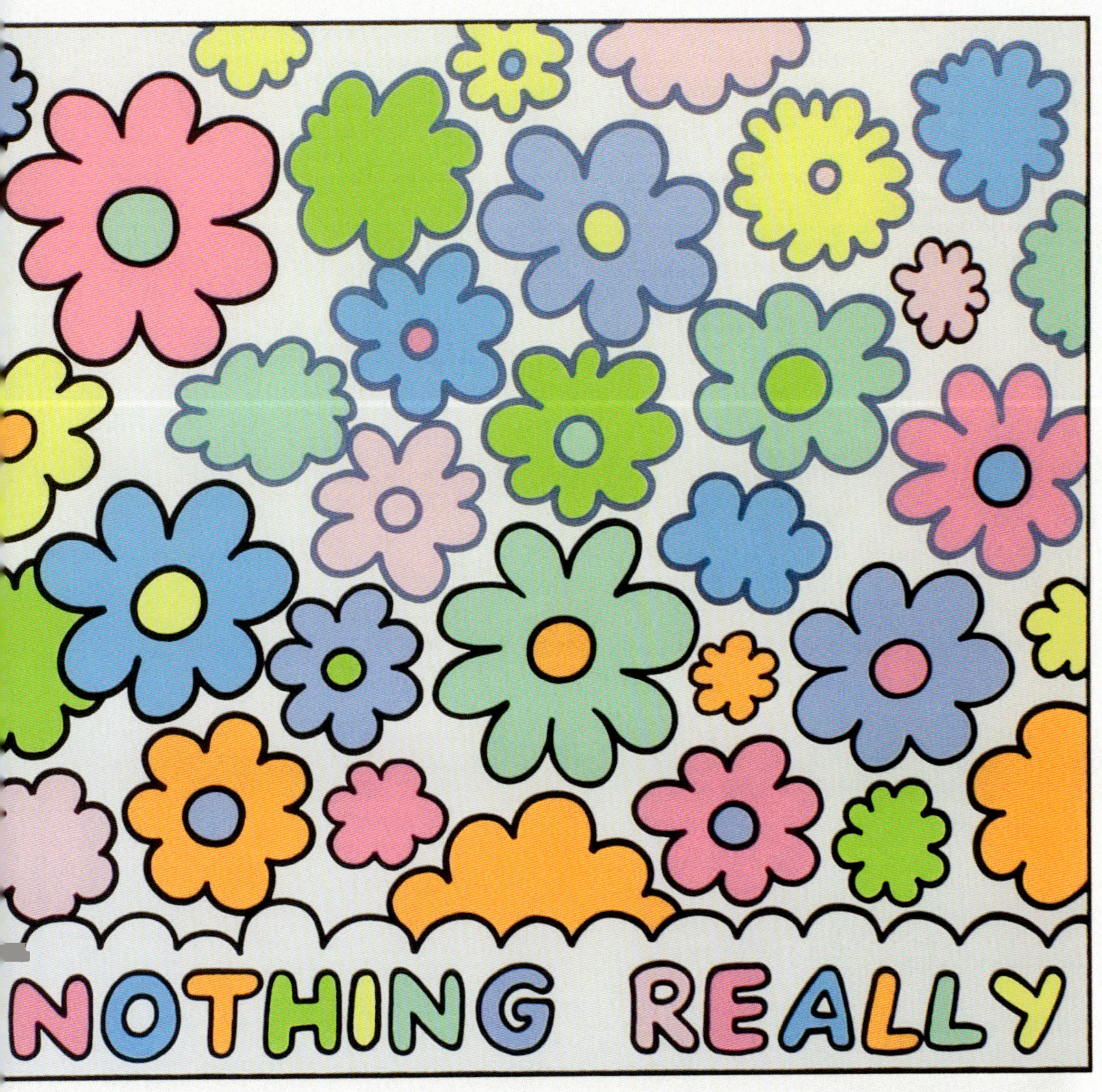
NOTHING REALLY

Atrium

Front cover, pages 3, 34–35, 68, 82–83, 120–121, 152–153, 172–173

Ground floor

Wade Guyton
Untitled, 2014
Altered steel chair
105.4 × 71.1 × 76.2 cm

Rob Pruitt
Esprit de Corps: Bench, 2006–2010
Blue jeans, rebar, cement
139.7 × 254 × 111.8 cm

Wade Guyton
Untitled, 2015
Epson UltraChrome K3 inkjet on linen
325 × 275 cm

Isa Genzken
Schauspieler, 2013
Mannequin, stool, shoes, wig, wood, fabric, plastic, metal
Dimensions variable

Richard Artschwager
Table Prepared in the Presence of Enemies II, 1992
Wood, metal, screws, formica
125.5 × 207.3 × 57.2 cm

First floor

Valentin Carron
Bleue bleue brune infâme, infâme, 2009
Styrofoam, fiberglass, wood, resin, metal, acrylic paint
220 × 220 × 30 cm

John Armleder
Of a Fisherman's Arrow, 2014
Mixed media on canvas
320 × 270 × 10.5 cm

Alex Israel
Untitled (Flat), 2011
Acrylic on stucco, wood and aluminum frame
259.1 × 152.4 cm

Second floor

Matthew Lutz-Kinoy
Horse illusion unhinged, 2016
Acrylic on unprimed canvas
173 × 285 cm

Laura Owens
Untitled, 2014
Oil, charcoal, gesso on linen
175.3 × 152.4 cm

Carsten Höller
Canary (2), (1), (7), (3), (5), 2009
Gravures in gold on paper
108 × 78 cm each

Third floor

Mathieu Malouf
This is the night when Christ broke the prison-bars of death and rose victorious from the underworld, 2017
Acrylic, pigment, and mushrooms on canvas
150 × 130 cm

Seth Price
Medium, 2014
Screenprint, acrylic, pigmented acrylic polymer, gesso on plywood
138.4 × 114.9 × 1.3 cm

General Idea
Ziggurat, 1986
Acrylic on canvas
160 × 160 × 6 cm

Seth Price
Untitled, 2016
UV-cured inkjet on dibond
119.4 × 119.4 cm

Antek Walczak
Culture XCIV, 2017
Silkscreen on aluminum sheet
160 × 120 × 3.2 cm

Fourth floor

Michael Krebber
Cartouche Painting N° 8, 2017
Acrylic on canvas
120 × 100 cm

Mary Heilmann
Cabrillo, 1995
Oil on canvas
122 × 122 cm

Christian Lindow
Gelbe Blume 4, 1980
Acrylic on canvas
183 × 220 cm

Olivier Mosset
Untitled, 1967
Acrylic on canvas
200 × 200 cm

Fifth floor

Eliza Douglas
You were built to burn, 2016
Oil on canvas
165 × 120 cm

Michael Krebber
Untitled (52), 2007
Acrylic and lacquer on canvas
105 × 75 cm

Calvin Marcus
Me with tongue, 2016
Oil stick, Cel-vinyl, liquid water color, emulsified gesso on linen/canvas blend
212.1 × 151.1 × 3.8 cm

Oliver Osborne
The Cloth Seller, 2014
Acrylic and silkscreen on linen
194 × 263 cm

Flyleaves

Trisha Donnelly
Untitled, 2014
Video in loop, 3’20
Dimensions variable

p. 3 (foreground)

Isa Genzken
Schauspieler, 2013
Mannequin, stool, shoes, wig, wood, fabric, plastic, metal
Dimensions variable

p. 4–5

Peter Fischli David Weiss
Untitled, 2010
Polyurethane
120 × 80 × 20 cm

Lutz Bacher
Camel, 2016
Mixed media
270 × 262 × 75 cm

Kerstin Brätsch
Unstable Talismanic Rendering [Psychotrops] with gratitude to master marbler Dirk Lange, 2016
Ink and solvent on paper
274.3 × 182.9 cm

p. 6–7

Tobias Madison
0, 2013
Paper towels, glue, metal
98 × 120 × 120 cm

John Armleder
Untitled (Furniture Sculpture), 1998
Wood, leather, acrylic on canvas
320 × 120 × 62 cm

Peter Fischli David Weiss
Untitled (Rio, Air France Jumbo), 1989–1998
C-print
124 × 185 cm

p. 14–15

Stephen Prina
Untitled, Exquisite Corpse: The Complete Paintings of Manet 248 of 556, Parisienne (Robe à Traine), (Parisienne) (Dress with a Train), 1875? Nationalmuseum, Stockholm, 2015
Cord, brass escutcheon pins
200.3 × 135.3 cm (left), 76.8 × 93 cm (right)

Judith Hopf
Exhausted Vase no. 8, 2009
Ceramic, lacquer
38.5 × 27.5 × 27.5 cm

Lutz Bacher
Dragon, 2012
Mixed media,
91.5 × 91.5 × 107 cm

p. 21

Rosemarie Trockel
Ostblock 2, 2009
Ceramic
72 × 72 × 21 cm

David Ostrowski
F (Between Two Ferns), 2013
Acrylic, lacquer, paper and cotton on canvas, wood
241 × 191 cm

p. 24–25

Günther Förg
Untitled, 1989
Acrylic on lead on wood
200 × 160 cm

p. 40–41 (background, left)

General Idea
PLA©EBO, 1991
Acrylic on wood
12.5 × 31.5 × 6.25 cm each

p. 46–47

Günther Förg
Untitled, 1990
Fabric on canvas
200 × 100 cm

Willem de Rooij
Untitled for Now (Pink), 2012
Unbleached linen and cotton on wood stretcher
215 × 135 × 5 cm

p. 56–57

Carol Rama
Guardiamo oltre…, 1966
Mixed collage on wood
60 × 60 cm

David Hominal
Untitled, 2015
Oil on canvas
220 × 180 cm

p. 60–61

John Baldessari
Object (with Flaw), 1988
Lithograph on three sheets of Somerset and Arches 88 cut paper and Plexiglas
142.2 × 257.8 cm

p. 72–73

Michael Krebber
Fanatic 274, 2011
Surfboard, lacquer, polystyrene, plastic
57 × 540 cm

p. 101

Rosemarie Trockel
Lisa, 1993
Photographs (6 parts)
100 × 75 cm each

p. 104

Juergen Teller
Joan Didion, Céline Campaign Spring Summer 2015, New York 2014, 2015
Lightjet C-print
177.8 × 127 cm

p. 105

Sylvie Fleury
A Royal Salute British Vogue December 2001, 2001–2002
C-print on aluminum
160 × 120 cm

p. 110

Anonymous
Historic African currencies, 19th century
Metal
Dimensions variable

p. 114–115

Sherrie Levine
After Edward Curtis 1–5, 2005
Photographs
48 × 33 cm each

p. 134–135

Cindy Sherman
Bus Riders (1–15), 1976–2000
Photographs
25.4 × 20.3 cm each

p. 140–141

Louise Lawler
Statue Before Painting, Perseus with the Head of Medusa, Canova, 1983
Photograph with text on mat
48.9 × 39.4 cm
She Wanted to Know More About this Statue, 1997–1998
Photograph with text on mat
33 × 26.6 cm
Hey!, 2012
Silver gelatin print with text on mat, 51.4 × 40 cm
A Pencil, 1991
Cibachrome with text on mat
41 × 35.5 cm
Skin from Angola, bought in Portugal, 2001–2010
Silver gelatin print with printed mat
36.2 × 29.2 cm

p. 144–145

Stephen Shore
Paul Morrissey, Edie Sedgwick, Lou Reed, 1965–1967
Photographs (3 parts)
32.4 × 48.3 cm each

Roman Signer
Tisch mit Sandkegel, 1998
C-prints (6 parts)
24 × 36.6 cm each
Nicht loslassen, 1983
Photographs on barrit paper (2 parts), 36 × 24 cm each
Zwei Ballone, 1983
C-prints (3 parts)
24 × 36 cm each
Wassersäule (Fontäne), 1976
Photographs on barrit paper on aluminum (6 parts)
23.4 × 16.4 cm each
Furka, 1993
Cibachromes on aluminum (4 parts)
50 × 75 cm each

p. 150–151

Roman Signer
Tisch mit Sandkegel, 1998
C-prints (6 parts)
24 × 36.6 cm each

p. 156–157

Henri Chopin
The Magic Tower, 1983
Ink on paper
29.6 × 20.7 cm
Le premier, 1987
Ink on paper
29.4 × 20.9 cm
Cerclés, 1983
Ink on paper
29.5 × 21 cm
George Orwell Monument, 1984
Ink on paper
29.7 × 21 cm

p. 160 (center)

Tom Burr
Double murder/suicide, 2013
Record sleeves, pushpins, wood, acrylic paint
120 × 120 cm each

Josef Strau
Samurai Among the Reeds, 2015
Tin, mother of pearl plates, and solder on canvas
120.5 × 80 × 3.5 cm

Jason Loebs
Untitled, 2012
UV-Curable four-color print on gessoed wood pannel
111.8 × 81.3 cm

p. 162–163 (left to right)

Jean Dubuffet
Le Roman burlesque, 1974 (detail)
Vinyl paint on cut-out plywood
Dimensions variable

Ellsworth Kelly
White Curve, Vevey, 1991
Acrylic enamel on composite material mounted on black marble
284.5 × 276.9 × 5.1 cm

Renaud Auguste-Dormeuil
I Was There, Power Black Out, January 30, 2009, Paris, 48°53'02.94"N_02°14'55.25"E", 2009
Lambda print mounted on aluminum
203 × 109 cm

p. 164–165

Marc Camille Chaimowicz
Screen Print VI (World of Interiors), 2008; Chapter One, III (World of Interiors), 2008; Chapter One, II (World of Interiors), 2008; Screen Print V (World of Interiors), 2008; Screen Print VIII

(World of Interiors), 2008; Chapter One, V (World of Interiors), 2008; Screen Print IV (World of Interiors), 2008; Screen Print IX (World of Interiors), 2008
All: hand-printed screen print, offset silkscreen, varnish
89 × 69 cm each

p. 169

Kelley Walker
A Black Star Press Distribution: Aquafresh plus Crest with Tartar Protection, 2002
CD, silkscreen
150 × 111 cm

Flyleaves

Valentin Carron
Untitled, 2006
Styrofoam, fiberglass, resin, acrylic paint
301 × 180.5 × 30.5 cm

Sturtevant
Pacman, 2012
DVD video, 1'15
Dimensions variable

Back cover

Blair Thurman
Gallery-Go-Round, 2010
Acrylic on canvas on wood
134.6 × 139.7 × 12.7 cm

Heimo Zobernig
Untitled, 1986
Black resin, linen, cardboard
60 × 80 × 7 cm

Tom Burr
Double murder/suicide, 2013
Record sleeves, pushpins, wood, acrylic paint
120 × 120 cm each

List of Artists Exhibited at the Quai des Bergues

John Armleder, Richard Artschwager, Lutz Bacher, John Baldessari, Mark Barrow, Martin Barré, Thomas Bayrle, Greg Bogin, Joe Bradley, Kerstin Brätsch, Tom Burr, Timothée Calame, Merlin Carpenter, Valentin Carron, Marc Camille Chaimowicz, Henri Chopin, Guy de Cointet, Thea Djordjadze, Trisha Donnelly, Eliza Douglas, Stan Douglas, Roe Ethridge, Cerith Wyn Evans, Hans-Peter Feldmann, Peter Fischli David Weiss, Sylvie Fleury, Günther Förg, General Idea, Isa Genzken, Wade Guyton, Richard Hambleton, Mary Heilmann, Candida Höfer, Yngve Holen, Carsten Höller, David Hominal, Judith Hopf, Roni Horn, Channa Horwitz, Alex Israel, Larry Johnson, Michael Krebber, Elad Lassry, Louise Lawler, Sherrie Levine, Klara Lidén, Linder, Christian Lindow, Jason Loebs, Matthew Lutz-Kinoy, Tobias Madison, Mathieu Malouf, Calvin Marcus, Paul McCarthy, Henry Moore, Olivier Mosset, Yoan Mudry, Marlie Mul, Oliver Osborne, David Ostrowski, Laura Owens, Martin Parr, Seth Price, Stephen Prina, Rob Pruitt, Sam Pulitzer, Carol Rama, Pipilotti Rist, Willem de Rooij, Thomas Ruff, Anri Sala, Cindy Sherman, Stephen Shore, Roman Signer, Valerie Snobeck, Lily van der Stokker, Josef Strau, Beat Streuli, Sturtevant, Stefan Tcherepnin, Juergen Teller, Blair Thurman, Wolfgang Tillmans, Rosemarie Trockel, Tseng Kwong Chi, Alessandro Twombly, Vincent Vulsma, Antek Walczak, Christopher Williams, Amy Yao, Heimo Zobernig

Photo Credits

Annik Wetter: cover, p. 3, 4–5, 6–7, 8, 14–15, 21, 24–25, 34–35, 37, 40–41, 46–47, 56–57, 60–61, 68, 72–73, 82–83, 97, 101, 108–109, 110–111, 114–115, 120–121, 134–135, 137, 140–141, 144–145, 150–151, 152–153, 156–157, 160, 164–165, 172–173, 181; and Marc Domage: p. 154; Philippe Fragnière: p. 54, 92, 96, 132, 133; Hans-Georg Gaul: p. 159; Serge Hasenböhler/Art Basel Photographic Services: p. 91; Thomas Humery: 95; Aurélien Mole: p. 185t; Timothée Nalet/© Peignée Verticale: flyleave (entrance, 163r); Fredrik Nielsen: p. 50tl, bl, 51; Georges Poncet: 162l; Christian Riis Ruggaber: 162r; Philippe Servent: p. 79; Nicolas Syz: p. 93, 177; Nicolas Trembley: p. 70-71; Robert Wedemeyer: p. 50tr, br

Courtesies

For all the works: Courtesy of the artists; and 303 Gallery, New York: p. 63, 64–65, 182; Air de Paris, Paris: p. 30, 31, 130, 158, 170–171, 185, 186–187; Balice Hertling, Paris, and Gavin Brown's enterprise, New York/Rome: p. 53; Mary Boone Gallery, New York, and Sprüth Magers, Berlin: p. 118–119; Christie's: p. 33; Paula Cooper Gallery, New York: p. 169; Elizabeth Dee, New York: p. 174–175; dépendance, Brussels: p. 23, 49; Essex Street, New York: p. 80; Estate of Guy de Cointet and Air de Paris, Paris: p. 154; Freedman Fitzpatrick, Los Angeles: p. 176; Lars Friedrich, Berlin: p. 58–59, 126; Galerie Andrea Caratsch, St. Moritz: p. 38, 43, 54; Galerie Buchholz, Berlin/Cologne/New York: p. 81, 116–117, 139; Galerie Buchholz, Berlin/Cologne/New York, and Hauser & Wirth: p. 77; Galerie Chantal Crousel, Paris: p. 36, 39, 75, 100, 123; Galerie Eva Presenhuber, Zurich: flyleaves (Donnelly, Carron), p. 9, 10–11, 42, 85, 146–147; Galerie Francesca Pia, Zurich: p. 26; Galerie Gisela Capitain, Cologne: p. 44, 66–67, 128–129, 179; Galerie Mezzanin, Geneva: p. 131; Galerie Nathalie Obadia, Paris, and Esther Schipper, Berlin: p. 22; Galerie Neu, Berlin: p. 12, 76; Galerie Thaddaeus Ropac, London/Paris/Salzburg: p. 28, 79, 105; Gavin Brown's enterprise, New York/Rome: flyleaves (Sturtevant), p. 89, 90, 113; François Ghebaly Gallery, Los Angeles: p. 155; Grassert Grunert, New York: p. 125; Greene Naftali, New York: p. 74, 88, 107; Hauser & Wirth: p. 13, 16, 148–149, 168, 183; House of Gaga, Mexico City: p. 20, 55, 124, 184; David Kordansky Gallery, Los Angeles: p. 50tr, br; David Kordansky Gallery, Los Angeles, and Massimo De Carlo, Milan: p. 50tl, bl, 51; Andrew Kreps Gallery, New York: p. 166, 167; Andrew Kreps Gallery, New York, and Mai 36 Galerie, Zurich: p. 99; Simon Lee Gallery, London: p. 48; Lehmann Maupin, New York/Hong Kong: p. 104; Metro Pictures, New York: p. 142, 143; Édouard Montassut, Paris: p. 122; Friedrich Petzel Gallery, New York: p. 86–87; Almine Rech Gallery, Paris: p. 180; Anthony Reynolds Gallery, London: p. 29; Esther Schipper, Berlin: p. 84, 91; Stuart Shave/Modern Art, London: p. 103; Sprüth Magers, Berlin: p. 27, 45, 136; Supportico Lopez, Berlin: p. 159

This book is published in collaboration with the SYZ Group on the occasion of the presentation of the Syz Collection at the Quai des Bergues, Geneva.

www.thesyzcollection.com

Editor
Nicolas Trembley

Editorial Coordination
Clément Dirié, Matthieu Neyroud

Proofreading
Clare Manchester

Design
Noémie Gygax

Typeface
Helvetica Neue

Color Separation & Print
Musumeci S.p.A., Quart (Aosta)

Printed in Europe

Published by
JRP|Ringier
Limmatstrasse 270
CH–8005 Zurich
T +41 (0) 43 311 27 50
E info@jrp-ringier.com
W www.jrp-ringier.com

ISBN 978-3-03764-548-2

JRP|Ringier publications are available internationally at selected bookstores and from the following distribution partners:

Switzerland
AVA Verlagsauslieferung AG
Centralweg 16
CH–8910 Affoltern a.A.
avainfo@ava.ch
www.ava.ch

Germany and Austria
Vice Versa Distribution GmbH
Potsdamer Str. 93
D–10785 Berlin
info@viceversaartbooks.com
www.viceversaartbooks.com

France
Les presses du reel
35 rue Colson
F–21000 Dijon
info@lespressesdureel.com
www.lespressesdureel.com

UK and other European countries
Cornerhouse Publications, HOME
2 Tony Wilson Place
UK–Manchester M15 4FN
publications@cornerhouse.org
www.cornerhousepublications.org

USA, Canada, Asia, and Australia
ARTBOOK | D.A.P.
75 Broad Street, Suite 630
US–New York, NY 10004
orders@dapinc.com
www.artbook.com

For a list of our partner bookshops or for any general questions, please contact JRP|Ringier directly at info@jrp-ringier.com, or visit our homepage www.jrp-ringier.com for further information about our program.

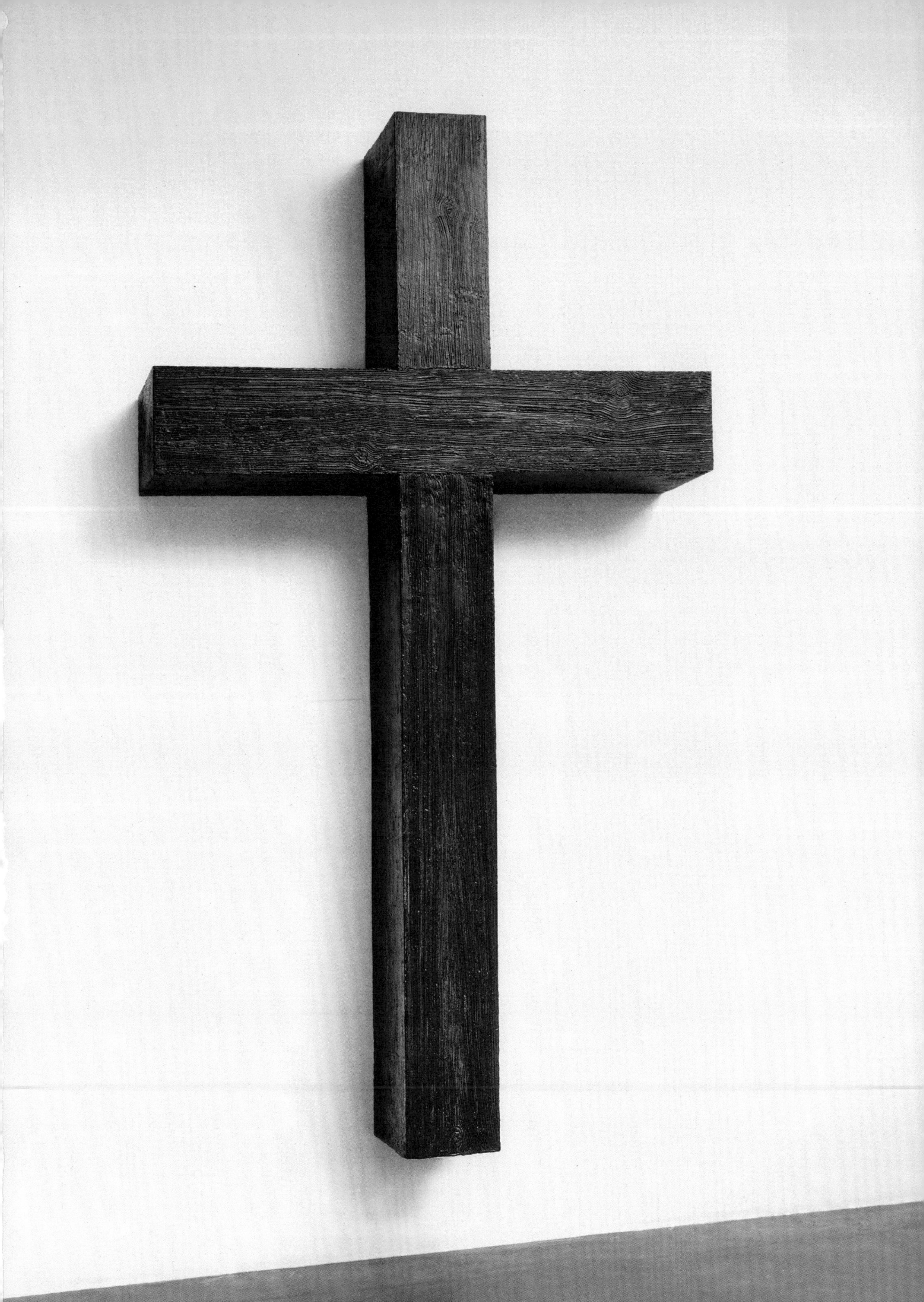

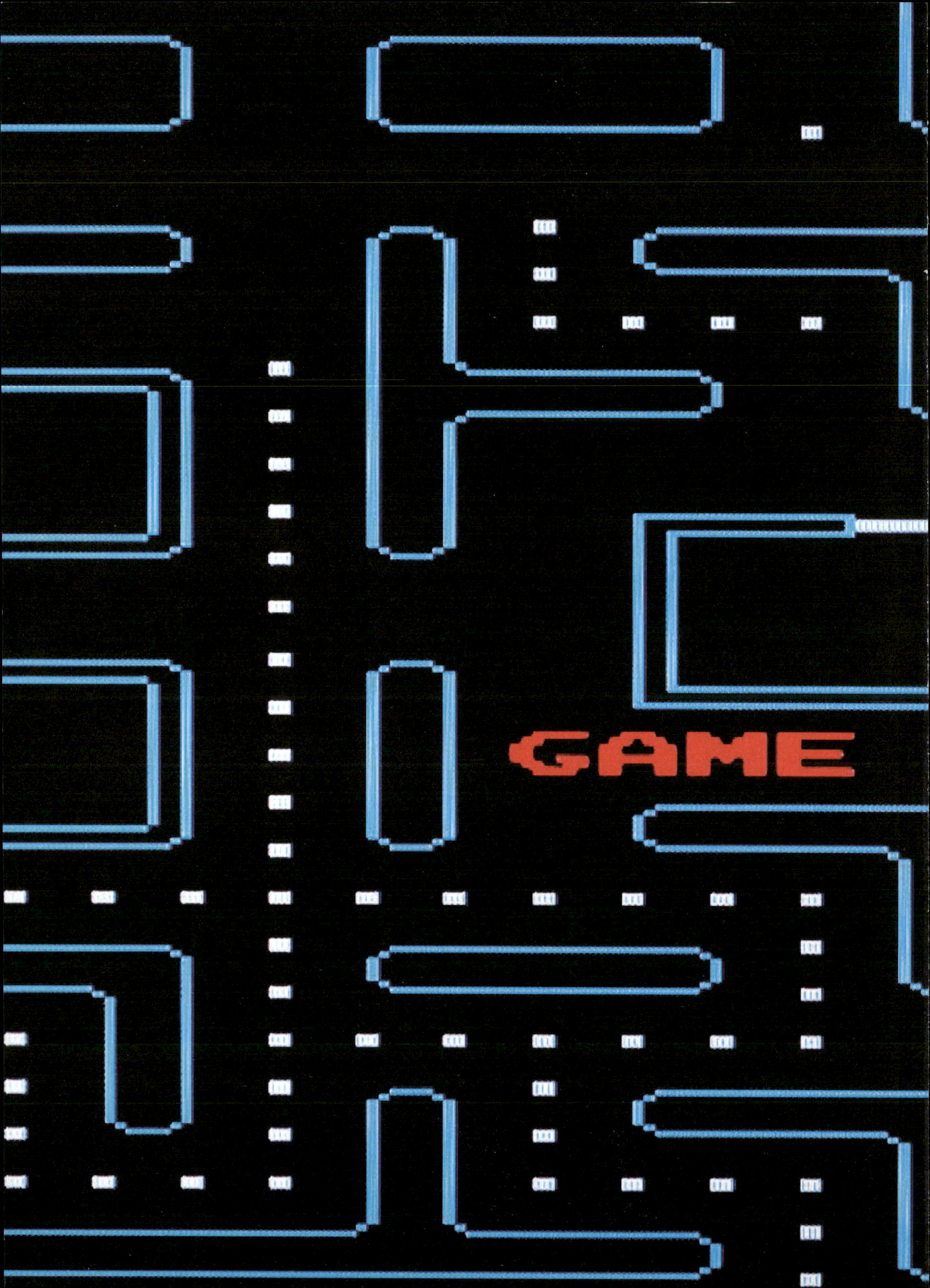
GAME